THE SECOND LIFE GRID™

THE OFFICIAL GUIDE TO COMMUNICATION, COLLABORATION, AND COMMUNITY ENGAGEMENT

KIMBERLY RUFER-BACH

WILEY

Wiley Publishing, Inc.

Senior Acquisitions Editor: Willem Knibbe
Development Editor: Candace English
Technical Editor: Glenn Fisher
Production Editor: Patrick Cunningham
Copy Editor: Candace English
Production Manager: Tim Tate
Vice President and Executive Group Publisher: Richard Swadley
Vice President and Publisher: Neil Edde
Book Designer and Compositor: Patrick Cunningham
Proofreader and Indexer: Asha Johnson
Project Coordinator, Cover: Lynsey Stanford
Cover Designer: Ryan Sneed
Cover Image: Patrick Cunningham

Library of Congress Cataloging-in-Publication Data

Rufer-Bach, Kimberly.
    The Second Life grid : the official guide to communication, collaboration, and community engagement / Kimberly Rufer-Bach. -- 1st ed.
       p. cm.
    ISBN 978-0-470-41291-6 (pbk.)
 1. Second Life (Game)--Social aspects. 2. Shared virtual environments. I. Title.
    GV1469.25.S425R84 2009
    794.8--dc22
                    2009009763

To Dennis and Gerrie Rufer (Grups!) and Russ Rufer and Tracy Bialik. With love.

ACKNOWLEDGMENTS

I'd like to thank

Everyone at Wiley, especially Willem Knibbe, Candace English, Patrick Cunningham, and Kelly Trent. Thanks for making me look so good.

My agent, David Fugate of LaunchBooks, who appeared out of the blue like a writer's dream.

Glenn Fisher of Linden Lab, who is a tireless and keen technical editor. Thank you, Glenn!

Catherine Smith, also of Linden Lab. Thanks for your help and trust.

The rest of the Lindens: Claudia L'Amoreaux, Cyn Skyberg, Gene Yoon, Joe Miller, John Lester, Madhavi Katikaneni, Robin Harper, Tom Hale, and Tom Verre, and too many others to list.

Everyone who let me interview them or take a picture of their avatar, and those who contributed sidebars and sent me tips and links.

My clients, from whom I have learned so much.

My staff, The Magicians: MAGI RULE!

Sam Sjogren, The Mighty Sammy (I meow at you repeatedly!).

Stephanie Sellers Sakasai . . . let's go out and hug a tree, but please (oh, please) don't bake a brie.

Russ Rufer and Tracy Bialik, for believing in my work, for the hardware, software, books, advice, putting up with reporters rearranging the furniture, and for taking care of me when I was sick, and all the rest.

The Grups, Gerrie (Moomar) and Dennis (Daddus) Rufer, for teaching me to read, write, walk, talk, and have a good time. Many parents would probably excrete a cupcake if their kid was trying to do something like write or play computer games for a living, but few could manage to give such good business advice at the same time. The last line of this book: Thank you, Grups!

ABOUT THE AUTHOR

Hi, I'm Kim.

Photo by Dennis Rufer

I got my start as a professional writer in 1984, when I took an article rejected by the editor of my high-school newspaper and sold it to a local weekly. I went on to sell a lot more writing over the years, mostly nonfiction for newspapers and magazines. In 1985 I became involved in early online communities (as a SysOp—node administrator—on FidoNet). Around the same time I worked on some of the first educational home-computer games, including *The First Men in the Moon Math* (Fisher-Price), which was a best-seller. Determined to be the best writer I could be, I applied to and was accepted to the Clarion Writers' Workshop at Michigan State University in 1988 (known by some as "boot camp for writers").

Eventually I went on to work with a partner of AOL (Writers Club/iUniverse.com), hosting online author events for large audiences. While I was doing that, one of my novellas, *Daddy's Girl*, which appeared in *Adventures in the Twilight Zone* (Ed. Carol Serling, DAW Books, Inc.), garnered recommendations for a Bram Stoker Award. I became involved in moderating various online communities, including working in-house at There as the community forums coordinator.

In 2004 I joined *Second Life*, where I built up an in-world business, at one time operating more than 20 virtual shop locations. In 2005 I started my Solution Provider company, The Magicians, hiring top content-creation specialists to work along with me to serve my clients' needs in *Second Life*. My first major client was UC Davis Medical Center, which hired me to create objects used in a simulation for training staff from the California health department in the deployment of emergency medical clinics in case of biological attack. This project was funded by the CDC. Some of my other clients have included the British Council, The University of Queensland, New York Law School, the Level Playing Field Institute, Global Kids, NASA, Wiley, and Strong Angel III. I have also given a lot of presentations about *Second Life*, some of them in *Second Life* itself.

My writing career and virtual worlds/online community career merged a couple of years ago when I coauthored *Creating Your World: The Official Guide to Advanced Content Creation for Second Life* (Wiley).

Aside from my career . . . I'm originally from the suburbs of Chicago, but when I was 17 my parents sold the house and cars and pretty much everything else, bought a travel trailer, and off the family went on a long, unforgettable adventure to "the land of milk and honey"—California—where we even got to live on a ranch for a while. Eventually I found my way to the redwood-forested mountains on the coast, where I live happily with Catawah Chicago (The Cat) in a cabin by a creek outside a small town, surrounded by good friends and neighbors.

When not working or playing in or writing about *Second Life* I like to hang out with my friends and watch the sunset or the moonrise, pet my cat, play the banjo (badly), hike, pet the neighbor's cow, smell the roses and eat wild berries when I'm walking into town, garden, read, watch the mergansers and red-shouldered hawks and steelheads and raccoons and deer and other wildlife in and around the creek, and (I hope, when this book is finished) sleep.

"The whole world is a circus if you know how to look at it." —7 Faces of Dr. Lao

INTRODUCTION

Welcome to my book, and thanks for reading.

This book has been in-process for a long time, since before my previous *Second Life* book, *Creating Your World: The Official Guide to Advanced Content Creation for Second Life*. Along the way there have been some changes in *Second Life*, many of them focused on making *Second Life* more useful for real-world organizations' projects. Linden Lab staff and I have been working together, right down to and past the planned deadline, to make sure that this book will be as current as possible, in order to give you the most assistance we can to help you plan and run a successful project using the *Second Life* Grid.

This book is full of information you can't look up somewhere else (though having that info all in one place should be helpful to you, too!). It's based on my five years of experience developing *Second Life* content for clients—and that is all built on my 24-year base of experience working on similar platforms, educational computer games, and online community management. It's also based on a wealth of information, some never before published, provided by Linden Lab.

I'm a specialist, a developer of virtual content and events and communities. While I do some marketing and have done more of it in the past, and while I do some teaching and have done more of that in the past, too, I know a lot of people who read this book are going to have much more experience in those and other areas than I have or will ever have. So I've chosen not to try to dazzle you with terminology. I don't sound like a marketing director, like the CEO of a huge multinational corporation, like an academic. I sound like what I am—a top *Second Life* Solution Provider who's also an author. So rest assured I won't try to sound like an expert in areas where I'm not one. I'll just tell you what I know about how to make your project work, as clearly and vividly as I can, and I hope that makes this material as accessible to you as possible, regardless of your professional background.

WHO SHOULD READ THIS BOOK

This book is for you if you are interested in or currently using the *Second Life* Grid for a real-world project. This includes educators, businesses, nonprofits, and government agencies. It's not written for people who want to have a hobby selling virtual goods or running a dance club just for fun (though if that's your thing, you might find this book useful). This book is for people who are using the Grid as a tool for their existing, nonvirtual goals.

I had the idea of writing this book because I was worried that I was going to burn out. Every day I was answering the same questions and giving the same advice to clients, prospective clients, reporters, etc. I knew that could go on for only so long before the quality of my work would be affected by repetition, and I felt that it would be better for me to put my time into actually building things rather than talking about them. So I decided I'd take enough time away from my work to write a book containing all my usual answers—sort of a giant paperback FAQ. I'd write the ultimate, definitive answers to the questions, and then I'd be able to hand out copies of the book to clients so they could look up things for themselves without having to contact me, and we could instead spend our time together on issues more specific to their individual projects. And I knew other readers would find this book helpful too—more of them than I could ever consult with on a one-on-one basis. I hope that I'm able to do some good, in these early days of virtual worlds, by shortening the learning curve and helping more organizations to get off to a good start.

The material for this book was drawn from many sources, but a lot of it came from my correspondence with my clients, project proposals, logs from Q&A events, and discussions with Linden Lab staff.

I went over all of those materials to see what I should cover, and made sure to include and explain all of the important questions, issues, and concerns my clients and others have asked me about repeatedly over the years. After reading this book, you should really understand the platform, what you're getting into, what the challenges will be, best practices, why it's vital to log in and try *Second Life* yourself right away, and ultimately how to go about having a successful presence on the Grid.

WHAT YOU WILL LEARN

There's a lot to cover here, and you'll find that some of it (though as little as possible) overlaps with other books about *Second Life*, including my own previous book. In general, though, this book is not intended to explain how to create content, or the basic user-interface and tools; it doesn't focus on things like how to set up your own account or how to make your avatar walk or sit. There are already tools and assistance for you right on the *Second Life* site, and there are other books to teach you those things. (*SL* has even gotten big enough to have its own *For Dummies* book.)

Instead this book focuses on what you need to understand about *Second Life* to plan, manage, and run a successful project using it. So instead of talking about "hit this button to make your avatar fly" or "here's how you build a chair," it's more about things like what you need to know to run a large event, attitudes of *Second Life* Residents toward corporate marketing or academic research projects in-world, and what sorts of resources and assistance are available for someone running a project like yours.

In general, the book focuses on the differences between private and public spaces, examples of how the Grid is already being used for real-world projects, what you need to know about *Second Life* Resident culture, and how to go about implementing your project.

PRIVATE VERSUS PUBLIC SPACES

The *Second Life* Grid contains the *Second Life* virtual world, and more. In other words, there are entire regions and whole continents that aren't connected to the mainland of the *Second Life* world, and avatars can't travel between all of them, or travel might be restricted to only approved avatars.

So your organization might keep its space private all the time, open to the public all the time, or somewhat restricted some or all of the time! You'll learn more about this in various parts of the book, such as Chapters 9 and 10.

USE CASES

Lots of organizations are already on the Grid, and some have been using *Second Life* for years now. Throughout the book, but especially in Part 1, you'll learn how organizations like yours are successfully using *Second Life* for their projects.

SECOND LIFE RESIDENT CULTURE

Anyone who does a project on the Grid needs to know about *Second Life* Resident culture. Even if you aren't going to be marketing to Residents, offering them a class, or interacting with them directly in any way, it's useful to know how people who have been using the platform for years manage unique social situations such as politely entering and exiting when, rather than knocking on a door, you simply teleport and appear at a meeting. Over and over throughout this book I will tell you, *you need to log in and try* Second Life *before you plan your project*.

There are use cases and overviews of technical and social know-how throughout the book. And there is a lot of straightforward, nuts-'n'-bolts how-to information. What should you be sure to do while preparing for a large virtual event, and what do you do if something unexpected happens during it? How do you know which Solution Provider to hire, or do you need one at all? Do you need to staff your virtual office around the clock, and how do you get a gadget you might use for on-call staff instead? You need to know all the background stuff first, but once you understand it, you need to know what to do with the knowledge!

WHAT IS COVERED IN THIS BOOK

This book is divided into four parts, which are detailed here.

The first part of the book gives examples and information about how various sorts of organizations use the Grid.

Chapter 1: What You Can Do on the *Second Life* Grid. This chapter talks in general about how organizations use the Grid, why Grid development may well not be something you can do in-house, what works and doesn't work, and what makes the *Second Life* Grid unique and perhaps the best tool for your job.

Chapter 2: Teach and Train. Starting with examples of educational use of the Grid, this chapter also focuses on assistance available to educational institutions, how to make sure the technology helps instead of hinders learning, what sorts of educational uses are best for the platform, and resources of use to educators.

Chapter 3: Government Agencies on the *SL* Grid. Government agencies face unique challenges on the Grid, but there are also special resources to help them. Learn about these and about successful government projects on the Grid.

Chapter 4: Nonprofits Reach Out. Lots of nonprofits are doing projects on the Grid, and we'll take a look at some success stories and at what sort of resources are available for nonprofit projects. This chapter also includes info about charity fundraising and home-grown *Second Life* fundraising efforts.

Chapter 5: Conduct Business. Learn about virtual meetings and conferences, prototyping and testing, why some marketing projects on the Grid have failed, and how to make sure that your project avoids their pitfalls.

The second part of this book is all about *Second Life* Resident culture and virtual-world etiquette.

Chapter 6: Your Avatar and Your Organization. This chapter is about avatars, the virtual representations of people. Learn what sort of avatars are appropriate for work or school, how to make sure your avatar is presentable, avoiding possible embarrassments, Resident subcultures, and how corporate HR policies might apply in-world.

Chapter 7: Understanding Social Interaction in *Second Life*. In this etiquette-and-culture chapter, you'll learn about the unique challenges of doing business in a virtual world, what's polite and what's not in this new culture, choosing the right communication interface, avoiding the many tempting distractions in-world, and keeping your work separate from them.

Chapter 8: Keep Up with Current Events. Learn why it's important to know what's going on in *Second Life* and the best sources for information about current events, downtime, changes, and more.

PART 3—DOING REAL WORK IN A VIRTUAL WORLD

The third part of the book is all nuts-and-bolts advice about how to get things done in-world.

Chapter 9: Manage Your Infrastructure. Learn about virtual land, permissions, inventory, and managing projects in a 3D world. This chapter is one you'll be using for reference, because it's full of information about how to get things done.

Chapter 10: Set Up a Virtual Office. This chapter will explain what sort of space is appropriate for business use (whether you want to set up a meeting space or a showroom), what you need to include, and more, such as discussions of privacy and security.

Chapter 11: Market and Sell Your Product. Marketing in-world has its own strengths and challenges. Learn how it's different from real-world marketing and how to use in-world marketing and advertising channels, how to bring in new *SL* Residents for your marketing experience, and what works and doesn't work.

Chapter 12: Run an Event. Here you'll learn what you need to know to put on a successful event in-world. Learn what sort of event space will work for your project, how to address scheduling issues, and how to promote your event. This chapter also covers moderation tools and techniques, what sorts of tools you need, and how to deal with problems during live events.

Chapter 13: Select a Solution Provider. This chapter gives you the tools to figure out when you need to hire someone to work with you on your project, and covers what's involved in that process, how you go about working with a Solution Provider, how to tell if a Solution Provider is the right one for you, and what can go wrong.

Chapter 14: Work in Teen *Second Life*. Learn what sorts of projects are allowed (or required to be) on the Teen Grid, what you need to do to work there, restrictions placed on Approved Adults, and all sorts of other useful tips for working in Teen *Second Life*.

Chapter 15: Locate Resources. Here you'll find tips about how to locate what you need, and an overview of tools that you might find useful for your project. You'll learn about tools you can simply buy from a Resident merchant in-world or that are relatively easy to build or purchase from a Solution Provider, tools for measuring the effectiveness of your project, and custom tools that require programming or assistance of Linden Lab or a Solution Provider.

PART 4—APPENDICES

Appendix A: Glossary. This appendix lists all sorts of new terms you'll encounter throughout this book and in *Second Life*, along with clear, concise definitions.

Appendix B: *Second Life* Community Standards. This appendix covers Linden Lab's policy regarding acceptable and unacceptable behavior on the Grid.

HOW TO CONTACT THE AUTHOR

I'd love to hear from you if you have feedback about my book, or suggestions for other books you'd like to see me write in the future. My email address is **Kim@TheMagicians.us**. You can learn more about my work in *Second Life* at my company's website, **http://themagicians.us**. Thanks again for reading this book. I sure hope you find it useful and enjoyable, and I look forward to meeting you in *Second Life*. Stop by Abracadabra and say hi!

Sybex strives to keep you supplied with the latest tools and information you need for your work. Please check their website at **www.sybex.com**, where we'll post additional content and updates that supplement this book if the need arises. Enter ***Second Life Grid*** in the Search box (or type the book's ISBN—**9780470412916**), and click Go to get to the book's update page.

CONTENTS

HOW YOUR ORGANIZATION CAN USE *SECOND LIFE*

06

07

08

09

10

11

12

13

14

15

You probably have a lot of questions about the *Second Life* Grid. What is the *SL* Grid? How many people use it? Are a lot of businesses, educators, nonprofits, and government agencies getting on the Grid? How do they use it for their projects, and why? What sorts of projects work best? Is the *SL* Grid right for your project? Read on for answers!

WHAT YOU CAN DO ON THE *SECOND LIFE* GRID

WHAT IS THE *SECOND LIFE* GRID?

You've probably read articles about *Second Life*, heard about it from a friend or colleague, or maybe you've even tried it yourself. A lot of people aren't clear on just what *Second Life* is and what it can do, but they know it looks like a game, which seems to conflict with the stories of government agencies and universities and corporations using it for serious and definitely nongame projects. So let's start with an overview of the *Second Life* Grid and the features it offers that might be useful to you for a project for your business, educational institution, nonprofit, or government agency.

The *SL* Grid is a platform that offers users the ability to create public or secure 3D online virtual spaces or to visit and use spaces created by others. The same technology is the framework of the popular virtual world *Second Life*, but the *SL* Grid contains the *Second Life* world, not the other way around. A convenient comparison: your space in *SL* is to the *SL* Grid as your company's website is to the World Wide Web. Additionally, while the *SL* Grid and world aren't games, they contain some games . . . along with classrooms, offices, auditoriums, and more (Figure 1.1). Again, compare this to the Web, which no one would consider a game, but where you can find games if you want them.

1.1 This doesn't look like a game to me!

You can keep your own space on the Grid private and allow only your own staff or students to access it, or you can locate your space in the *Second Life* world and allow community members—known as Residents—to visit and participate. It's easy to use the *SL* Grid's tools to control access to your space. You can even decide whether to allow your own staff or students to access the *Second Life* world within the *SL* Grid, and create a custom signup and orientation experience for your staff, students, or customers. Additionally, a new offering on the horizon will allow you to set up stand-alone virtual spaces, even behind your own firewall. Still other tools in the works will facilitate participation in your virtual meetings, classes, and other activities via a web interface or an instant-messaging client, or by calling a phone number.

And, of course, the *SL* Grid includes powerful tools for content creation, so you can develop what you need to make your space attractive and functional. Additionally, you can tap into the wealth of Resident-created content, which you can purchase from shops in the *Second Life* world using Linden dollars, the convenient microcurrency of this virtual world.

Once you're on the Grid and have your space set up, you can use it for all sorts of projects, or even at any time repurpose the space with surprising ease and speed and at a reasonable cost.

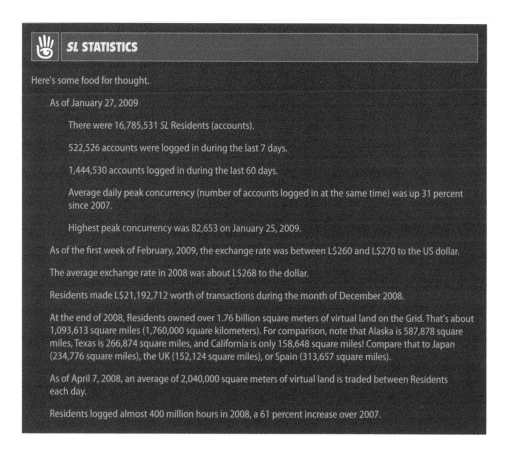

SL STATISTICS

Here's some food for thought.

As of January 27, 2009

There were 16,785,531 *SL* Residents (accounts).

522,526 accounts were logged in during the last 7 days.

1,444,530 accounts logged in during the last 60 days.

Average daily peak concurrency (number of accounts logged in at the same time) was up 31 percent since 2007.

Highest peak concurrency was 82,653 on January 25, 2009.

As of the first week of February, 2009, the exchange rate was between L$260 and L$270 to the US dollar.

The average exchange rate in 2008 was about L$268 to the dollar.

Residents made L$21,192,712 worth of transactions during the month of December 2008.

At the end of 2008, Residents owned over 1.76 billion square meters of virtual land on the Grid. That's about 1,093,613 square miles (1,760,000 square kilometers). For comparison, note that Alaska is 587,878 square miles, Texas is 266,874 square miles, and California is only 158,648 square miles! Compare that to Japan (234,776 square miles), the UK (152,124 square miles), or Spain (313,657 square miles).

As of April 7, 2008, an average of 2,040,000 square meters of virtual land is traded between Residents each day.

Residents logged almost 400 million hours in 2008, a 61 percent increase over 2007.

FEATURES OF THE *SL* GRID

In Chapters 2 through 5 we'll look closely at how educators, nonprofits, government agencies, and businesses use the Grid for their specific needs. But first let's consider the possibilities. Here's a high-level overview of what's in store on the Grid.

MAKE YOUR SPACE PUBLIC OR PRIVATE

When you set up a space of your own, you can control it via in-world tools (which you'll learn to use in Chapter 9). You can purchase virtual land from Linden Lab or from another *SL* Resident, or rent anything from a small shop all the way up to whole islands and continents. Terraform and landscape your land, or hire a developer to do it for you, and you can have a tropical paradise, a mountain retreat, or just about any other sort of terrain you like. You can locate your space on the *SL* world's mainland, where things are especially crowded and busy, or on a private island where you have more control, or you can maintain a presence in more than one location.

As mentioned earlier, you can even control who has access to your space: allow members of the *SL* community to visit it, or restrict access to only avatars you choose. (You can easily switch this setting, if you want to be "open" only some of the time.) Using the Registration API, you can create a custom *SL* account-creation web page and have new avatars logged in directly to your location in-world. You can decide whether you want those avatars to be restricted to your island or if they'll be free to visit the rest of the *SL* world. If a visitor is causing trouble, you can quickly and easily eject them from your space, and even ban them from returning.

You have options for age restrictions, as well. There's a special place for *SL* users age 13 to 17, called Teen *Second Life*, which is separate from the rest of the Grid and has plenty of rules and technical restrictions in place to make sure that it's a safe space for teens to interact.

For the ultimate control over access and communications, the upcoming offering I mentioned earlier will allow you to run your own stand-alone virtual space, behind your organization's firewall if you wish. At press time, little information was available, but it should prove very useful, particularly for organizations that are concerned about keeping private conversations private.

REPRESENT LOCATIONS AND THINGS

Want to make a scale model of your office, part of a real-life city, or your product? With the Grid's built-in tools, a few assets imported from external programs, and some skill, you can do just that.

Want to put your favorite chair on the lunar surface? No problem! Would it be useful to you to re-create long-gone places, like an ancient Egyptian village or a Roaring Twenties speakeasy? You can bring the past to life in 3D and, if you wish, invite others to visit and explore, or you can give away or sell copies of these assets or even rent spaces to tenants.

You can even develop—or have developed for you—things that don't yet exist, such as a prototype of a hotel you envision. And of course you can create places and things that aren't possible in real life, like undersea cities, magical flying furniture, crystal trees, and floating castles. Some *SL* Residents create works of art entirely within the *Second Life* world, display them in galleries, and sell copies—or originals.

BE YOURSELF OR YOUR *OTHER* SELF

Your representation on the Grid is called an avatar. This 3D character can have almost any appearance you choose. You can use photos to create an avatar that looks just like you (but maybe a tad thinner or younger, if you like!). Or maybe you want to look a bit different. Be an elf, an Inca, or a space pirate, or model yourself after a celebrity or historical figure.

It's easy to change what your avatar wears, so you can have a businesslike avatar that looks like the real-life you for a meeting, then turn into a talking bird, a robot, or Abraham Lincoln—within seconds.

Artists create all sorts of clothing and accessories for avatars to wear or carry, and animations so that your avatar can dance, take a bow, shake hands with a client, or fly like a superhero. You can have custom work created for you, or you can shop the amazing array of existing user-created content.

CREATE INTERACTIVE EXPERIENCES AND TOOLS

The Grid not only offers the ability to shape the space around you and the avatar that represents you; it also includes support for scripts written in a proprietary programming language called the Linden Scripting Language, or LSL for short. Make interactive displays, working vehicles, curtains that open or close, vending machines, and more. When your needs exceed what's practical to do with LSL, you can make your in-world scripted objects talk to an external server. Another book in this series, *Scripting Your World: The Official Guide to Second Life Scripting* (Wiley, 2008), is an excellent scripting resource.

PARTICIPATE IN THE ECONOMY

The medium of exchange in *SL* is the Linden dollar, or L$. Offering things for sale to avatars, and buying objects, scripts, avatar parts, or even land is as easy as checking a box and setting or paying a price, or using a user-created vendor (Figure 1.2).

1.2 User-created content can often be purchased from vendors.

How do you get L$ to spend? Avatars with a Premium *SL* account (which costs as little as US$6 per month if you pay a year in advance) receive a weekly stipend of L$300. If that's not enough for your needs, you can purchase L$ on the LindeX currency exchange or from a third-party reseller. (Beware of purchasing L$ on eBay because of the potential for fraud.) Many *SL* Residents earn L$ by selling content they have created, selling or renting real estate, performing services, or winning competitions. Some of them cash out their L$ earnings by selling them for US$. Many Residents are hobbyists, but some take this work as seriously as running any real-life business, and earn a good real-life living. For example, in December 2008, 205 *SL* Residents made US$5,000 or more from L$ transactions. You'll learn more about the in-world economy in Part 2.

Some nonprofit fundraisers in *SL* bring in substantial donations, such as the American Cancer Society's Relay for Life, which in 2007 involved more than 1,700 participants in-world who brought in a total of US$118,000 (yes, that's US dollars, not Linden dollars). In 2008 the relay raised nearly US$200,000.

REACH OUT TO THE COMMUNITY

The *Second Life* world is a very sociable place, with tens of thousands of Residents in-world at any time. They create content and sell it, shop, join support groups for real-life concerns, date, play, relive a better childhood, roleplay, take or teach classes, explore, compete, research—there are almost unlimited possibilities, few restrictions, and a lot of creativity. Type almost anything into Search, and you will find *SL* Residents who share your interest.

Some organizations find a lot of value in the community and locate on the mainland, are open to the public at their own island, or even become involved directly with Resident activities and groups. Some sponsor popular communities or events, seek out popular places for product-placement opportunities, conduct or participate in job fairs, set up focus groups, solicit feedback, do scientific research, or offer information.

You can also use the Grid's group tools to start a community of your own within the *SL* world, or a private community, separate from the rest of the Grid, for which you control access and signups.

IMPROVE COMMUNICATIONS

The Grid includes many channels of communication: text chat, voice, instant messages, and group messages. Additionally, you can post on the official forums; put up signs and banners; list an event on the official calendar; purchase an in-world classified ad; and fill out your account profile, group profile, or a description of your project. Trade calling cards with other people and maintain a contact list. Search functions make it easy to find information in-world. There's also a wealth of user-generated resources on the Web, such as *SL*-specific newspapers, magazines, and photo-sharing sites.

New communications features we're likely to see soon include expanded abilities for the SLim client, which is an external instant-messaging application that can be used to communicate with *Second Life* Residents, including via voice calls. And soon there will be new ways to share your *SL* events, meetings, and classes with people who aren't logged into *SL* at all.

Second Life Residents hail from all parts of the globe, and there's text support for many languages. You can even pick up a free translation gadget that will, on the fly, help you to communicate with those around you. And with logging tools built into the Grid, you can keep a record of everything that was said in text chat. Using a third-party application, you can easily capture audio and video, too.

More and more real-world organizations are making use of the *SL* Grid's communication tools to reduce travel costs (Figure 1.3). For example, IBM holds many internal meetings on the *SL* Grid rather than flying employees all over the world. Some University of Queensland students telecommute to classes held in the virtual world.

Many people prefer avatar-based communication to a regular teleconference because the voice feature in *SL* makes it easy to see who's talking. Avatars can make voice or text chat seem more personal, affording some of the same social cues that are important in real life, such as eye contact and proximity. Particularly when communicating with people already familiar with online worlds, games, or other activities, communications and activities on the Grid can be especially engaging. Would you rather sit in a classroom looking at a diagram on a chalk board, or do you think you might pay more attention if your avatar and those of the other people at the meeting were all instead walking around in a 3D virtual model?

Don't forget that you can use *Second Life* for 3D data visualization. Even something as simple as a bar graph can be made more compelling if you can walk around in it virtually and watch the bars grow and shrink in real time!

SHARE MEDIA

Suppose you want to share video with your students or a podcast with your customers or a website with your colleagues. You can do all of these things on the *SL* Grid, with the ability to stream media in-world. You can stream audio, video, or view web pages.

Although there was not much info available at press time, we can look forward to a new feature (probably near-term) that will allow true collaborative web browsing in-world. And if you have an immediate need to share your documents, video, or even a view of your computer's desktop, you can try a solution like Immersive Work Spaces, which I'll discuss more in Parts 2 and 3 of this book.

1.3 IBM uses this space for events at their Almaden island.

KEEP YOUR RIGHTS, PROTECT YOUR CONTENT

On the *SL* Grid you own the intellectual property you create. You can decide who may use your things, and how. Using simple check boxes, you can set permissions for who can move or modify your creations and whether those creations can be transferred or copied. Similarly, you can choose who is able to put content on your land, whether they are allowed to run scripts there, and just how long they can visit. You can even charge admission.

WHAT WORKS AND WHAT DOESN'T

With so many useful features and powerful tools, the *SL* Grid is a great match for a wide range of projects. But even the best hammer in the universe doesn't make such a hot screwdriver! It's important to understand what sorts of things work best on the Grid, what challenges you might face, and what ideas might need to go back to the drawing board. Throughout this book we'll discuss many of these things in detail, but here's an overview.

WHAT WORKS TECHNICALLY

A virtual world is a marvel of computer technology, and that means it is complicated. The Grid is more complicated than most virtual worlds, largely because of one of its distinguishing and strongest features, the ability for every user to add unique content at any time.

A world where all of the content is already prepared and loaded from a CD requires less bandwidth than the Grid, of course, where brand-new content must be streamed constantly. Unlike the case in so-called 2.5D sites, everything on the Grid must be rendered in true 3D so that you can see all sides of it. This means the graphics are, in most cases, less advanced than those of a static game. Otherwise, everything would be very, very slow. It also means that to use the Grid you need to have broadband and a pretty good computer—one with plenty of memory and a fast graphics card.

Everyone you want to access your space on the Grid must meet the hardware and bandwidth requirements, too. Be sure to check that your staff or students can meet them. If you set up a custom account-creation portal, make sure the requirements are clear. If you intend to run a live event on the Grid, make sure all participants have logged in with the computer and Internet connection that they'll use; that way you can be sure all will go well.

What if your computer only barely meets the requirements? You can edit your *SL* Preferences to trade off graphics quality for better performance (Figure 1.4).

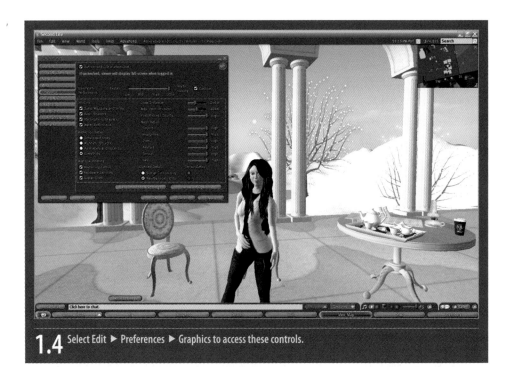

1.4 Select Edit ▶ Preferences ▶ Graphics to access these controls.

Keep in mind that even if you and your team have the most screamin' machines in town, many *SL* Residents don't, and they might not be able to see or take advantage of some of the more-advanced features you enjoy. If you want them to visit or participate in your project, it's important to develop your space in a way that will look and function well for your audience. It's no fun to visit what others tell you looks like a magical glowing fairyland when you can't see the glow yourself.

Keep the following considerations in mind to make your space accessible to users with less-capable systems and to keep things from *lagging*—performing slowly—for everyone.

Don't crowd your space. If you put fewer things on your land, everything will run better for everyone. This goes for avatars, too. More avatars mean things will run slower for everyone there.

Spend your construction resources carefully. Just because you can make everything incredibly detailed doesn't mean it's always a good idea. Complex things create more system load. Save your resources for key objects or areas and simplify the rest.

Consider including text options. The Grid offers a voice feature that is used successfully for a lot of educational and business purposes. However, it requires added bandwidth and memory from your visitors' systems. If you want to make your project accessible to the greatest number of visitors possible, keep this in mind.

Offer alternatives to your video stream. Those with less bandwidth or less-capable computers may not be able to view streaming video in *SL*. If possible, offer a way to view the stream externally, or plan a different way to allow participation or to impart your information.

Expect delays. If someone has less bandwidth than you do, keep in mind that it takes longer for them to see your text in chat or IM, and longer for their reply to show up for you. The same goes for other things that have to be rendered or loaded, such as signs and sounds.

Remember viewing distances. If someone has their Preferences turned down to maximize performance, they can't see very far. If you want everyone who arrives at your island to see a certain sign, don't put it more than 64 meters away (the minimum *draw* or rendering distance).

DEVELOPMENT TOOLS

Although it's possible to create almost anything on the Grid, there are some limitations. With careful design and planning, it's possible to greatly reduce resources used and increase functionality. What might have seemed impossible can become possible if you truly understand all of the quirks of the development tools (or your developer does, if you don't do the work yourself). This is why, although you might have programmers or artists on your staff, it's usually wise to work with a Solution Provider that specializes in developing for the Grid.

On the Grid we use a combination of proprietary, built-in tools and external programs to develop content. The following list covers their strengths and limitations.

Prims. Structures, furniture, trees, vehicles, jewelry . . . almost everything you see on the Grid—other than avatars and the land, sea, and sky—is made from shapes called *primitives* (*prims* for short). Prims come in a variety of basic shapes (Figure 1.5) that may be cut, stretched, hollowed, twisted, textured, and linked together. These shapes are created within the Grid and there is not an easy way to export them to other programs. A newer feature, *sculpted prims* (or *sculpties*) start out looking like other prims, but when you use an importer to bring in a NURBS (non-uniform rational B-spline)-based model from an external program such as Maya or Hexagon, you can apply it to the sculpted prim to have the prim take on the new shape. There are limitations to how complex this imported model may be, however, and it requires more system resources to render than a regular prim does. Even on a fast system, you'll probably see blobs for a few seconds before sculpted prims load completely. Support for actual meshes is in development (meaning you'll soon be able to import 3D models created in an external program), though at press time it was unclear how this will work.

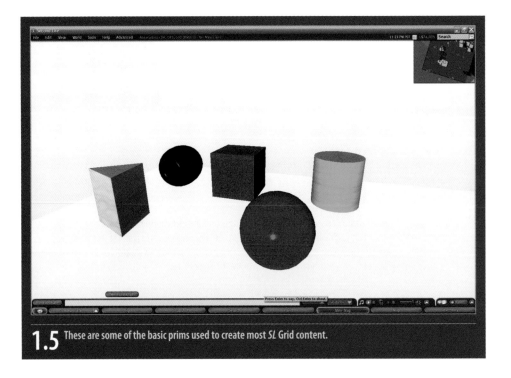

1.5 These are some of the basic prims used to create most *SL* Grid content.

Textures. Once your prim, regular or sculpted, has been shaped, you apply a texture or a color to it. Textures must be created using an external program such as Photoshop or Gimp. Each texture that must be rendered increases system load, and the larger the texture the greater the impact. For this reason, it's a good idea to keep textures small and to use as few as possible. Good news for those used to baking shadows into their textures or using additional dark prims to give the appearance of shadows: Linden Lab intends to offer support for dynamic shadows soon, which means that objects in-world will cast shadows based on the virtual light sources around them.

Scripts. Scripts must be written in the proprietary Linden Scripting Language (LSL), though you can use an external script editor to write your code. LSL is an object-oriented scripting language that some programmers compare, because of its tiny allowable script memory, to embedded-systems programming. This is one of the reasons that it is difficult to create complex programs entirely within the Grid. Fortunately, in most cases it is possible to put multiple scripts into one object, and scripts can send data via email, and both export and import data to an external server. For projects that involve databases, for example, it's often best to use LSL to script the user interface and ship your data to an external server. It's possible to have too many scripts, though. If many scripts are running in one area, they may be unable to run at the appropriate speed.

Avatars. Avatars are shaped using an editor built into the Grid. There are limits to how tall or short one may be, although there are some ingenious workarounds involving, essentially, wearing stilts or folding up your avatar's arms and legs. An avatar's surface (or skin) can be color-adjusted using the editor, or a custom skin texture may be created in an external 2D graphics program and imported to the Grid. Eyes are colored or textured the same way. Hair and beards may be made using the internal editor, but for better-looking results they're usually built from prims and textures, then attached to an avatar. You can even get long, manicured fingernails, a wagging tail, or a nice pair of flappy wings. Of course, each prim and texture adds to the rendering load for you and everyone around you. While some Residents might think it's more important to look good than to feel good, most people won't appreciate being paralyzed while waiting for a room of overly elaborate hairstyles to load.

Clothing. Most clothing on the Grid is made of a combination of a few very limited meshes modified using built-in tools and imported textures. In some cases prims may be used—for things such as belts, shoes, and hats. Clothing looks best on avatars of the size for which the clothing was made, because the textures may distort on larger or smaller shapes. Prim clothing may need to be resized or otherwise adjusted . . . one size may fit "all," but usually not well!

Animations. Avatars may be animated so that they can do things like dance, sip a cup of tea, shake hands, or pose for a picture. Each animation can be up to 30 seconds in length, created in an external program like Poser or Avimator and then imported. In most cases, a scripted object controls the animation, triggering it and perhaps syncing animations that affect one or more avatars (for something like a handshake). There's no automated way to make animations line up perfectly when they sync, and like clothing, animations work best for avatars of the size for which they were created. For animations, the developer's skill level makes a big difference.

Audio. You can create audio clips in an external program and import them into the Grid, but they can't be longer than 10 seconds and must be in `.wav` format. It is possible to use a script to chain together audio clips to, for example, play an entire song. However, especially for those with slower systems or network connections, this doesn't always work out ideally. There is usually a lag while audio clips load.

Land. If you own a parcel of virtual land in an area where terraforming is allowed, you can terraform your land, change its texture, plant trees, and include areas of water. In fact, you can even decide the time of day, controlling the moon and sun's placement in the sky. Land tools also allow you to control access to your land, to decide who is allowed to leave objects on the land or run scripts there, and to eject or ban avatars. However, in some places, and often when renting instead of purchasing land, you may be able to do only some of these things. Also, certain tools are available only to the land owner, which may make it tricky to delegate certain tasks, like changing the source of streaming media on the parcel or backing up the terraforming.

The number of prims you may have on your land is linked to the size of your parcel. Media streams are also limited—one per parcel. Fortunately, you can subdivide your land to accommodate more than one stream. There is also a limit to how many avatars you can have together at one time: typically 40. There are workarounds for some of these situations, and new features on the way to help, potentially allowing hundreds or even thousands of participants at your virtual event—I'll talk about them in detail in Part 3.

WHAT WORKS SOCIALLY

Second Life is primarily a place where people interact, so it's important to understand the social scene before designing projects that will involve *SL* Residents.

MULTICULTURAL, MULTINATIONAL

Less than half of *Second Life* Residents log in from in the USA, and plenty of them don't speak English or log in during prime-time US hours. Depending on what sort of project you intend to do in *SL*, you might need to get a translation device (a scripted object available in-world), hire multilingual staff, or have signage created with messages in more than one language (Figure 1.6).

At press time, *SL* is undergoing a large localization project. Currently you can access it via sites in German, Japanese, and Korean, and localization volunteers speak about 32 different languages. With Residents from all over the world, you might have to take time zones into account. It's often a good idea to plan events, meetings, or classes at the most inclusive time that will fit your own schedule. Occasionally you'll contact a particular person who informs you that it's outside their business hours. Some people put that information right in their avatar's in-world profile.

1.6 This sign, located at the Estonian Embassy in *Second Life*, has buttons to click to receive a notecard in English or Estonian.

Linden Lab has modified some of its policies to accommodate *Second Life*'s multinational user base. For example, they now charge European Residents Value Added Tax on purchases or fees paid to Linden Lab in real-world money, not L$. Additionally, it's forbidden to display Nazi iconography in-world because it's forbidden in Germany. For the most part, though, expect things to be based on US law.

ANONYMITY AND IMMERSION

Most *SL* Residents value their privacy very highly, and a lot of them strive to keep their real lives and second lives separate. Some view the *SL* world as just that—a world—and one in which they are a different person. This has ramifications that will likely be important to you.

The woman avatar with whom you're chatting might be a man in real life. The dog sitting next to her might insist he really is a dog, growling angrily if you press him to talk about his real life. There are all sorts of subcultures with their own lands—whole continents—where not roleplaying along or showing up with your avatar garbed inappropriately is a social faux pas, or even a crime that will get you banned from that area (Figure 1.7).

This commitment to anonymity and immersion, while not shared by every Resident, is widespread enough to make some *SL*-project plans, like many others made by mice and men, go awry. For example, suppose you wanted to create a virtual shop where Residents could, via an in-world interface and using L$, buy your real-life product and have it shipped to their real-life home. You'd have to ask Residents for real names and contact info, and a lot of them just won't give it up. Keep in mind that any time you plan something that requires real-life info and breaks immersion, you'll be limiting your audience to only part of the community.

1.7 According to the rules at the Avilion Hinterlands area, my business-casual attire isn't appropriate.

WHY NOT SPEAK UP?

Not all Residents use the Grid features you might consider very useful, such as the voice feature. It's valuable to understand why.

As many as half of Residents don't use the voice feature; they prefer to type. There are a lot of reasons for this. Some Residents value their privacy and immersion in their alternate world too much to let their real-world voice be heard. After all, you'd know that big, buff lumberjack was really a young woman if you heard her voice! And if your avatar is, for example, a cartoon rabbit, it might be difficult for you to make your voice sound appropriately rabbity.

Other Residents eschew the voice feature for reasons that have nothing to do with roleplay. Some people don't want to be overheard by or disturbed by other people nearby in real life. In fact, you can't always count on other Residents having their speakers turned on. Still other Residents are hearing-impaired in real life, and enjoy the ability to be just like everyone else while logged in. People communicating in a non-native language often find it easier to understand text, in which their own thoughts are accentless. Others find that, with the ability to scroll through a conversation, text is more conducive to multitasking, or they like to use the text-logging feature built into the Grid.

THERE'S NO GOLD RUSH

An awful lot of articles in recent years have referred to a *Second Life* "gold rush," particularly when talking about marketing projects. And it was that way for some real-life organizations that were early adopters. Not that they made a bundle selling their products to people via their *SL* world avatars! No, the "gold" was in the form of press coverage, when mainstream media outlets reported that these companies were involved in *SL* at all. It made great "news of the weird." Most early projects were designed for photo opportunities and press releases, and tended to look like the real-world stores and other locations they were intended to promote.

After a while it was no longer a novelty for companies to set up virtual stores, and companies that came along in the next wave didn't get so much press. Yet many continue to come to *SL* with projects that would appeal only to mainstream media or staff members unfamiliar with *SL*, rather than being geared toward existing *SL* Residents. These projects don't do so well, and that's why there's been a media backlash that claims *SL* wasn't such a great marketing venue after all and that it was probably not much good for anything except virtual infidelities.

The problem was not with the Grid or the *Second Life* world. The problem was that so many projects weren't designed to appeal to *SL* Residents. Of course they didn't succeed in selling anything to anyone in-world!

WHY SOME RESIDENTS AREN'T WELCOMING

Early adopters of *SL* tended to be a particularly smart, technically able, creative bunch. They also, as a group, were a bit impatient with corporations and governments and any sort of marketing. Many of them didn't want their second lives, which so far had been relatively free of corporate branding and the like, to be cluttered up with ads and marketing pitches. They felt they were bombarded with enough advertising in their real lives, and said so on the forums. So when the first organizations came into *SL* to work, some Residents went as far as having their avatars carry protest signs.

The *SL* world's user base is broader now, but in part because of some of the early mistakes made by some organizations hoping to strike it rich in the marketing "gold rush," there are still some negative feelings about real companies and institutions in *SL*. However, organizations that learn to fit in with *SL* Resident culture can overcome this bias. (I'll discuss this more in Part 2 of this book, and cover how to undertake various types of projects in Part 3.)

Similarly, some of the first educators and researchers in *SL* were a bit clumsy in their approach. There were early incidents in which Residents felt—rightly—that they were being spied upon or treated like guinea pigs rather than human beings. Imagine how you would feel if an entire class of students set up right next to your vacation hideaway, left trash lying around, logged your conversations, and posted them on the Internet with criticism and mean-spirited comments. This is exactly what happened to some early Residents. Things have improved greatly in the years since then, but sometimes *SL* Residents are still subject to that kind of inconsiderate behavior. For example, a constant stream of researchers (often students) posts on the *Second Life* official forums requesting that Residents please take their surveys. Most of these surveys include the same questions that have been asked over and over. Often they aren't spell-checked, or refer to *SL* as a game—a sure way to irritate a substantial number of Residents. Some Residents make a hobby of critiquing these surveys, pointing out how the questions and their wording make it clear that the researcher isn't familiar with *Second Life*. Some post outright that they are sick of badly planned surveys and suggest that the researchers log in and do their own research.

Ow. Doesn't sound like the locals are going to rev up their welcome wagon and rush to greet you, does it?

But some organizations do get a warm welcome to the Grid, along with everything from volunteer help to free custom-developed content. Next you'll learn what they're doing right, and how you can go about doing the same thing.

GAINING ACCEPTANCE

What do the American Cancer Society, NASA, and John Wiley & Sons, Inc. have in common? All of these organizations have received remarkable support from *Second Life* Residents. What did they do right?

Rather than a gold-rush boomtown on the wild frontier, try viewing the *SL* world as a quickly growing city that's been around for a few years. There's infrastructure; there are land barons who got in and claimed valuable property early; there are established local brands, institutions, and traditions; and there are Residents who are pillars of the community.

Once a city has reached this stage, the opportunity to open up the first bakery or barber shop in town is already long gone. If you've ever lived in a small town, you know what it's like when someone wants to come in and compete with the local merchants. You'd better offer something new or better, and you need to fit in with the locals—offer them something they value without stepping on their toes. Maybe join the chamber of commerce so that you can network with and get the assistance of the local community. Get to know your neighbors and introduce yourself to the local press.

The American Cancer Society (ACS) established its Grid presence the right way, with a project in *SL* run by respected Residents who enlisted the volunteer assistance and support of other well-known merchants, content creators, and celebrities. The ACS's activities in *SL* are many, including various fundraising projects and support-group meetings. What really set them apart early on, though, was their in-world Relay for Life project. The annual event in *SL* is treated just like real-life Relay for Life events, with L$ donations converted to US$. And that real-world similarity is probably what makes the ACS's presence such a success. Residents (despite some avatars' outlandish appearance) appreciated being treated the same way as people in the real world. No one from the ACS condescended to them. No one called *Second Life* a game. Residents were approached like any real-life community and asked to participate in a good cause that they could really get behind.

Although the ACS has its own island on the Grid, its presence is ubiquitous. All over the Grid, in all sorts of Resident shops, you might encounter donation kiosks or advertising for fundraisers (Figure 1.8). By making a thoughtful entry into SL, the ACS is now a real part of the community.

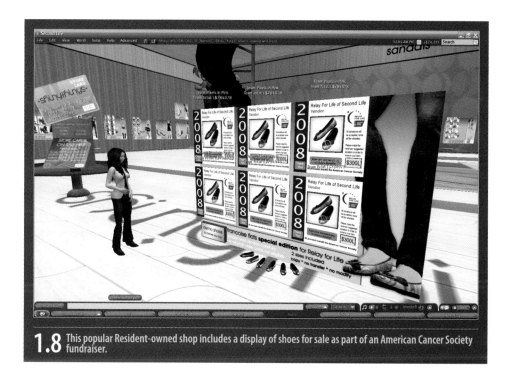

1.8 This popular Resident-owned shop includes a display of shoes for sale as part of an American Cancer Society fundraiser.

Similarly, NASA got its start in *SL* by asking for help from Residents. A grassroots project run by Residents, the International Spaceflight Museum (ISM), exhibits scale models of spacecraft, mission control, the solar system, and more. It's one of the most celebrated destinations on the Grid, and has even established itself as a real-life nonprofit organization.

Rather than going into competition with the ISM, NASA representatives approached the museum's management and asked for help, acknowledging the experience and expertise of the established ISM community. That was the right thing to do. That way no one was worried that NASA was going to compete with or overshadow the ISM. Residents liked the plans NASA had for their project, and the opportunity to give their input and assistance to bring valuable displays and events to the community. It wasn't long before NASA had placed its own island adjacent to the ISM (Figure 1.9). Resident consultants and developers—some of them professionals—volunteered to help to create much of NASA's *SL* content. In fact, my own company designed, developed, and donated the NASA CoLab Headquarters building. Why? Because we wanted to be a part of something good—good for the *SL* community and for our real-life community.

John Wiley & Sons, Inc. is another organization that has been very successful in connecting with the *Second Life* community. In fact, I have heard Residents say things like, "Wow, Wiley gets it! I bet their *SL* books are pretty good." This is, don't forget, coming from a community that historically has distrusted corporations. What did Wiley do right?

Some Wiley staff already had a good understanding of *SL* because they'd been publishing books about it for a couple of years. They logged in and became familiar with the world, its features, and its Residents. That put them ahead of a lot of companies. When they hired me to promote their products in *SL* and I asked, "If you could be any kind of animal, what kind of animal would you be?" they caught on instantly. Pretty soon they graduated from their stigmatizing "newbie" avatars and transformed into cute, cuddly cartoon animals—a leopard, a hippo, and a penguin wearing teensy Wiley-branded jackets. They had a good time racing around on their ice skates and snowball-fighting with Residents at their events. But more importantly, Residents had a good time with them. These weren't evil corporate stuffed shirts who just wanted their money—they were *SL* Residents, too.

1.9 This bridge connects the Resident-owned International Spaceflight Museum and NASA's CoLab.

Wiley's speakers at their events, as well as my event staff and I, were respected community members. We gave away fun goodies and tools that were useful to Residents who wanted to create their own content or run their own events. There was even an ad for the International Spaceflight Museum in the slide rotation between events. Wiley "got it" and fit in.

You'll read more about the *SL* Resident community in Part 2, but for now the take-away is this: if you want to succeed with *SL* community, you need to be a part of it.

HOW TO PLAN SUCCESSFUL PROJECTS

It takes a bit of knowledge about the Grid and—for some projects—about *SL* Residents to plan and develop something successful. Many ideas don't work out because they are based on approaches that would work in real life or the Web rather than what works best on the Grid. This book will give you a great start on understanding what will work and what won't.

Sometimes you'll need to hire a professional Solution Provider to help with your project. For some projects you can buy user-created content or build a few things yourself and have enough for a prototype; in other instances you might be able to do all the work yourself. Sometimes Resident volunteers can help.

Many people find it a good idea to start out small, first exploring, then starting with a small parcel of land where they can experiment a bit before committing to a large project that requires a great investment of time and money. Some even start with a scale model (Figure 1.10).

The first thing you need to do to make your project a success—something that everyone in the aforementioned examples did—is to make an *SL* account yourself.

1.10 This is a scale model used to plan an island in development for The University of Queensland.

LOG IN AND TRY IT

The concept of this section can't be emphasized enough: *You must log in and try things out.*

There's really no way to understand what you are getting into without making an account and wandering around *SL* yourself. You could read hundreds of pages, but until you log in and try it, you won't truly get it.

Sure, some organizations hire a developer, tell them what to do, and that's that. But if you do that, your odds of success are low. Some developers are very good at what they do, and others are not. Some have experience in related fields, but that doesn't always mean they know *SL* much better than you do. There have been some spectacular failures—some developers really need the work, and will agree to build whatever you think up, and they may never mention or even realize that the plan isn't well suited to the Grid.

Spending some time in *SL* yourself will let you understand what is likely to work, and allow you to judge whether anyone you hire to work for you on the Grid really knows what they're doing.

WHY *SECOND LIFE?*

This *Second Life* stuff may be more complicated than you thought. How will you ever get a handle on all of these technical considerations, plus learn your way around the Resident community? Is it really worth all of the time and effort? Maybe there's an easier virtual world to use, or maybe you could just do this stuff on your old website?

Sure, there are other virtual worlds, but none of them offers the same flexibility and the diverse user-created content available to you on the *SL* Grid. It offers more useful features and freedom than any other platform of its kind. Because of its many strengths, the Grid is complex. And the social challenges are simply the nature of the virtual-world type beast rather than a *SL*-specific issue.

Websites are very valuable, and the Grid certainly won't replace them any time soon. However, it offers an entirely different experience from looking at a website. Visitors go to your site and look at it. Visitors go to your space in *Second Life* and interact with one another and share the experience. The same social immersion that can make some things a challenge is one of the Grid's great strengths.

Read on for examples of how organizations like yours are already successfully using the *SL* Grid for their projects.

CHAPTER 02

TEACH AND TRAIN

What sorts of educational projects are going on in *Second Life* now? Is there assistance for educators who want to do their own projects in-world? Can you really get credit for a course you attend in a virtual world? What sorts of projects work best in *SL*? Is it hard to get funding and approval? This chapter will answer these questions and more!

WHAT ARE EDUCATORS DOING IN *SL*?

Distance learning, simulations, social experiments, prototyping, scientific visualization, corporate training, public lectures, and collaboration; these are just some of the uses educators have found for the *Second Life* Grid. Some institutions currently using the Grid include Harvard University, Princeton University (Figure 2.1), Stanford University, Edinburgh University (UK), The University of Queensland (Australia), University of Hamburg (Germany), Toulouse Business School (France), Fontys University of Applied Sciences (Netherlands), Lazarski School of Commerce and Law (Poland), Loyalist College (Canada), The Hong Kong Polytechnic University, Massachusetts Institute of Technology, Sungshin University (Korea), and many others all over the globe. You can see a partial list of educational institutions and organizations that have a *Second Life* Grid presence on the SimTeach wiki at **www.simteach.com/wiki/index.php?title=Institutions_and_Organizations_in_SL**.

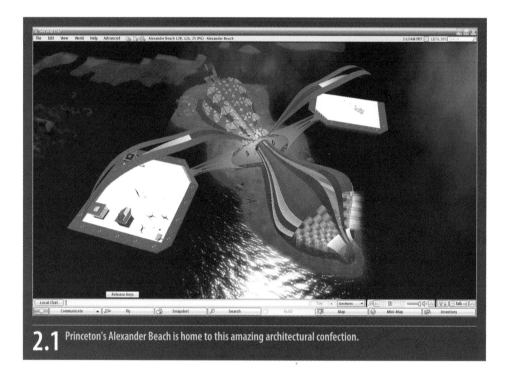

2.1 Princeton's Alexander Beach is home to this amazing architectural confection.

There are thousands of educators in-world and hundreds of private regions dedicated to educational projects. According to "A Spring 2008 'snapshot' of UK Higher and Further Education Developments in *Second Life*,"* a report by John Kirriemuir and funded by the Eduserv Foundation, "While an accurate figure is difficult to determine (partially due to the non-public nature of some developments), as a rough estimate some three-quarters of UK universities are actively developing or using *SL*, at the institutional, departmental and/or individual academic level."

Says Rafi Santo, virtual community manager with Global Kids (*SL* avatar Bhikku Beeks in the Main Grid, Rafi GKid in Teen *Second Life*), "Educators dealing with almost any content area can use *SL*'s flexibility as a platform and its content creation tools to bring in content related to their educational objectives. On top of this, there is an incredibly enterprising, innovative and collaborative *Second Life* educators community that provides support and examples for educators that are interested in utilizing the space."

* http://www.eduserv.org.uk/foundation/sl/~/media/Foundation/sl/uksnapshot052008/final%20pdf.ashx

Educators pioneered the use of the *Second Life* Grid for real-life projects. Let's take a closer look at a few educational projects in *Second Life*.

MEDICAL TRAINING: UC DAVIS MEDICAL CENTER IN *SL*

Way back in 2005 I was hired by the University of California, Davis, Medical Center to work on their project in *SL*. That was the first instance I am aware of in which *SL* was used for a real-life project that wasn't only an experiment. UC Davis was, in fact, my first client. What was Davis doing in *SL*? They had a few projects going on, but the first one I worked on was a simulation funded by the US Centers for Disease Control and Prevention and used by the State of California's health department to train its staff in the deployment of emergency medical clinics that would be used to distribute antibiotics in case of biological attack. The project modeled some real-life locations that would be commandeered by the state health department and used as clinic sites, such as a gymnasium and an expo center, along with their furnishings and the supplies and tools that would need to be deployed. This way, real-life workers would be familiar with the locations—if you told them to turn left at the water fountain, they'd know just what you meant, because they had been there and seen that water fountain in the virtual world. They'd familiarize themselves with the equipment they'd deploy and practice how to arrange that equipment for optimum traffic flow in specific clinic locations.

Although this simulation is located at a region that's not open to the public, you can see some of it in a video at **http://news.com.com/1606-2-6099774.html**.

Davis had a lot going on, and it wasn't long before I was working on an improved version of their Virtual Hallucinations project, which allowed visitors' avatars to wander through a re-creation of the university's mental-health clinic while experiencing what it was like to be schizophrenic (Figure 2.2). This was a downright creepy experience—and very educational. The latest version of the project is in a private region, but you can still visit the original Virtual Hallucinations at **http://slurl.com/secondlife/sedig/27/45/22/**.

2.2 At the original version of Virtual Hallucinations, visitors experience re-creations of actual hallucinations reported to researchers.

UC Davis is just one of many educational institutions and nonprofit organizations using *Second Life* for medical projects. Some others include Ann Meyers Medical Center, a medical-training simulation for practicing diagnostic skills; Second Health, a fully equipped hospital simulation; Heart Murmurs, where you can listen to and learn about heart sounds; and The Gene Pool, a virtual location for learning about genetics.

RELIGIOUS STUDIES: THE UNIVERSITY OF QUEENSLAND

Rather than the body or mind, some institutions study matters of the spirit. The University of Queensland started out using the *SL* Grid for distance learning. Postgraduate students Daniel Walker (*SL* avatar Merryn Beck) and Morgan Leigh (*SL* avatar Thaiis Thei) meet with supervisor Dr. Helen Farley, lecturer in studies in religion and esotericism (*SL* avatar Rupert Uriza) and two other students via the *Second Life* Grid. Morgan, who lives in Melbourne, far from the university, says, "It is hard to remain motivated when you never leave your house and spend all day every day in front of your computer—not much outside stimulus. You miss the happy accidents of meeting people that you get at an actual university. But being able to use *Second Life* as a place to meet has been a help." Dr. Farley adds, "I think it has made us feel connected and like a small research community. Of course it not the same as being in a room together, but it's the next best thing."

Dr. Farley meets with these students at a private region called EdTech Island, which is owned by another university (Figure 2.3). She explains, "That's because I did a course through Boise State University about teaching in *Second Life*. That was a great course run by Lisa Dawley. It was a wonderful way of finding out what was possible in *SL* and seeing what other people are doing. It has been great to experiment with and try things out."

Dr. Farley has also used *SL* as a venue for teaching meditation, just to see how it would work out. Then she and Dr. Rick Strelan (*SL* avatar Nansar Blessed) sought approval and funding for purchase of an island for a more ambitious use of the *SL* Grid. Says Dr. Farley, "We send students out to religious spaces in real life, but there are issues with insurance, transport, and so on. And not all religious spaces are available to us in real life. Not every religion is represented here [in Brisbane, Queensland]. Still, I worried about sending students to religious spaces in *Second Life*. I thought that maybe religious practitioners would feel like zoo animals. With students

2.3 The University of Queensland's temporary location is hosted by Boise State University.

watching them and looking at them. That's when I started thinking about having an island with buildings resembling religious spaces. This would also have the advantage of being able to provide information, but most importantly, students could roleplay and re-create rituals. But we lacked the expertise to build those things ourselves. I wanted to learn how to do it and that was the original plan, that I would build them. But it quickly became obvious that I wasn't up to the job—skillswise and timewise. That's when we recruited an experienced and talented builder and her team—that was a great decision!"

She adds, "Because of the level of interest in this project we thought it was important to have a build that was very professional—another good reason to get an experienced builder. We hope to use the island in a number of our courses—obviously because of the large number of buildings. I think that helped when it came to getting funding—this had a wide application for us.

"We hope to take classes into *Second Life* and have them perform rituals or roleplay or take part in other activities. We hope to use the space for novel forms of assessment. Maybe we could ask students to make a piece of machinima instead of write an essay, or there are some interesting quiz tools available too. But we also want students to be able to go into *Second Life* in their own time and wander around the buildings. I want to provide resources to make that worthwhile. I also feel that this environment will help with equity. We have a reasonable number of students who don't have English as their first language. I think having the option of communicating in text will help them. But also being able to return to the builds and pick up on the information they missed first time round will be helpful. Also, a lot of students work. Most of our students are doing some work and it makes it increasingly difficult for them to get to class. They'll be able to go to the build or meet other people there and do the activities they couldn't do in real time.

"In August, we'll be hosting a conference called Alternative Expressions of the Numinous. I've had a few people ask if they can present in *Second Life*—so that's something that we're looking at too."

Dr. Farley, Dr. Strelan, and their students aren't the only ones exploring the use of the *SL* Grid for religious studies. In fact, Dr. Farley was one of the presenters at The Future of Religions/Religions of the Future, a two-day in-world conference in June 2008 hosted by Extropia and the Al-Andalus Caliphate Project.

LANGUAGE LEARNING: THE BRITISH COUNCIL IN TEEN *SECOND LIFE*

The British Council has its own multiregion estate in Teen *Second Life* where teens can visit its self-learning resources to practice their English, learn about UK history and culture, or just hang out and have a good time. The island is full of locations from UK history and legend, and even the future—complete with flying cars.

"I was working as a consultant on a podcasting project for the British Council and . . . had been introduced to *SL* through an article in *Wired*. . . . As soon as I was in [*SL*] I got it," says Graham Stanley, *Second Life* project manager, the British Council (*SL* avatar Baldric Commons on the Main Grid, Graham Bluecoat in Teen *Second Life*).

He continues, "It was the freedom that *SL* seemed to offer an educational project that appealed, and the look of it. I tried a few other worlds too, but they didn't feel right. And then I realized that the main educational action is all taking place in *SL* with so much support and work being done in universities even back then—now it's all the more apparent.

"At first the plan was to take one [private region] and to do stuff ourselves. We were given four hours a week to work on it. Then the directors of the British Council got wind of what we planned. [We were] told to upgrade the project and make sure it looked good. That's when we started to look around for professional developers.

"The space is principally a very attractive place to spend time, and then there's the quests. The idea is for the learning to take a back seat but to be present, but the main drive would be to attract students through the use of story or through game learning. If we can intrigue them enough then they'll do what they can to understand, and with language learning this is the key (Figure 2.4). We are having problems pitching the level. This is why we want to make it multi-layered, with the possibility that low-level language-learners can follow but also that the higher-level learners don't get bored. So we are using text and audio and also hiding things to get the students searching around the island. Something [our developer, Kimberly Rufer-Bach] said early on was key to this—that in your designs if you have hidden features, then people will come back and explore more."

2.4 The British Council offers fun learning experiences in Teen *Second Life*.
Image courtesy of the British Council

"Essentially this is what we are doing, and we have chosen a UK theme because of the nature of our organization," Stanley says. "We also can repurpose a lot of the British Council's output elsewhere on the Web and link to it, etc. We are experimenting, as everyone else is, with the uniqueness of the environment, trying to learn from experience (and from others) how best to use it for education. That's why conferences like . . . SLanguages are so important. I've also met a whole new group of educators that I'd never have met if it hadn't been for *SL*. My horizons have been broadened considerably, which is a great thing." We'll take another look at the British Council's *SL* Grid project in Chapter 14, "Work in Teen *Second Life*."

Stanley is in good company—he was one of the presenters at the second annual SLanguages conference in-world (**www.slanguages.net/home.php**). Language learning is one of the hottest uses of the *SL* Grid for education, and not only by universities and nonprofits like the British Council. Another of my clients, Languagelab .com, is a business that offers immersive language classes in *Second Life*.

There's a multitude of fascinating educational projects on the Grid, covering a wide range of subjects. Some educators even make a project of cataloging educational projects in Second Life (Figure 2.5).

RESOURCES FOR EDUCATORS

There's a lot of information to gather and assimilate if you want to do an educational project on the *Second Life* Grid. Fortunately, there's a growing number of assistance sources offering educators everything from free and discounted land to tools and in-world classes.

ASSISTANCE FROM LINDEN LAB

Linden Lab offers special assistance for educational projects in *Second Life*. These include discounted private-region pricing and other resources for information and support.

2.5 International Schools Island, a project of The Education Project Asia, is home to a 3D index of educational venues in *Second Life*.

Linden Lab offers a substantial discount for the purchase and maintenance fees of private regions used for educational and nonprofit projects. At press time, the purchase price for a full region is reduced from US$1,000 to US$700 and the monthly maintenance charge is reduced from US$295 to US$147.50. For homestead regions, which are private regions with the same amount of space but fewer resources, the discount reduces the normal setup fee of US$375 to US$262, and the maintenance fee is reduced from US$95 to US$66.50 monthly. Now that's a bargain! However, to receive the discounted rates, you will need to fill out a Special Order Form and allow Linden Lab to verify your status as an educator or nonprofit. You'll also be required to pay your region's maintenance fees for either six or twelve months in advance when you purchase the region. Keep in mind that this special pricing applies only to purchases of private regions.

You can learn more about the Special Order Form at **https://support.secondlife.com/ics/support/default .asp?deptID=4417&task=knowledge&questionID=4897**. Note that you may need to log in with your *SL* account to access that page.

In addition to discounted land, Linden Lab offers educator resources including a blog, mailing lists, and more. Your first stop, according to Claudia L'Amoreaux (aka Claudia Linden), should be the *Second Life* Grid website at **http://secondlifegrid.net/**.

Additionally, Linden Lab sponsors the *Second Life* Education Blog, better known as the SLED Blog, which is edited by Sarah Robbins, a Ph.D. candidate at Ball State University (*SL* avatar Intellagirl Tully). This resource is a virtual crossroads where educators discuss their *SL* projects and other aspects of education in *SL*, offering one another advice and assistance. It includes a calendar of upcoming educational events, and can be viewed at **www.sl-educationblog.org/**.

Linden Lab also maintains some mailing lists specifically for educators:

- *Second Life* Educators, also known as SLED: This mailing list is very, very busy. Here you'll find information and announcements from Linden Lab of interest to educators. But what really keeps this email forum so active is the participation of over 5,000 members (according to L'Amoreaux in May, 2008) discussing the use of *Second Life* for education and training: **https://lists.secondlife.com/cgi-bin/mailman/listinfo/educators**.

- Educatorsandteens: Primarily for those working with teens aged 13 to 17, this list includes information and announcements from Linden Lab, as well as discussion among educators and academics, and even a few teens: **https://lists.secondlife.com/cgi-bin/mailman/listinfo/educatorsandteens**.

- Healthcare: This list is primarily for people interested in or currently using the *SL* Grid for healthcare support and education: **https://lists.secondlife.com/cgi-bin/mailman/listinfo/healthcare**.

- *Second Life* Researchers: This list is a great way to keep in touch with others who are using the *Second Life* Grid for research projects: **http://list.academ-x.com/listinfo.cgi/slrl-academ-x.com**.

OTHER SOURCES OF ASSISTANCE

Linden Lab isn't the only source of assistance you'll find on the *Second Life* Grid. Nonprofits, Solution Providers, *Second Life* Residents, and fellow educators all offer resources for educators in *Second Life*. A few are listed here:

- The New Media Consortium's NMC Campus (Figure 2.6) is one nonprofit that's giving educators in *SL* a huge boost. You can view the consortium's *Second Life*-specific information at **http://sl.nmc.org/**. NMC offers a wealth of resources to educators on the Grid, including grants, subsidized virtual-land rentals, classes, tools, settings for use by researchers, and more. You'll learn more about NMC in Chapter 4, "Nonprofits Reach Out."

- Eduserv, a UK nonprofit, also awards some grants, offers conference space, and more for projects in *Second Life*: **www.eduserv.org.uk/foundation/sl**.

- SimTeach, operated by Jeremy Kemp, an instructional designer at San Jose State University (*SL* avatar Jeremy Kabumpo) offers a wiki for *SL* educators and researchers. It's an unparalleled informational resource: **http://simteach.com/**.

- *SL* Library 2.0 is a project of the Alliance Library System and Online Programming for All Libraries (OPAL) and offers informational resources and land rentals for educators. You'll learn more about it in Chapter 4, but you can check it out now at **http://infoisland.org/**.

- SciLands (Figure 2.7) is a virtual continent on the *SL* Grid that includes over 20 science- and technology-related organizations. Members meet to share ideas and help one another, and they share various resources, such as meeting spaces. Learn more and check out the calendar at **www.scilands.org/**.

- RezEd is an online hub for educators working in virtual worlds, and the site at **www.rezed.org/** is full of useful information about education using the *SL* Grid.

- The International Society for Technology in Education has a presence on the Grid, along with an in-world group and events: **www.iste.org/Content/NavigationMenu/Membership/Member_Networking/ISTE_Second_Life.htm**.

- Discovery Educators Network offers weekly events in *Second Life*: **http://blog.discoveryeducation.com/secondlife/**.

- Metanomics, a project of Cornell University, offers weekly events of interest to educators: **http://metanomics.net/**.

2.6 The NMC Campus hosts many events for educators.

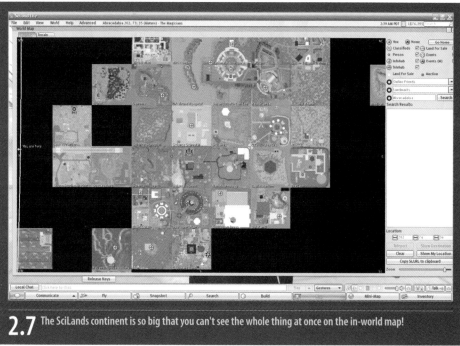

2.7 The SciLands continent is so big that you can't see the whole thing at once on the in-world map!

There are numerous other in-world groups to join, including Real Life Education in *Second Life*, *Second Life* Research, K-12 Educators, Community Colleges in *SL*, Educators Coffee House, Schome Educators, and UK Educators. Information about each of these groups, including how to join, can be found in *Second Life* by using the Search feature.

Keep an eye on
the SLEDevents
calendar at **http://
sledevents.blogspot
.com/**. It shows
one or more edu-
cational events
going on in *SL* just
about every day.

Some educators find it valuable to join lots of groups and attend the weekly events some groups hold. Group members usually receive announcements reminding them of meetings, but if you are in too many groups that send in-world announcements or one that sends a lot of announcements or group instant messages, they can disrupt your work. Meetings may be useful for learning about best practices and what mistakes to avoid, but that information is usually more efficiently accessed via blogs, mailing lists, and websites than via in-world meetings. Meetings are great for networking and socializing, though, and sometimes you'll see an interesting demo. Just don't fall into the trap of spending your entire workday at meetings and events rather than working on your own project.

If you want to attend a real-life *SL* educational conference, you'll be interested in the *Second Life* Education Community Conference (SLEDcc), which is part of the Official *Second Life* Community Convention. If you can't attend in real life, you can still attend the in-world portions of the conference. Learn more at **http://sledcc .wikispaces.com/**.

CREDIT AND INTERNSHIPS

Numerous institutions offer for-credit courses in *Second Life*; the SimTeach wiki lists hundreds of universities and community colleges offering for-credit courses. Internships are offered by organizations as diverse as the University of Southern California, Global Kids, and NASA.

Rafi Santo, the virtual community manager at Global Kids (*SL* avatar Bhikku Beeks on the Main Grid, Rafi GKid in Teen *Second Life*) says, "We offer community-service hours for teens that participate in programs that in some way serve the larger Teen *Second Life* community."

"We are looking to work with universities in order to provide internships," says David Schwartz, Ph.D. (*SL* avatar Benton Wunderlich), founder and president of Music Academy Online (Figure 2.8).

2.8 This Museum of Women Composers is located at the Music Academy Online's island in *Second Life*.

"*Second Life* is a virtual microcosm of the real world that includes the entire gamut of real-world businesses and organizations," says Barbara McMullen, Dean of Online Learning at Monroe College, in an article in *The Greentree Gazette*.* "So why shouldn't our students have an opportunity to work for these businesses?" As of November, 2007, a dozen Monroe College students had participated as interns in *Second Life*, and five of them interned a second time. The nature of the students' internships varied, with IT students focusing on content creation and design, including scripting, while business students pursued projects like in-world marketing, sales, and customer relations. "One of our graduates is now employed in *Second Life* by the company she interned with and is earning an income," McMullen says.

WHAT PROJECTS ARE A GOOD MATCH FOR *SL*?

Good projects for the Grid are immersive, interactive, and social. *SL* offers 3D graphics, the option to communicate via text or voice, custom immersive environments (which can often be developed inexpensively and quickly), preexisting content, a community of educators and Residents, streaming media, and the ability to log in from anywhere to interact with people far away. While the *SL* Grid isn't an ideal platform for reviewing or collaborating on documents, for example, or for holding events with huge audiences, there are workarounds and tools to allow those things, and it's certainly useful for reviewing or collaborating on artworks, displays, demonstrations, and exhibits, and for smaller events.

It's important to learn what works best on the Grid before you start your project. "I have seen other organizations jump in and start a project without getting to know the environment . . . they decided they needed to be in *SL* and so built a replica of their school. Exactly the kind of thing that most organizations (ourselves included) think they need to do before they really understand *SL*. So they (and others) have a nice replica of their RL [real-life] building and other parts of the city . . . but now realize that it's not very practical in *SL* or very useful to them other than being a glorified advert. So, I think that's the key . . . immersion in *SL*," says Graham Stanley. He continues, "I understand why there are buildings and classrooms in *SL*, but personally prefer other settings. However, there is a strange logic sometimes in using a familiar setting like a conference room, such as at the SLanguages conference. You don't have to explain to everyone what to do, where to sit, etc., and everyone knows that they are going to watch a slide presentation—it is effective and saves time. I think there's room for both, but I'm personally attracted to more interesting, exciting environments in *SL*."

Dr. Helen Farley agrees that re-creations of familiar educational settings aren't the best use of *SL*: "I don't see the point of re-creating classrooms or lecture halls in *Second Life*. In *Second Life* you can do anything you can imagine. *Second Life* provides the perfect environment for immersion. I can stand in front of a class and talk about a religion. I can show them some pictures and they might learn some more. But if I take them to a religious space, let them participate in the rituals [Figure 2.9]—well, that's an experience they won't forget. It will give them a much fuller understanding of what it means to an adherent of that religion. Empathy and immersion—that's what I think *SL* can offer to students of studies in religion."

You'll find a lot of learning environments in-world that don't look anything like a classroom, and creative ways of mixing educational content with fun. Claudia L'Amoreaux says, "You can just have everyone sitting in chairs and do straight lectures, and there can be times when that's even useful. But I think where it really shines is when you come up with interesting ways to get people participating." She cites an example of an event about immersive education where the event facilitator stood on a diving board while many of the other attendees floated in inner tubes in a swimming pool. "There is this ability to have a lot of fun and really play—bring play into learning. I like it when I see that really being taken advantage of," she says.

2.9 When an avatar enters this synagogue at The University of Queensland's region, a scripted object reminds them to wear a headcovering and where to get one if needed.

 AN OVERVIEW OF MATHEMATICS IN *SECOND LIFE*

BY DR. HENRY SEGERMAN, POSTDOCTORAL LECTURER AT THE UNIVERSITY OF TEXAS AT AUSTIN (*SL* AVATAR SEIFERT SURFACE)

As with most of the sciences, the mathematics activity in *SL* is generally in the form of exhibits made by educators and experts. There isn't much in the way of classes being taught or students building their class projects in *SL*. There are separate reasons for each of these:

First, in terms of lecturing in SL, the current state of the technology behind *SL* makes it difficult to, for example, draw on a whiteboard, write mathematical notation and so on. Powerpoint-style presentations are possible, but time-consuming to put together, and communicating with students when questions come up will be difficult.

There are some experiments involving freehand drawing with prims or particles, but nothing that you'd want to write anything down with.

There is also a set of prims with symbols on them (by Leandra Kohnke) which are a very simple although slow solution to the problem: one can arrange an equation just by rezzing blocks with the symbols on them and moving them around. The lack of good support from the client itself may change quickly once web content is well integrated with *SL*, as there are solutions to this kind of problem on the Web. I might still not want to lecture with these kinds of tools, but at least I could have a conversation with a student using mathematical notation.

Second, class projects built in *SL*: it is certainly possible to make interesting and informative mathematical exhibits in *SL*, but it isn't easy. As with the other sciences, getting students to make those exhibits themselves will go likely too far into the technical issues of getting *SL* to do what you want it to do, rather than spending time on the content of the course.

On the positive side, you can get a better sense of a three-dimensional construction by being able to walk around inside of it, being able to turn it over in your hands, or rather with your camera. Xah Lee (*SL* avatar Xah Toll) writes at **http://xahlee.org/3d/viz.html** extensively on where the state of the art is in scientific visualization, and where it should be within 10 years:

"Perhaps due to the evolution of our perception system, the experience of actually walking on or inside a math object is vastly different than just seeing it as zero-thickness abstract lines and sheets rotating around its center."

I would add another plus, in that multiple people can be present in different locations around an object, discussing it from different angles.

So the potential is certainly there, but what can we do currently? One can generate (albeit a little slowly) arbitrary parametric surfaces using **www.lslwiki.net/lslwiki/wakka.php?wakka=LibraryParametricSurfaceRezzer**, and many people have made polyhedra, geodesic domes, and so on. I have also had success with animating a rotating four-dimensional hypercube, generating the Lorenz Attractor, building various fractals and knots, and making the "crooked house" from a short story by Robert A. Heinlein, which is a house with eight cubical rooms, connected as the three-dimensional faces of a four-dimensional hypercube.

There are, no doubt, many ideas out there yet to be realized (virtualized?), and the possibilities for mathematical content can only increase as the tools improve.

Obviously, some projects are better suited to the *SL* Grid than others. And still others may need to be modified to work well in-world. Like any other tool, the *Second Life* Grid has both strengths and weaknesses. Some of these are technical considerations, and others are social. In Part 2 of this book we'll take a close look at Resident culture in *SL*, and in Part 3 we'll study the nuts and bolts of doing a project on the *SL* Grid.

 EDUCATORS' FAVORITE ADVICE FOR EDUCATION IN *SECOND LIFE*

Sage advice from *SL* educators:

"Experiment with your own private property first, make your own projects and promote those before you try to teach something to your students." —Nadja Franz, freelance teacher at the University of Applied Sciences Kiel, Ph.D. candidate, University of Potsdam (*SL* avatar Nadja Revnik)

"My number-one piece of advice is, immerse yourself. Take the time to learn as much as you can about *SL* by experiencing it. The lessons you will learn are invaluable when you begin to construct your own project." —David Schwartz, Ph.D., founder and president, Music Academy Online (*SL* avatar Benton Wunderlich)

"Have clear goals from the very beginning. Realize that the implementation details will undoubtedly change over time, as you'll be learning more and more as you spend time experimenting in *SL*. Be focused on your goals, but be flexible in your thinking. Also include a study of outcomes in your project. Quantify success as much as possible. And publish your results!" —John Lester, leader of Linden Lab's Proactive Mentoring Program in Education and Healthcare (*SL* avatar Pathfinder Linden)

"Do not be in a rush. Spend time in *Second Life* becoming acclimated to the environment. This will inform you how best to use it in a course. Attend courses yourself—there are always many on building, etc. and most of these are for free. The teachers of these courses are adept at using *SL* for delivering content." —Steven Hornik, lecturer, University of Central Florida, Kenneth Dixon School of Accounting (*SL* avatar Robins Hermano)

"Be flexible! The way you thought that your project would turn out in *Second Life* may not match up exactly to how it actually gets implemented, but just keep your eye on your broader goal and be open to changing how you think those goals will be reached. Also, be sure to reach out to other educators to bounce ideas off of. There are a lot of people with a lot of experience, and there's a lot to be learned in terms of best practice from prior projects. (Not to mention many mistakes that can be easily avoided by asking a couple of key questions!)" —Rafi Santo, virtual community manager at Global Kids (*SL* avatar Bhikku Beeks on the Main Grid, Rafi GKid in Teen *Second Life*)

"The more one knows about how it all works, the better. It is also more convincing when trying to sell it to potential fund-providers." —Dr. Rick Strelan, senior lecturer in studies in religion, The University of Queensland (*SL* avatar Nansar Blessed)

LEARNING YOUR SUBJECT VERSUS LEARNING THE INTERFACE

As you'll hear over and over if you talk with other educators or participate in one of the education-related mailing lists, *Second Life* does have a learning curve. One of the challenges of using the *SL* Grid to teach is designing your project so that students' need to learn how to use *Second Life* doesn't overshadow their primary subject of study. You can do a number of things to make the *SL* learning curve less steep.

It's important to offer a good orientation experience that teaches your students the *SL* skills they'll need to participate in-world. New *SL* Residents start their virtual lives at Help Island with an in-world web browser open to the New User Tutorial. However, sometimes it isn't ideal for educators' purposes. Help Island offers self-teaching experiences in some skills, but they may not be applicable to the course you are teaching. Also, if you use the Registration API, which we'll discuss further in Part 2 of this book, your students will log in directly to your private region, without any prior orientation experience.

Your avatar's Inventory may contain copies of parts of Linden Lab–created orientation stations, but they are far from complete and as of this writing they don't offer practice in some of the newest features available in-world. That means you may need to create an orientation experience or have one created for you.

 A NEW STUDENT'S PERSPECTIVE

"We didn't have any students who had spent any significant time in-world. So, our first class was essentially learning how to operate and move. We had prepared avatars for them beforehand, which saved a lot of time. Then we went through a brief phase when the students explored the 'game' aspect of flying, teleporting, changing clothes, etc. By the third class, we were pretty settled, and could operate the tutorials more smoothly."—Daniel Walker, postgraduate student, The University of Queensland (*SL* avatar Merryn Beck)

 A FEW WORDS ABOUT ORIENTATION

"I think the perfect *SL* orientation experience has yet to be made. It's almost like searching for the Holy Grail. I think it's really difficult because of the difference in experience of people. Lots of people who set up accounts in *SL* are impatient to leave orientation (I know I was) but then realize that it was probably worth spending time learning the basics. I created another avatar and went back!" —Graham Stanley, *Second Life* project manager, the British Council

Another way to make it easier for your students to get started learning something other than *SL* skills is to use tools that make it easier for them to participate without them. For example, Dr. Helen Farley, lecturer of studies in religion at The University of Queensland, recommends using a Pied Piper gadget, which makes a number of seats appear behind your avatar and follow you. She says, "Then when you move, the students follow without having to walk. It removed the need for them to be able to do everything perfectly from the get-go."

When working with people new to the Grid, carefully designed spaces and interfaces really make a difference. Boxes can unpack themselves, information kiosks may whisper to passersby to have them click the kiosks for further information, and structures should be built so that they're easy even for a "newbie" to navigate. You can create maps that will instantly teleport your students to their classroom or a lecture hall. Some convenient tools or scripts can be found in-world, available for free or for purchase with Linden dollars. But in many cases, it might be worthwhile to consider engaging a Solution Provider with experience in creating customized, newbie-friendly user experiences for educational *Second Life* projects.

Graham Stanley, *Second Life* project manager, the British Council, says, "Especially as we are registering students and they are turning up on our island, they don't have the option of an LL orientation, and they found the learning quests too difficult. We have responded to the feedback, asking [The Magicians, the author's company] to build us an orientation area [Figure 2.10] to make the quests easier and provide more support for them. This is why we have started putting teleport maps around the island and also adding things like cartoon guide intros to the quests. Aesthetically I'd prefer not to, but I think there's a need for this. . . . I think that this is the thing about *SL*. It's a dynamic environment. You can try something out and then change it without too much trouble. Nothing is set in stone . . . except, that is, Excalibur on our island."

2.10 Avatars learn how to use *SL* features at the Orientation Stations on the British Council's Teen *Second Life* estate.

The first step for anyone planning a project on the Grid is to learn how to get around it yourself. "Get to know the *Second Life* Grid technology before planning a project," advises L'Amoreaux. "Whoever is reading this has taken the right first step by getting this book and reading it, because hopefully that will provide a lot of answers as well," she says, but adds, "I think that your most important resource is the community itself."

CONDUCTING RESEARCH

An amazing array of research projects is underway in *Second Life*. Some of these include studies of how the appearance of an avatar affects test performance, financial experiments utilizing the *SL* Grid's monetary system, and surveys . . . lots and lots of surveys, often posted on the official *Second Life* forums. Unfortunately, many *SL* Residents have become tired of filling out surveys there. If you must use an in-world survey, be prepared for heckling and pointed questions.

Linden Lab used to have a specific research policy, and they required approval of each research project in-world. Now, probably because of the sheer number of research projects on the *SL* Grid, this research policy appears to have been scrapped. Today, researchers just have to abide by the Terms of Service* and Community Standards.**

RESEARCH IN *SECOND LIFE*

BY SARAH ROBBINS, PH.D. CANDIDATE AT BALL STATE UNIVERSITY AND FOUNDER OF THE *SECOND LIFE* RESEARCHERS LIST (SLRL)

As Edward Castronova has made us aware, virtual worlds have the capability of serving as a sort of "petri dish" for research. Not only can we create simulations and models of complex concepts for study; we also have, in the case of *Second Life*, access to thousands of people from various backgrounds with which to interact and learn from.

However, much to the chagrin of many eager researchers, gathering data in *Second Life* isn't as simple as merely jumping in and gathering information. The ethics and concerns that researchers in "first life" consider when dealing with human subjects must still be respected in *Second Life*, of course. But there is another level of insight necessary for research in a virtual world: cultural literacy. Virtual worlds, such as *Second Life*, have their own unique developing culture as well as mechanical limitations. Researchers, whether academic or business, must spend time in the culture to understand how Residents interact and live, as well as [to develop] a deep understanding of the world's mechanics.

It's not enough simply to create an account and begin research. Researchers must think of *Second Life* as a culture unto itself. For example, one could not study fashion in *Second Life* without an understanding of how clothing is produced, worn, purchased, and rendered.

Virtual worlds offer researchers readymade populations of captive subjects, but we still have a lot to learn about the natives in these spaces, and research methods will have to adapt as quickly as the technology.

GETTING APPROVAL AND FUNDING

It's becoming less difficult for educators to receive approval and funding of their *SL* projects because others have broken trail for them. In the early days of education in *SL*—a whole two or three years ago—it was hard for educators to launch projects in *SL* because administrators and accountants often viewed them as wildly experimental. Most projects were started by dedicated, adventurous educators who experimented using mostly or entirely their own time and money. Once they were able to show results, they were better able to seek approval and funding. Now, however, because the *SL* Grid is becoming recognized as a legitimate teaching tool that gets results, this approach isn't always required.

Increasing numbers of educators are able to tap their schools' budgets in inventive ways. Some have a leg up because someone in another department already has gotten the school involved in *SL*. There are more and more students already in-world, able to help. And the pool of educators in-world willing to collaborate and share resources is growing. Plus, of course, as discussed earlier in this chapter, now there are numerous nonprofit groups offering educators assistance and even funding.

*   http://secondlife.com/corporate/tos.php

**   http://secondlife.com/corporate/cs.php

The following are tips from *SL* educators on how to secure project approval and funding.

"Get to know your Course Development people and be very nice to them, especially the lab management who will need to put *SL* on lab computers. There are many wonderful stories, blogs and videos (machinima), I'd suggest posting a request to the SLED list and see how others have done this." —Steven Hornik, lecturer, University of Central Florida, Kenneth Dixon School of Accounting (*SL* avatar Robins Hermano)

"It is far easier for someone to believe your idea is doable and has merit if they can see details about other projects that are going on and successful." —John Lester, leader of Linden Lab's Proactive Mentoring Program in Education and Healthcare (*SL* avatar Pathfinder Linden)

"Get into *SL* and really figure things out from the inside out; spend time in here exploring and understanding and asking questions; above all, do some lecturing or teaching—it is always trial by fire in here when you present a lecture or teach a class." —David Schwartz, Ph.D., founder and president, Music Academy Online (*SL* avatar Benton Wunderlich)

"Highlight other successful educational projects in *Second Life*; there are many of them out there." —Rafi Santo, virtual community manager for Global Kids (*SL* avatar Bhikku Beeks in the Main Grid, Rafi GKid in Teen *Second Life*)

"Spend time in *SL* and get to know it so you can answer questions, or have a more experienced person help with presentation for approval; acknowledge the problems and challenges of *SL* up front; you need to show it to your group—many people just don't understand unless they see it." —Lori Bell, director of innovation, Alliance Library System (*SL* avatar Lorelei Junot)

"Combine it with marketing for the university." —Nadja Franz, freelance teacher at the University of Applied Sciences Kiel (*SL* avatar Nadja Revnik)

"We have spent a lot of time on educating people internally, the people who make decisions about money, etc., trying to show them what it's all about. We have been lucky to have [found] some *SL* champions this way in our organization . . . because unless you can sell it to them, then the project remains on paper. Apart from demos, I recommend using video. It helped us a lot. You can show the best features in little time." —Graham Stanley, *Second Life* project manager, the British Council (*SL* avatar Baldric Commons in the Main Grid, Graham Bluecoat in Teen *Second Life*)

GOVERNMENT AGENCIES ON THE *SL* GRID

What are government agencies doing on the *Second Life* Grid? What specific challenges do government agencies face coming into an environment like *SL*? What resources are available? What are the best ways a government or government agency can use *SL*? This chapter will address these questions, so keep reading!

WHAT ARE GOVERNMENT AGENCIES DOING ON THE *SL* GRID?

There's still a perception among some people that *Second Life* is a game. That's becoming less common, though, especially for government agencies. When the first government agencies began projects on the *Second Life* Grid, they had to go even farther than most other organizations to overcome the idea of *SL* as a game. A government employee who spearheaded a project in *SL* once reported that, while he was cleared to attend meetings in the *SL* world, while doing so he was required to close and *lock* his office door so that no one would walk in and, presumably, risk seeing a naked avatar.

Those times are, as I said, passing. That same person now manages an official government project on the *Second Life* Grid, with an entire island of interactive content that is open to the public. Government agencies in-world are multiplying, and assisting one another to get on the Grid. There was even a US Congressional hearing in-world in April, 2008.

However, there are still challenges, as illustrated by the difficulties I encountered in trying to get permission to quote government employees about their work in-world. Nor can I, in most cases, talk about my own experiences developing *SL* content for government agencies on the Grid. Many organizations have concerns about image and security, but government agencies are usually the most restrictive. Despite this, some very valuable government projects are going on in *SL* right now.

Most government projects in *SL* involve communication with the public, or collaboration with other agencies or companies. There are training projects in-world, as well (like the one I worked on for UC Davis Medical Center, which was funded by the CDC to train state health-department staff in California, as mentioned in the preceding chapter). Let's look at some more examples.

NOAA

The National Oceanic and Atmospheric Administration (NOAA) was one of the first government agencies working in *SL*. They started off with one private region and a small amount of content that was created in-house, along with what appeared to be prefab content acquired in-world. To choose a Solution Provider to develop the custom content they required, in 2006 the agency invited a few well-known content-development companies to create proofs of concept. Then a panel of NOAA staff judged the proposals. Although all of the developers were paid for their entries, the winning company received a contract to continue development.

Since then, NOAA has expanded to 12 private regions. The agency's islands include educational exhibits like the oil spill shown in Figure 3.1, a submarine ride, a tsunami simulation, whales, a real-time weather display, a volcano, and an airfield. A block of 9 new regions purchased by NOAA was added and developed in 2008.

NOAA collaborates with other organizations, such as Global Kids, via *Second Life*. In association with that nonprofit, NOAA brought some of their content to Teen *Second Life*, where teens can check out things like an interactive global-warming exhibit.

The manager and motivating force behind NOAA's *SL* Grid project is Erik Hackathorn (*SL* avatar Hackshaven Harford). He's a key figure among government employees working in-world, and he has made it easier for other agencies to bring their own projects to the Grid.

3.1 The teleport map at NOAA's Okeanos island allows you to visit educational exhibits such as the oil spill shown here.

NASA

The National Aeronautics and Space Administration's (NASA's) Ames Research Center is another government agency that's been very active in *SL*, but their approach was very different from NOAA's. Rather than building in-house or hiring a development company, NASA representatives approached an established *SL* Residents' grass-roots organization, the International Spaceflight Museum (ISM). The ISM, which I'll talk about in more depth in Chapter 4, "Nonprofits Reach Out" (the ISM now has nonprofit status), was already hosting space-themed events, including guest speakers, and they had displays such as scale models of rockets and the solar system, plus offered a rocket ride and other attractions. NASA asked the ISM for guidance and assistance, and explained that they wanted to involve the public in this project, and further that their CoLab project in *SL* would serve as a way for the public to give NASA input.

Many ISM members volunteered to help NASA establish their presence on the Grid (Figure 3.2). My own company contributed the NASA CoLab Headquarters building. NASA's private region is located next to that of the ISM, forming the original nucleus of the SciLands, a virtual continent of science-themed regions operated by government agencies, nonprofits, and educational institutions.

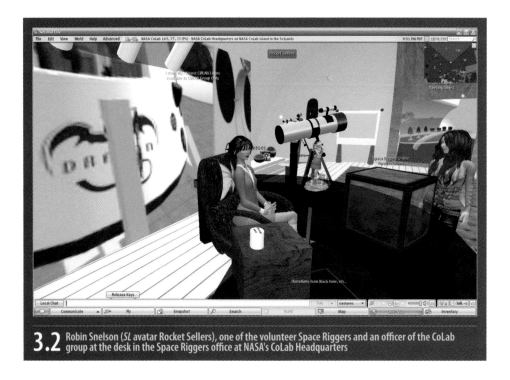

3.2 Robin Snelson (*SL* avatar Rocket Sellers), one of the volunteer Space Riggers and an officer of the CoLab group at the desk in the Space Riggers office at NASA's CoLab Headquarters

The centerpiece of NASA's CoLab island is its CoLab Headquarters building, which has offices for its collaborators. The island hosts an educator resource center, an Oregon L5 Society lava-tube exhibit, an office of the National Space Society, a Return to the Moon planning area, a nature trail, sandboxes for development and collaboration, and spaces for meetings large and small. NASA has many events at the island, including weekly meetings for CoLab group members.

The Ames Research Center paved the way for the NASA Jet Propulsion Laboratory's (JPL's) entry into the Grid. The JPL started out in one of the office pods in the CoLab building, and went on to develop their own region on the Grid, Explorer Island. Also part of the SciLands, the JPL's region is open to the public, but was still under development as of mid 2008. However, it will include meeting spaces, exhibits about robotic space missions, and a Mars Mountain area in which there will be rides such as rovers and "Mars airbags." Giant dust devils roam randomly in this area, and aside from being very cool to see, one of them will seat three avatars at a time for a wild ride, allowing the public to experience, virtually, the Phoenix Mars Mission (Figure 3.3).

3.3 This is the Phoenix Mars Mission exhibit at NASA's Explorer Island. It's still under construction—pardon their spacedust!

NPL

Another government agency residing in the SciLands is the UK's National Physical Laboratory (NPL; Figure 3.4). The NPL's approach to developing their *SL* projects has been much more traditional than NASA's. The NPL hired developers to build their content right from the start.

The NPL has developed a variety of interesting projects, and has even become so familiar with the Grid as to become a service provider. The NPL now works to develop other organizations' projects, such as (along with fellow service provider the New Media Consortium) the Imperial College, London's Second Health project (Figure 3.5). Instigated by Dave Taylor (avatar Davee Commerce), the programme lead for virtual worlds and medical media at Imperial College, it includes a virtual hospital and a series of machinima documentary films created using it as a set, intended to show a patient's experience of healthcare in the future.

Collaborative projects are common in *SL*. The NPL and the University of Denver created their joint Nuclear Power Station project at the university's Science School region. How did this come about? Dave Taylor and Jeffrey Corbin (avatar zazen Manbi), University of Denver physics and astronomy research assistant, were neighbors on the SciLands continent on the Grid. While having a neighborly chat, it occurred to them that a US-UK collaboration could be very valuable. They went on to plan and work together to develop the project, which received a grant from the US Nuclear Regulatory Commission.

3.4 This National Physical Laboratory of the UK exhibit is on a rented parcel at the International Spaceflight Museum. You don't need to buy a whole private region to establish a presence on the *SL* Grid.

3.5 Dave Taylor's avatar shows off Imperial College, London's Second Health project.

CDC

The Centers for Disease Control and Prevention (CDC) was investigating the *SL* Grid early on. In fact, as I mentioned earlier, they funded UC Davis Medical Center's early forays onto the Grid. Since then, they have developed a region of their own, which offers all sorts of health information to *Second Life* Residents.

When I visited, a robot flew up to me and offered me the opportunity to comment on the region. Figure 3.6 provides a sense of the place; there's a kiosk that distributes health-awareness wristbands for avatars, a conference center and an area that provides information about mobility and dexterity. Numerous signs are placed along a scenic walkway, and when clicked these open web pages that contain information about specific medical issues, ranging from workplace safety to heart health. This is a nice of example of how an agency can link to their existing online assets as part of their project in *SL*.

3.6 The CDC's region offers useful health info in accessible, nonthreatening ways.

ESTONIAN EMBASSY

Although a lot of government projects in *SL* focus on science and health, another way governments use *SL* is for virtual embassies. Estonia has a particularly interesting region, Virtual Estonia. One of the things that makes it special is that it's actually staffed during Estonian business hours. Additionally, it includes numerous interesting art installations (Figure 3.7), many of them interactive, and it hosts events related to technology and culture. I had never thought about Estonia as a high-tech place, but now I sure do!

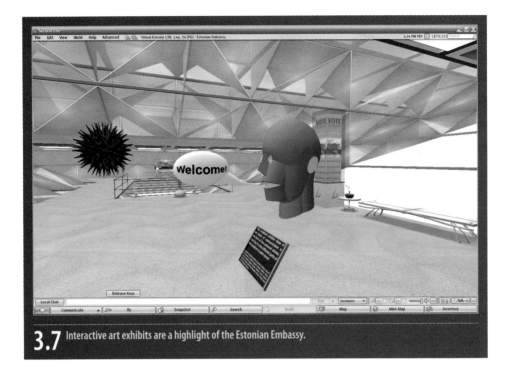

3.7 Interactive art exhibits are a highlight of the Estonian Embassy.

SWEDISH EMBASSY

Another embassy on the *SL* Grid is maintained by Sweden. The Swedish presence in *SL* is especially appealing visually, and includes modern architecture in a beautiful natural setting that invites just hanging out, science exhibits in the Linnaeus Room (Figure 3.8), and even an Ikea.

STRONG ANGEL

Strong Angel is a biannual disaster-response practice involving governments, nonprofits, and corporations. Along with practicing real-world tasks like getting emergency power and communications in place, distributing food, and checking out the latest in emergency shelters, many of the participants bring the best in cutting-edge technology. Together they experiment and collaborate to both develop new solutions and to practice how best to work together when responding to actual disasters. Some of the Strong Angel participants in 2006 included the Naval Postgraduate School, Microsoft, Bell Canada, Cisco Systems, Google, Sprint Nextel, and Office of the Secretary of Defense. The full list is available at **www.strongangel3.net/organizations**.

My company was hired to develop the Strong Angel region on the *Second Life* Grid. The idea was to explore how the Grid might be used to aid communications during a disaster, for visualization of the site, and even for things like tracking refugees. After the project, the *SL* region would remain as a location for further experimentation and demonstration, and for public information.

3.8 The Linnaeus Room at the Swedish Embassy

I was asked to create a region of ruins with an appearance similar to those of the ancient Agora of Athens. It included components like exact scale models of ruined temples converted to conference areas or auditoriums, complete with screens displaying streaming video (Figure 3.9). To showcase the detail possible, we added mythological creatures lurking around the island in out-of-the-way places (a nest of baby dragons, a sheep-eating Cyclops, fish swimming in undersea ruins) and scripted objects to show the interactivity available in-world (such as an oracle). Throughout we included information kiosks, which offered Strong Angel III shirts for avatars, an informational notecard, and a link to the Strong Angel III website. The public was to be encouraged to visit the island, and the Strong Angel group hoped that it could be used as a place to not only disseminate information to the public, but also as a venue in which visitors might meet some of the people heading up operations at Strong Angel III.

As part of this project, I was a participant at Strong Angel III in San Diego, California. I spent most of a week at the command center of the disaster-response simulation, where I demonstrated my technology and discussed how it could be combined with technology that others brought to the real-world command center. Some of the ideas generated during discussions at Strong Angel III included using the *SL* Grid to quickly and inexpensively prototype a site so that troops could explore it and familiarize themselves with it, simulating the landscape and structures around an airport to study locations that might be too convenient for terrorists, and using a stream of live data to move avatars or other representations of people around a 3D space to track the movements of refugees. One SA III attendee suggested using a private region like Strong Angel as a virtual command center in the case of a real emergency. Although it would be difficult or impossible to gain enough bandwidth for someone in the midst of a disaster area to log in to the Grid, it might still be a great way for remote specialists to participate in briefings, view video, and study models.

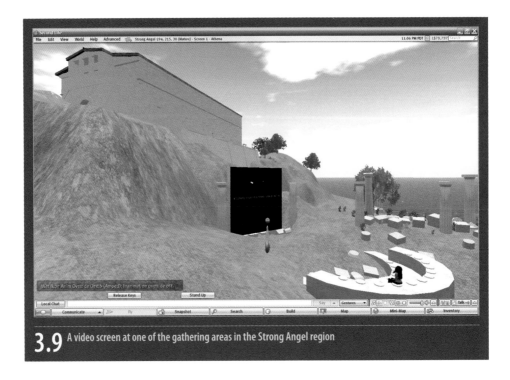

3.9 A video screen at one of the gathering areas in the Strong Angel region

RESOURCES FOR GOVERNMENT AGENCIES

There's assistance awaiting you from a variety of sources if you are considering launching a government project on the *Second Life* Grid.

Linden Lab offers a discount on virtual land to educational institutions and nonprofits, and this applies in some cases to government agencies. You can learn about current prices at **https://secure-web11.secondlife.com/ land/privatepricing.php**. Linden Lab also has a mailing list called Real Life Government in *Second Life*. It's a great resource for asking questions, discussing projects, and seeking collaborators. You can learn more about it, view archives, or sign up at **https://lists.secondlife.com/cgi-bin/mailman/listinfo/governmentinsl**.

Real Life Government in *Second Life* is also the name of an in-world group for those who are working on or interested in government projects on the *SL* Grid. You can find more information about the group and sign up via Search ▶ Groups in-world.

Many government projects are located in the SciLands, a continent of science-themed private regions on the *Second Life* Grid. To view a list of government agencies, educational institutions, and nonprofits that are part of the SciLands, go to **http://spreadsheets.google.com/pub?key=pw9J7oeB9L2Y5CNH0kz3HfA**. The contact for government agencies who'd like to learn more about the SciLands is Erik Hackathorn, of NOAA (*SL* avatar Hackshaven Harford).

The *SL* Wiki offers more information about government on the grid at **http://wiki.secondlife.com/wiki/Real_Life_ Government_in_Second_Life**.

CHALLENGES FOR GOVERNMENT AGENCIES

As I mentioned at the beginning of this chapter, it was difficult to get permission to conduct interviews for this chapter, and in some cases I was unable to write about my own involvement in certain government projects on the *SL* Grid. That's because working with government agencies is simply different from working with anyone else on the *SL* Grid.

THE AGENCY–CONTENT CREATOR RELATIONSHIP

In my experience, government agencies have had lower budgets than many civilian organizations doing similar projects. But there are low budgets for other types of projects, too, and budgets are certainly on the rise. However, no matter what the budget, hacking through governmental red tape—and delays caused by it—can be very time-consuming for a developer. Tendering a proposal for a government project is, in most cases, much more complicated than it is for any other sort of project in-world. The agreements government agencies ask developers to sign are, unsurprisingly, downright baroque. Rights demanded to the works created are usually all-encompassing, whereas for other projects there's usually more room for negotiation. And then there's that NDA, which in some cases restricts or entirely removes the benefit of mentioning the developer's work on the project in promotional materials or to the press.

Additionally, many projects in *SL* are started by one early-adopting evangelist who may work on the project on their own outside of business hours. These people are usually employed as "techies" themselves, not in the legal department. In one such case, an eager government employee working to launch a project in-world offered Solution Providers a deal that sounded great. But when that agency's legal department caught wind of the project, they suddenly came up with a much different agreement, in black and white, involving buying all rights to things the Solution Providers had been told would be open source. It was such a change that the developer nearly bolted, and plans had to be scaled back radically. It's crucial for government employees to make themselves aware of what contractual agreements are likely to be called for officially, even if they start off the project working unofficially or informally.

So, for developers, many government projects in *SL* mean lower-than-usual pay, lots of red tape and hassle, and giving up all rights to their work or even to take credit for their work (Figure 3.10)—at least, without seeking special permission, which is likely to take longer than they'll have if they're about to be interviewed by a reporter. Some developers are happy to take on government projects despite all the restrictions, but other developers turn away from government projects altogether. And that has an impact. The pool of competent, reliable developers for the *SL* Grid is not huge (though it's growing), and the refusal of some developers to take on government work means the pool is even smaller for government projects. I know of one government-project director who was nearly to the point of begging for proposals, because he had to have at least three bids, and he had received only one.

Some government agencies turn to volunteers. This can work out great, but it's risky for both the workers and the agency soliciting the work. For the agency, there's the chance that uncontracted developers will lose interest and never complete the work. And for the workers there's a chance their efforts will go unrewarded at all. At least one governmental agency has managed to anger a formerly supportive group of *SL* Residents. Having initially promised future financial assistance to the group in exchange for the group's volunteer assistance and custom content development, that agency seemed to have forgotten all about it. This is terrible for the agency's image, and doesn't do wonders for the in-world perception of that government in general. Such a situation is particularly sad for a project that was, in large part, planned and implemented to reach out to the public.

The takeaway: It's vitally important to know what you're really going to be able to deliver before making a deal, whether you're representing the soliciting agency or whether you're a contractor.

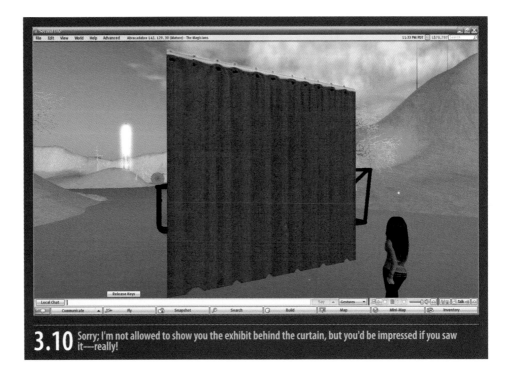

3.10 Sorry; I'm not allowed to show you the exhibit behind the curtain, but you'd be impressed if you saw it—really!

SECURITY IN A VIRTUAL SPACE

Security is important to government agencies—in some cases that's their whole job! So, how secure is the *Second Life* Grid? That depends on what sort of security we're discussing.

It's unlikely that someone is going to hack your system or give you a virus via *SL*. (Although there was once a QuickTime exploit that might affect *SL* users if they viewed streaming video, Linden Lab put safeguards in place right away to warn Residents who didn't get the software patch immediately.) No, as far as that kind of security goes, *SL* is pretty darn good.

What about controlling who sees your stuff, who gets to poke at it, and especially who can access conversations you have in-world? That's a little more complicated. It depends, in large part, on where you are.

Linden Lab staff may be able to view your chat or access anything you have in-world, just as your mail provider's staff can see your mail, and employees of the company that runs your favorite IM service can see your IMs. The exception is if you choose to host *Second Life* regions behind your own firewall. An offering from Linden Lab that's on the horizon at press time will enable an organization to purchase a stand-alone deployment of *Second Life* technology, which will allow the organization complete control over who has access to the virtual spaces it hosts and all data and activities within it. Those who take advantage of this offering will be able to choose whether to connect their small grid of regions to the *Second Life* Grid. Governmental agencies have often asked for this ability, and its availability will be a boon for those concerned about privacy and security.

Not everyone will want or need a stand-alone solution, though. If you don't, what about other *SL* Residents? How much prying can they do if you don't run a grid behind your firewall?

If you have a plot on the mainland—not your own private region—your privacy options are limited. Any avatar within 20 meters can see regular chat, and voice conversations carry even further. You can, however, instant-message instead, using text or voice, and no one but the person you're IMing with will be privy to the conversation. And if you have a private region without an adjacent region that you don't control, and if you restrict access to your region, then no one but Linden Lab can see or hear your discussion.

What about keeping someone from poking at your gadgets or studying them? The bad news here is that anyone within visual range of your objects can try clicking on them or looking at their content. Walls don't keep avatars out, and don't necessarily block their view. You can see anything within 64 to 512 meters (or more with scripted tools) (Figure 3.11), even inside of buildings, if you are good at managing your camera controls. You can see the names and types of items inside of an object, too. How can you stop someone from doing this? Again, you need a private region with restricted access and no neighboring land that doesn't enforce the same controls.

3.11 I can see a floating building in the clouds over the neighboring island. The second picture was taken with my avatar in the same location, but I used the camera controls to peek in the neighbor's window!

NOTE

It's possible to script a remote listening or logging device (a "bug") to pick up and repeat or record text chat. You can make sure unauthorized avatars can't put things on your land, but you still must watch out for neighboring land owned by someone else. Instant messages are immune to bugging.

NOTE

It is possible to stop unauthorized avatars from interacting with your scripted objects, but that restriction has to be designed and coded right into your objects.

In general, unless you choose a behind-the-firewall solution, don't count on the *SL* Grid for anything you want to keep top secret.

WHAT ABOUT THOSE NAKED AVATARS?

So, what about them? The naked avatars, the casinos, and all of that stuff that was sensationalized in the press a while back . . . are these things really all over the place in *SL*? Won't they reflect negatively on government projects in-world? In a word: no.

Regions on the *SL* Grid have ratings: M or PG. On PG-rated land, there's no "adult" content, and even on M-rated land, adult content must be kept out of view of passersby. Gambling on the Grid was outlawed in 2007. And as for the possibility of a naked avatar wandering into a virtual governmental office . . . well, someone may show up at a government location in real life and act inappropriately, as well. It's a simpler matter to eject and ban an avatar than it is to deal with a similar situation in real life! And, of course, if you have a private region with controlled access, especially without uncontrolled neighboring regions, you can be pretty sure you won't have any naked avatars running around the place!

It's helpful to think, in this case, about the Web. There are naked pictures all over the Web, but that doesn't keep government agencies from having websites!

WHAT WORKS BEST FOR GOVERNMENT ON THE *SL* GRID

It is impossible to list here all of the government agencies that have a presence on the Grid. From the 12 islands of NOAA to the Virtual Canadian Defence Academy proof of concept, and from the NASA: Fifty Years and Beyond mixed-reality event that was a part of the 42nd Annual Smithsonian Folklife Festival in June 2008 to the State of Missouri Job Fair (Figure 3.12) in-world the same month, there are all sorts of government projects on the Grid.

3.12 The State of Missouri's IT employment center is located at EduIsland 3.

For the most part, the best uses of the *SL* Grid for government projects are those that don't require a lot of se-crecy and security (unless you choose a behind-the-firewall solution when it becomes available). Projects that work out well reach out to the public, to inform, to educate, to solicit feedback. Projects that involve collabo-ration in-house and between governments and government agencies, or with other sorts of organizations, also are a good match for the *SL* Grid. And, of course, there's the ability to quickly and relatively inexpensively create prototypes and simulations!

I think back to a conversation I had with someone from the US government while I was at Strong Angel III. He wanted to know if I could re-create a particular building on the Grid. Yes, of course, I said. He asked about scale, how detailed it could be, accuracy—could I simulate darkness? (I'll talk about such components more in Part 3 of this book.) He was impressed to learn that what he wanted could be created on the *SL* Grid. Then he asked me how much it would cost, just a ballpark figure—a million? A hundred thousand? His lowest guess was high by one or two figures.

It doesn't cost much to get on the Grid—you can try it for free, and even if you want a permanent installation, something really simple can cost about US$75 a year. The payoff can be great, with a much smaller investment than would be required to develop your own solution from scratch.

CHAPTER 04

How are nonprofit organizations using the *Second Life* Grid? Are there any pitfalls or benefits nonprofits need to know? What sort of assistance is available for nonprofit projects? What sort of charity fundraisers and support groups are in the *Second Life* world?

Nonprofits in-world exemplify the cooperative aspect of the *Second Life* Grid. This chapter discusses how nonprofits can use the *SL* Grid, and also what some in-world nonprofits offer to other organizations on the Grid.

NONPROFITS
REACH OUT

WHAT ARE NONPROFITS DOING ON THE *SL* GRID?

As you might have gathered by now, there's a lot of crossover between educational, governmental, and nonprofit projects on the *Second Life* Grid. There's a ton of collaboration going on, and many organizations build or offer tools or resources for other types of organizations. That makes neat categorization of projects nearly impossible.

But this is due to one of the great things about using the *SL* Grid for your project: loads of connections and collaborations are born at in-world conferences and events or through chance meetings on the Grid. It's just like networking in real life. However, most organizations in-world are especially open to working together. As more than one person I interviewed commented, these are early times for virtual-worlds technology, and therefore the early adopters are especially open to collaboration rather than competition. Additionally, *Second Life* is, by its nature and culture, a collaborative space.

Nonprofits have found many uses for the *Second Life* Grid, including the following:

▶ Fundraising

▶ Education

▶ Resources for Residents

▶ Resources for other organizations in-world

▶ Support group meetings

▶ Community outreach

HOMEGROWN NONPROFITS

Nonprofit projects in *Second Life* have a long tradition, predating the entry of real-world nonprofits into *SL*. They have become an integral part of the fabric of *SL* culture. Let's look at two pioneering groups of Residents that have set precedents for nonprofit projects on the *Second Life* Grid: VERTU and the ISM.

VERTU

The first fundraising group organized in *Second Life* was Virtual Economies Realizing True Usefulness, or VERTU. Founded by a Resident named Bhodi Silverman with the support and assistance of other prominent *SL* Residents, and in partnership with Gaming Open Market (a company that provided a monetary exchange between US$ and L$), the group's goal was to raise money for real-world nonprofit organizations.

The group's first campaign, in 2004, raised US$1,768 for the Electronic Frontier Foundation. That was followed by a successful campaign to raise funds for Heifer International, then one that raised over US$5,000 for the Red Cross to help the victims of Hurricane Katrina.

Fundraising events included dances and auctions of in-world merchandise and "dates" donated by *SL* Residents, some of them held in a re-creation of New Orleans. VERTU's fundraising efforts had an impact far beyond that of the thousands of dollars raised for charities. This was a turning point not only for *Second Life*, but also for virtual-world technology. Prior to this, *Second Life* was generally viewed by Residents and outsiders as "just a game." But now *SL* Residents had made an appreciable impact in the real world and had shown that the *SL* Grid could be used for "serious" purposes. Many of the Residents involved in VERTU have gone on to volunteer their efforts for other charity projects in-world.

INTERNATIONAL SPACEFLIGHT MUSEUM (ISM)

The International Spaceflight Museum—or ISM—is another nonprofit in-world that has served as a model for real-world organizations that have come to the grid later, assisting some of them with their entry to the virtual world. This organization is especially dear to me—I was on the planning committee.

According to its website (**http://slispaceflightmuseum.org/blog/**), "The International Spaceflight Museum is a virtual museum presently located in the virtual world of *Second Life*. It hosts exhibits and events about real-world spacecraft, rockets, and space travel."

The group's founders did not foresee the institution the ISM has become today. According to Katherine Prawl, CEO of the ISM Corporation (*SL* avatar Kat Lemieux; see Figure 4.1), "It began as an arbitrary art festival project, then when someone suggested we start a museum based on the space station we'd built, we agreed it would be a good idea, so we did it. Other *SL* Residents saw what we were doing and wanted to play along, so our group grew until now we have over 75 members and two islands full of informative exhibits." The ISM has now become a real-life nonprofit corporation, presently working on its application for tax-exempt status.

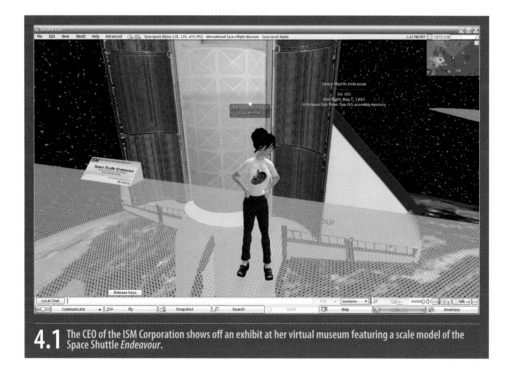

4.1 The CEO of the ISM Corporation shows off an exhibit at her virtual museum featuring a scale model of the Space Shuttle *Endeavour*.

Today the ISM has two islands and plans are under way for its third. Katherine says, "The International Spaceflight Museum is a publicly supported volunteer project, but one with some very stringent guidelines, which we've developed over the life of the project. For instance, we attempt to make all of our exhibit items (rockets, space-probe models, etc.) full-scale, so people can really grasp the actual size of them. We also do our best to make them true to life in terms of being accurate representations of their appearance. We see our museum as being a real museum that just happens to exist only in a virtual world. The mission of the museum is the same as RL [real life] museums—to inform the public about our subject and to promote support for (in our case) space exploration. We believe that showing the public models of objects and information about space and spaceflight will make them more excited about it, and better prepared to support it in RL."

Funding for the ISM comes from Resident donations, fundraising activities such as selling donated virtual items in the organization's gift shop, and support from other organizations. "We've received help from organizations such as NMC (New Media Consortium) and NPL (the UK's National Physical Laboratory), as well as substantial contributions from individuals. Our second island was paid for by an individual who is not on our board of directors, for instance," says Katherine. The ISM also rents space on its islands to real-world organizations that display space-related exhibits there and hosts events with expert speakers and streaming video feeds.

One fundraising experiment that is of particular interest is the ISM's unique sponsorship program. Individuals and organizations bid on eBay for the opportunity to sponsor their favorite rockets. Winning bidders' names or logos are displayed on plaques next to the in-world exhibits.

The ISM was instrumental in assisting NASA in establishing their NASA CoLab on the *SL* Grid. The SciLands continent, dedicated to regions for science and technology education, coalesced around this nexus. More than 20 organizations, including government agencies, universities, and museums, call the SciLands home today.

Learn more about the ISM and its current and upcoming activities at **http://slspaceflightmuseum.org/**. More information about the SciLands is available at **www.scilands.org/**.

CHARITY FUNDRAISING EFFORTS

From grassroots beginnings, charity fundraisers in *Second Life* have grown and now raise very substantial funds for a variety of organizations. Let's take a look at some examples.

RELAY FOR LIFE OF *SECOND LIFE*

In 2004 an *SL* Resident named Jade Lily organized an event and silent auction that raised US$2,000 for the American Cancer Society (ACS). Later that year, Jade and ACS's *SL* representative RC Mars planned together to expand fundraising events, and in 2005 organized a Relay for Life (RFL) walkathon in *Second Life*. The event was similar to any other RFL event in a small town, and raised US$5,000 that year. In 2006, RFL of *SL* raised US$41,000, and donations totaled US$118,500 in 2007.

Raising funds isn't the only goal, however. As Synergy Devonshire, the ACS's *SL* public relations and marketing chair, says of RFL of *SL*, "We always have more donors who come to the individual team events, but we really want to convert some of those donors into activists and supporters. Our goal is to raise awareness of the other ACS activities in *SL* so cancer information and support is available to every *SL* Resident."

Along with the traditional walk, which covered 35 *SL* regions in 2008, RFL activities in *SL* include live entertainment, auctions, Giant Snail Races (Figure 4.2) hosted by RacerX Gullwing (in which the racers themselves become giant snails and run a special-effects-filled course), and sales of special in-world merchandise including household goods, avatar clothing and accessories, vehicles, pets, and more.

Some Residents make very substantial donations. For example, in 2008 one virtual dress created by Resident Eshi Otawara was auctioned for L$460,000 (about US$1,700) to two *Second Life* models—avatars Kay Fairey and Clarabelle Cazalet—to benefit ACS. As remarkable as that may seem, a one-of-a-kind virtual sports car created and donated by Resident Francis Chung went to an anonymous Resident in 2006 for L$600,000, or about US$1,850 to US$1,950.

You can learn more about Relay for Life of *Second Life* at **www.rflofsl.org/**.

4.2 RacerX Gullwing shows off trophies awarded to winners of his Relay for Life Giant Snail Race. Yes, he's a rabbit.

 RFL OF *SL*: FUND-RAISING AND AWARENESS-RAISING

RFL OF *SL*'S TEAMS CHAIR CAROL PFEIFER (SL AVATAR TAYZIA ABBATOIR) AND EVENT CHAIR AVATAR FAYANDRIA FOLEY TALK ABOUT THEIR FUND- AND AWARENESS-RAISING IN *SL*.

What made you choose SL *for your project?*

Foley: I have cancer, and my discovery of *SL* happened at the same time I was facing the fear of death and the physical deterioration cancer and/or the treatment can cause. *SL* seemed a way to me for me to fight cancer no matter the condition of my body.

Pfeifer: So many more people from all over the world can be reached in far less time here in *SL* than could be in [a small town in] RL and yet at the same time have a real sense of community and camaraderie.

What specific challenges do nonprofits face coming into an environment like SL*?*

Foley: Integrity. People are apprehensive about giving their money. They fear being scammed, and rightly so.

Pfeifer: One specific challenge is conveying to some the legitimacy of the fundraising that is being done in an online venue when you are raising hundreds of thousands of dollars. Of course, when you are fundraising for the ACS, we can provide proper documentation and accounting to show legitimacy. Other challenges include, of course, technical challenges and overloads with avatars' presence at fundraisers that could cause sim crashes, etc.

continued

How long did it take and how much did it cost to develop your SL project?

Foley: ACS rents 35 sims for the Relay to be held on, but that is the only cost. Volunteers do the rest.

What are the best ways a nonprofit can use SL?

Foley: Awareness. Let people know they are around and what they do.

Pfeifer: Nonprofits can reach out and provide support, produce awareness, raise funds, and so forth, to a vast audience all over the world. Meetings can be held with people from all over the world joining in without ever having to hop a plane or pay travel expenses.

Does your organization have guidelines for in-world behavior and dress?

Foley: Yes, we follow the same rules and guidelines as a Relay in the real world.

Pfeifer: Yes, we ask that all fundraising events be kept at a PG rating.

How do you measure the effectiveness of your project?

Pfeifer: The numbers speak for themselves; the amount raised for the American Cancer Society each year is monumental for an online world such as this, and the outreach, comfort, and information that cancer survivors and other volunteers can provide for other Residents looking for answers is unmeasurable.

SAVE THE CHILDREN

The first UK charity participating in *Second Life* was the nonprofit group Save the Children. This organization had a unique fundraiser on the *Second Life* Grid in 2006. They sponsored a contest in which *SL* Residents built yaks (yes, yaks). Copies of the prize-winning bovine were offered for sale for L$1,000 each, and all proceeds were converted to real money and donated to a real-life fund to purchase yaks for people in Tibet to use for milk, wool, and pulling plows.

SUPPORT GROUPS

Another way nonprofits and *Second Life* Residents use the Grid is for in-world support-group meetings and to offer and access related information. These plentiful resources cover topics ranging from depression over the death of a pet to Internet addiction. The following are some examples:

The American Cancer Society has a region on the Grid that provides support-group meetings for cancer patients, survivors, caregivers, family, and friends—anyone touched by the disease or seeking to learn more about it.

Twelve-step groups, including Alcoholics Anonymous, also meet in-world.

SupportForHealing maintains a region on the *SL* Grid where a wide variety of support groups have weekly meetings. Support is offered for people with depression, anxiety, and panic disorders, as well as neuropathy, HIV/AIDS, and many other health issues, particularly mental health–related issues. More information about SupportForHealing is available at **http://supportforhealing.com/**.

Project Brigadoon, founded by John Lester (*SL* avatar John Prototype), president of BrainTalk Communities, Inc., offers a safe, private, customized environment on the *Second Life* Grid for people dealing with autism or Asperger's Syndrome. Learn more at **http://braintalk.blogs.com/brigadoon/2005/01/about_brigadoon.html**.

ShockProof, founded by Karen Gans (*SL* avatar The Sojourner) is a group for stroke survivors. This group works closely with Project Brigadoon's mainland Brigadoon Explorers under the aegis of the Dream Travelers group. Karen—Soj to her friends in-world—did much to focus attention on support groups and other nonprofit activities on the *SL* Grid, including organizing and running the annual Dreams Fair held in the Dreams regions (Figure 4.3). The 2008 Dreams Fair participants included over 50 health, support, education, and arts groups and featured information booths, rides, games, more than 75 events, and other interactive experiences over a two-week period. Soj is no longer with us; she passed away a little over a month after the fair in 2008. Her impact on the *SL* Grid and its culture, nonprofits, and educational institutions, as well as her impact on the lives of many, will be remembered.

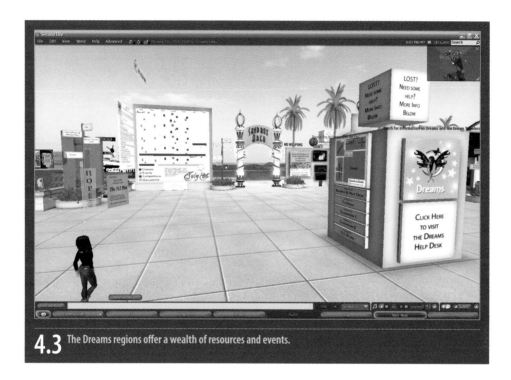

4.3 The Dreams regions offer a wealth of resources and events.

Some question whether it is useful to attend online support-group meetings. In fact this issue is brought up on the *Second Life* forums with regularity. Each time, Residents who have been helped by these groups post refutations. It's hard to disagree that it is much better to attend a virtual support-group meeting than not seek help at all, and that virtual meetings may lead one to real-life resources. Many who would hesitate to attend meetings in real life or who might be too ill to do so find that the ability to remain anonymous and the easy accessibility of the *Second Life* Grid make it much easier to find support and resources.

You can read some interesting statistics about support groups in *SL* at **http://john-norris.net/2008/10/19/statistics-for-second-life-support-groups/**.

OTHER NONPROFIT USES OF *SECOND LIFE*

Nonprofits use the *SL* Grid in too many ways to present here; one could probably write an entire book on the subject. However, this section presents a few representative examples.

NEW MEDIA CONSORTIUM (NMC)

You've already read about some of the New Media Consortium's work in *Second Life*. The NMC is an international nonprofit consortium of over 300 education-oriented organizations that focuses on new media and technologies. The NMC is a powerhouse (Figure 4.4). Its in-world NMC Campus project, launched in June 2006, is a collaboration that includes more than 125 institutions and offers assistance to other organizations and individuals on the Grid, bringing value to the entire *Second Life* world. Its activities are many: events, classes, sponsorship of art shows and performing arts, creation and distribution of useful tools, symposia, provision of meeting spaces, an *SL* orientation area, and more. The organization rents land in its NMC Campus islands to educators and to fellow nonprofits.

4.4 Dr. Larry Johnson (*SL* avatar Larry Pixel) of NMC at NMC Campus's renowned orientation area

NMC Campus has been self-sustaining for over two years, with more than 14,000 individuals from 50-plus countries registered at press time. Some of its projects include the immersive *Macbeth* project (with University of Sydney), the Second Health project (with Imperial College, London, described in the preceding chapter), and the Yale Architecture & Environmental Studies Project (an interactive model of a real-life library used to plan remodeling). When I asked my interview subjects who else I should talk to, the most common answer was Dr. Larry Johnson at NMC! This is no surprise—in 2008 Dr. Johnson even accompanied Linden Lab founder Philip Rosedale to testify to Congress about virtual worlds.

Dr. Johnson says, "*Second Life* is a fantastic platform for not-for-profits to deliver services to members. Our effort, the NMC Campus project, is directly aligned with our mission and purpose, and has a simple but clear vision: to comprehensively support colleges and universities who wish to experiment with virtual worlds. The original campus, located on a single sim, was a test bed for needed research and demonstration activities. As the project grew to 87 regions, at every turn, keeping the vision in focus, e.g., to inspire and influence future development, to expand working knowledge, to showcase creativity and ideas, and to encourage collaboration both inside and outside of *Second Life*, has always been an extension of our real-life work in emerging technologies."

In May 2008 the organization announced its Virtual Learning Prize, a competitive award program with a budget of US$100,000. Awardees receive US$5,000—a cash incentive of $500 plus $4,500 in development assistance to develop innovative open-source educational projects in virtual worlds. The first round of awards went to diverse institutions: the University of Canterbury; the University of British Columbia; the National Oceanic and Atmospheric Administration; Metropolitan State College of Denver; Seton Hall University; University of California, Berkeley; University of Pittsburgh; and Stark State College of Technology.

To learn more about the Virtual Learning Prize, visit **www.nmc.org/virtual-learning-prize**. For more information about NMC's work on the *Second Life* Grid, see **http://sl.nmc.org/** or join the in-world NMC Campus group.

ALLIANCE LIBRARY SYSTEM AND INFO ISLANDS

Librarians have become an important part of the *SL* scene, thanks to the Alliance Virtual Library, a project of the Alliance Library System and Online Programming for All Libraries (OPAL). The Alliance Virtual Library offers a multitude of events on the Grid, including book talks and discussions open to all Residents, sometimes in collaboration with Resident groups such as the library in the steampunk Victorian Resident "country" of Caledon. The ALS operates on a shoestring budget, and is working to make their Info Islands in *SL* sustain themselves through activities such as renting land to librarians and educators, pursuing grants, and holding events such as the Stepping into History and Stepping into Literature conferences for educators and librarians, hosted in partnership with LearningTimes (**http://learningtimes.net**). More information about these conferences is available at **www.steppingintovirtualworlds.org/**.

Lori Bell (*SL* avatar Lorelei Junot), Alliance Library System's director of innovation, heads up the Alliance Virtual Library project on the *Second Life* Grid, including the Info Islands continent and Edulslands. She says, "Info Islands have collaborative library services such as reference and collections programs for Residents of *Second Life*. There is an active community of librarians who work together to provide these services and also to help libraries set up their own presences. Info Island Archipelago has over 40 partner islands of nonprofits, educators, and government agencies. We bring educators and libraries together on some of our islands. We all work together to investigate and provide library services and programs in virtual worlds, with libraries, educators, nonprofits, and government agencies who work together in *Second Life*." Any Resident can access library services and any library can join.

I am a huge fan of the Land of Lincoln project, and made my own period ball gown for my avatar so I could attend a ball at the White House and dance with Honest Abe himself. The experience was surprisingly touching. Abe and the First Lady, played by library staff (Figure 4.5), conversed by pulling from a pool of prepared quotes, but these came off very naturally. In this setting, with period music and avatars in costume, one can experience living history in a vivid way. Although reading about something like the outbreak of the Civil War is informative, it's not the same as "being there" virtually when Lincoln receives telegrams about the attack on Fort Sumter and discusses it with his wife while cannons fire in the distance.

The Info Islands include more than 40 islands, half of which are rented to or belong to other organizations. The following are some of the many exhibits and resources hosted on the Info Islands:

▶ ICT Library, run by avatar Milosun Czervik on one of the Info Islands, which offers free and low-cost tools and scripts for educators. You can learn more about it at **http://ictlibrary.googlepages.com/**.

▶ Info Island International, which includes resources for people learning languages and celebrates various cultures. The info desk here is staffed with live help 80 hours a week. You can find more information at **http://world.secondlife.com/region/3d0432ee-86fb-4297-8ab6-7532526e7dd7**.

▶ Auditoriums, including those on Cybrary City, Cybrary City 2, Edulsland, and Info Island, and a theater in the Infotainment region, all of which are free to use, though events must be scheduled in advance.

4.5 Land of Lincoln manager Roberta Zerrahn (*SL* avatar Daisyblue Hefferman) roleplays Mary Todd Lincoln at the White House.

▶ A public library with reader advisory collections and exhibits.

▶ Investing InfoIsland, funded by a grant from Financial Industry Regulatory Authority (FINRA) and American Library Association (ALA) and aimed at baby boomers, offers information about finances and investment.

▶ Infotainment Island includes Jazz Cat nightclub and has played host to rotating exhibits, including one on the British Invasion, and another on women in rock.

▶ Only Yesterday, a 1930s-themed region where one can visit a Hooverville (Figure 4.6), Gatsby's, a dance club with period music, and shops. You can even rent a place for your avatar to call home.

▶ Commonwealth (Figure 4.7) is made up of several islands that provide free space in *Second Life* for progressive organizations and nonprofits, like Greenpeace and the ACLU.

You can learn more about the Info Islands and upcoming events at **http://infoisland.org**.

4.6 Only Yesterday manager Rolig Loon gives a tour of Hooverville, a re-creation of the Depression-era shantytowns called Hoovervilles.

4.7 The Commonwealth Islands host progressive organizations.

GLOBAL KIDS

In 2006, Global Kids (Figure 4.8), a nonprofit based in New York City and supported by the MacArthur Foundation, was the first organization to work in Teen *Second Life*. Focused on empowering teens through education about how to become activists in their community, this organization has found the *SL* Grid to be a great place to engage teens, as well as a safe space for teens to practice newfound skills.

4.8 This iconic volcano, the centerpiece of the Global Kids regions, has a hidden cave at its center.

Since my company developed Global Kids's first island in Teen *Second Life*, the organization has expanded to five islands. Global Kids hosts major events that offer teens the opportunity to meet and interact with world leaders and other experts in many fields. Additionally, the organization offers a wealth of resources and classes for teens in which the teens themselves use the *SL* Grid to create videos, interpretive displays, and educational games.

A major force in *SL* Grid youth educational projects, and one of the first organizations to become deeply involved in using the Grid, Global Kids has expanded its program to offer various sorts of assistance and training to other organizations, including land rentals for educators of teens. Global Kids often collaborates with other organizations, such as hosting a copy of NOAA's interactive global-warming exhibit in Teen *Second Life*.

Global Kids maintains RezEd, a site with the mission of being "an online hub providing practitioners using virtual worlds with access to the highest quality resources and research in the field to establish a strong network of those using virtual worlds for learning," according to their site at **www.rezed.org/**. The site includes blogs focused on different types of education in virtual worlds and related concerns, podcasts, discussions, and more. Visit the site for more information or to sign up.

You can learn more about Global Kids projects for teens at **http://holymeatballs.org/**.

LEVEL PLAYING FIELD INSTITUTE (LPFI)

The Level Playing Field Institute is an organization that strives to level the playing field so everyone has the same opportunities, regardless of race, gender, or orientation. The LPFI was one of my earliest clients, and one of the pioneers of using the *SL* Grid for real-life corporate training. My company developed a 3D scale replica of their office's kitchen, which was used as a setting for creating machinima (video shot in-world) for education, as well as a meeting location where avatars could be seated to view and discuss it.

We went on to work together to develop an informational space on the Main Grid. The largest part of the area is the Unlevel Playing Field game (Figure 4.9), in which visitors are randomly confronted by closed doors that block their upward progress—a great metaphor for what can happen in education or the workplace. Players receive information about which LPFI program can help them to metaphorically unlock the door that blocks their way, and the virtual door model fades away, allowing them to continue the game. Along the way, players can click symbols such as a university seal and a statue of justice for further information, and there's a prize at the end, along with a full-scale model of the iconic UC Berkeley Sather Tower.

4.9 The Level Playing Field Institute's unique Unlevel Playing Field game offers information about educational and career resources.

Other features of the build are information kiosks with links to the Web, video screens, a photo booth and display, a survey machine that offers multiple-choice questions and gathers anonymous results, and more.

FRONTIER SPACEPORT

There are a lot of aerospace projects in *Second Life*, each with its own goals. Robin Snelson (*SL* avatar Rocket Sellers) heads up the Frontier Spaceport, which was started by the Space Studies Institute and Space Frontier Foundation. It focuses on real rocket and space projects, and has a spaceport that isn't a museum. Says Snelson, "It's an extension of the real-world nonprofit organizations' work to expand the way people think about our future in space, with emphasis on commercialization and industrialization. The idea was to establish a beachhead for that community, provide a big sandbox, resources, and creative vision—then see if it would build itself. It's a research project to explore the potential for outreach and social networking, and to lay groundwork for virtual conferencing and distance learning."

With a motto of "Always Under Construction" the Frontier Spaceport spans three regions in *Second Life*. Al Differ (avatar Differ Darwin) is the founder of an advanced high-altitude airship company, and he's designing and testing a full-scale model at the spaceport. Robert McBrayer (avatar Adluna Dagger) built and scripted X Prize Foundation Lunar Lander Challenge rockets here. Jim Botaitis (avatar Jimbo Perhaps), a prizewinning model maker and decal artist, built a full-scale model of the *Mir* space station in the virtual sky to support a documentary about space entrepreneurs by Space Frontier Foundation advocate Michael Potter (avatar Potter Raymaker). He also built and scripted solar-power satellites to support a National Security Space Office study led by Colonel Coyote Smith (avatar Coyote Watanabe).

Snelson says, "The scene setting, big sandbox, and editorial guidance are producing the desired effect. A community is forming. People know they are free to create their own events, set up a project in the sandbox, an enterprise on the spaceport, so long as it serves the topic and fits the theme. It's still early, we're all early adopters and researchers in here. A great community is growing on the western border of the SciLands on the space frontier."

RESOURCES FOR NONPROFITS

Some great resources are available for nonprofits on the *Second Life* Grid.

HELP FROM LINDEN LAB

If your organization is a qualified nonprofit, Linden Lab offers the same break on land-purchase and maintenance fees as those available to educators, which I discussed in Chapter 2.

Linden Lab also maintains a listserv for those interested in nonprofit projects in-world. You can learn more about the Nonprofits mailing list, read the archives, or sign up at **https://lists.secondlife.com/cgi-bin/mailman/listinfo/nonprofits**.

OTHER RESOURCES

Some nonprofit organizations in-world are there primarily to help other nonprofit organizations, educators, and other entities. Three of the biggies are NMC, the Alliance Virtual Library Project, and Global Kids, discussed earlier in this chapter. We'll take another look at Global Kids in Chapter 14.

The Nonprofit Commons group in-world is made up of employees of nonprofits, and volunteers interested or involved in nonprofit projects on the *Second Life* Grid. The group has weekly meetings on the Grid and provides free space to nonprofit organizations. Check out their blog at **www.nonprofitcommons.org/**.

CHALLENGES FOR NONPROFITS

Early fundraising projects run by Residents in the *SL* world faced and surmounted a variety of problems. For example, much more controversy once surrounded issues such as accountability: in a world where Residents used mostly anonymous avatars, how could one be certain that funds raised would actually go to the intended charity? These fears were initially allayed by the involvement of Gaming Open Market, a trusted company that managed a money exchange, converting L$ to US$. Since then, more and more Residents have given up their anonymity or work with recognized real-world organizations. Some Residents have become so well known that they are anonymous only in the sense that a famous author or actor who uses a pen name or stage name is anonymous.

There have been and continue to be scams related to charity. A more common problem is the occasional fraudulent placement of invisible boxes over donation kiosks; donors unknowingly end up paying their money via that box to a crook rather than to the actual charity.

 DETECTING DONATION-KIOSK FRAUD

Before you pay a donation kiosk, check the owner of the object and if they are really associated with the organization to which you intend to donate. Also, it's a good idea to use the Highlight Transparent feature to see if there's an invisible box owned by someone else sitting over the kiosk!

Fundraisers in-world are now a constant feature of the *Second Life* world's social scene. There are always donation kiosks for worthy causes, as well as fundraising events. But nonprofits raising funds in-world face problems that, while not new in the real world, are relatively new on the *SL* Grid. Some *Second Life* Residents, burned out from volunteering—sometimes full-time—reduce the time they spend volunteering, or stop volunteering altogether. Also, some Residents feel a sort of donation fatigue; they're displeased that their fun virtual retreat has become a place where they are constantly tapped for donations or where they are unable to escape real-world issues. As one Resident and cancer survivor says, "I came in-world to relax and have fun and to try to distract myself from how ill I felt and worries about my latest pathology report, not to be reminded about cancer over and over. It gives me flashbacks." This resistance to the real world impacting the virtual one is not uncommon, although it is more often directed at corporate marketing campaigns; nonprofits are rarely hindered.

WHAT WORKS BEST FOR NONPROFITS

When asked about how nonprofits can best use the *Second Life* Grid, Katherine Prawl of the ISM says, "That really depends on what the object of the NPC [nonprofit corporation] is. In the case of the ISM, we are an educational nonprofit, so our primary objective is to present information in a way that is accessible to the greatest number of visitors. For groups who sponsor research and need to fund that, *SL* may be a way to raise money, but given the perceptions of the currency as being worth more than it actually is in RL terms, meaningful donations are not usually obtained in-world. Rather, it can be a platform to educate potential donors about the goals of charity so they might support it in RL."

Most importantly, though, make sure you're familiar with *Second Life* before you attempt to establish your nonprofit organization. Synergy Devonshire of RFL of *SL* advises, "You have to understand the community first. If you do not, then any and all offerings are going to fall short of expectations." Consider the donation figures quoted earlier in this chapter; certainly it's worth getting to know a few avatars and letting them get to know your organization!

05

What sorts of businesses are on the *Second Life* Grid? How are they using it? Are virtual meetings all they're cracked up to be? What about conferences? Can the Grid be used for prototyping and testing products? What's the best way to use the *SL* Grid for marketing? Do businesses face any special challenges using *SL* for projects? What sorts of assistance are available to help my business with a project on the *Second Life* Grid? This chapter will answer these questions and more.

CONDUCT BUSINESS

WHAT ARE BUSINESSES DOING ON THE *SL* GRID?

Marketing—the first obvious business use of the *SL* Grid—has been outshone by less glamorous uses, and some of those uses are big money-savers or efficiency-increasers for corporations sharp enough to be early adopters of this new technology. In general, think about uses that involve social interaction, 3D interactive models, or ways of accessing information.

Although there have been some experiments in using the Grid as a venue for selling real-world products (Circuit City and Dell have tried it), so far the approach hasn't taken off. Perhaps it will be more successful when Linden Lab introduces the Linden dollar API (which will be used for making purchases in L$—using the L$ as microcurrency on external websites, for example—so you could purchase with L$ without having to convert them to US$). Also, while a few enterprises have offered virtual goods for sale, usually in conjunction with in-world marketing projects, there have been no big successes in this area—certainly nothing that compares with sales of virtual goods by Residents.

Some effective business uses of the Grid are as follows:

▸ Meetings and conferences

▸ Recruiting and interviewing

▸ Prototyping and testing

▸ Marketing

▸ Training and simulations

▸ Market research

The following sections discuss some of these uses in detail.

VIRTUAL MEETINGS AND CONFERENCES

The business use of the *Second Life* Grid that's really on the rise lately is meetings and conferences, including job interviews. With the increasing cost of gas and of travel in general, and an already established familiarity with phone conferencing, the use of the *SL* Grid instead of traveling is one that some companies are rushing to embrace.

One good example is ArcelorMittal, the world's largest steel company, which held a mixed-reality event for shareholders on the *Second Life* Grid in 2008. About 60 *Second Life* Residents logged in and attended at the company's location in-world (Figure 5.1), where they viewed a live video stream of the shareholder meeting. In-world participants included shareholders and potential shareholders who were able to pose questions for board members via instant message and access various related reports with a simple mouse click.

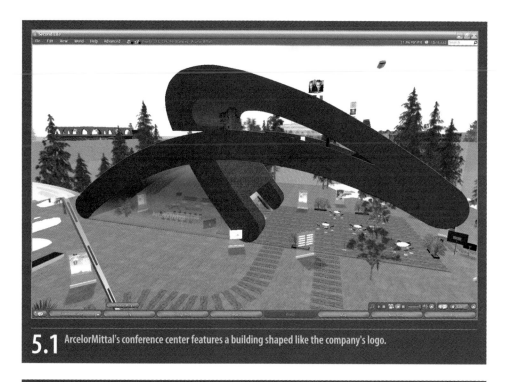

5.1 ArcelorMittal's conference center features a building shaped like the company's logo.

 VIRTUAL CORPORATIONS ON THE GRID

The state of Vermont passed a law in June of 2008 that opens the way for the formation of virtual corporations. Vermont Liability Limited Corporations may now exist only on the Internet and conduct board meetings using an electronic or telecommunications medium. Other states must recognize these LLCs. New York Law School's Virtual Company Project hopes to offer infrastructure to facilitate the formation and management of these virtual businesses. For more information, go to **http://dotank.nyls.edu/VisualCorporation.html**.

Companies such as Manpower (Figure 5.2) and Kelly Services (Figure 5.3) have led the way in using the *Second Life* Grid as a way to connect with potential hires. Indeed, this seems to be one of the most successful uses of the Grid lately, and one into which various organizations of all sorts are expanding, including government agencies. Additionally, companies that are focusing their *Second Life* projects primarily in other areas, such as marketing, are also setting aside a space in their *Second Life* builds where Residents can access job-opportunity information. Job fairs are becoming regular events in the *Second Life* world, and the Eye4You Alliance even organized a college fair in Teen *Second Life* that included booths set up by more than 20 colleges and representatives of organizations as diverse as Amazon, NASA, and Squirrelverse.

5.2 To kick off the launch of their project, Manpower held an event featuring a panel of experts on doing business on the *SL* Grid.

5.3 Kelly Services offers employment opportunities in a fun way on the *SL* Grid, using cartoony interactive exhibits and a heads-up display.

IN-WORLD MEETINGS AND EMPLOYEE RECRUITMENT

MICHAEL BOLTZ (*SL* AVATAR BOOTSIE BLINKER), AVIVA USA EVP AND CHIEF INFORMATION OFFICER, DISCUSSES SOME BUSINESS USES FOR *SL*.

Tell me a bit about your Second Life *project.*

We created a presence in *SL* for an Aviva USA island. The primary driver is to leverage innovative technology to attract new life-insurance and annuity sales agents to Aviva USA. At Aviva USA we pride ourselves as being an innovative company, and *SL* was the perfect medium to get the message out. . . . We also plan to leverage our *SL* presence for agent education and training.

What specific challenges do businesses face coming into an environment like SL*?*

The major hurdle is companies jump in too fast with expectations that are too high, particularly around e-commerce. There is a buzz about *SL*, but the commercial environment within *SL* has not yet been widely adopted or accepted by its members. I do think there is commercial potential as the platform evolves, still to be determined.

How much of your project did you build in-house?

We had a cross-functional Aviva USA project team that collaborated with IBM to develop the island. Our in-house team developed the requirements, helped with the design, and provided project management. IBM facilitated the design and did the development. It was very cool to hold our project team meetings inside *SL* as our island was being constructed!

Do you think it's important to log in and try SL*, or could someone just hire a developer cold?*

I always recommend you try before you buy. Well prior to seeking project approval, we were experimenting in *SL* to determine viability for our objective to leverage innovative technology to attract new professionals.

How long did it take and how much did it cost to develop your SL *project?*

I don't want to state the costs, but it was economically feasible from a cost/benefit perspective and the project was funded out of our IT R&D budget, so not a huge investment. The entire project from inception to implementation took five months.

What's your view on "griefing" and possible clashes with existing SL *Resident culture?*

You have to deal with the world you live in, real world and virtual. The security aspects of *SL* have improved considerably over the past year. We also have our island secured and only open to agents who register with us. We have the island staffed with Aviva USA avatars who are customer-service associates.

What are the best ways a business can use SL*?*

There are endless possibilities and lack of creativity is the only barrier. There are numerous training, education, collaboration, commerce, social, and other capabilities that *SL* offers.

Do you have any tips about getting approval and funding for an SL *project?*

Find a business driver for establishing a *SL* presence, not a "just for fun" project. You need something with teeth that makes a compelling business case for doing a project. You are much more likely to gain support. Also, start small. Don't invest millions of dollars in the platform until you have some small wins to establish credibility. Walk before you run.

Do you usually have someone online at your SL *location, or specific office hours?*

We do staff the island during normal business hours of 8 a.m. to 5 p.m. During off-hours we have mailboxes that provide easy interaction.

Along with corporate presences on the *Second Life* Grid come unions. In fact, there's a region called Union Island (Figure 5.4), which is a project of New Unionism Network, TUC, and UNI Global Union, and supported by Connect, Prospect, RSU IBM Vimercate, Unison, and ver.di. The group sponsors in-world events such as a May Day celebration. One organization that is part of this coalition, RSU IBM Vimercate, drew almost 2,000 demonstrators who logged in to participate in an online show of solidarity with IBM Italy workers at seven IBM locations on the *Second Life* Grid. The protest received a lot of press coverage, including video footage on the evening news in Italy. You can learn more about Union Island at **http://www.slunionisland.org/**.

5.4 At Union Island you can check out an exhibit of historical photos.

PROTOTYPING AND TESTING

One of the first product prototype tests on the *Second Life* Grid was for a 3D model of a robot character for the 2005 movie *The Hitchhiker's Guide to the Galaxy*. Much time and expense was saved by using the Grid for this rapid prototyping. Testers were able to pose the model in various ways to decide how it should be posed in images for a marketing campaign.

Crompco LLC was another company that made early use of the *SL* Grid. The underground-gas-tank-inspection firm trained gas-station inspectors using traditional methods, such as sketches on a chalkboard. When they developed a 3D model in the *Second Life* world to use instead, the results were remarkable. Quickly and relatively inexpensively, Crompco was able to model the gas station, the switches, the underground lines, and the tanks. They even developed scripted interactivity to highlight various parts of the gas stations' workings. Trainees responded very well. After all, this was a lot more attention-getting than a chalkboard!

One of the hottest uses of the Grid is for prototyping real-life architecture. A successful use of the *Second Life* Grid for prototyping was undertaken by Starwood Hotels. The company hired a developer to create a model of their new aloft hotel, which was yet to be built in real life. *Second Life* Residents were invited to visit the hotel, sit in the chairs, hang out in the lobby, investigate the guest rooms, and attend events on the grounds. And they were asked to submit feedback and suggestions. This data was incorporated into the final design of the actual aloft hotel when it was built. When the *Second Life* project was complete, Starwood donated their region to the nonprofit TakingITglobal, which provides (according to its website) "opportunities for learning, capacity-building, cross-cultural awareness, and self-development through the use of Information and Communication Technologies."

The Tech Museum of Innovation's project The Tech Virtual is, according to information they provide at the entrance to their museum in *Second Life*, "not only a museum in *Second Life*, it is also a collaborative design platform for science and technology museum worldwide. The purpose of this platform is to generate concepts and content for use in museum exhibits." Content created as part of the project is licensed under a Creative Commons Attribution license, so participating designers and curators are able to use the content by citing author credit. International teams are able to collaborate to produce low-cost prototypes for testing. You can learn more about the project at **http://thetechvirtual.org/**.

TIP

The Arch is a blog covering architecture and design in virtual environments. Check it out at **http://archsl .wordpress.com/**.

Many more companies are also using the *Second Life* Grid to prototype and test their products and procedures in private regions closed to the public.

MARKETING

Marketing projects on the *Second Life* Grid have gone through some real changes—and necessarily so! The marketing approach that first worked on the Grid just can't cut it anymore, because it was all about novelty; using *SL* for marketing stopped being new a couple of years ago.

The first companies to use the *SL* Grid for marketing confused a lot of *Second Life* Residents, who posted on forums taking potshots at some of the early marketing efforts. At the time there was very strong resistance to corporate use of *Second Life*—in fact, there was broad-based resistance to almost anything that might disrupt the immersion and roleplay enjoyed by many (if not most) Residents. They didn't want to see real-world brand logos all over the place and there was a lot of jeering at the re-creations of real-world shops.

One of the first of these was American Apparel, which did indeed look very much like the chain's real shops. It also sold some no-nonsense, plain merchandise, like T-shirts in various colors. Many Residents, aside from their distaste for the corporate world intruding on their virtual world, also felt that the build lacked imagination and that the shirts offered were not any better than those available from Resident shops, often for lower prices—and why support the corporate newcomers over the hometown artists (despite the fact that a Resident artist was hired to create these things)? Some expressed confusion: did this company really think they were going to sell these plain virtual shirts to anyone in-world? There were even a few incidents of "griefing"—armed Residents causing trouble in the virtual-world location. Although it's not possible to actually harm avatars, they can be inconvenienced, and it just doesn't look right to have armed protesters in your store!

However, American Apparel's campaign was a huge success. The company was not really targeting in-world shoppers at all. American Apparel was after press in the real world, which picked up on the novelty of their virtual shop and gave them lots of coverage. And for those unfamiliar with a virtual world, a shop that looked just like a real shop, with shirts just like the real shirts available for sale was news, and it was something the average news reader would understand when they saw a picture! American Apparel did a great job with this campaign.

Other companies were successful with campaigns that leveraged real-world media, too. As more and more corporate marketing folks became aware of what was going on—it was pretty hard to miss—there was a great rush to establish an *SL* presence for real-world marketing purposes. Lots and lots of companies put up replicas of their real-world shops and sent out press releases about them; unfortunately they offered little or nothing of real value to *Second Life* Residents. And it was not long before the press and the reading public got tired of talking about which company had just set up a shop in *Second Life*. It wasn't big news anymore.

That was when we saw a backlash, where more and more noise was being made about how *Second Life* marketing projects didn't work, that *Second Life* was no good for businesses, and that it was all a bunch of hype. Yes, there was hype—businesses created it themselves and others fell for it.

But negative press fills pages and attracts readers, and it's a great out for those whose projects failed (not due to their error in judgment, of course—it was all the fault of this virtual-world platform!). So then there was negative hype, and it was just as full of misleading info as the first wave of positive hype, as some of the companies whose marketing departments had missed the first wave folded up their virtual shops and left. In some cases, the Solution Providers they'd hired left as well.

The good news is that some companies appear to be doing quite well with current marketing projects on the *SL* Grid. They do well because they aren't trying to court the real-world press. Instead the people running these projects—the corporate marketing managers and the *Second Life* Solution Providers they hire—actually market to avatars and base their campaigns on extensive, solid knowledge of the target market (something I'll cover in depth in Part 2 of this book).

One good example is John Wiley & Sons, Inc., the publisher of the book you hold in your hands. They didn't need to do a *Second Life* project to stir up the real-world press. They needed to sell their line of how-to books about *Second Life*. Right there they had an advantage—their product was one that was obviously a good match for the audience in-world. But what really sets Wiley apart is their approach to marketing to avatars; although they started out a few years back with a shop that looked like a real-world bookstore full of nonfunctional shelves etc., they went on to have in-world events that were designed not to look good in screenshots for the media, but rather to function as events of use, entertainment, and interest to *Second Life* Residents.

We'll take a closer look at this campaign in Part 3, when I discuss how to go about producing successful events on the Grid. But here we can look at one simple point that will make it clear why Wiley has succeeded where others have not: the Wiley event advertising I designed, including invitations, posters, and other event announcements in-world and in *Second Life*–specific publications, all made it clear that all subcultures of *Second Life* Residents were welcome at the events, that there was seating for avatars of all sorts (including those of large size, such as dragons, which often aren't welcome at events), and that there was going to be a big snowball fight afterward! In other words, it was made very clear that this was an event planned for Residents. Event attendance sometimes exceeded our two-region capacity, and many Residents were left with the idea that Wiley gets it, and that their books were worth checking out. In 2008 Wiley began expanding their *Second Life* presence to include promotions for non-*SL*–specific lines of books, starting with how-to books for software commonly used by Resident content creators, such as Photoshop and various 3D-modeling platforms.

The secret to Wiley's success is that they got to know Residents and hired a Solution Provider who knew Resident culture. Other publishers have found *Second Life* a lively location to promote books with displays and author events, some of them hosted at Publishing Island, home of the annual *Second Life* Book Fair.

Entertainment promotions have done quite well in-world. Early on, Suzanne Vega performed live in *Second Life*, and musicians including Ben Folds and Journey (Figure 5.5) have followed in her footsteps. An *Iron Man* film campaign featured a screenshot contest where Residents posed wearing free Iron Man avatars. Another campaign that did well by offering value to Residents was the 2007 promotion of the IMAX version of *Harry Potter and the Order of the Phoenix*. About two dozen *Second Life* avatars dressed in distinctive uniforms and roamed the *Second Life* Grid, giving away IMAX-branded items such as T-shirts, chairs, and 3D glasses. The *Second Life* marketing campaign was credited as a key reason the movie broke all IMAX box office records. Again, this campaign gave something of value to Residents, and the product marketed (a fantasy-genre movie) was a good match for the *SL* audience. Similarly, television tie-ins have generated a lot of traffic, and online communities have been developed in the *Second Life* world to promote *The L Word* and *Gossip Girl*. In fact, community-building is an important way to establish your brand in-world.

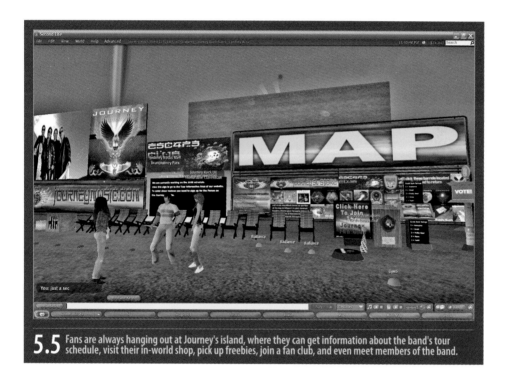

5.5 Fans are always hanging out at Journey's island, where they can get information about the band's tour schedule, visit their in-world shop, pick up freebies, join a fan club, and even meet members of the band.

Some other notable marketing ventures on the Grid include L'Oreal, who had a multicampaign yearlong presence and was a hit with Residents when they distributed free avatar skins in the *Second Life* world. These were decorated with makeup similar to effects one might want to achieve with the company's products in the real world. Evian experienced similar success with the same kind of skin-distribution program. The Weather Channel offered Residents the opportunity to have their avatars try extreme sports under various weather conditions, which helped build a relationship with the brand.

Telecommunications or ISP enterprises like Orange (Figure 5.6) and Big Pond have also developed thriving communities on the Grid, with lots of interesting events and places to investigate.

Adventurous avatars enjoy visiting re-creations of exotic destinations such as Visit Mexico and Dublin (Figure 5.7), sponsored by tourism agencies. This gives visitors a taste of the real thing, perhaps planting the seed of the idea for a real-world vacation.

5.6 Orange Island hosts a lot of great events for *Second Life* Residents.

5.7 *Second Life* Residents can tour a Guinness brewery at one of the Dublin islands.

ASSISTANCE FOR BUSINESSES

Enterprises usually start out on the Grid with more funds than educators and nonprofits, but they also have some special needs. Fortunately, there's assistance available.

LINDEN LAB PROGRAMS

Linden Lab offers assistance specifically for or of interest to businesses developing a presence on the *Second Life* Grid. The following are some examples; see Chapter 15, "Locate Resources," for a more in-depth discussion of such programs.

▶ The Enterprise Level Support program is a fee-based membership program offering top quality, quick response, and help available 24 hours a day, every day of the year. Learn more about it at **http://secondlifegrid.net/programs/elsp**.

▶ Custom surnames are available for a fee, so your staff can have your company's name as their avatar's last name.

▶ The Corporate Use mailing list facilitates discussion via email. Sign up or view archives at **https://lists.secondlife.com/cgi-bin/mailman/listinfo/slcorporateuse**.

▶ The Registration API can be used to develop your own custom *Second Life* registration and first log-in experience for your staff or customers. Learn more or sign up at **http://secondlifegrid.net/programs/api/reg**.

▶ The Marketing section of the *SL* wiki is full of useful information for business uses beyond marketing: **http://wiki.secondlife.com/wiki/Marketing**—good for stuff other than marketing—good for all bizfolk.

▶ If you're looking for *Second Life* market data, check out **http://wiki.secondlife.com/wiki/Market_Data_Portal**.

▶ If you'd like to build a customized or branded *Second Life* viewer or sign up to be informed about any future *Second Life* Grid server licensing, look at **http://secondlifegrid.net/programs/licensing**.

▶ If you contact Linden Lab about content creation, event facilitation, or consultation on your project, they'll probably refer you to the Solution Provider Directory. Check it out at **http://secondlife.com/solution_providers/listings.php**.

▶ Think Linden Lab might want to partner with you? Find information about that at **http://secondlifegrid.net/resources/business**.

OTHER SOURCES OF ASSISTANCE

Along with resources offered by Linden Lab, other sources of help are available for businesses that want to launch projects on the *Second Life* Grid.

A number of companies offer market research based on interviews with *Second Life* Residents. You can find more information about this at **http://wiki.secondlife.com/wiki/Market_Research_Suppliers**.

Some in-world groups, such as the RL Work in *SL* group, cater to businesses. When in-world, go to Search ▶ Groups.

The best source of help, other than in-world groups for new Residents, may well be an experienced Solution Provider you hire to help you develop your *Second Life* presence. In Part 3 you'll learn more about what Solution Providers offer and how to pick the best one for your project.

CHALLENGES FOR BUSINESSES ON THE GRID

The biggest challenge faced by businesses on the *Second Life* Grid is simply familiarizing themselves with the Grid and Resident culture. Almost every project that has failed has done so because its basic design was wrong. Time and again I have been approached by corporations that wanted to do projects that just did not make sense.

One large corporation hurt their image by hiring "ad farmers"—in-world businesspeople who blight residential neighborhoods with billboards. Some ad farmers do this not to make revenue from the ads, but instead to put exorbitant prices on land that hosts purposely ugly or distracting displays; they make their money by selling the land to neighbors who just want to get rid of the eyesore. The aforementioned large corporation hired some of these ad farmers to promote their product, probably thinking "banner ad" rather than "extortion," and it led to the corporation being attacked by in-world Residents and on blogs. This ad-farming practice, by the way, is no longer allowed in the *Second Life* world, although similar, more subtle schemes continue to be a problem.

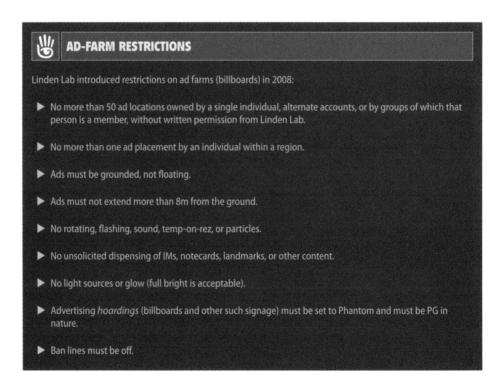

AD-FARM RESTRICTIONS

Linden Lab introduced restrictions on ad farms (billboards) in 2008:

▶ No more than 50 ad locations owned by a single individual, alternate accounts, or by groups of which that person is a member, without written permission from Linden Lab.

▶ No more than one ad placement by an individual within a region.

▶ Ads must be grounded, not floating.

▶ Ads must not extend more than 8m from the ground.

▶ No rotating, flashing, sound, temp-on-rez, or particles.

▶ No unsolicited dispensing of IMs, notecards, landmarks, or other content.

▶ No light sources or glow (full bright is acceptable).

▶ Advertising *hoardings* (billboards and other such signage) must be set to Phantom and must be PG in nature.

▶ Ban lines must be off.

Some other large corporations have hurt their images by hiring inept developers who put together buildings that were the *Second Life* equivalent of shoddy construction. Picture a building where sections of the floor have gaps between them, and where, if you click on an interactive kiosk, all you get is an error message. How could a big company end up with a build so bad that it leads to bad press and derision? It's almost always a failure to log in and have a look around to see what is possible in-world or to check out previous builds by their developer to see how they looked in comparison with top-quality work.

Still other companies have commissioned what they believed was top-quality work that was problematic because the things created looked great in a screenshot, for example, but were so wasteful of in-world resources that they hurt the Grid's performance for everyone in viewing range. One much-discussed example was the poor *SL* performance for everyone around Residents wearing resource-hogging shoes created as part of a marketing campaign.

Another issue businesses face on the Grid is trademark infringement. Many Residents create knock-offs of real-world goods or put popular trademarked logos on their virtual creations, either for their own use or even for sale. This is an issue faced by plenty of organizations that don't have an official *Second Life* presence, but it's particularly obvious if you spend some time in-world. The Grid is filled with user-created content, and plenty of it is "fan" work or otherwise re-creates real-world objects and brands. Some of it is available for sale in-world for Linden Dollars, usually not with official sanction from the copyright holder.

Companies do have recourse: they can file a Digital Millennium Copyright Act takedown request. You can find information about how to file a notification with Linden Lab at **http://secondlife.com/corporate/dmca.php**. However, this means you have to discover the offending objects and then Linden Lab has to find all of them. There are millions of assets on the Grid, which makes this very difficult.

Some companies have taken another approach—one that is less likely to offend Residents who feel they are doing a brand a favor by bringing it into the virtual world. For example the iconic Playboy logo graced many unsanctioned items for sale in the *Second Life* world. Rather than doing the obvious thing, Playboy developed an island of their own on the Grid—one shaped like their logo (Figure 5.8). On that island they offered official branded merchandise. Playboy representatives dressed in Playboy Bunny avatars roamed virtual shops in the *Second Life* world to scope out instances of trademark infringement, and reportedly even offered a marketing partnership to some Resident shop owners who were making quality merchandise.

◥ NOTE

You'll learn more about the social aspects of *SL* in Part 2, and the technical aspects of the Grid in Part 3. But suffice it to say you need to log in and spend some time in-world before you begin to plan anything.

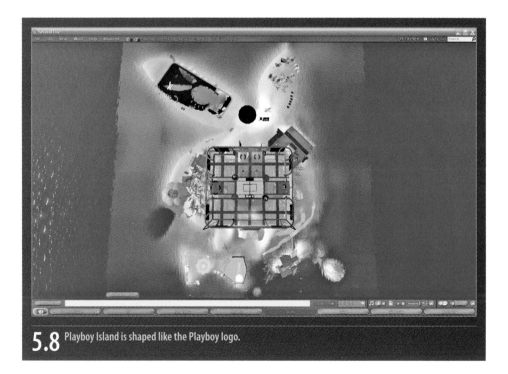

5.8 Playboy Island is shaped like the Playboy logo.

Coca-Cola went a step farther than this. The *Second Life* world was already full of unauthorized Coke-branded items, chief among them a Coke vending machine that was passed around freely between Residents. Rather than filing a takedown notice, Coke responded with a contest for *Second Life* Residents, challenging them to design a new Coke machine. With this came permission for the Residents to use the Coke logo and branding in-world. Some unauthorized virtual merchandise that had previously been pulled from sale was reinstated. In this way, Residents voluntarily augmented the company's official Virtual Thirst campaign (Figure 5.9).

5.9 Coca-Cola's Virtual Thirst area is located high in the sky.

WHAT WORKS BEST FOR BUSINESSES

So, with all of that in mind, what's the best approach for enterprises on the Grid? Here are some key points:

▶ Meetings and conferences, including job interviews, are one of the best uses of the Grid. You can learn more in Chapter 10, "Set Up a Virtual Office," and Chapter 12, "Run an Event."

▶ Spend some time on the Grid before you begin planning your project.

▶ Design marketing offerings that present something of value to Residents in-world, not only for attractive screenshots and sound bites for real-world media. You'll find information on how to go about this in Chapter 11, "Market and Sell Your Product."

▶ Make sure the products you market are carefully targeted to Residents' interests.

▶ Select a Solution Provider who's familiar with Resident culture and who has a good reputation in-world.

▶ Be certain that content created for your project is quality work that balances its appearance and functionality with its impact on in-world resources.

CULTURAL FUSION: YOUR ORGANIZATION AND THE *SECOND LIFE* GRID

06

Why's it so important to log in and try *SL* before you plan a project? What sort of avatar appearance is appropriate while on the job? Should your avatar look like your real-life self? How do you change an avatar's appearance, and where do you get the parts to do it? Is it expensive? What avatar-related pitfalls are there, and how can you avoid them? What's fashionable in-world? Are certain types of avatars better received by Residents? How will your business's HR policies apply on the *SL* Grid? You'll find out in this chapter.

YOUR AVATAR AND YOUR ORGANIZATION

WHY YOU NEED AN AVATAR IN-WORLD

Would you hire a consultant to open an office for you in a country no one from your organization had ever visited? No, of course not! You'd want to send someone there to have a look around in order to gain a better understanding of the local culture, what locations might be best for your purposes, who the movers and shakers are, and what challenges and benefits you're really facing. The same thing applies to a virtual world like *Second Life*. Although you can hire a consultant to build whatever you need, to run your events—to do almost all the work involved in some sorts of projects—it would be foolhardy to "buy before you try."

And just as you can't gain a good understanding of a real-life community by spending a few hours at a visitor information center or a Chamber of Commerce office, neither can you really understand what's going on in the *Second Life* world by logging in and poking around an orientation area for a few hours. You (or someone from your organization) need to log in and spend an appreciable amount of time exploring to see what organizations like yours have already done and what's possible, to understand the local (if virtual) culture, to make some contacts with Residents and understand their needs, and to investigate the "builds" or projects of Solution Providers you might consider hiring.

At first you might feel it's frivolous to dedicate time (either yours or your employees') to something that looks like a game, but how can you invest in it otherwise? View the *Second Life* world as a foreign land, and this book as your travel guide to an exciting, rich, and different country in which you might establish a business presence—if you can find a way your organization's culture and that of *SL* Residents can mesh.

 **ACCOUNT OR AVATAR?**

An *account* is what you create when you register to use *Second Life*. It has a name associated with it, which you choose during sign-up (and which you cannot change). You can register more than one account.

An *avatar* is your virtual representation in *Second Life*. You are always represented by an avatar while logged in—you can't be in-world without visual representation. At any time you can change parts of your avatar (such as skin or eyes), or your entire avatar (instantly changing from a human to a bear, or from a bear to a robot, for example). You can even use duplicate avatars for different accounts.

Additionally, Residents don't usually say, "His avatar's a robot." Instead they'll likely say, "He's a robot" or, "He's wearing a robot avatar."

To do this you need to have an avatar: a visual representation of yourself that can move through the *Second Life* world and interact with other avatars and objects. And although we've all heard the adage "you can't judge a book by its cover," we also know that people do it all the time. In a situation like this, where you can choose to look like just about anything, from your real-life self to a talking tree, such judgments have some interesting ramifications, and not only because of the reactions of people who interact with you. For example, some researchers have found that subjects who used an avatar that was generally considered attractive behaved more assertively—not only while using the avatar, but for some time afterward!

It's possible to change your avatar's appearance nearly instantly, but other people will get used to a particular appearance and recognize you by it. You might not want to change too often—otherwise some people might be confused. One *SL* Resident has even formally registered her avatar, Aimee Weber, as a trademark.

It's important to log in and try *SL*, and it's also important to put some time and care into the appearance of the avatar you choose to represent you and your organization.

WHAT SORT OF AVATAR IS APPROPRIATE?

Second Life Residents take on all sorts of forms. Sometimes it's even hard to recognize that they're not just part of the scenery. Will Segerman's avatar, Art Laxness, looks exactly like a default prim—a wooden cube. He's employed by my company, and he wears this avatar while he works. Is this sort of avatar the right one for you? Probably not, and it's been done already anyway!

Your avatar can be human or not. It can look very realistic or cartoonish. It can look like a supermodel or like an average person or even like your real-world self. What are the benefits and drawbacks of different avatar types, and are they different in different situations?

This section covers the considerations that should come into play as you choose an avatar for work.

DO YOU HAVE TO BE A HUMAN?

Most avatars look like human beings, but not all of them do. You can be an animal, a creature with both human and animal traits, a mythological being, an inanimate object, a space alien, a robot . . . just about anything. Figure 6.1 shows a whole range of avatars. It's a good idea to try different types during your early *Second Life* experimentation. It will give you a better understanding of what Residents experience, what's possible, and the technical challenges involved in wearing or creating different forms.

6.1 Avatars can take on many forms.

Some people wear nonhuman avatars for business and educational purposes. The CFO of Linden Lab, John Zdanowski (avatar Zee Linden), recently spoke to a meeting of Solution Providers in-world while he was a very cute beagle. Kara Williams (avatar Jessamine Harrington) is an elf, as you can see in Figure 6.2, and runs in-world support-group meetings for ShockProof. Although most people you'll meet in *Second Life* business and educational situations are humans, a sizeable minority aren't.

6.2 Kara Williams wears this avatar while running support-group meetings.

IS IT OKAY TO BE SILLY?

In the *Second Life* world, creative self-expression goes to extremes on a regular basis, and if you look like a plain old everyday realistic person, well, that's kind of dull unless it's very, very well done—to stand out, you'll need remarkable quality if you're not displaying a lot of creativity.

I routinely caused a bit of a stir a couple of years ago by showing up at in-world meetings and events in an avatar with a strong resemblance to my real-life self dressed in a business suit. However, now there are plenty of real-looking avatars in suits, and you have to do a little something different to stand out. And most people do. Even a human avatar in a suit might accessorize with sneakers that have blinking lights.

I've seen people at meetings or running classes while dressed up as cartoon animals or amorphous, shifting blobs, and aside from a few comments at the outset on the fashion statement or the quality of the work, it's usually not caused a disruption. There are a few exceptions, such as the following:

▶ Your avatar is really huge, gets in the way of others' view, and can't fit on a normal chair. Full-size dragon avatars, for example, are often not welcome at events.

▶ Your avatar is very complex, made out of many attached parts and textures and scripts, and requires a lot of resources in order to be rendered by other people's systems. This slows down system performance for those around you, which is looked on with disfavor. You'll learn more about etiquette related to your avatar's consumption of resources in the next chapter.

▶ Your avatar glows in the dark and messes up the effect of the build you're visiting or even causes other Residents to sit there squinting in real life against the blaze of light produced by your avatar.

▶ Your avatar has parts that stick out and poke into others' personal space or even through other avatars.

▶ Your avatar has a lot of large blinking lights on it or is otherwise very distracting.

So when is it best to be a human, and are there any situations in which it's beneficial to be something else? When dealing with "newbies"—people unfamiliar with the *Second Life* world, such as clients who are logging in for their first meeting—it may be wise to be a human in mundane dress. It can be jarring to have a serious conversation with a fairy or a fish if you're not used to it, and some people might not know how to relate to you, particularly if your avatar doesn't have a face.

However, if you're dealing with established Residents or people accustomed to massively multiplayer online gaming, it can be beneficial not to look like a "suit." The decision isn't always clear-cut. You might be a human in a suit but have an animated tail that is scripted to pick up on cues from your chat text and automatically punctuate the chat by wagging or drooping the tail. Maybe you're a bunny in a business suit. Or maybe you're a human in a suit that would have been worn in Victorian times.

And if you're just exploring, familiarizing yourself with the world? Well, be whatever you like!

SUPERMODELS

In a world where you can take on any appearance, some people choose to look like supermodels. Is this necessary? Not really. In fact, a lot of these avatars end up looking alike because they're as close as possible to a certain real-life cultural standard of attractiveness. It's a look that requires a lot of elaborate assets—clothing, hair, shoes, eyelashes, and more. Most of these avatars have very high rendering costs. It might be a better idea to look a little bit imperfect, like a regular person—you'll look less like a doll, be more approachable, and be less likely to cause slow performance for those around you.

There is debate among Residents about whether supermodel avatars perpetuate unrealistic notions about personal appearance in the real world. Some discount this, and say that if they have the chance to be slim and gorgeous, they're going to take it! Lately, though, there's been a growing trend of Residents, particularly those with female avatars, attempting to make their avatar shapes more like average people. Their avatars are shorter, broader, droopier, and curvier than supermodels. We're also seeing a growing number of male avatars with bald spots or paunches, and shoulders that actually fit through a standard doorway!

DOES YOUR AVATAR HAVE TO LOOK LIKE YOUR REAL-LIFE SELF?

Although many people have human avatars, they rarely look just like their real-life selves. My avatar, for example, usually looks a lot like me . . . but younger. I didn't even do this on purpose. It used to be near impossible to make a realistic avatar that looked older unless you wanted to spend a lot of money, and no off-the-rack avatar parts were available to allow me to do it while looking like my real-life self. I got used to my avatar's youthful looks, and haven't ever felt motivated to look older. Despite the age difference, I have been recognized in real life by people who had only seen my avatar, so I guess it's close enough! Most people who have avatars that look like themselves idealize their avatars somewhat. They make their avatars younger or thinner or with more hair or a smaller nose.

Plenty of human avatars don't look at all like their owners, and this is not considered strange by Residents (or by most businesspeople and educators in-world). Some prominent Residents and people doing real-life work in-world don't even share the same gender as their avatars. Don't be surprised if you attend a meeting and find a man's voice coming from a female avatar, or vice versa.

Of course, there are some situations in which it's beneficial to look like yourself. For example, if you were a celebrity appearing in-world for a promotional appearance, it would probably be a good idea to have the appearance your fans expect!

⬎WARNING

Keep in mind that once you have chosen a name for your *Second Life* account, your avatar will be stuck with it forever. To change names you'll have to get another account, and many *Second Life* assets are not transferrable from one account to another. Some considerations are how difficult the name is to spell, how long it is to type, and whether there's already a Resident with a name very similar to yours.

OFF-THE-RACK AND CUSTOM AVATARS—OR DO-IT-YOURSELF!

Most Residents put a lot of time, effort, and money into customizing their avatars. For many, shopping for and dressing their avatars is a hobby in itself. Avatar parts, clothing, and accessories are the top-selling content in the *SL* world. Self-expression is important, and other types of content require land to host it. Not everyone has land, but everyone does have an avatar.

⬎ TIP

Go to Inventory ▶ Library ▶ Clothing to find some looks to try.

When you log into *Second Life* for the first time you'll have a default avatar and access to a selection of avatars provided to every Resident in the Library folder of your Inventory. From it you can select a variety of looks, including a human avatar in a business suit, a small dragon, or even a silly robot with a cardboard box for a head. These will do for a start, but using one of them will mark you as a "newbie."

That's not so important while you're just exploring and learning your way around. However, if you show up at an event representing your organization while wearing one of these, Residents will notice. The common assumption will be that you are a newbie, that you don't care enough about *Second Life* to bother to work on your avatar and customize it, and that your organization's just out for a quick buck at Residents' expense. Residents may even gossip about it in-world and on *Second Life*-specific forums.

While wearing one of these "newbie" avatars, expect reactions ranging from eager (and authentic) offers of assistance to improve your looks, offers too good to be true from those who'd like to offer you the virtual-world equivalent of the opportunity to buy the Brooklyn Bridge (such as investment schemes), and (particularly in situations where you're trying to sell or promote something) condescension. These reactions will probably be magnified if you also haven't yet learned to make your avatar walk, fly, or sit and you bump into walls and other avatars.

Most Residents start out by modifying the default avatar and clothing using the in-world Appearance tools. It's difficult to make a good-looking avatar using these tools without practice, and not everyone has the talent or develops the skill to do it. You're likely to end up with a rough-looking avatar at best, or one that's downright misproportioned. This is likely to get an even stronger reaction than using one of the Library avatars, because it will stand out more.

Fortunately, you don't have to make your own avatar from scratch. You can either hire a Solution Provider to create a custom avatar for you, or buy one from a Resident—whole or in part.

A Solution Provider can make an avatar that looks very like your real self, though the necessary simplification of avatars that keeps us from needing supercomputers to render them means it won't look *exactly* like you. Rates for something like this can range from around a hundred Linden dollars at the very low end to hundreds of US dollars for an avatar with features like a custom photosourced or hand-drawn skin. With a range like that, quality can vary a lot, so you'll want to check out more work from the artist you're considering. You'll learn more about choosing a Solution Provider in Part 3 of this book.

Some shops in-world sell complete avatars, some already dressed in suits. These can be a good starting point, but share drawbacks similar to using an avatar from the Library. If you don't like the idea of showing up at a party in the same outfit as a couple of other people, imagine arriving and finding yourself face-to-face with your twin, or triplets!

Most Residents create their avatars from a selection of parts they purchase from other Residents in-world, which they often modify themselves. You can get a shape, a skin, hair, eyes, and other attachments and adjust them to create a unique look. This goes for nonhuman avatars, as well!

AVATAR PARTS

Your avatar is made up of a few basic parts that you can customize or purchase. These include its shape, skin, eyes, and hair.

The basic framework or outline of an avatar—its 3D model—is called a *shape*. You start with a default shape, which you can modify by using the Appearance Editor (Figure 6.3). Its slider-style controls adjust height, body fat, hand size, nose length, and just about every other proportion. To try this, select Edit ▶ Appearance ▶ Shape.

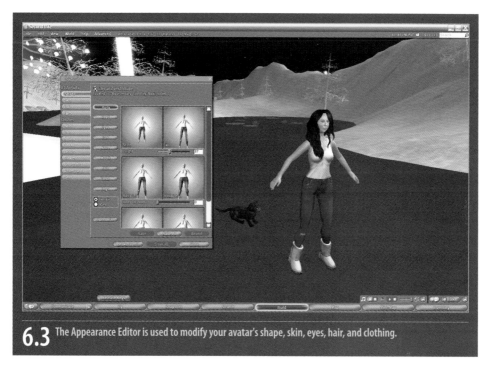

6.3 The Appearance Editor is used to modify your avatar's shape, skin, eyes, hair, and clothing.

⬎ WARNING

Before you edit your avatar using the Appearance Editor or by putting on new body parts, make sure you've saved a backup. Go into Appearance mode then select Make Outfit. Check the boxes next to all of the parts you want to save, and be sure to label your backup so that you can find it later. You'll find a folder with the name you chose nested in the Clothing folder in your Inventory.

Some shops in-world sell premade shapes, which you can usually adjust yourself. Sometimes when you purchase a skin it comes with a shape that is made to match.

SKIN

The surface texture of an avatar is called a *skin*. There are two main types of skins. One is a *slider skin*, so called because it is created using default textures that are adjusted using sliders in Appearance mode. To access these controls use the Skin tab. This sort of skin is often used as a base for avatars that are made from attached prims.

The other main type of skin is made of textures created in an external graphics program, such as Photoshop. These are uploaded and applied in Appearance mode on the Tattoo layer, then saved as a complete skin. High-quality skins are created this way. Some are hand-drawn, others are made from photographs, and the best are usually created through a combination of these sources.

Some skins are made in these ways, but with some transparent or translucent parts. This allows the wearer to adjust their color somewhat using the Appearance sliders.

The skin is typically the most expensive part of an avatar. As illustrated in Figure 6.4, you can change your avatar's appearance dramatically simply by changing your skin. However, particularly when skins have a lot of detail or shading, they are not a natural match for every shape. It might take some careful shopping to find a skin that works for your shape, or you might choose to adjust your shape to work well with a skin you like. At most shops you'll find sample skins to try for free or for L$1.

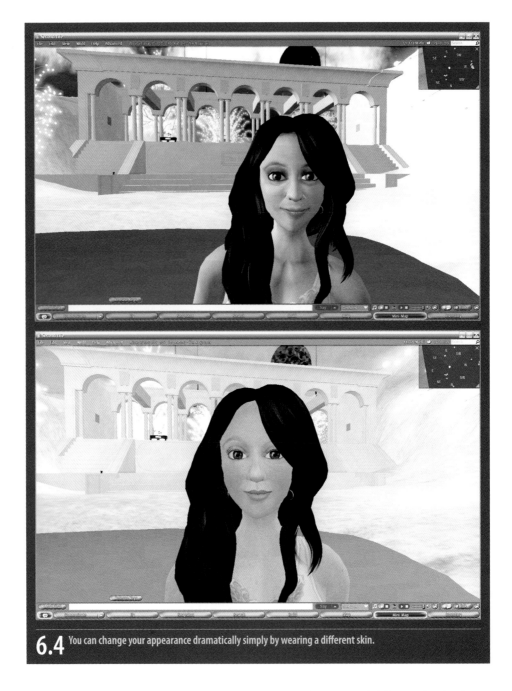

6.4 You can change your appearance dramatically simply by wearing a different skin.

Most skins are available in a variety of colors, some with or without freckles or with different-colored eyebrows. If you have a male avatar, keep in mind that, except for slider skins, your facial hair is usually painted right onto your skin. Some skin creators offer multiple versions of a skin with a variety of facial hair. If you have a female avatar, your makeup is probably painted on, as well. Most skin creators offer the same skin with a variety of different makeup styles.

Keep in mind that you will rarely be able to edit skins you purchase, though you will probably have the right to make copies.

By the way, many avatars in the *SL* world sport tattoos. With the exception of those that are part of a custom skin, they're as easy to put on or take off as a shirt. In fact, they usually *are* shirts or socks or other articles of transparent clothing worn over the skin layer.

EYES

Your default eyes can also be edited in Appearance mode. However, there are a lot of eyes available for sale in-world, in just about every color and style imaginable. Like good-quality skins, these are made from textures created in an external program and you probably will not be able to edit them. Some, made of prim attachments, are even animated or glow in the dark. Eyes are rarely editable by buyers, but are usually copyable.

HAIR

Two main types of hair are available to avatars. The first type, called *slider* or *system* hair, is created and edited in Appearance mode, similar to default shapes and skins. This hair is usually very simple in appearance and cannot be made into fancy styles. It rarely looks realistic.

The other type is *prim hair*. This is attached to your avatar's head over a base of transparent or very short slider hair. Prim hair can be very complex, and may even have flexible parts. Many styles are available at Resident shops, and for some Residents hair-shopping is almost a vice. While many Residents never change their shape and rarely change their eyes or skin, many change their hair style much more often than they would in real life.

Prim hair shops usually offer samples to try, and prim hair you purchase is almost always editable using the Object Editor. This way you can resize and often recolor your hair to match your avatar. It's also usually copyable but not transferrable. Be sure you copy your hair before you start editing it, in case something goes wrong.

CLOTHING

You'll find some outfits to wear in the Library, but so will everyone else. Most people want a more unique, self-expressive look. Unless you really need to have a specific outfit custom-created for you, or something like a jacket with your company's logo on it, you can probably find something appropriate at a Resident-owned shop.

Like skins, clothes can be made either using Appearance sliders alone or using textures imported from an external graphics program. Some are hand-drawn and others are photosourced. Usually you won't want to mix photosourced and hand-drawn clothing and skins, because the styles clash and you'll end up looking like a cartoon person in a real shirt, or vice versa!

Some clothing is sold with the right to modify it, which is really handy if it's a light or neutral color that you can edit in Appearance mode. Clothing you purchase is either copyable or transferrable, and most vendors will be labeled to indicate this. It is especially important to pay attention to the copy/transfer rights if you're considering buying something as a gift for a friend. I'll talk more about the permissions system in Part 3 of this book.

Some avatars don't wear clothes. For example, realistic animals or robots usually go without. So do a lot of human avatars, either because of their amorous activities or because of their virtual lifestyle. There are a lot of nude beaches in the *Second Life* world.

Some regions in *Second Life* don't allow nudity for human avatars (or anything else that has humanlike bits to expose). At the top of the viewer, next to the region name, you'll find a rating of PG (suitable for general use) or M, Mature. Nudity isn't allowed in PG regions. Some owners of Mature regions don't allow nudity, either.

How do you find
all these clothing
and avatar-part
shops? Click on
the Search button
at the bottom of
the viewer and
select a tab ap-
propriate for what
you want to find:
a place to shop, a
group to join, an
avatar you want
to send a message
to. Then enter your
search words in
the box—such as
hair or *suit*—and
click the Search
button.

When that's the case, you usually will be informed by a sign, a chat message, or a notecard that you receive when you arrive.

MATURE VS. PG

The *Second Life* Community Standards (**http://wiki.secondlife.com/wiki/LL:Second_Life_Community_Standards**) state the following:

INDECENCY

Second Life is an adult community, but Mature material is not necessarily appropriate in all areas (see Global Standards below). Content, communication, or behavior which involves intense language or expletives, nudity or sexual content, the depiction of sex or violence, or anything else broadly offensive must be contained within private land in areas rated Mature (M). Names of Residents, objects, places, and groups are broadly viewable in *Second Life* directories and on the *Second Life* website, and must adhere to PG guidelines.

GLOBAL STANDARDS, LOCAL RATINGS

All areas of *Second Life*, including the www.secondlife.com website and the *Second Life* Forums, adhere to the same Community Standards. Locations within *Second Life* are noted as Safe or Unsafe and rated Mature (M) or non-Mature (PG), and behavior must conform to the local ratings. Any unrated area of *Second Life* or the *Second Life* website should be considered non-Mature (PG).

Clothing includes shirts, pants, skirts, underpants, undershirts, socks, shoes, gloves, and jackets. These are the labels of the *clothing mesh* or layer, not the actual article of clothing. For example, a shirt worn untucked so that its tails are outside of the pants will probably actually be worn on the jacket layer. The skirt layer is used for the lower portion of many jackets.

AVATAR ATTACHMENTS

Many objects other than prim hair can be attached to an avatar, and (predictably) these are called *attachments*. You can't attach them just anywhere—you have to wear them on one of a selection of specific *attachment points*. To put on an attachment, find it in your Inventory, right-click it, and select Wear. The item will appear at its last specified attachment point. If you'd like to change its attachment point, right-click it in Inventory and select Attach, then choose from the list of attachment points you aren't already using. To remove an attach-ment, right-click it in Inventory and select Detach.

You can use the Object Editor to revise an attached object's location by right-clicking it and selecting Edit, then dragging it into place. It's a good idea to make a backup copy first, if possible.

FASHION ATTACHMENTS

Most attachments are intended to accessorize your avatar, but some avatars are made almost entirely from attachments. Here are some of the types of attachments avatars wear to alter their appearance (loosely arranged in the order you might shop for them, put them on, or adjust them):

Hair. As we already discussed, most avatar hair is an attachment worn over a slider hair base.

Facial hair. Although most avatar facial hair is a part of the skin layer, some avatars sport attached mustaches, beards, or sideburns.

Sometimes you'll
attach something
to your avatar and
not be able to see
it. This is usually
because its attach-
ment point was
set for an avatar
of a different size
from yours. Even
though the object
is still the same
distance from the
attachment point,
it is embedded in
your avatar. To fix
this, attach the
object to a differ-
ent, easier-to-get-
at point, use the
Object Editor to
move it away from
the point, then
reattach it to the
original location.

Shoes. Slider shoes just don't have the same realistic, detailed look as shoes made from prims. Like prim hair, prim shoes are worn over a slider base. Many in-world shops offer sample shoes to try. Unlike real-life shoes, these will probably not be available in multiple sizes. Instead, you resize your avatar's feet in Appearance mode so that they will fit into the shoes. Boots are usually made up of four attachments— one for each foot and one for each lower leg—plus a slider shoe base.

Clothing parts. Some clothing includes added details made of attachments, such as epaulets, buttons, cuffs, tails, or even flowing, flexible skirts. These often require adjustment to fit your avatar properly, and most shops do not offer samples to try. If you haven't had any practice with editing objects, you might find this difficult!

Fingernails. Fingernails are part of your skin, and you can also purchase clear gloves with nails painted onto them. However, some fingernails are made of prims. You wear an attachment of five prim nails on each hand. These contain scripts and animations so that your avatar's hands will remain in the proper pose for the nails to appear placed correctly. You might have to resize your hands to get the correct fit.

Eyelashes. An increasingly popular type of prim attachment, eyelashes come in a variety of styles. They'll usually attach to one of the points on your avatar's head. So far no one has figured out how to script these so that they blink in time with an avatar's eyes, so be aware that you might not look entirely natural with your eyes closed!

Jewelry. Although you'll find the odd necklace painted onto a clothing layer, most jewelry is in the form of prim attachments. Some of it can be very elaborate, and certain top designers even sell limited-edition jewelry for prices that might surprise you!

Belts. Some trousers or skirts include a belt on the texture layer, but a lot of belts are attachments.

Ties. Like belts, some ties are textures on a clothing layer, but these days more and more of them are prim attachments—some are even flexible and move in the breeze.

Wings. These are one of the first attachments most avatars try. After all, *Second Life* avatars can fly, so it makes sense that many would like to wear wings. A large variety is available, and some wings are even scripted to flap.

Ears and tails. Like wings, some ears and tails are scripted for functionality. Your catlike ears might perk up or droop, and your tail might wag when it picks up from your chat that you've said the word *happy*.

Hats. There's no such thing as a slider hat! Hats are made from prims and attached to your head.

Handheld objects. If you see an avatar holding a fishing pole, a gun, or a cup of tea, it's an attachment, probably worn on the hand attachment point.

Pets. Through the "magic" of attachments, you can have a little dragon perched on your shoulder, a kitten in your arms, or even a glowing cartoon fish circling your head.

SCRIPTED ATTACHMENTS

Some attachments aren't intended to be seen at all, or not primarily, but are instead worn for functional purposes. They might be worn attached to your avatar's body, or on special attachment points called *HUD attachment points*. HUD is short for Heads-Up Display. For example, see the HUD in Figure 6.8. Things you wear on your HUD points are not visible to anyone but you. Here are examples of some sorts of scripted attachments (listed roughly in the order I'd deal with them in-world):

Animation override. This attachment, also called an *AO* for short, may take the form of a HUD you control by clicking its buttons, or as an attachment worn on the avatar or a HUD attachment point that you control by entering commands in chat. It replaces the default animations that pose your avatar while standing, walking, sitting, running, flying, landing, jumping, or hovering. You can buy an animation override attachment with a full animation set already in it, or you can select specific animations at an in-world shop. The way your avatar moves can really lend it a lot of personality, and make you seem aggressive, casual, or even allow you to run on all fours like an animal.

Flight assist. The height to which your avatar can fly is usually limited to about 300 meters. But Residents build a lot of interesting things in the sky and you don't want to miss them! A flight assist attachment will allow you to fly higher, and some also allow you to increase your acceleration or overall speed.

Scanner. Sometimes called *radar*, this is a gadget that scans the area around you and reports what avatars are nearby and how far away they are. Some HUD-based scanners even use visual markers to indicate avatar locations.

Finder. Enter the name of the avatar or object you want to find, and this will find them. Some gadgets of this type will even direct you to the target with a stream of particles you can follow.

Weapons. There are all sorts of weapons in the *Second Life* world. Some of them act on their targets by *pushing*, or applying force that can knock your avatar a short distance, or even so high into the air you might wonder if you're headed for orbit. *Pushguns* or weapons that do this are sometimes called *orbiters*. Other weapons cause varying degrees of *damage*. If an avatar takes enough damage, it *dies*—is sent to its *home point* with no penalty. Still other sorts of scripted weapons interact with one another, similar to real-world laser tag games, and don't affect any bystanders who aren't also using compatible equipment. Landowners on the *Second Life* Grid can disable push or damage. We'll learn more about that in Part 3 of this book.

Defensive attachments. Where there are weapons, there are defenses. Some are anti-push attachments, which help to keep you from being shoved around. Others are shields that repel damage.

Bloghud. This HUD allows you to compose blog entries in-world and send them straight to a blog for posting.

Facelight. You probably know how much time and effort the theater and film industries put into carefully lighting their stars. In *Second Life*, many people do the same for their avatars, purchasing and wearing invisible objects that shed light on their avatars. A good facelight, properly adjusted, can improve appearances in certain situations. Unfortunately, there are a lot of facelight attachments that are way too bright, so that the wearer goes about surrounded by a blinding glow.

Handshake attachment. This attachment is scripted to animate your avatar and another you select so that you shake hands.

Hug attachment. Similarly, this attachment lets you hug another avatar.

Typing replacer. This is a specialized animation override that makes your avatar perform a different action than the standard typing motions as you enter text.

Dance attachment. Some Residents play their dance animations directly from their Inventory's Animations folder. Others load their animations into an attachment, allowing them to easily switch or select dances on the fly. Some dance attachments also allow you to offer to animate other avatars around you.

Translator. This handy gadget will do a quick-and-dirty language translation in real time. You'll encounter people from all over the real world while in the *SL* world!

Emoter. This attachment can trigger different facial expressions, poses, audio clips, or all three. Some of these are HUD-based, but others operate on chat commands or even by picking up and responding to words you say in text conversations.

Multitool. Rather than wearing a whole bunch of different scripted attachments, you might consider purchasing a multitool, which combines multiple functions.

DO YOU HAVE TO SPEND A FORTUNE?

Although there are a lot of things you can buy to improve your avatar, you don't necessarily need all of them. As you spend some time in-world learning your way around, you will discover what sorts of things you do and don't need for your own purposes.

Most of these things are available at reasonable prices. For example, you can find a nice suit in the range of L$200 to L$500. That amounts to under US$2. Even a skin, the most expensive thing you're likely to buy for your avatar, probably won't cost you more than L$1,000, and often substantially less. It's possible to spend a lot more, though, particularly if you want custom work done. On the other hand, you can find many free items that will serve temporarily or even for a long time. Some of these, by the way, are distributed promotionally by real-world organizations. Evian and L'Oreal are two companies that gave away free, quality skins, for example.

If you don't have a lot of time to shop, you can ask your Solution Provider for assistance. I've created custom avatars and made over client avatars using off-the-rack assets. In one case, to quickly prepare for an in-world public appearance, I assisted my editor from Wiley in transforming from a leopard Tiny that looked like a cuddly stuffed animal into a dashing businessman in a classy suit. I pulled a few things from my Inventory, teleported him around the Grid to some good shops, and helped him get his clothes and attachments in place. He was all ready to go, with quality shoes and a tie in just the right shade, and even an AO, in under an hour.

ONE AVATAR OR TWO?

Most *SL* Residents have more than one avatar outfit in their Inventory, changing their clothes and hair and makeup, or even changing into completely different sorts of creatures for certain occasions. Some Residents change their look more often than they change clothes in the real world—sometimes even as the punchline to a joke. And, of course, some change for reasons like those of the librarian we saw in Part 1, who dresses up as Mary Todd Lincoln for educational events. At the Stepping into Literature conference in 2008, where participants learned about using virtual worlds to teach about and promote books, some organizers dressed as characters from famous books. Event guests asked them questions, which they answered in character. The guest who surmised the identity of the most characters won a prize.

ALTERNATE ACCOUNTS

For some Residents, the ability to shape-shift isn't enough. Many have more than one *Second Life* account. Reasons for this vary, including using the alternate account (or *alt*) to test scripts or object permissions, to hold backups, or as a sort of bank to store spare L$. Others use an alt to explore different facets of themselves or the Grid, participating in different *SL* subcultures with each one. They may or may not keep the connection between their avatars secret. There are less positive uses for alts, as well, such as spying—it's the ultimate in disguise. Some Residents, intent on hiding their identity, go as far as to log in more than one alt at a time, making sure the avatars are seen together and taking care to not log in too quickly with one after logging off another.

Letting this sort of thing worry you is a sure way to make yourself miserable. Pretty soon you'll end up wondering about half the people you meet. I usually take avatars at face value unless I have a specific reason to do otherwise.

⬎ WARNING

If someone sends you an object or other asset while you're marked as Busy, it will automatically be refused.

Keeping work and play separate is one popular and often valuable reason for maintaining an alt. Sometimes you want to do something in-world besides work. Don't expect others to either know about or honor your regular business hours. Not only might they be in some other time zone, but many people do business in-world during hours other than between 9 a.m. and 5 p.m. I receive business-related instant messages at, say, 1 a.m. on a Sunday, from people who know what time it is where I am. Although you can mark your avatar as Busy so that someone who sends you a message at an inconvenient time will receive an Away message, this also blocks all incoming content and instant messages, so you can't shop or receive a message from a friend.

This is why some use one avatar for work and one for play. This has drawbacks, though. Many assets can't be copied or aren't transferrable, and invariably you'll find that the shoes or the vehicle you wanted to use are stuck in the Inventory of your other avatar. Plus, you'll still want to interact with some of the same people, and if this goes on long enough you're likely to find that your nonbusiness alt receives business instant messages, too.

However, having a dedicated work avatar can still be useful. It makes it easy to keep your personal assets and L$ separate from those of your employer. If you leave your company, someone may take over that account and have access to its no-transfer assets. Also, if your organization has purchased a custom last name, your lone avatar will still bear that name even if you move on. Additionally, some activities you might want to explore in-world may not be those your organization wants to endorse or be associated with. Some might not mind that the group NOOD XXX SeXoRama CluB appears in your profile, but others certainly will!

Sometimes an organization or in-world group will even create a shared-use avatar that holds and manages resources such as land or L$. I'll cover this more in Part 3 when I discuss managing project inventory and the permissions system.

AVOIDING AVATAR EMBARRASSMENTS

It's not easy being a newbie. You have to learn to walk without even a crawling stage to help you ease into it. You'll miss doorways and run into the wall, fall over the sides of staircases, and plummet from platforms in the sky. Flying takes practice, too, and until you have some you'll find yourself smacking into buildings and trees and fellow avatars. Even sitting isn't always intuitive.

Let's review some of the most common challenges you'll face as you get used to your avatar. Maybe you can avoid some of these embarrassing situations!

Accidental flashing. Several common situations can lead to your avatar exposing more flesh than you'd like:

▶ Taking flight: Most female avatar skins are anatomically correct. In other words, they're not smooth like Barbie dolls—the details are all there. In a virtual world where you can fly, always remember: if you're wearing a skirt, double-check before you take off to be sure you're wearing underwear.

▶ Animated chairs: Scripted chairs may contain animated poses, some of which are not very modest for avatars dressed in skirts. Be sure you're wearing underwear! If you aren't certain what sort of animation seats will contain at a meeting or an event, consider wearing slacks.

▶ Change of clothing: You can change your outfit by dragging its folder from Inventory and onto your avatar or by right-clicking and selecting Wear. Everything you're wearing will be replaced by the items in the folder. If the folder doesn't contain pants, guess what happens? You don't want this to happen in public. Also, make sure that if there's a skirt in the folder, there are also underpants. One way to avoid this embarrassing situation is to right-click the outfit in Inventory and select Add to Outfit. This will replace like items (skin for skin, socks for socks) but will not remove items for which there's no replacement.

▶ Slow-rendering clothing. Beware when changing clothes in public in areas that contain a lot of textures and avatars. Because rendering them takes a lot of resources, things can appear slowly. This includes your clothing. You could accidentally flash onlookers while you make your wardrobe transition. Some shopping areas offer changing booths, or you can teleport home to change. By the way, some Residents don't care if you see their avatar without clothes, and they won't bother with modesty!

⟶WARNING

So you think that avatar over there is pretty silly-looking, huh? Make very sure its wearer is in on the joke before you comment. For all you know, it's intended to match that person's real-life appearance!

Unmarked poseball. *Poseballs* are spheres that contain a script and an animation. You right-click and choose Sit (or another action) from the pie menu, and your avatar is placed and animated. Maybe you're seated on a chair or you're animated so that you appear to be painting a fence. Beware of unmarked poseballs in strange places. Many *SL* Residents participate in adult activities that involve poseballs, and you don't want to do so by accident!

The cheap seats. Most quality chairs in *Second Life* are scripted so that you will automatically be seated in the correct spot, facing the expected direction. However, some are made poorly or don't contain scripts. You may find yourself facing the wrong way or unable to sit at all. This can be really stressful if you're trying to take a seat for an important meeting! To sit on an unscripted object, step away from it a little bit, turn to face it, right-click exactly where you want your avatar's rear to end up, and select Sit. This should seat you on the object, facing the place you had been standing. If this fails, one workaround is to rez a prim, sit on it, and then move it into the desired position.

Accidental attachment. Sometimes when you rez an object by dragging it from Inventory, rather than dropping it on the ground you might accidentally drag it onto yourself. Suddenly it's an impromptu attachment. The default attachment point used to be the skull, which led to an embarrassing newbie rite of passage involving wearing things like houses and vehicles on their heads. Nowadays the default attachment point is the right hand, but you'll still hear lots of jokes about newbies with boxes on their heads.

Invisible attachment. Some new Residents, upon first undressing their male avatars, are somewhat surprised to find that their avatar seems to be missing something. Fortunately for those who feel the need for these missing parts, they can be purchased at shops in-world and attached. However, clothing layers conform to the avatar shape and can't be made to conform to prims. So that bit pokes right through. However, many of these attachments are scripted so that they can be commanded to become invisible, relieving the wearer from having to detach and reattach. Figure 6.5 illustrates what an invisible attachment looks like to someone who has selected View ▶ Highlight Transparent. Oops!

⟶NOTE

Some Residents view their avatars as dolls of sorts. Others identify closely with their avatars, seeing them as extensions of themselves. There's not always a correlation between these views and whether or not these folks are upset when you accidentally see their avatar without clothing, but you can guess how it probably goes.

6.5 This invisible top hat glows red when Highlight Transparent is on.

SECOND LIFE STYLES

Like any large community in real life, the *Second Life* world contains many subcultures. Residents involved in a subculture tend to share a similar sense of style or certain specific traits of appearance, and some maintain regions or even large continents dedicated to their shared vision. It's useful to know what associations people might assume you have based on your avatar's appearance before you choose how you want to look.

MAJOR STYLES OR SUBCULTURES

Countless subcultures thrive in *SL*—so many that it would be easy to write an entire book about them. Some people make a full-time job of virtual fashion, and there are many publications about them, similar to real-life fashion magazines. You'll learn more during your own exploration of the *SL* world, but for now let's have a look at some of the Grid's most prominent styles and subcultures.

6.6 Animal avatars like this are created using a combination of poses and attachments.

Armies. Sometimes dressed in military costumes and other times outfitted in the ragtag castoffs found in postapocalyptic settings they frequent, some Residents like to play war games and develop more and more powerful weapons and increasingly intricate defenses. Be careful when you visit their regions, because they're likely to be damage-enabled.

Cyberpunks. If you find yourself in a location that looks like something out of *Blade Runner* or you notice the avatar you're talking to sports a robotic eye or arm along with her black leathers, you might have stumbled upon a cyberpunk location. A popular science-fiction genre in the 1980s, cyberpunk is one of the most popular clothing fashions and architectural styles in the *Second Life* world.

Dragons. They're often as big as a house, made from prim attachments, and impressively detailed, and they breathe fire (or sometimes other elements, like ice crystals). You might encounter smaller dragons, too, but they're usually just babies!

Elves. The pointed ears are an obvious clue that cloak-wearing avatars you might encounter are elves. They tend to look the way you'd expect an elf to look after you've seen *Lord of the Rings*. A lot of Residents try out the look and even stop by to participate in a drum circle or other in-world elven event, and many decide to make it their virtual lifestyle. Some of them form clans ruled over by royalty and nobles.

Fandom-based. Some people always wanted to be Jedi and others are Dr. Who aficionados. In *Second Life*, such fans have their chance to not only create fan art, but to live it. Wander around a bit and, sometimes even in re-creations of their native habitats, you'll encounter Stormtroopers, Starfleet officers, and scarf-wearing magic students who look an awful lot like characters from the *Harry Potter* series.

Ferals. Some Residents wear avatars that look like animals—birds, wolves, lions, apes, or just about any animal you can imagine (see Figure 6.6). These avatars are created by using animations to mimic poses and movements of real animals, and prim attachments to create an animal's shape. Animal avatars that walk on four feet are sometimes called *quads*. Some who wear these avatars, but not all, belong to a subculture of *Ferals* (not to be confused with the Lost Ferals brand of Feral avatar for sale in-world).

They roleplay animals. Humans and other non-Ferals aren't allowed to visit some of the Ferals' lands, where they hunt and defend their territory and consult shape-shifting shamans.

Furries. A *Furry* is an anthropomorphic animal—in other words, it's shaped like a human and walks on two legs, but it has the head and maybe the paws and tail of an animal. Some popular anthropomorphized animals are foxes, skunks, and wolves. Not everyone who wears this type of avatar is part of the Furry subculture, which has been around a long time both online and in real life. But there are a lot of Furries living in dedicated sims where they often participate in roleplay, weaving themselves entire lives and histories.

Goreans. This subculture is based on a series of novels by John Norman set in a land called Gor. It's a bit controversial, because along with often beautiful, well-made regions, much of Gorean roleplay revolves around sexuality and (consensual) slavery roleplay. Gorean fashion indicates the roleplayer's status: including skimpy, translucent silks for slaves, and loose, full-coverage gowns with veils for freewomen.

Kids. *Second Life* (with the exception of Teen *Second Life*) is only for those 18 and older. So when you see an avatar that looks like a kid, perhaps missing teeth and with a bandage on the knee, you're seeing a real-life adult who has chosen to roleplay a child (Figure 6.7). Along with other Residents, some roleplay entire extended families and even attend school or summer camp. If you want to know where to find the best toys, ask an *SL* kid.

6.7 *SL* kids dress and act like the real thing.

Mafia families. Sharp dressers, fiercely loyal, and heavily armed, mafia families are an online phenomenon that goes back long before they started carving out their turf in *Second Life*. Once I attended an in-world mafia-family wedding, and shortly after the vows one of the guests said the wrong thing—what a shootout! Apparently even the bride had a gun tucked into her garter.

Mer. With scripted prim tails and beautiful undersea regions, Mer are worth a visit. They keep to themselves, but perhaps that's because most regions aren't submerged!

"There's a lot of misconceptions about child avatars as a whole, with many assuming some horrible things about us all. As a result, a lot of people ask me, "Why be a kid in *Second Life*?". There are a whole lot of answers: it's a chance to recapture one's youth, or get the toys you missed, or gain things once lost or never had. It's also a whole lotta fun. It's like the old *Twilight Zone* episode where a group of octogenarians regain their youth— literally—by playing the child's game "kick the can." And really, how is my choice of avatar any different, really, than appearing as a dragon, a Furry, or even the girl next door?" —Marianne McCann

Neko. Drawn from Japanese anime, a neko (*cat* in Japanese) is a cute human with cat ears and a tail (Figure 6.8). Neko tend to behave in a catlike way, too, often meowing and accessorized with bell collars and mousetraps. You can tell them from Furries because they don't have prim heads; they have regular avatar faces. Sometimes they wear skins with stripes or spots, though.

6.8 Neko have the ears, tails, and sometimes paws of cats. Compare the neko in this picture to the quad snow leopard.

Parents of prim babies. Sooner or later you will encounter a pregnant avatar. Some in-world businesses facilitate this, selling pregnant-avatar shapes and maternity fashions. There are even subscription services of sorts, which send a new, larger shape every few days or weeks. Expectant-avatar couples even attend roleplay Lamaze classes and get checkups, and when the big day comes they may go to a virtual maternity center. Animations for the mother, father, and doctor simulate the delivery. The parents can then purchase a baby made from prims, and carry it, put it to bed, or wheel it in a stroller. Some Residents who are unable to conceive or who have lost a child find this roleplay to be a very meaningful experience that helps them work out their real-world issues.

Real-life cultures. Some Residents like to dress in the style of or live in a real-life culture of which they may or may not be a part. Visit a Zen garden and see avatars in beautiful kimonos or fighting with samurai swords! Travel back in time, virtually, to Renaissance England, 1930s America, the Old West, or ancient Rome. There you'll find avatars dressed in the fashions of the day.

Steampunk Victorian. Top hats, waistcoats, corsets, and bustles are some of the things worn by avatars who are involved in the steampunk Victorian subculture, and by some who just enjoy the look (Figure 6.9). There's a bit of retro science fiction thrown into the mix, with some avatars riding clockwork horses or building difference engines in their spare time. You'll find dozens of regions full of Victorian architecture dedicated to this virtual lifestyle, where many interesting events are open to the public. These Residents tend to use formal forms of address, such as Mr. and Miss.

6.9 Residents of Caledon include a clockwork man and many others who put a lot of creativity care into their appearance.

Tinies. Tinies (Figure 6.10) are avatars smaller than those you can normally create with the shape sliders. A special AO folds up their limbs, which are enclosed in prim attachments, giving them the appearance of cute little animals. They tend to be very playful, and in regions they own or frequent you'll probably find lots of Tiny-sized furnishings, homes shaped like giant mushrooms or cute cottages, and shops full of Tiny clothing and accessories. Tinies can't wear regular avatar clothing because it won't conform to their prims, so they have to wear clothes fashioned from prim attachments.

Vampires. Clad in fashions of a bygone time, usually in black or other dark colors, and perhaps accessorized by large jewels, vampires tend to live in richly appointed, atmospheric regions where it's always night. Scripted attachments allow them to use their fangs to bite their victims.

You'll find there's a lot of crossover between styles and subcultures. Perhaps you'll meet a steampunk Victorian dressed formally, down to his pocket watch, but with the head, tail, and paws of a skunk. You might encounter a neko *SL* kid, or a Tiny fox in a kimono and carrying a samurai sword. Some Residents have more than one avatar, with each involved in a different community. And, of course, you'll find plenty of Residents dressed in jeans, T-shirts, and sneakers, looking pretty much like they do offline.

6.10 Tinies are usually whimsical.

IN-WORLD PREJUDICE

Real-life discrimination makes its way into the virtual world just as it finds its way onto the Web, along with racist slogans, sexist comments, and bigoted attacks on people of all religions and cultures. In *Second Life* such acts are usually perpetrated by *griefers*—people who seek ways to upset others for their own entertainment. We'll take a closer look at this phenomenon in Chapter 7, "Understanding Social Interaction in *Second Life*."

One unfortunate result of this is that some avatars are mistreated because their appearance shares some traits with avatars that Residents are used to seeing griefers wear. If, for instance, your avatar is dressed in freebie clothes, is very tall, has a lot of body fat, and is grossly misproportioned, many Residents will be wary because of the association with griefers.

There's also prejudice against various in-world subcultures. If you look like a member of a mafia family, a lot of Residents will expect you to act like one, and many don't appreciate gunplay. If your avatar appears to be pregnant or is carrying a prim baby, others might avoid you because many attached babies (or even pregnant bellies) are scripted to announce when they need a diaper change, when they are hungry, or when the mother feels a kick. Some Residents get pretty tired of hearing this chatter.

Furries have it the hardest. Their complex social interactions, their characterizations, their motivations, and storylines that in some cases extend back years before the advent of *Second Life*, are sometimes foreign even to other *SL* Residents. On top of this, a particular online community that some consider organized griefers decided Furries make a nice target. Attacks on Furry regions and on individual Furries, nasty comments, and rude forum posts are frequent. Others looking for a cheap laugh at someone else's expense contribute, as well. Despite unfortunate instances like these, however, *Second Life* Residents tend to be more tolerant than most people in the offline world.

On the flip side, certain types of avatars almost always get a positive reception. Steampunk Victorian style seems to go over well just about everywhere, for example (perhaps it's those Victorian manners), and nearly everyone likes a Tiny.

HOW WILL YOUR ORGANIZATION'S HR POLICIES APPLY?

At your workplace in real life you might be used to wearing business-casual attire, or maybe you wear a suit every day but Friday. How does this translate to a world where you might be teaching or doing business with leopards and elves?

Some companies have specific policies regarding in-world behavior. IBM has a written policy for in-world employee conduct that includes wearing a human avatar and business-casual clothing. Global Kids's policy exactly mirrors their real-world policy. One Solution Provider required an *SL* content creator they hired to change from her *SL* kid avatar into an adult avatar while working. On the other hand, my staff includes, along with various other humans, an *SL* kid, a box, a Tiny warthog, a neko, an alien, and one team member who might take on any form, from horse to human to grizzly bear.

Is it a good idea to require your staff to be humans in suits, or should you allow them more freedom—and how much? Is it a good idea to restrict groups your employees or students may join and regions they may visit in-world to those that are PG-rated? Suppose you hire someone who already has a *Second Life* account. Can you legally restrict what that avatar does outside of business hours? If you want to restrict their activities, would you be better off having them use a different avatar created specifically for when they're on the job? Is it legal to tell someone their avatar must be of a certain age or gender as a requirement of employment? This is a new area—there's not much precedent.

One thing is for certain: you or someone from your organization needs to log in, have an avatar, and take a look around so you can make informed decisions!

07

What are the unique social challenges involved in doing business in a virtual world like *Second Life*? Which of the communications interfaces in-world is best for a given situation? What are the rules regarding chat logs? What languages are supported in-world? How is event etiquette different from everyday in-world interactions? What kinds of unique social situations might you find yourself in, and how should you handle them? What's griefing, and what can you do about it? Are intimate in-world activities and gambling serious distractions for real-life organizations? That's what we'll discuss in this chapter!

UNDERSTANDING SOCIAL INTERACTION IN *SECOND LIFE*

SOCIAL CHALLENGES FOR VIRTUAL-WORLD BUSINESS

It's easy to imagine the kinds of technical challenges involved with doing business in a virtual world (and some of them have been discussed in earlier chapters). But less obvious and sometimes harder to understand are the social challenges faced by real-life organizations that do business in a virtual world like *Second Life*.

Most people you'll deal with in-world, even those who are also doing work for real-life organizations, are probably working remotely all or part of the time. They're not in an office at a corporate headquarters or an educational institution. This means that often you'll find even real-life businesspeople working in-world at hours outside of standard business hours for their time zone. Unless there's a statement about business hours in your profile (and even then, because many people won't think about checking it) most people won't know whether you're in-world at a given time to work or play, so they'll IM you.

Additionally, with people from all over the globe in-world, sometimes it's hard to coordinate meetings across time zones. Expect to have someone IM you about business at, say, 3 a.m. on a Sunday morning, or at some time in the evening. People may even try to get you to come to a meeting on a Saturday afternoon.

All of these remote workers and others logging in from home have countless things going on around them in real life, of course. The dog is barking, the kid needs feeding, there's someone at the door, there's a TV in the background. Sometimes the phone rings, and there is certainly no receptionist to grab the call. So often people have to go "Away from Keyboard," or AFK.

There are many social conventions like this one that aid remote communication. As you might know from IMs and teleconferencing, there are ways around the lack of visual clues you get in face-to-face interactions. Expect to see lots of emoticon use and people typing LOL. Also, avatars will use *gestures*—combinations of animations, audio clips, and text—which can indicate things as varied as happiness, boredom, laughter, and even applause. Additionally, some Residents wear *emote* attachments of various types. These can automatically trigger gestures by picking up text-chat cues, or they can be accessed manually by clicking buttons on a HUD.

Another area of online interaction *SL* Residents have honed to a high art: multitasking. In *Second Life*, multitasking is almost constant and it's expected. It's common for someone to be conversing with avatars around them at an event, talking with a couple of others in IM, and also answering email or working on something in another application. It's not considered rude, and even during very serious conversations you might notice a delayed response while the other person is fielding an IM or you might hear them typing in the background while you're in a voice chat.

If you're not able to keep up with many different conversations or activities at once, it's perfectly OK to tell someone that you're busy and that you'll get back to them later!

COMMUNICATION INTERFACES

A few different communication interfaces are built into the *Second Life* Grid, and lots of Residents use external tools to keep in touch, as well. Each has its pros and cons.

Use the Gestures pull-down to access some gestures, as shown in this image. If they don't work, it's because they aren't enabled. To enable them, go to Inventory ▶ Gestures, select the gesture you want to enable, right-click, and choose Enable.

TEXT CHAT

Most conversations in *Second Life* are text-based. (Voice is a relatively new feature, and some established Residents who have been around for a while still prefer text chat.) Here's what you need to know:

▶ Text chat has a range of 20 meters. All avatars within that range can view your text. If you want to talk to someone who is farther away, you can shout to be "heard" for 96 meters. However, just like in real life, there are lots of situations in which shouting is considered rude. You wouldn't want your business meeting interrupted by someone yelling in the distance, would you? And if you don't want those around you listening in (reading), try an instant message instead.

▶ I don't have to tell you that people's typing ability varies. Some type very slowly, and that can really make a meeting drag! Some Residents are very fast typists. Get a couple of them in a chat together, and you'd better be a very fast reader! You may find it hard to follow a couple of conversational threads at once if you're at an event where a lot of avatars are chatting. You're not expected to always follow all of them. It's just like real life—you might hear what the people standing a little ways off are discussing, but you can't always participate in that conversation.

▶ It's common for people to type at the same time, one responding to something the first person said as the first person continues typing. If it were a voice conversation, they'd be talking over one another. In text chat you'll see this a lot. Some who've done it for a long time pick up the habit of doing it in voice chat as well—for example, typing responses while someone is using voice chat.

HOW TO SHOUT

Enter some text and use the Say pull-down to either broadcast your comment normally or to shout, as shown here. As of press time, avatars can't whisper but scripted objects can, and when they do their text is viewable only within a 10-meter range.

⊿ TIP

If you type /me and hit Return in chat or IM, *SL* will make your name appear in chat. For example, if my avatar Kim Anubis were to type "/me slaps you with a trout," the text would appear as, "Kim Anubis slaps you with a trout."

▶ You'll occasionally encounter chat speak, such as *u no wut i m33n*. In some circles that's considered déclassé, but in others it's the norm. It's also often used for humorous purposes. If you don't want to chat-speak, remember that reading a lot of short lines of chat is more engaging than waiting around for a whole paragraph, so consider pressing Enter after each sentence.

▶ You can log your chat in *SL*, either by copying and pasting from chat history, or automatically. Go to Preferences ▶ Communication to enable automatic chat logging (Figure 7.1). Be aware, however, that the rules of *Second Life* prohibit publishing or sharing logs without the permission of everyone included or without at least omitting names or identifying statements.

INSTANT MESSAGING

Instant messaging is the way to speak privately with another *SL* Resident or with a group across the Grid. You can IM a group or you can put a bunch of calling cards into a folder and IM all of those Residents at once. The following bullet points lay out the basics of IM.

▶ While everyone nearby can read your regular text chat or hear your voice chat, instant messages are seen or heard only by the participants you send them to. In Preferences you can adjust whether your IMs appear alongside regular text chat or if you see the text only in an IM window.

▶ If you respond to an IM then teleport to your IM partner's location, it's standard to switch to regular chat rather than continuing to use IM. Be sure to click somewhere outside of the IM window to initiate an open chat before you start typing.

7.1 The Communication tab lets you turn logging on or off as well as enable email forwarding of instant messages you receive while you're offline.

- ▶ Before you send a sensitive IM, always double-check which window you're in before you press Enter. Everyone eventually sends text to the wrong Resident at some point, and it's often very embarrassing. Always double-check!

- ▶ Instant messages are usually an interruption. Keep in mind that people you're IMing probably aren't hanging out waiting for an IM from you—they're busy with something. Realize that you likely aren't getting a slow response because they don't want to talk to you, but because they're multitasking.

- ▶ Don't overuse group IMs. Most groups have rules against "spamming." Be sure you've read the group charter and that your IM is appropriate. If a group IM spins off a private conversation between you and another avatar or two, take it to a private IM just between you.

- ▶ Sending an IM to an avatar standing right next to yours is usually considered odd unless you have a specific need for privacy. Otherwise you'll be assumed to be a newbie, a scam artist, or about to make a pass if you do this out of the blue. It's normal to converse in open chat first if you're near one another (if you aren't at an event).

- ▶ If someone IMs you or you IM them and you aren't near one another, it's not an automatic invitation or request for one of you to teleport to the other's location. Remember, there's a good chance the other person is multitasking. So if you ask them if they'd like a teleport (TP) and they say no, don't take it personally. They might be slapping together prims to meet a deadline, or in the midst of trying to dress their avatar!

- ▶ You can log IMs in the same ways you can log chat.

- ▶ Some Residents prefer to use external IM platforms, such as Yahoo! or AIM. These are handy for those who aren't always logged in or who use various alts.

VOICE CHAT AND VOICE IM

Voice chat is used much of the time by those doing real-life work in-world, but many Residents—half, by some estimates—don't use it. Some don't have a headset or are already pushing the limits of their computer's performance or don't have enough bandwidth as it is. But most who don't use voice have nontechnical reasons. Consider the following:

▶ Most people are not logged in from an office, and a lot of them log in during the evening. They don't want to wake their kids or spouse. They don't want to be overheard by housemates. They don't want you to have to hear the background noises of their real-life location.

▶ Plenty of Residents don't want you to hear their voice because their real-life voice doesn't match up with their animal avatar or the gender or speaking style of their *SL* self. A lot of Residents prefer to do as much as they can to maintain anonymity, and others simply don't want to ruin their in-world representation.

▶ With so many languages spoken in-world, voice chat can be more problematic than text. Most people type and understand written second languages better than they speak them. Additionally, attachments such as Babbler can translate text chat on the fly, but there's nothing similar for voice chat. Furthermore, there are plenty of hearing-impaired Residents who, naturally, prefer text chat.

▶ Voice is prone to chewing sounds, background noise, and cross-region restrictions.

▶ Voice chat can be great for getting through a meeting quickly and for certain types of multitasking, such as coordinating a team during a text-chat event or while building things in-world. For other types of multitasking, though, it isn't so great. You can have only one voice conversation at a time, and you can't scroll back to see what you missed!

▶ It's usual to ask before starting a voice chat or voice IM. Don't assume that even people with a voice indicator over their avatar's heads (Figure 7.2) actually have headsets connected. And if someone doesn't want to use voice chat, don't pressure them—you never know why they're not using voice.

7.2 The glowing white dot here indicates that my avatar has voice enabled. The green curves around the dot indicate that I'm speaking right now.

TIP

Voice chat doesn't carry across region borders if the regions aren't part of the same estate. In such a situation, use the voice feature within an IM or use text chat instead. Voice IM is heard only by the individual or group you've included in the IM, and only if they have voice enabled themselves. If you think you will need to use voice IM at an event, meeting, or class, be sure to make arrangements ahead of time to include everyone in a group.

▶ Because in-world voice can be heard for a very long distance (up to 60 meters from your listening position), some Residents don't like to use in-world voice chat even though they will use other voice platforms. The solution is usually voice IM or an external voice client, usually Skype.

OTHER SOLUTIONS

Residents communicate in a bunch of ways aside from those three main communication channels. Some of these are unique to *Second Life*.

▶ One common way to talk to other Residents is the offline IM. When you log in, you'll find any IMs you received while you were offline. You can also have them forwarded to you automatically by checking the Send IM to Email box in Preferences ▶ Communication, as shown in Figure 7.1. Now when someone IMs you while you are offline, the message will be emailed to the address you provided when you registered for *Second Life*. The number of offline IMs you can receive in-world is capped, so it's very important to activate automatic forwarding.

TIP

If you find that in-world voice-chat audio quality is poor and you have another voice application open (such as Skype), try shutting down the other program. Also, bandwidth limitations have a strong effect on voice-chat quality.

▶ Notecards are a good way to present a large block of text to someone in-world, but the formatting options are very limited. You can create a notecard yourself or find one in the Notecards folder in your Inventory.

▶ Some Residents will give you an email address you can use to contact them (or even provide one in their profile). However, don't expect this. Many Residents like to keep their second life in *Second Life*.

> **OFFLINE IM VERSUS NOTECARD**
>
> Busy Residents receive a lot of offline instant messages. These are *capped*—not saved—if you receive more than 100 before you log in. While that seems like a lot, that number includes things like messages from scripted objects, system messages, and group notices, so functionally you'll reach the limit well before 100 communications from Residents. For this reason, many prefer that you instead contact them by sending a notecard. Others hate to be contacted in this way, though, and would rather get the IM. Some Residents even prefer direct email. It's a good idea to check your intended recipient's profile to see if there's a preference stated. It will usually be included on the General tab of a person's profile or as one of the items listed in their Favorites.

I'll discuss additional ways of communicating with Residents in Chapters 9, 11, 12, and 15, but for reference, here are a few:

- Group notices
- Region/estate notices
- Notecard-giving objects
- Objects that speak in chat or IM
- URL-loading objects
- Signs
- Media (Web) on a prim
- Streaming audio
- Streaming video

ETIQUETTE

When you visit a foreign country, you expect social rules to be a little different from those back home. The same is true about visiting a virtual world like *Second Life*. Some conventions you'll probably already know from interacting via instant messages or spending time in other virtual worlds, but others are specific to *SL*.

SL-specific etiquette might not seem important to you if you simply want to hire a developer and have them take care of things for you. However, if you appear in-world and Residents find that you do things like chat with them with your avatar's back turned or while invading their personal space, it will reflect negatively on your organization. Word gets around fast, and even some *SL*-specific media outlets can make some pretty pointed remarks about real-life organizations' staff members that don't care enough to learn about their world. It is exactly this sort of rude behavior that causes projects to fail.

GENERAL *SL* ETIQUETTE

Etiquette varies a bit depending on *SL* subculture and context, but this section provides some general points to keep in mind:

▶ When you offer someone a teleport (Figure 7.3), remember that when they accept it they'll appear in front of you and slightly above the ground. Don't teleport someone so that they'll land on top of someone else or in a wall, or so that they'll fall—find an appropriate location before offering the teleport. If you're hovering in the air, be sure to tell the person to select Fly before they accept your teleport offer.

7.3 Teleport offers appear as a blue system message popup.

▶ It's considered polite to ask before offering someone a teleport. A "blind" teleport offer that comes without warning, particularly from a stranger, is likely to be ignored.

▶ Just because you notice an area is build-enabled doesn't mean it's OK to take out objects from Inventory or build them there. Sometimes a posted notice or the description of the parcel provides information about what's allowed in an area. If the landowner is there and you're not in a designated sandbox area, it's polite to ask permission to rez something. Otherwise, use common sense—don't rez a car in the middle of someone's store or on top of their Telehub. And be sure to pick up or delete your things before you leave!

▶ Many feel it is inconsiderate to build things that go right up to a shared parcel line, particularly if it crowds a neighbor's build. Similarly, noisy builds, builds with flashing lights, builds that don't fit in with the existing neighborhood, or those that use up a disproportionate share of the region's resources are not going to make your neighbors love you.

▶ If there are no ban lines (which indicate you aren't allowed access) around a parcel, when's it OK to enter and have a look around? Businesses are usually fine to visit anytime, as are sandboxes, parks, and other places that might be public in real life. Homes, however, are a different story. Many Residents will be happy if you explore the home they built, and others will be upset. A good rule of thumb is to not enter a house that has avatars in it unless you were invited. You've got no idea what they're up to in there!

▶ To gain a little privacy, some Residents build *skyboxes* like the one in Figure 7.4. These are builds up off the ground, usually 200 to 700 meters up. These might be used for meetings, intimate encounters, or development of new products. It's a bad idea to poke around in someone's skybox without permission.

7.4 This skybox is located about 500 meters above the ground and has no obvious entrance, so it's probably a private space.

▶ If you go to visit someone's build to check it out at their invitation, they are unlikely to be upset and they'll probably even expect you to use your camera controls to look around beyond the area where your avatar is standing. However, *camming* through the walls to spy in a build where you haven't been invited is considered terribly rude.

▶ Many Residents consider it polite to ask before offering friendship or calling cards, but it's not considered universally rude to make the offer without asking. Your offer might well be rejected if you don't first have at least some conversation with the person, though. If your offer is rejected, it's not necessarily personal. Some Residents don't like having to deal with managing additional inventory items, including calling cards.

▶ It's considered polite to ask before starting a voice chat or IM. Don't try to pressure anyone into using voice.

▶ When you IM someone you don't know well, especially if it's an offline IM, don't simply say "hi." State your business briefly and don't be surprised if you don't receive an immediate response.

▶ If your real-life location is noisy, be sure to mute your microphone. Don't leave your mic locked open; use the push-to-talk functionality instead.

▶ If you ask a Resident, "Where are you from?" and they name the sim where their avatar lives instead of a real-life state or country, don't be surprised. It's considered rude to press for real-life details.

▶ When you arrive at an unfamiliar area, look around for any posted rules. You might also receive some information about the rules of an area from a scripted object via IM or notecard. Rules are likely to include dress code (such as period clothing or at least some kind of clothing), use of weapons, or use of profanity.

▶ Always ask permission to publish or distribute chat logs.

▶ Each Resident can be a member of up to 25 groups at a time. If someone refuses your group invitation, it is rude to pressure them to drop another group to make room for yours. It's not rude for them to drop your group.

▶ It's impolite to pressure someone to give you rights to edit or manage their objects or land—such rights are unusual unless you know the other Resident very well.

▶ It's considered polite to have your avatar face the avatar with whom you're conversing, although this is not quite the same as it is in real life. Particularly due to certain animation-override poses or animated seats, your avatar might not be able to turn its head. However, if you're standing and talking with a group of people, your avatar should be aimed in their direction.

▶ People like to have personal space around their avatars. This is almost the same as it is in real life—stand at about the distance you would if you were in a similar real-life situation. It's considered rude to allow your attachments to poke through other people's avatars (Figure 7.5). Because some builds are tricky to navigate, due to sudden waves of lag or unfamiliarity with the platform, avatars bump into each other more often than people do in real life. It's not taken as personally in-world, but it's still considered polite to apologize.

7.5 I should apologize for skewering my friend's avatar with my fishing pole!

▶ When you first appear at a location, it might take a while for things to rez (load). The buildings are likely to appear before avatars do, so if you start walking around too soon you run the risk of unknowingly bumping into people or even shoving them down stairs. Either wait until you're sure everyone has rezzed, or use the minimap to navigate (Figure 7.6).

▶ If you're traveling the Grid with someone and have just been teleported to a location but it's taking a while to rez, make sure you tell the other person. They may be all rezzed and ready to go. It's polite to wait for those for whom things rez more slowly. Don't complain!

7.6 Avatars are invisible when they first appear, and as they load they are represented by glowing clouds. The green dots indicating avatars on the minimap in the upper-right corner of this figure show that there are many more unrezzed avatars to bump into here!

▶ Residents use the term "stalking" very loosely, usually for humorous reasons.

▶ Times and dates in *SL* are often given in *Second Life* Time (SLT). This corresponds with Pacific Time. If you mention a time to someone in-world, it's polite to either state it in SLT or to convert it for their time zone.

▶ It's polite to mention that you're going away from keyboard (AFK). Others will probably reply with OK, K, or KK. HB means "hurry back." Pay attention to your avatar's surroundings; if you're blocking a door or a stairway, step out of the way before you go AFK. Also, if you're going to be gone for a very long time, it's good to let others know it'll be a while. It's not unusual to leave an avatar AFK for a long time rather than logging off, because you can come back and review chat history and be caught right up. When you return, say that you're back, and others will welcome you, perhaps by typing WB ("welcome back"). If the group of people you were with has moved elsewhere while you were away, IM one of them and ask for a teleport (TP).

▶ Although almost everyone is excited to discover the ability to play sounds, gestures, and animations, playing them incessantly is considered rude. No one wants to hear the same 10-second audio clip over and over and over, and watching a newbie try out every gesture available to them loses its charm pretty quickly.

EVENT ETIQUETTE

In-world events involve etiquette of their own, much of it having to do with reducing rendering cost and background noise. Event etiquette usually applies to any large organized gathering of avatars, including classes, lectures, meetings, and live concerts.

- If you receive an event invitation that specifies formalwear, period attire, or some other type of dress, it's polite to comply. In many cases the folks putting on the event have invested a lot of time and effort into creating an immersive experience that would be disrupted by inappropriate clothing. Often an event host will provide or be able to direct you to some free or inexpensive clothing. If you have questions, send an instant message.

- Some event advertising and invitations will specify that you should not wear prim-heavy (or *primmy*) attachments or avatars. Some will even say to not wear hair attachments. Avatars are the most resource-intensive things rendered in *Second Life*, and many wear a variety of scripted attachments, which can take a lot of resources to render. This can be a real problem at a heavily attended event, especially for those with slower computers or broadband. Sometimes exceptions are made for Residents who are full-time Furry or animal avatars, who would be uncomfortable or unwilling to attend in an unfamiliar form.

- At events where there is voice chat, live music, or some other audio stream, many Residents consider it polite to precede each line of chat with a slash. The slash keeps your avatar from making typing noises.

- If you're in the audience at a voice event, make sure your microphone is inactive so you don't contribute unnecessary background noise. Stories are still shared about one unfortunate person who, during the first week that the voice feature was enabled, fell asleep at an educational event and snored for the duration into an open microphone while event attendees attempted to awaken her by shouting.

- At a text-based event, it's best to take private discussions to IM. However, at voice-based events audience members will text-chat among themselves or even directly to the event host or participants (who will often respond in kind). This is called *backchat*.

- Unless you're at an event where dancing would be appropriate in real life, it's probably not appropriate in *Second Life*, either. It's also polite to sit in one of the seats provided for the audience. You might see a newbie who stumbles onto the stage and asks, "What's going on here?" or a griefer who hops up there and starts dancing and shouting, but the event host will probably remove them at once.

- Rather than getting up on stage and asking what's going on, send an instant message to a member of the event staff or even to someone else nearby.

- If someone's giving a presentation, don't send them an instant message (unless they've asked the audience to submit questions that way). Also hold your friend requests and inventory offers until after they're done. All of those blue system messages can be really distracting!

- Avoid performing gestures that play sounds (except for applause), and also remove or avoid using attachments that "spam" in open chat. For example, some attachments might be scripted to advertise, like "Joe's Coffee: You can get free coffee at Joe's!" while others will impart status info to their owners, like "Flight Box: All systems go!"

- Applauding is appropriate just as it is in real life. You can use a clapping gesture or you can type something in chat like **/me applauds** or ***applause***.

- *Poofers* are particle-generating attachments that allow an avatar to appear or disappear in a puff of smoke or hearts or other symbols or images when teleporting. These are really disruptive at events, so try to remember not to wear your poofer when you attend an event.

- If you find yourself at an event where there's dancing and you don't have dance animations of your own, look around for a *dance ball* or *dance machine*. These are scripted objects you click to have your avatar animated. If you don't see one, ask someone nearby. You might also encounter someone wearing a scripted attachment that you click to dance with them. For couples dancing, you'll also find dance balls in pairs (usually a pink one and a blue one), as shown in figure 7.7. Right-click one of these and select *Dance*.

7.7 You and a partner can dance together using dance balls like these.

▷ Many Resident DJs, live musicians, event hosts, and other event staff aren't paid a salary. So for them, and to augment the pay of others, there are *tip jars* (Figure 7.8). To use one of these, right-click and select Pay, and then choose your amount. You'll also find tip jars at in-world locations such as art installations, amusement parks, and even shops. Charging admission is very rare in-world, and prices for most in-world goods and services are very low. Tipping to show your appreciation helps to keep expenses paid.

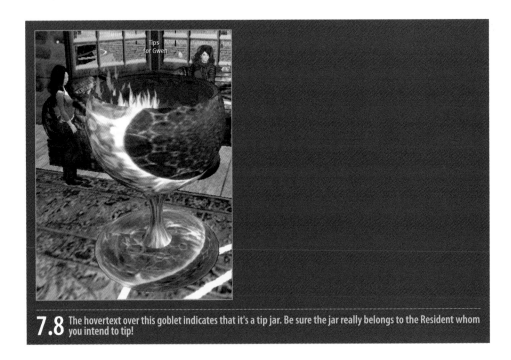

7.8 The hovertext over this goblet indicates that it's a tip jar. Be sure the jar really belongs to the Resident whom you intend to tip!

UNIQUE SOCIAL SITUATIONS

During your adventures exploring *Second Life* or among Residents who come to visit your own corner of it, you'll probably find yourself in social situations that aren't like anything you've experienced. *Second Life* Residents are part of a community made up of people with all different views of just what their virtual world really is, what it should be, and what it means to them. Henrik Bennetsen, a Stanford University researcher, summarized these by describing two main viewpoints: augmentationist and immersionist. The first group is made up of people who view the *SL* Grid as a platform that assists them in performing certain tasks, extending their real-life abilities. Immersionists, on the other hand, view *SL* as a world, often one in which they play a different role than they do in their life outside of the Grid.

Most Residents do not fit solidly into one category or the other. You might encounter an SL kid (that is, an adult roleplaying as a kid) with a virtual family, who does development work for real-life companies while her avatar is dressed in a school uniform and Mary Janes and holding a lollipop. You could meet a real-life university researcher who's a Furry residing in a region that's ruled by a feudal lord.

Of course, you aren't required to involve yourself this deeply, though it's very helpful to understand it if you want to relate to other Residents. It is important to know what to expect and how you're expected to react.

Most *Second Life* Residents keep their real life and their virtual life separate to some degree. Some take on the form of a person of the opposite sex or someone of a different age, economic status, or profession. They might not be of the same race as their real-life self. They might not be human, or they might live, virtually, in a different historic period. Although more and more Residents are including real-life information in the First Life tab of their profiles, often because they work in-world, many will leave that tab blank or include an image of their avatar instead of a photo. It's important to respect their wish for privacy and to resist prying. Unless you've read otherwise in their profile or been told directly, address them and treat them as if they are what they appear to be in-world.

> **⊾WARNING**
>
> It's against the *Second Life* Terms of Service to disclose real-life information about a Resident without their permission.

ROMANCE AND FAMILY

It's a good idea to check out the profiles of avatars with whom you'd like to converse, so that you can learn whether they're likely to want to talk about their real life or if they are keeping that out of the picture. Other important information you'll find in a profile includes whether an avatar has a Partner (Figure 7.9). This is a field on the first tab of the profile. Residents can pay a small fee to Linden Lab in order to have their romantic or business partner listed—or to dissolve the partnership. Take the Partner tab seriously—don't be flippant about the relationship.

Much noise has been made in the press about virtual romantic and sexual relationships. Some people do not consider it cheating to have a virtual romantic relationship while they're married to someone else in real life. However, in practice the results of this are often about as bad as they'd be if the whole thing happened offline. There are plenty of exceptions, though. There are also countless jokes about people who have fallen for another avatar, only to find out that in real life their romantic interest isn't of the same gender or age as their avatar. Despite this, many do find real love in-world, and some relocate to be together or even get married. Some in-world neighbors of mine had a mixed-reality wedding, complete with simultaneous in-world and real-world ceremonies so that the friends who were there when they met in-world and as their love blossomed could also attend.

Other in-world relationships include virtual families—not mafia-style roleplay families (which do exist on the Grid), but Residents who will take on traditional nuclear-family or even extended-family roles. This is most common among *SL* kids, who might have a mom, a dad, or siblings. Other Residents often roleplay or genuinely view their closest in-world friends as siblings or parents or children. Even if this strikes you as odd, it should be respected.

7.9 This avatar profile indicates the name of the Resident's Partner.

Similarly, if you encounter someone with a prim baby (a scripted baby made from prims), keep in mind that this could be a way in which the virtual parent is working through a real-life loss or dream—be polite about it. Go ahead and ask the baby's name, and tell the proud parent that it's cute, or (as my parents always taught me) if you can't say something nice, don't say anything at all.

POLITICS AND DRAMA

Some *Second Life* Residents view *SL* as a world governed by Governor Linden (an administrative Linden Lab avatar), rather than as a Grid run by a company. Additionally, some Residents involve themselves in virtual in-world governments, sometimes viewing these as states within the country or world ruled by Linden Lab. Some regions or continents are managed by these governments, and they take all forms, from democracy to feudalism with royalty and nobility.

Related to this, you may encounter (particularly in forum posts or blogs) accusations of Linden Lab playing favorites. When a Resident or their company contracts to do work for Linden Lab or makes a business arrangement without an open bidding process (or sometimes despite such a process), some Residents will react as if it is a matter of government corruption. They feel that certain other Residents receive preferential treatment and that it's not fair, even in cases where preferential treatment would normally be the case (for premium-account holders who pay more, or Solution Providers who need access to specialized support channels, for example). Residents who are allegedly receiving favors or who have a perceived too-close relationship to Linden Lab might be referred to as *FIC*, an acronym for *feted inner core*, a reference first popularized by a Resident named Prokofy Neva. Believers in the FIC, or inner circle of Linden favorites, assume that FIC Residents get a quicker response to their support tickets or Abuse Reports, and that their Linden minions will do many special favors, and even harass or ban their enemies on their behalf.

Other Residents label this sort of thing *drama*. In the *SL* context, drama is unnecessary excitement over things that just aren't such a big deal, or spending a lot of time gossiping or discussing in-world interpersonal relationships. Sometimes the term is used by those who consider in-world goings-on to be less real than what happens in offline life. However, relationships in-world can be just as deep and complex as those offline (and indeed, often offline relationships start or end online). You probably know people with plenty of drama in their real lives. What you're less likely to see in real life is a sign designating a location a *drama-free zone*.

FANTASTICAL ROLEPLAY

Sometimes you'll find yourself among roleplay less familiar to you than governments or families. For example, what do you do if a bunch of crossbow-toting medieval warriors runs up to you and asks you to point out a place where they can hide from the enemy army that's pursuing them? My approach is usually to go along with their roleplay, because . . . well, it's fun! Who wouldn't want to watch them ambush the gang that shows up dragging a catapult? However, if you're about to host a business meeting, you can just tell them so, and ask them to go. Even if I'm busy, I might play along in telling them so: "Alas, I am unable to assist you in your defense, for ambassadors of a foreign city-state are about to arrive here to parley. I'm sorry; this is not a good location in which to make your stand, but best of luck to you, warriors. Fight mightily elsewhere!"

Some roleplayers, especially those who are involved in a roleplay sim (region or simulation) may wear *titlers* (Figure 7.10), attachments that allow them to have words hovering over their head, similar to their name and group tag. So you might learn that a person wearing the *quad* (quadrupedal) wolf avatar is specifically a young female wolf who's a member of the Lightning Den and is slightly wounded, with a bite on her hind leg. As the figure shows, this information is often presented in a cryptic way, usually with abbreviations or codes. Otherwise, your view might be blocked by paragraphs of backstory hovering over each adventurer's head! Sometimes you'll be required to wear a titler yourself when you visit roleplay regions, so that everyone can see by the message over your head that you're a noncombatant or a visitor.

7.10 A titler displays some roleplay information over this Resident's head.

BUSINESS

In-world business activity can be confusing. Some in-world businesses are real-world businesses through which Residents are able to cash out enough L$ micropayments to make a nice real-life living. Many more are hobby businesses, and some are just plain roleplay. The distinction is made in various ways. For example, the *The Metaverse Messenger*, a virtual-worlds newspaper that mostly covers *Second Life*, offers different ad rates depending on whether an ad is purchased to promote a completely in-world organization, a real-life organization, or a real-life organization with an in-world presence.

The reason for the varied ad rates is because there's a disconnect between the perceived and actual value of Linden dollars. Typically, there are around 265 Linden dollars to the US dollar. However, a L$100 shirt might be too expensive for many, and a L$500 shirt had better be something very, very special. For many Residents, L$1,000 is a lot, even if it's only a few real-life dollars.

GRIEFERS

⬂NOTE

There are plenty of jerks around who like to cause trouble, but most days in the *SL* world I do not encounter any of these problems. I'm more likely to have to deal with someone who rudely left litter around or who doesn't know how to behave at an event than with someone who harasses me by calling me names or shooting at me! And remember, no one can actually harm your avatar, so most griefing is only a nuisance.

Griefing describes troublemaking activities someone undertakes to get a rise out of the people around them. Someone who does this is a *griefer*. If you've spent much time online, you've probably run into this sort of thing: on message boards, a griefer might be called a *troll*. Griefers are usually not seeking financial gain. It's all about upsetting people for laughs. There are different sorts of griefers and griefing techniques, and what you can and should do about them varies accordingly.

TYPES OF GRIEFING

Most griefers just stir things up for a lark—it's a casual thing, not a hobby to which they're dedicated. However, there are griefers who put a lot of time, effort, and thought into how to cause trouble. Some claim they're really valuable members of the community because they expose weaknesses of the platform. That's not why they do what they do, though!

Some griefers band together. In fact, there are large griefing-based organizations, which generally are older than the *Second Life* platform. They not only target *Second Life*, but also do their best to cause trouble on other interactive sites. For example, some of them are known for getting together to slaughter other characters in massively multiplayer online games, regardless of whether they're going to gain points or treasure. They just want to kill off someone's cherished character. Alternatively, they might get together to block a door or path. They discuss their griefing strategy on their own forums, in-world, or in text chat elsewhere, and then log in to effect their plans. Afterward, they will describe or even post pictures of what they've done, for amusement of and accolades from their griefing peers.

Some people grief because they are bored, others behave like boors because they do it all the time in real life, and some wreak havoc accidentally because they don't understand the rules. Maybe they think they've signed up to play a shooter game? Many griefers will go away if you explain the rules, give them something better to do, and make sure they know they aren't allowed to shoot people, etc. The real problem is the dedicated griefers, especially those that are organized.

There are lots of griefing techniques. Loosely, they break down into chat griefing, avatar griefing, object griefing, and land griefing. Let's take a look at those forms and then at the best ways to deal with the issue.

Harassment in chat or IM is a common form of griefing. You've seen it from bullies on the playground when you were a kid—name-calling, for example. However, in-world griefing goes beyond someone telling you that you have cooties (neener neener).

A griefer who mouths off to you in chat might continue to hassle you in IM if you walk, fly, or teleport away. He or she might send the same phrase over and over, quickly, flooding you with chat so that you can't converse with anyone else. Related griefing methods include sending you objects, group invitations, friendship offers, etc. over and over and over. Some griefers create or acquire scripted objects that will do these things on their behalf.

AVATAR GRIEFING

Some griefers will go after your avatar, shooting you with weapons, using a *cage gun* or *cager* to trap your avatar, or simply bumping into you to shove you around.

Others create avatars designed to upset people. Some griefers plan to grief you with the name of their avatar. They'll select a name intended to offend. Another approach is to use cartoonlike, offensive depictions of various racial groups. If someone speaks up about it, the griefer will almost certainly accuse them of racism, usually while speaking in a style chosen to fit their offensive stereotype. One unfortunate result of this type of griefing is that it makes some Residents wary of avatars of certain races if they're linked to brand-new accounts or if those avatars don't exhibit much personalization or expense put into them—the assumption is that they belong to griefers.

When a griefer finds someone who is a good target—who responds in a gratifying way to griefing—or against whom they've developed a grudge, they might make an avatar especially for the occasion, registering a new account with a name similar to yours.

OBJECT GRIEFING

Along with using weapons to make others around them miserable, griefers create or acquire other objects that they find useful for getting a rise out of people. These are often called *griefer objects*.

A griefer object does something to disrupt the activities of those around it. One common type text-shouts an offensive or nonsense phrase over and over. Others repeatedly play an audio clip. Some spew particles—images without substance that float around and obstruct everyone's view. Sending out a multitude of these particles makes it difficult for computer systems to render them all, creating lag. Some of these objects are self-propelled, and even sense and follow avatars.

The worst griefing objects are *self-replicating objects*, also sometimes called *grey goo*. These objects usually do one or more of the usual griefer tasks, but also automatically generate copies of themselves. Imagine if such an object makes only 10 copies a minute, and each of those makes 10 copies a minute. You can envision the chaos of these things bouncing around, making noise, spewing particles, and shouting in chat. Some of them are scripted to drift around the Grid, spreading like evil dandelion seeds. If they aren't stopped quickly enough, self-replicating griefer objects can not only put such a rendering load on someone's system that the *Second Life* viewer crashes, but they also can cause a region or multiple regions to crash.

The earliest grey-goo attacks brought down part or all of the Grid. Since then, Linden Lab has instituted new methods of containing such attacks while working to remove the griefer objects. Additionally, the consequences for griefers who undertake this sort of denial-of-service attack have become much more serious; in recent years Linden Lab has taken to reporting them to the FBI.

↘TIP

If someone shoots you with a cage gun and traps your avatar, it's easy to escape. Right-click on the nearby ground, a chair, or another object, and select Sit. Or simply teleport away.

↘WARNING

If you witness an attack of self-replicating objects, immediately submit an Abuse Report so that Linden Lab can stop it before it spreads. If there are so many griefer objects to render that you find yourself lagged and unable to check the name or owner of them, instead submit a support ticket via the *Second Life* website.

Land-related griefing is one of the most destructive forms. It can lower property values or even damage or destroy your build. Fortunately, it's also the type of griefing against which there are the best defenses, and if you manage things properly you should be just fine.

Some griefers like to cause trouble by having a negative effect on your virtual real estate. Some do things like put up nasty signs. Others might rez a giant box on top of your sign so that no one can see your property or even find it.

An even worse problem is when a griefer discovers that a landowner has left incorrect permissions on their land or objects on it. The griefer might then be able to ruin the land's terraforming, vandalize or delete buildings, or raise the terrain in the region so high that all of the buildings are sunk into the ground and automatically returned to you, ruining the whole place. Other griefers will purchase land next door to someone with a nice build or someone they consider a likely target and then build something purposely offensive, hideous, or distracting.

One type of griefing is motivated by profit. The griefer purchases a small piece of land, puts a purposely upsetting or view-destroying build on it, and then sets it for sale at a ridiculously high price. The idea is to make the neighbors miserable enough to finally be willing to pay to get rid of the eyesore that's blighting the neighborhood. Sometimes a griefer will purchase a piece of land, subdivide it into the smallest parcels possible, and then put high prices on each of them (sometimes along with hideous objects). This is often referred to as *land cutting*, which is not allowed by Linden Lab. When these tiny parcels have advertising kiosks or signs on them, it's called *ad farming*.

Some land cutters, in response to Linden Lab's rule against the practice, do not mark the blighted land for sale, and instead attempt to sell it less directly. Some ad farms are not created specifically for the purpose of extorting payment, but instead are full of banner ads. Compare this to someone putting up a bunch of giant billboards (which sometimes spin, animate, or light up at night) in the middle of a nice residential neighborhood in real life. As of press time, Linden Lab was planning to roll out a zoning program to help with this sort of situation.

 THE INFAMOUS ATTACK OF THE FLYING BODY PARTS

A lot of people outside of *SL* have read, seen images or video of, or just heard about an occasion when an *SL* real-estate mogul's in-world interview by a real-life media outlet was interrupted by a swarm of flying body parts. Because much of the coverage of the occurrence was by people who didn't understand griefer objects and how they can be controlled, these stories presented an undeservedly negative view of the *SL* Grid. This wasn't an example of how inappropriate *SL* is for real-life meetings and events. It was, rather, an example of mismanagement by event staff. The attack could have been stopped within seconds or made entirely impossible if land-management settings and training of or assistance to the event host had been handled properly by the developer.

HOW TO STOP GRIEFING

Most of the griefing activities discussed here are against the *Second Life* Terms of Service. You can file an Abuse Report, and Linden Lab (and possibly the owner of the region where the problem was reported) will respond. You will receive a form email letting you know that your report was received and resolved, but for privacy reasons Linden Lab will not tell you more about what happened. Sometimes you can read about how things were handled in the incident report at **http://secondlife.com/support/incidentreport.php**.

Necessarily, response time varies. A reported grey-goo attack will probably get a quicker response than a report that someone said you had a nose like a pig's! Fortunately, there are other ways in which you can respond to griefing.

If someone is typing offensive things you don't want to read, mute them. You can right-click the avatar then select Mute. Muting will not only keep you from having to see chat and IMs from the person, but also will mute chat from objects that belong to them. You can mute voice chat, as well. Whatever your approach, don't engage the griefer. They're in it to see you blow your top, so don't.

Once you've muted the griefer, or if you've decided to simply ignore them or to teleport away, you can contact the owner of the land where the problem occurred and explain what happened, including the name of the offending avatar and any objects they used to grief you. If you own the land where the problem is happening, you can ban the griefer from it, stop sounds from entering from the neighboring land, and remove all of the griefer's objects. You can also prevent unauthorized avatars from creating objects on, bringing objects onto, or using scripted objects on your land. If you own the region or are an estate manager, you also have the ability to stop scripts from running, and to suspend physics. In Part 3 we'll take a closer look at how to access your land-management tools and the permissions system.

There are also scripted objects that can aid you in your defense against griefing. Some are used to control access to land, and others give avatars other than the land owner the ability to eject and ban troublemakers. There are even scripted objects available to make you (nearly) impervious to virtual weapons.

Some Residents have formed networks that share ban lists so that known troublemakers can be kept away. These are very controversial.

HOW TO SUBMIT AN ABUSE REPORT

It's easy to submit an Abuse Report, or AR. Go to Help ▶ Report Abuse and fill in the fields.

CRIMINAL ACTIVITY

There are crooks all over the place in real life and on the Web, and naturally they find their way to the *SL* world, as well. Distinct from griefers, these crooks aren't in it for the amusement value or notoriety, but for the money. Most of their activities are fraud-based, and not unique to the *SL* Grid. A few varieties of crime to watch out for:

- ▶ Pyramid schemes

- ▶ Fake charity kiosks

- ▶ Hijacking existing real charity kiosks or tip jars, usually with a clear prim set over the actual kiosk or jar, so that you are paying it (and its owner) instead of the person you intended to pay

- ▶ Intellectual-property theft

- ▶ Group invitations offered in hopes that you'll accept before you notice the exorbitant membership fee

- ▶ "Selling" or renting land that someone else owns

- ▶ Pretending to be shop staff and taking your money

- ▶ Phishing, particularly for your *SL* login information, to clean out your account

If someone tries to pull one of these numbers on you, be sure to file an Abuse Report!

ON-THE-JOB DISTRACTIONS

Some people have the impression that every acre of the *Second Life* world is full of casinos, naked avatars going at it, and all sorts of other distractions inappropriate for your workplace. They join *SL*, walk up to the first attractive avatar they see, proposition them baldly and rudely, and quickly find themselves *booted* (ejected from the area) and smacked down with the *banhammer* (banned). They shouldn't have believed everything they read about *Second Life*!

Sensational stories sell papers (or get page hits). Some reporters seek out sensationalist material. I've been interviewed about the work I did on a UC Davis Medical Center project funded by the CDC that was used to train health-department staff in how to respond in case of terrorist attack, educational use of the *SL* Grid for a MacArthur Foundation–sponsored essay contest by respected nonprofit Global Kids, and my company's involvement in the Strong Angel III international disaster-response practice, among other serious *SL* projects with which I've been involved. And for years there always came a point during the interview when the reporter would lower their voice, look at me sidewise with something like a leer, and ask me about avatars doing the nasty. Similarly, they'd ask about things like gambling, or so-called Internet addiction. They usually had ulterior motives for the interview, and sometimes they'd even quote part of what I said out of context to support their agenda. So I'm not surprised at all that someone who hasn't been in-world might expect to find a social cesspool. But it just isn't the truth, and the press is starting to do less of this sort of scandalmongering. The last few reporters who interviewed me didn't even ask for my views on virtual extramarital affairs! It's pretty sad that I should find that to be notable.

That said, there are avatars who live a nudist lifestyle, and there are Residents who use the Grid technology to have virtual intimate relations with one another. However, most of this activity takes place in avatars' private homes or regions, and you don't have to visit those places.

Some regions are rated PG and others are rated Mature. No nude avatars or foul language should be displayed in PG-rated regions. On the mainland, mature activities aren't supposed to go on in the open, where they can be seen by casual passersby. In private regions, rules are set and enforced by the estate owner. You're not likely to find avatars doing the horizontal bop when you go to a university's private region to attend a lecture, or in the middle of a company's virtual meeting! To avoid most sights and activities inappropriate for your workplace, just don't teleport to anyplace with a name like TrixieSexxiHonee's XXX Escort Club.

And if you do want to check out TrixieSexxiHonee's establishment but don't want it to reflect negatively on your organization, do what other *SL* Residents do: log in with an alt! After all, you wouldn't use your business email address for "hot" correspondence, would you?

It goes (almost) without saying that you shouldn't be visiting Trixie's place during business hours. Nor should you be off checking out the local casino during work hours, online or off. By the way, Linden Lab made a rule against gambling in *SL*, so if you do find an illicit casino, stay out or run the risk of being banned from the Grid.

Some employers might be concerned that they can't keep their staff out of these places. And they probably can't, any more than you can tell your employees that they are not allowed to ever buy an adult magazine. You can control only what your staff does during business hours and with an avatar provided by the company.

Just as it is possible to have your company's tech-support department block access to certain web content in a real-life office, it's possible to have Linden Lab or your developer assist you in setting up restrictions to keep your staff's or students' avatars from leaving your private estate. However, this can't be undone, so if you ever want to go to a meeting at another company's island or take your students on a virtual field trip to an in-world museum, you have to allow them a bit more freedom. In most cases a social contract and the use of good judgment are the real answer here.

And, as we've already discussed, it's possible to restrict access to your land or region. If you like, you can keep out everyone but your own staff or students or a selected list of specific avatars, or eject and ban anyone who doesn't conform to your rules of conduct. (And soon you'll be able to select a stand-alone solution and run your own minigrid with complete control!) To do this, of course, you or someone else has to enforce those rules and maintain access and ban lists. I'll discuss how to go about this in Part 3. This is one of the ways in which *Second Life* is more like a real-life location than like a website.

If you're concerned about your organization's image being affected by *SL* having things like escort clubs, think about the Web. There are plenty of unsavory sites on the Web, but that doesn't keep businesses from having websites!

08

Why is it important to keep up with current events in the *Second Life* world? What are the best sources of information from Linden Lab? Are there some good *SL*-specific publications to read? How about some online discussion forums? Where can you find out about upcoming in-world events? How do you know when Linden Lab plans some downtime for the *SL* Grid? This chapter will answer these questions and teach you how to keep up with what's going on in the *Second Life* world and on the *SL* Grid!

KEEP UP WITH CURRENT EVENTS

WHY KEEP UP WITH VIRTUAL CURRENT EVENTS?

It's really important to know what's going on in a place where you intend to invest time and effort! Some reasons for this are obvious, and others aren't.

First, you need to make sure that whatever project you're planning isn't just a reinvention of the wheel. Someone unfamiliar with what's going on in *Second Life* might think it would be really cool to develop based on what they believe is a unique idea, not knowing that it was done well by someone else just last week! This book is a good overview of what different organizations are doing in-world, but you'll want and need to do some research yourself; *SL* changes quickly.

Also, you need to know if that odd glitch you just encountered was a sign that your computer thinks it's time to retire, or if it's just a temporary Grid instability. There are places where you can find out about current issues being repaired, and planned downtime.

You'll also probably want to keep up with what trends are big and those that are just starting to take off, as well as what new features Linden Lab has in store for us, not to mention brand-new Resident-created tools that might prove very useful to you. The *SL* Grid is a place of constant innovation, and you never know what goodies are going to come along.

It's also important to keep up with what your competitors and colleagues are doing, what big events are planned in-world, and more. Fortunately, with the informational channels Linden Lab keeps open, as well as Resident and other news sites that focus on *Second Life* news, you can keep abreast of the action.

This is especially important if you intend to interact directly with the *Second Life* Resident community. You won't be able to follow conversations without knowing the hot news of the day. And as I've already discussed, Residents are likely to notice if you don't know what's up. That can hurt your organization's image very badly in a virtual world where many Residents are tired of feeling as if real-life organizations view them as mere cash cows on a virtual ad farm.

THE OFFICIAL *SECOND LIFE* BLOG

Most important news from Linden Lab is announced or discussed on the official *Second Life* Blog, which you can view at **http://blog.secondlife.com/**. There you'll find posts from various Linden Lab staff members, who report on what they're up to. The blog includes metrics, new features, requests for feedback, introductions of new staff members, explanations for changes or problems, features about projects that are good examples or just worth checking out, and more.

RESIDENT NEWSPAPERS AND BLOGS

There's a multitude of *Second Life*–specific online publications, as you can see displayed at the in-world news stand in Figure 8.1. Some of them have in-world editions (Figure 8.2) with pages that turn, but many more are web-based. These include everything from traditional magazine or newspaper formats to blogs. Most of those I list here are supported by advertising, both from in-world Resident businesses and organizations that are based primarily outside of the *Second Life* world. Some publications put out an annual hard-copy edition coincident with the annual Resident-run *Second Life* Community Convention (or SLCC) where they are distributed. You'll learn more about some of these publications in Part 3 of this book, when I talk about marketing.

8.1 This newsstand houses a variety of kiosks Residents use to access *Second Life* news sources. Newspaper displays are housed in the little building, while the kiosks around the edges of the courtyard link to various magazines and newspapers.

8.2 Even leopards are welcome to visit the offices of the magazine *Second Style* to peruse back issues or to pick up the latest edition.

Here are some of the *SL*-specific publications that I read regularly.

CNN's iReport.com. This venerable news outlet has a Stories from *Second Life* section at **http://www .ireport.com/ir-topic-stories.jspa?topicId=1307**. Check it out for Resident-posted stories, some of which get picked up for their regular news reports. You can visit in-world, too . . . CNN moved to a bigger, better in-world location in February 2009.

Massively. You can catch up on your daily MMO news, including *SL*-specific stories at **www.massively .com/category/second-life/**. This is a good site for details of major breaking news stories.

Metanomics. Read about business and policy in virtual worlds, including lots of *Second Life* news, at **http://www.metanomics.net/**.

The Metaverse Messenger. Check out the granddaddy of *SL* newspapers at **www.metaversemessenger .com/**. The *MM*, as it's called, offers a nice balance of business and social news on a weekly basis. The *SL* equivalent of a real-life local newspaper, it tends to be a bit less sensationalistic than some other Resident-run publications.

New World Notes. Formerly Linden Lab's embedded journalist in the *SL* world, Wagner James Au now blogs at **http://nwn.blogs.com/nwn/**. You'll find some thoughtful essays and interesting news here, along with occasional photo competitions, polls, and weekly event recommendations.

Not Possible in Real Life. Also called NPIRL and located at **http://npirl.blogspot.com/**, Bettina Tizzy's blog will keep you up to date on the latest developments in the *Second Life* art world.

Reuters *Second Life* News Center. Located at **http://secondlife.reuters.com/**, this is an especially good source for those interested in using the *SL* Grid for their organization's projects—it's very business-oriented. (At press time, Reuters has stopped posting new material about *SL* but they have not pulled the site. It's unclear whether regular updates will resume.) You can also attend Eric Reuters's office hours in-world at the Reuters Atrium (Figure 8.3)—there's information and a SLURL at the site.

RezEd. If you'd like to check out a site for *SL* educators full of useful tips, visit **www.rezed.org/**.

***Second Life* News Network**. Updated irregularly (usually every day or three), this site, also known as SLNN, often focuses on interesting niche stories that other publications overlook. Check it out at **www.slnn.com/index.php**.

Second Style. Like fashion magazines or want to know what stylish avatars are wearing this season? Go to **www.secondstyle.com/**.

Second Thoughts. This blog, at **http://secondthoughts.typepad.com/**, is the virtual soapbox of Prokofy Neva, sometimes called the "infamous antagonist." Often this is the first source of info about important *SL* trends; expect occasional strong language and stronger opinions from this *SL* commentator.

SLCN.TV. If you'd rather watch the news than read it, check out **http://slcn.tv/**. This site offers straight news, sports coverage, music news, fashion, talk shows, and even a game show.

SLED Blog. If you're interested in what educators are up to in *SL*, check out the official *SL* educators' blog at **www.sl-educationblog.org/**.

Additionally, although they aren't *SL*-specific publications, you can often find interesting news of *Second Life* in *Wired* and CNET, at **http://www.wired.com/** and **http://news.cnet.com/**, respectively.

8.3 Reuters hosts a weekly discussion of current events at this island in the *Second Life* world.

POPULAR WEB FORUMS

While some Residents work hard to bring you the news, others just want to discuss that news, to get advice, to sell their services or goods, or to have some fun. Many of them turn to web-based forums. You can learn a lot by reading them, and even more by participating.

Second Life Residents discuss current events, post how-to information, help each other by answering questions, and post event announcements, product promotions, and service ads on the *SL* Forums. Residents can access the forums at **http://forums.secondlife.com/**.

Along with the official forums operated by Linden Lab, Residents have created many unofficial forums on which to discuss *Second Life*–related news and topics. There are two that I read from time to time, where I sometimes find some interesting breaking news or information.

One is the venerable SLUniverse community, which you can visit at **www.sluniverse.com/php/vb/**. This forum has been a touchstone of the *SL* Resident community for years. Keep in mind that on this forum you may encounter material or links to material that you might not want someone to read over your shoulder at your workplace.

A newer forum, but still full of longtime *SL* Residents and well worth a look, is Second Survivor, at **http://secondsurvivor.com/SecondSurv/**. Not only will you find news of current events here, but sometimes the ideas for those events are born during discussion, and plans begin right here. You might encounter some not-safe-for-work material here, as well.

When you visit Resident-run forums, keep in mind that you are visiting a community with a history of its own, and be sure to read the FAQ or other rules before you post.

NEWS FROM LINDEN LAB

Linden Lab maintains a lot of communications channels, including some that facilitate two-way discussions with Residents. Their blog is just a start; it often links to a discussion on the forums. Let's have a look at some other official news sources.

THE OFFICIAL *SL* EVENTS CALENDAR

Hundreds of events take place in the *Second Life* world every day. These include live music, philosophical discussions, grand openings, fashion shows, art shows, plays, dances, contests . . . the sheer number and range of events is nearly overwhelming.

Residents are able to list their events on the Official *Second Life* events calendar at **http://secondlife.com/events**. You can also access the calendar in-world. Go to Search ▶ Events. Event listings may be sorted by date and time, or by type of event (Figure 8.4).

8.4 You can search in-world to find in-progress and upcoming events.

Many Resident sites list best-of or niche-specific events. Some of the best of these are at SLEDevents at **http://sledevents .blogspot.com/**. Also check out the event recommendations from the *Metaverse Messenger* and New World Notes.

LINDEN OFFICE HOURS

Dozens of Linden Lab staff members—Residents call them *Lindens* because their avatars all share that surname—maintain regular office hours in the *Second Life* world, where Residents are welcome to show up and chat for an hour, usually once a week. Of course, each Linden has their own area of expertise. Additionally, sometimes there are pre-announced discussion topics.

You can find a listing of Lindens who have office hours and on what they focus at **http://wiki.secondlife.com/wiki/Office_Hours**. There's also an office-hours calendar at **http://www.google.com/calendar/embed?src=c2g7djaua9j4he8c6d0iu7n7k8%40group.calendar.google.com**.

Don't expect to find a Linden Lab representative wearing a suit and sitting behind a desk. You're much more likely to encounter a Linden who looks like a typical *SL* Resident in a location like Qarl Linden's mazelike giant cube in the sky, Torley Linden's brightly colored watermelon-themed island, or Claudia Linden's peaceful outdoor sanctuary. Usually these meetings are pretty informal.

Linden office hours are not a tech-support channel. They're just a way to talk directly with Linden Lab staff members who are building the platform's features and guiding its community and other programs.

LINDEN LAB MAILING LISTS

Linden Lab offers a variety of public mailing lists for discussion of specialized *Second Life* topics, such as using the *SL* Grid for education, software-development issues related to *Second Life*, and how to use *SL* for live musical performances. You can learn more about the mailing lists at **https://lists.secondlife.com/cgi-bin/mailman/listinfo**.

Some lists are much more active than others—in fact, some of them, like the Educators list, might fill up your inbox all by themselves! Fortunately, there's an option to receive these in digest mode (so that you receive all of the new posts in a daily email rather than throughout the day), or you can simply read archives sorted in various ways. To access archives, go to the mailing lists URL in the previous paragraph, click the name of the list that interests you, then find a link to that list's archives.

The best use of these lists is for discussion among peers, although there is direct participation by Linden Lab staff members on some lists. Keep in mind that some of what you'll read on these lists is partially or entirely rumor—it's important to know the source of the information and to double-check with Linden Lab when it's something important.

SECOND LIFE STATUS

Like most things on the Web, *Second Life* or certain parts of it sometimes have to be shut down briefly for maintenance. Additionally, sometimes Linden Lab notifies Residents that the Grid is experiencing technical difficulties and provides information about what's going on and the estimated repair time. Typical of Linden Lab's policy of remarkable transparency, they include interesting details and explanations.

If you simply want to know whether the Grid has gone down or if it's just you, you can access the *Second Life* Grid Status Reports page at **http://status.secondlifegrid.net/**.

Another very useful feature of the Status Reports page is the *Second Life* Planned Outages Calendar, which can also be accessed via **http://www.google.com/calendar/hosted/lindenlab.com/embed?src=Grid-downtime%40lindenlab.com**. This calendar lists all planned downtime as well as of specific in-world and website features. Be sure to check it before scheduling events, classes, or meetings!

MESSAGE OF THE DAY

Linden Lab posts a Message of the Day (MOTD for short) right on the Grid's loading screen. MOTDs are usually notices about important events, impending downtime, or other newsworthy announcements.

OTHER CHANNELS FOR LINDEN LAB NEWS

Linden Lab works hard to keep information flowing. Here are a few more sources to check out:

Town-hall meetings. From time to time, Linden Lab's CEO or other Lindens will appear in-world to talk about important issues or developments. These gatherings usually are held at an event stage in the Pooley region. Although town-hall meetings were once text-chat events that were simulcast via text repeaters at Infohubs and Resident parcels across the Grid, these days they are usually conducted in voice chat simulcast as streaming audio and made into a podcast for those unable to attend.

Linden Village. Many Lindens maintain their virtual homes or offices in this area, in the Ambleside and Waterhead regions. Other highlights include an art gallery, a hot-air balloon tour, orientation stations, and the Linden Lab Recruiting Center, where you can learn about *Second Life* and Linden Lab employment opportunities (Figure 8.5).

8.5 Linden Lab Director of Marketing Programs Glenn Fisher (*SL* avatar Glenn Linden) shows off the Linden Lab Recruiting Center in the Waterhead region, part of the Linden Village.

Infohubs. These spaces, developed by Resident volunteers and located throughout the mainland of the *Second Life* world, include a variety of Linden information kiosks and Resident-created content (Figure 8.6).

8.6 Infohubs are Linden-owned locations (many built by volunteers) that offer information to Residents. Anyone can set their Home location at an Infohub, which is great for those who don't own land.

DOING REAL WORK
IN A VIRTUAL WORLD

03

Why pay for imaginary land? Should you own or rent? Are there breaks for educators and nonprofits? What should you consider when shopping for land? How do you administer it? How do you manage other in-world assets, including people and inventory objects? Can you control intellectual property in *SL*? How do you manage a project in a virtual world? This chapter will answer all of these questions.

MANAGE YOUR INFRASTRUCTURE

LAND

Everything on the *Second Life* Grid takes place on virtual land (or in the sky over it). Although it's possible to undertake certain types of projects without owning or renting some land, you still need to understand a few things about it.

◥ NOTE

This is one of the most important chapters in this book; in fact, sharing the information in it was my original inspiration for writing a book about *Second Life*. Just about every client and prospective client with whom I have ever discussed a *Second Life* project has at some point needed help with some aspect of this material. If you intend to do any sort of project in *Second Life*, you need to read this.

◥ NOTE

As discussed in Chapter 2, "Teach and Train," Linden Lab offers discounts on land for qualified educators and nonprofits, although taking advantage of this may require you to have a parcel in a specific area—usually this is the case when taking advantage of other special programs, like those offered by the New Media Consortium.

WHY PAY FOR IMAGINARY LAND?

Some people have a hard time accepting the idea of buying virtual land. After all, they say, it isn't real! But that's a misconception. It certainly is real; it just isn't *land*.

The purchase of *Second Life* land really means that you agree to rent some resources on the *Second Life* Grid that you can administer and use based on the guiding metaphor of "land."

In other words, you're renting server space and the opportunity to control what goes on there, along with various support services and administrative tools. It's a lot like paying for a web-hosting package that includes site-building tools and support.

OWN, RENT, OR HIRE A MANAGER?

If you want some land for your project, you can purchase it or rent it from a *Second Life* Resident or a Solution Provider with whom you work. Naturally, there are pros and cons to each of these options.

If you purchase your land, you have control over it, including the ability to select others to whom you can give administrative powers. However, Linden Lab remains a landlord of sorts for the land you buy. There's the one-time, up-front expense of purchasing the land, plus you'll have to pay a monthly *tier fee* tied to the size of the parcel, unless you own 512 square meters or fewer (or pay a monthly maintenance fee for a private region). That much tier is included with a Premium *Second Life* membership, which, in turn, is required to own land (but not to rent it). If you purchase an entire region, you'll have even more control, such as broader powers related to terraforming and access, plus you can select its Grid location and name, and specify whether you'll allow other islands to be adjacent to your own.

Many Residents and some organizations choose to rent land rather than own it. Some companies specialize in virtual property management. Usually there's no up-front purchase price, and you pay the rent in Linden dollars. Some companies will accept alternative forms of payment, such as PayPal. This can be a real benefit, because it might be a little simpler for your accounting department. Another nice aspect of renting is that you don't have to figure out how to sell your land if you decide not to keep it. Downsides are that there may be limitations on what you're allowed to build on the land, neighbors might use a lot of region resources (say, if they often host well-attended events), and you'll have access to fewer administrative tools than you would as a landowner. In addition, if you need land-related support, you will have to count on your landlord to either deal with it or to contact Linden Lab on your behalf, which can be a problem if your landlord doesn't happen to be around at the time!

Some Solution Providers will be happy to rent you a parcel on an island they already own, or to rent or purchase land and sublet it to you. This is usually figured into the overall cost of your project and is likely to include administering the land for you. In some cases, the Solution Provider acquires the land, develops it, and then transfers it to their client.

If you need a region for only a short time (for example, to host a big event), you can rent one or more directly from Linden Lab.

Linden Lab does not currently allow anyone to own an Openspace or Homestead unless they have a regular region. So if you want only an Openspace, you'll have to rent it. These can be converted into Full Regions for a fee (or vice versa), so if you buy one and find you need more resources, you can upgrade for US$100.

⬐TIP

See the latest land prices and policies at **http://secondlife .com/land/index.php.**

PRIMS, GLORIOUS PRIMS!

I've talked a little bit about prims—the basic building blocks for almost everything in *Second Life*. There's a limit to how many prims a Full Region can support (not counting those attached to avatars): 15,000. This works out to 3 prims for every 16 square meters—which is the smallest parcel into which *Second Life* land may be subdivided. A Full Region will support up to 100 avatars at once.

A Homestead region offers reduced performance. It supports only 3,750 prims, and up to 20 avatars.

An Openspace, although the same size as other regions (Figure 9.1), supports only 750 prims and 10 avatars. You're not allowed to post event listings or classifieds for parcels on an Openspace, and Openspaces are restricted to light use (such as scenery).

However, Homesteads and Openspaces both cost a lot less than a regular region! If you're thinking about getting a region for privacy reasons rather than because you need to build a lot of things on it, and if you don't need to have a lot of avatars in the region simultaneously, a Homestead may be right for you. However, if you need a lot of prims, want to run more than a few scripts, or will have more avatars on your land at once, you need a Full Region.

These limitations are subject to change; you can read the latest at **https://support.secondlife.com/ics/support/ default.asp?deptID=4417&task=knowledge&questionID=3952**.

9.1 The car in the foreground gives an idea of the size of this region.

How many prims you'll need to support depends not only on the things you want to have in-world but also on how they are built. Everything you put on your land will use up some of your prims, but your content developer's approach makes a big difference. For instance, in Figure 9.2, the shape on the left is one red prim. The shape on the right is made of four prims of different colors. If those prims were all red, the shape on the right would look exactly like the one on the left. But you could put a lot more of those one-prim objects on your land!

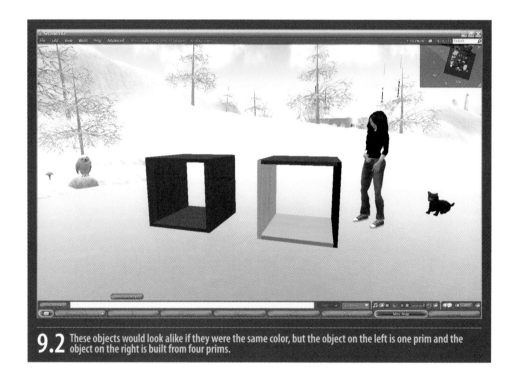

9.2 These objects would look alike if they were the same color, but the object on the left is one prim and the object on the right is built from four prims.

In general, the skill of the content developer who creates your objects, along with the complexity of the objects, will greatly affect the prim count required for your project. A good Solution Provider can discuss your project specifications with you and estimate how many prims you need before you go shopping for land.

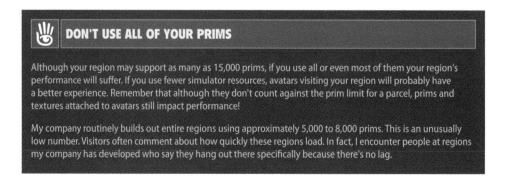

DON'T USE ALL OF YOUR PRIMS

Although your region may support as many as 15,000 prims, if you use all or even most of them your region's performance will suffer. If you use fewer simulator resources, avatars visiting your region will probably have a better experience. Remember that although they don't count against the prim limit for a parcel, prims and textures attached to avatars still impact performance!

My company routinely builds out entire regions using approximately 5,000 to 8,000 prims. This is an unusually low number. Visitors often comment about how quickly these regions load. In fact, I encounter people at regions my company has developed who say they hang out there specifically because there's no lag.

Keep in mind that many of the techniques used to reduce the number of prims needed to build an object will require other resources, usually textures. Each texture needs to be rendered by the computer of each visitor who sees it, and if there are too many textures, or very large textures, this can cause lag. So can too many prims, or complicated prims (which require more system resources to render). Even if your island can technically support 15,000 prims—or even if your builder can work miracles with few prims and lots of textures—it's far better to keep your resource consumption down.

Scripts and the physics engine are also managed at the region level, so if you have too many scripts or too many moving parts within one region—including avatars—performance will suffer. This is why your frame rate drops at a packed event. It's also why there's a limit on the number of avatars allowed in a region. The region owner can increase this number, but it's a balancing act—one I'll discuss further in Chapter 12, "Run an Event."

LOCATION, LOCATION, LOCATION

Along with prims, another main consideration when selecting land is location. Depending on the location you choose, you may get more or less foot traffic, a better view, more resources, or even a prestigious region name. It's a big decision, because it can be costly or even entirely impractical to move your build.

Linden Lab charges US$150 to relocate a private region. Regions cannot be rotated, so if you want to change your layout it might take a fair bit of work. Renaming a region costs US$50, plus you'll have to change all of your landmarks and SLURLs (*Second Life* Uniform Resource Locators, but no one calls them that!), so think carefully about your region's name. Linden Lab does not allow regions to be named after real-life places. However, there are regions that predate this rule, with names like Amsterdam and San Diego. Sometimes a preowned region will cost more because its name is that of a real city or is desirable for some other reason, just like a URL.

If you rent a region, you'll have to negotiate with the landowner if you would like to move it. And if you own mainland (discussed later in this chapter), you can't move it. You'll have to get some other land and have your build moved or reconstructed at the new location.

MATURE SIMS VERSUS PG SIMS

Region owners or Linden Lab (on the mainland) can select whether a region is rated PG or Mature. In PG regions (PG does not mean "parental guidance suggested" in *SL*, but only that the region is not Mature-rated), Residents must not engage in sexually explicit language or behavior, swearing, or violent behavior or imagery. Some Residents feel that based on enforcement, PG is more akin to a G movie rating than a PG movie rating.

Even in Mature regions, there are limits. For example, explicit material shouldn't be out where passersby will see it, and adult behavior is expected to be kept "behind closed doors."

It's easy to check the rating of a region. Just look at the top of the viewer, between the coordinates and the name of the parcel.

MAINLAND VERSUS PRIVATE REGION

In most mainland regions, you can terraform plus or minus four meters. However, in some of them you can't terraform at all, and a few are less restrictive. In private regions, including Openspaces and Homesteads, you can terraform plus or minus 100 meters. Mainland parcel owners can use the About Land tools, but not the Region/Estate tools available to private-region owners (including things like making a backup of your terraformed terrain or changing the texture of the ground). Why buy mainland, then? Foot (or flyby) traffic is high in certain areas of the mainland, especially around popular Infohubs and Resident builds. The mainland offers some areas of nice infrastructure, too, like roads and even themed areas, such as Bay City, which has a mid-20th-century style. And if you buy mainland, your "landlord" is Linden Lab, meaning there's no go-between to deal with in the event of a technical problem.

NOTE

Be aware that Linden Lab has been considering limits on scripts, similar to those on prims, and that Openspaces and Homesteads are likely to have greater restrictions than Full Regions.

NOTE

Although Linden Lab used to occasionally duplicate a private region and the build on it, they no longer offer this service.

NOTE

At press time, Linden Lab was testing a new stand-alone offering that will allow you to operate your own mini-grid, even behind your firewall. If privacy and security are especially important to you, this might be your solution.

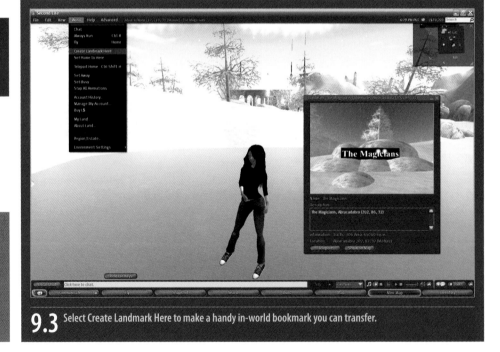

TIP

Preowned land, particularly on the mainland, can be difficult to identify as having already been terraformed. This means you might buy a low-lying island with plans of, for example, terraforming a hill in the middle of it, only to find that the land has already been raised to its highest allowable limit. To find out whether the land you're purchasing can be terraformed further, contact the seller.

TIP

If you paste a SLURL into chat or IM, other Residents can click it to open the map.

NOTE

Landmark icons in Inventory come in two colors. Bright-red landmarks indicate that you have used them. They'll be a dimmer shade of red until you have.

If you buy mainland or rent any kind of land, you have no control over what the neighbors put next door and how it'll affect your view. If they clutter their land with too many prims and textures or have a lot of events, it will affect performance for visitors to your parcel. Even if the rented land's covenant says the neighbor isn't allowed to build a 20-story skyscraper with blinking ads on it, that helps only if the landowner enforces it!

SLURLS AND LANDMARKS

Landmarks and SLURLs are the *Second Life* equivalent of bookmarks.

SLURLs are URLs that can be clicked to bring up the in-world map with a teleport beacon at a particular location. To create a SLURL, click the Map button then type the region and coordinates into the map. Then click Copy SLURL to Clipboard, and paste the SLURL into an IM or chat in *SL*, or into other documents. When someone clicks your SLURL, it will bring up a web page with a link that opens the *Second Life* map directed to your chosen location. If you would like to create a more elaborate SLURL with additional information, go to **http://slurl.com/** and click the Build Your Own SLURL link. This will allow you to add things like a description and image to the page that pops up when someone clicks your SLURL.

SLURLs are great for including on websites, but landmarks are usually more useful in-world. To create a landmark, go to the location you wish to mark. Then go to World ▶ Create Landmark Here (Figure 9.3). Your new landmark will appear in Inventory in your Landmarks folder. You can rename your landmark from there, but you cannot change its destination; instead you'll have to create another.

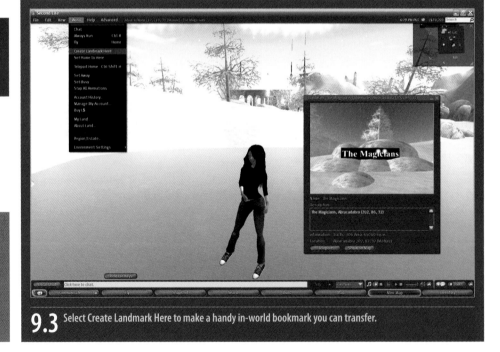

9.3 Select Create Landmark Here to make a handy in-world bookmark you can transfer.

Landmarks are great because you can pass them to other avatars as Inventory items, scripted objects (such as a *landmark giver*) can distribute them, and you can embed them in notecards by simply dragging and dropping. Most Resident merchants include landmarks with things they sell, so that you can easily return to their shops.

Traffic (formerly called Dwell) is intended to be a general indication of the popularity of venues in *Second Life*. To see a parcel's Traffic score, click on its name at the top of the *SL* viewer while you are standing on the parcel. You'll see the Traffic score on the General tab (shown in the "About Land" section later in this chapter).

The way in which Traffic is calculated is a bit of a mystery. It's based, at least in part, on the percentage of a visitor's *SL* day spent at the parcel. Very brief visits don't count, so just logging in for a minute is not supposed to affect Traffic.

Traffic is very controversial among Residents because it is one of the factors used when calculating a location's rank in Search results. Naturally, most want their parcel to be at the top of the list. Over the years, various techniques (including camping and the use of bots) have been developed for boosting a sagging Traffic score.

Camping is facilitated by *poseballs* or seats avatars use to be paid a small amount of Linden dollars, usually referred to as *camping chairs*. For example, you might seat your avatar in a camping chair that pays you L$10 per hour, so long as you don't time out (log out automatically due to inactivity) during that time. The landowner feels that the cost of paying campers is worth the boost in Search ranking. Some camping chairs aren't chairs at all, but instead are poseballs that animate avatars so that they appear to be painting, sweeping, busking, or modeling fashions. Camping is frowned upon by many Residents because it artificially skews Traffic scores. Other Residents, though, rely on camping to earn Linden dollars to purchase things like clothing and hair for their avatars. In fact, some camping equipment pays in merchandise rather than in Lindens.

It might seem silly that someone would sit their avatar somewhere for an hour for 10 Lindens. However, most campers are doing something else while their avatar is camping—they might be logged in doing something else using another account, or they might be asleep while their avatar is earning a few Lindens. Then the question is whether the electricity used to keep the computer on is worth the Lindens earned!

Some Residents cut out the middleman and sit a bunch of avatars on their own land to pump up their Traffic. To do this, they use *bots—Second Life* avatars driven by third-party software run on a server outside of the Grid. The bots aren't very smart, but standing around on a piece of land to raise the Traffic score, without timing out, is well within their abilities. If you find a seemingly deserted region with a ridiculously high Traffic score, then notice a skybox full of silent default avatars, you have probably come across a bunch of Traffic-boosting bots. As you might imagine, most Residents who aren't engaged in this activity themselves are not too pleased about it, and many have called for a ban on bots.

There are lots of other ways to improve your parcel's rank in Search, and some of them are just as shady as bots. For example, since Search takes into account how many avatars list a location in their Profile Picks, some Residents have taken to paying people for listing their build!

PERMISSIONS

Various permissions systems are used for administrative tasks in *Second Life*. There's one for controlling land, another for managing groups, and a third for controlling assets. Together, you use these to manage how others can access and use your in-world land and other assets.

PARCEL AND ESTATE PERMISSIONS: HOW TO RULE YOUR VIRTUAL DOMAIN

Two control panels are used for controlling land in *Second Life*, About Land and Region/Estate. You may access the latter only if you own a private region or if the region owner has made you an estate manager.

To administer land on the parcel level, its owner or a group member with an appropriate role uses this panel. Right-click the ground of the parcel and select About Land to access these controls. The About Land panel has six tabs: General, Covenant, Objects, Options, Media, and Access.

The General tab (Figure 9.4) shows basic information about the parcel.

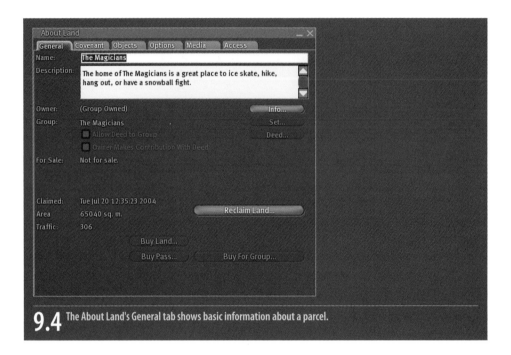

9.4 The About Land's General tab shows basic information about a parcel.

Name: You can rename the parcel using this field.

Description: The text you type here is the description used for Search and is used by default for Profile Picks and landmarks.

Owner: This field names and links to information about the avatar or group that owns the parcel.

Group: The Set button allows you to associate the parcel with a group.

Allow Deed to Group: Use this feature to transfer ownership of the parcel to a group. You'll need to make sure the group has enough tier to support the parcel. It's also a good idea to double-check which group members will then be able to administer the land (see "Groups: How to Organize People and Hand Out Power" later in the chapter for more on groups).

Deed: Use this button to give the parcel to a group of which you're a member.

Owner Makes Contribution with Deed: Check this to automatically contribute tier to support the parcel.

For Sale: If the parcel is for sale, this field will list the sale price and the name of any specific avatar who might be allowed to purchase the parcel if it is not offered for sale to just anyone.

Sell Land: Click this button to open the Sell Land window, which will allow you to set the price, select a specific avatar to whom you would like to make the sale (if desired), or choose to sell all transferrable objects currently on the land along with the parcel.

Buy Land: If the land is set for sale, click this button to buy it.

Claimed: This is the date the parcel was last transferred, merged, or subdivided.

Area: This is the size of the parcel, in square meters.

Traffic: The number here indicates an estimate of how popular or active a parcel is.

Reclaim Land: The region owner may click this to reclaim land. This button appears when you are the estate owner and the parcel is held by someone else.

Abandon Land: Give up ownership of the land without receiving any payment. This button appears when you are not the owner of the estate on which you hold a parcel.

Buy Pass: Click this button to enter a parcel that requires an admission fee.

Buy for Group: Allows purchase of the land for a group.

The Covenant tab (Figure 9.5) shows the name of the parcel, the estate, and the estate owner, along with the covenant itself. The covenant should show any rules to which land purchasers or renters must agree.

⬎WARNING

If you use the Sell Objects with Land feature, be sure to keep backups of any objects you sell with your land, and be very sure of the permissions of the objects you're transfer-ring. It's very easy to ruin a build this way, and glitches during transfer aren't unheard of. Some Residents avoid using this feature.

⬎WARNING

There's no Undo button for land sales, purchases, group deeds, or land abandonment!

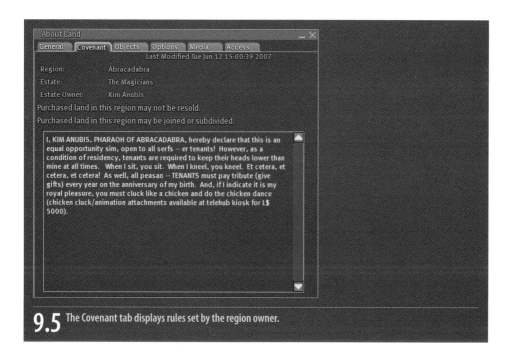

9.5 The Covenant tab displays rules set by the region owner.

The Objects tab (Figure 9.6) is used for administering objects on a parcel. It includes the following:

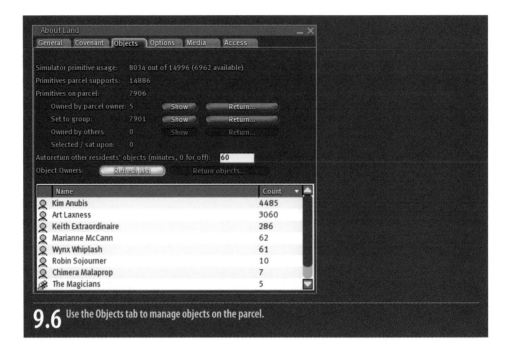

9.6 Use the Objects tab to manage objects on the parcel.

Simulator Primitive Usage: This shows how many prims are supported by all parcels you own in a region and how many are currently in use and available. You can use these on any parcel you own in the region, but not in other regions.

Primitives Parcel Supports: The number of prims you can have on the parcel at once.

Primitives on Parcel: How many prims are currently on this parcel. This is broken down in fields indicating how many belong to the parcel owner, how many are set to the group associated with the parcel, how many are owned by others (not set to group), and how many are currently selected or being used as seats. Click the Show button to highlight prims in one of these categories.

Autoreturn Other Residents' Objects: The number here corresponds with how long objects not owned by the parcel owner or the group are allowed to remain on the parcel before being automatically returned. The minimum is one minute. A zero means Autoreturn is off.

The Objects tab also includes a list of all Residents who have objects on the parcel. To highlight an avatar's objects, click their name; you can return their things by clicking the Return Objects button on the Object Owners line.

The Options tab (Figure 9.7) allows you to control what people can do on the parcel, as well as allowing you to publicize it. This tab includes the following:

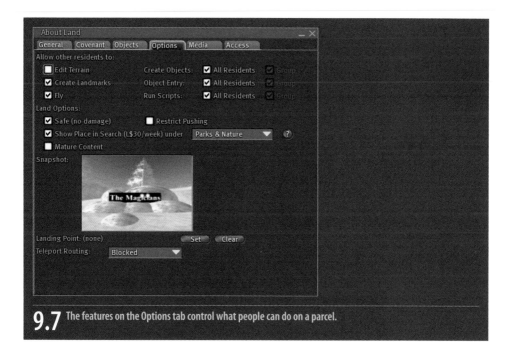

9.7 The features on the Options tab control what people can do on a parcel.

Edit Terrain: When checked, anyone can terraform the parcel. You'll almost never want to leave this checked, because any passerby or griefer could mess with your terrain!

Create Landmarks: Uncheck this to keep visitors from creating landmarks here.

Fly: Uncheck this if you don't want avatars to fly here. Avatars who arrive airborne will still be able to fly until they land.

Create Objects: Check these boxes to control who can rez objects on the parcel—anyone, group members, or no one.

Object Entry: Check these boxes to control whose objects can enter the parcel from neighboring land. This doesn't stop vehicles, by the way! To keep them out, you'll need to read about the Access tab (shown later in Figure 9.9).

Run Scripts: Use these check boxes to control who's allowed to run scripts. If someone arrives wearing a scripted object that is already running, that object may continue to function.

Safe: Check this to disable the damage system on this parcel. Otherwise, avatars who fall down the stairs, get shot, or have a big prim dropped on their head may "die"—be teleported to their home location.

Show Place in Search (L$30/week) Under: For L$30 a week, you can have your parcel description and image appear in in-world Search in the category you choose.

Mature Content: Check this to indicate if your parcel contains adult content. Some Residents will Search only areas without it.

Restrict Pushing: This disables a script function that can be used to apply force to avatars and objects. It will stop use of certain types of weapons, but it breaks some useful and fun things, like trampolines.

Snapshot: Drag and drop a texture from your Inventory, which will appear along with the parcel description in Landmarks, Picks, and Search.

Landing Point: Stand where you would like avatars to appear, facing in the direction you'll want them to look when teleporting to your parcel, and click the Set button.

Teleport Routing: Select whether avatars may arrive only at the landing point (a specific location you select, at which avatars will arrive when they teleport to the parcel), anywhere on the parcel, or if they are blocked from teleporting onto the parcel.

The Media tab (Figure 9.8) is used to control media on the parcel:

9.8 The Media tab's controls allow you to stream audio, video, and web pages.

Media Type: *Second Life* will attempt to automatically detect the type of media you are streaming, but you can set it manually here. This can be a web page or a video stream.

Media URL: The URL of the media you want to stream on the parcel.

Description: Describe the stream here.

Replace Texture: Drag a texture from Inventory to this box. Anywhere that texture appears within the parcel, it will be replaced by whatever visual stream is located at the URL you chose.

Media Options: You can choose to have the image automatically scaled, have the streamed file loop, or hide the URLs of the streams so they won't be displayed in About Land for unauthorized visitors. You can define the size of the displayed media, as well, though it doesn't work for video streams.

Music URL: Type the URL of the audio stream you'd like to play at the parcel.

Sound: Check Restrict Spatialized Sound to This Parcel to keep from hearing sounds from the neighboring parcel.

Voice: Select the channel used for the voice feature or disable it.

The Access tab (Figure 9.9) controls who's allowed to visit your parcel. You can choose to let in only members of the group associated with the parcel, or you can select specific avatars who are allowed to enter the parcel. Other avatars will not be allowed to enter the parcel. This tab also offers the option of setting a price and duration for temporary passes for avatars not in the group or on the access list. The Banned Residents field allows you to keep 300 specific avatars from entering the parcel. You can also use options on this tab to restrict access based on Residents' *Second Life* payment status.

9.9 The Access tab allows you to control who can visit your parcel.

Avatars not allowed access to a parcel cannot approach it at lower than 50 meters above the ground. However, Residents actively banned will not be able to approach at lower than 768 meters.

REGION/ESTATE

The Region/Estate panel offers tools for administering regions and estates (a group of regions with the same owner). To access these controls, you must be the region owner or an estate manager empowered by the owner. To access these controls, go to World ▶ Region/Estate. This window has six tabs: Region, Debug, Ground Textures, Terrain, Estate, and Covenant.

The Region tab (Figure 9.10) offers administrative tools for the specific region you are in when you open this window. It includes the following:

9.10 The Region tab on the Region/Estate panel offers administrative tools for a region.

⬐ TIP

Along with Teleport Home One User on the Region tab, you'll find a number of the tools on the Debug tab and the Access tab very useful for dealing with griefers. If you're planning to host an event, make sure you know where to find these tools in a hurry! You can disable a weapon or even stop bullets in midair, put a stop to self-spawning grey goo, or give a griefer the boot . . . forever.

Block Terraform, Block Fly, Allow Damage, and Restrict Pushing: Check these to override settings at the parcel level (from About Land).

Allow Land Resell and Allow Land Join/Divide: Check these to change settings for all parcels in the region.

Block Land Show in Search: Check this box to keep the parcel from showing in Search.

Agent Limit: Increase or decrease the number of avatars allowed in a region. The default is 40. Remember, if a region contains too many avatars, performance will suffer.

Object Bonus: You can increase the number of objects each square meter of the region is allowed to support. This doesn't increase the number of prims you can have in a region, just the number per parcel. This is why you might see a "double-prim parcel" for sale.

Maturity: Toggle the region's rating between PG and Mature.

Teleport Home One User and Teleport Home All Users: These controls are used to kick avatars out of the region.

Send Message to Region: Everyone in the region will see your message in a blue pop-up.

Manage Telehub: Click this to open a window that will allow you to set up and manage your Telehub and its features.

The Debug tab (Figure 9.11) offers tools for troubleshooting performance problems:

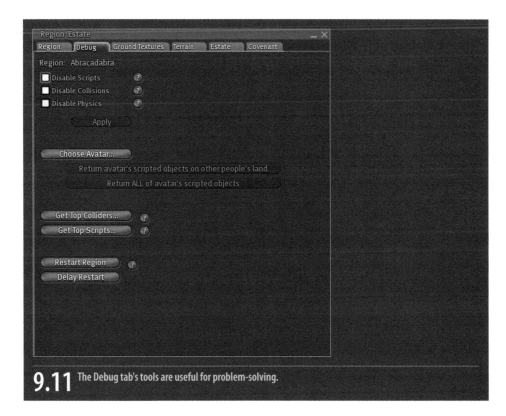

9.11 The Debug tab's tools are useful for problem-solving.

Disable Scripts: Check this to stop all scripts in the region.

Disable Collisions: This stops physical-object collisions in a region.

Disable Physics: This disables the physics engine in the region and will even stop avatars from walking.

Choose Avatar: Click this button to select an avatar so that you can use the buttons below it to return their objects that are on land belonging to others, or all objects they own anywhere in the region.

Get Top Colliders and Get Top Scripts: Use these to open a window that will show what objects and scripts are having a major impact on the region's resources. You can also use this feature to set a beacon on these objects or to return them.

Restart Region: Click this to restart the region.

Delay Restart: Click this to delay the restart by 60 minutes.

The Ground Textures tab (Figure 9.12) is used for setting terrain textures for a region. There are four texture levels, and you can drag and drop a texture onto each one. The textures must be 512×512-pixel 24-bit TGA files (you can find some in the Library). Using the texture-height controls, you can adjust the maximum and minimum height of each texture for every corner of the region; the textures average out in the center.

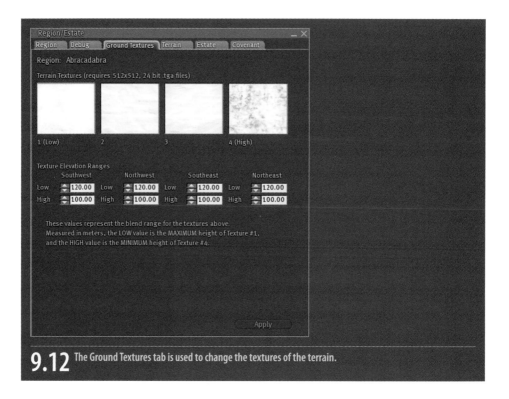

9.12 The Ground Textures tab is used to change the textures of the terrain.

The Terrain tab (Figure 9.13) offers some terraforming controls:

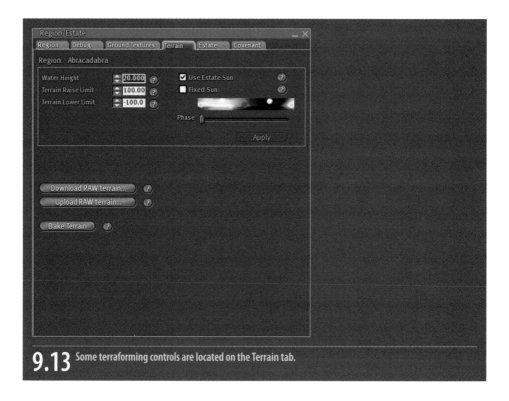

9.13 Some terraforming controls are located on the Terrain tab.

Water Height: Adjust the height at which water will be rendered in the region. The default is 20 meters, and if you set it differently your water level will probably not match that of the neighboring region, as seen in Figure 9.14.

9.14 The gap in the water is due to different Water Height settings in neighboring regions.

Terrain Raise Limit and Terrain Lower Limit: This controls how much terraforming may vary on parcels within the region.

Use Estate Sun and Fixed Sun: Make the day cycle match throughout all regions in the estate using Estate Sun. You can lock in the time of day for just this region by using the Fixed Sun check box.

Download RAW Terrain: Click this to export your terrain for backup or modification, or to duplicate it in another region. It's always a good idea to back up your terrain!

Upload RAW Terrain: Import terrain you have modified or created in an external application.

Bake Terrain: Click this to set the current terrain as the region default.

The Estate tab (Figure 9.15) offers an array of tools for administering your entire estate:

Estate Managers: Add or remove other avatars to whom you grant the ability to use most of the Region/Estate tools for this estate. Estate managers don't have the ability to deed land or access About Land or to download or upload RAW Terrain files.

Use Global Time: Keep the region's day cycle in sync with the mainland.

Fixed Sun: Keep the sun from moving.

Phase: Select the time of day (if Fixed Sun is checked).

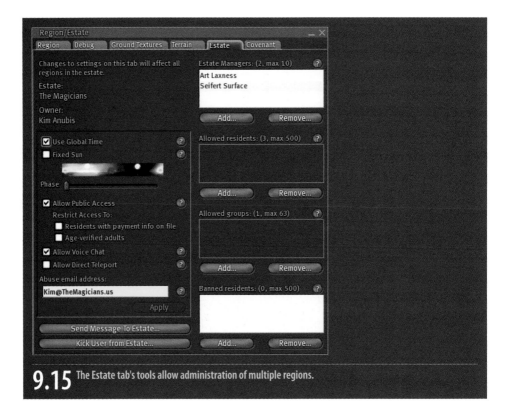

9.15 The Estate tab's tools allow administration of multiple regions.

Allow Public Access: Check this box to allow anyone to visit the estate, except those on the Banned Residents list. You can also use check boxes to restrict access to Residents who have payment info on file with Linden Lab, or to age-verified adult Residents.

Allow Voice Chat: Check this box to allow use of voice chat in this estate.

Allow Direct Teleport: Allow avatars to teleport directly to any point. Landing point routing in About Land overrides this. You can also disable Direct Teleport and set up a Telehub.

Allowed Residents and Allowed Groups: Add or remove avatars or groups that will be allowed entry when access is restricted.

Banned Residents: Add or remove avatars that you don't want to allow in the region or estate.

Send Message to Estate: This works like Send Message to Region, but on an estate-wide basis.

Kick User from Estate: This ejects a specific avatar from all regions in this estate.

The Covenant tab (Figure 9.16) lists the name of the region, the estate, and the estate owner. The owner posts the rules of the region here, and they'll appear in About Land.

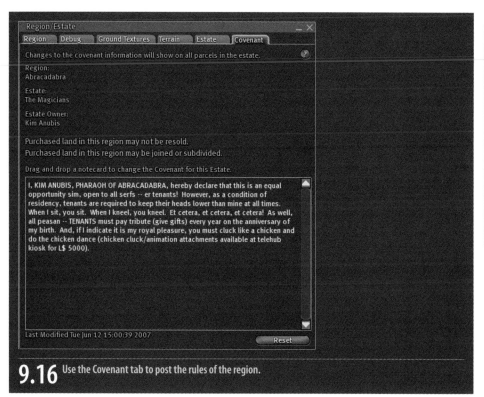

⟍TIP

Want to learn more about administering parcels and estates, choosing land, terraforming, and designing resource-efficient, functional builds? Check out my other book, *Creating Your World: The Official Guide to Advanced Content Creation for Second Life* (Wiley, 2007).

9.16 Use the Covenant tab to post the rules of the region.

GROUPS: HOW TO ORGANIZE PEOPLE AND HAND OUT POWER

The *Second Life* Groups feature offers many administrative tools, and you are sure to need them. You can join a maximum of 25 groups. This can be a touchy issue for some Residents, because many have reason to be in more than 25 groups and some are offended if you leave or refuse an invitation to their group. It can be a real problem to manage a lot of shop locations, client locations, or other land if you need to be in a different group for each and you don't have enough groups available, and deciding which friend's or client's group to drop can be very problematic. Groups are used for many purposes, including property management for Resident homes and shops, real-life organizations' projects, clubs and special-interest groups, *Second Life* families, product updates, collaborative building, and more. Many Residents don't have a *free group*. In other words, they already have 25 and can't add another without making a difficult decision. That's why it is important to learn about how to use the Groups feature to create different group roles rather than creating multiple groups!

To see a list of the groups you're in, click the Communicate button, then the Groups tab (Figure 9.17). This tab offers some useful buttons:

IM/Call: Start a group IM with the selected group.

Info: Open the group's Group Information console (Figure 9.18).

Activate: Change which group you're associated with at the moment.

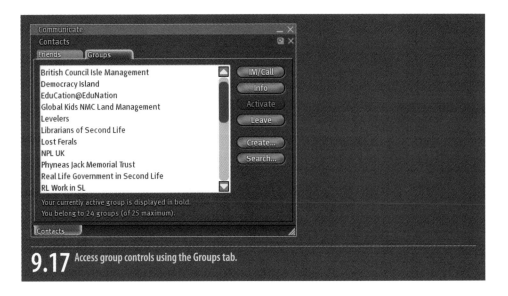

9.17 Access group controls using the Groups tab.

Leave: Quit the selected group.

Create: Open the Group Information console for a new group. Starting a group costs L$100, and if you don't have at least one other member within 48 hours the group will be disbanded. Groups must always have two or more members.

Search: Open Search with the Groups tab selected.

The Group Information console has five tabs: General, Members & Roles, Notices, Proposals, and Land & L$.

The General tab (Figure 9.18) includes the name of the group and its founder, a field for the group charter, and a roster of members with their titles and the time of their last login. Only group members can see all of this information; for example, some group members might choose not to appear on the member list, and only members can see the last login time.

⊾WARNING

Be sure that you don't have the Open enrollment option checked in the Group Preferences section if you don't want strangers to join your group.

This tab also offers a Group Preferences section, with options like whether the group shows up in Search, if members need an invitation to join, the ability to set an enrollment fee, and whether the group shows up in your profile. You can also use pull-down menus to select whether the group description contains Mature content (for Search listings) and which of your group titles you would like to wear, if you have more than one. Drag and drop your logo or another texture onto the Group Insignia box.

The Members & Roles tab (Figure 9.19) contains three other tabs. The first of these, Members, includes a list of all group members, any tier they have contributed to support any group-owned land, and the time of their last login. Select a name and click Eject from Group if you want someone to be expelled immediately. If you'd like to add a member, click Invite New Person (this brings up a new window that lets you select an avatar and designate a role for the invitee). When you highlight a member, the roles to which they are assigned are checked in the Assigned Roles list, and their group-member powers show on the Allowed Abilities list.

The Roles tab (Figure 9.20) lists all of your group's roles. You can have up to 10. There are three default group roles: Owner, Officer, and Everyone. The last of these has very restricted abilities and is the default role for group invitations or open enrollment. The Owner role has all abilities.

9.18 The Group Information console's General tab allows you to display group information viewable by other Residents.

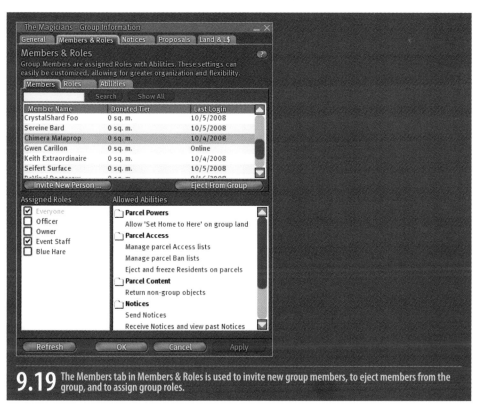

9.19 The Members tab in Members & Roles is used to invite new group members, to eject members from the group, and to assign group roles.

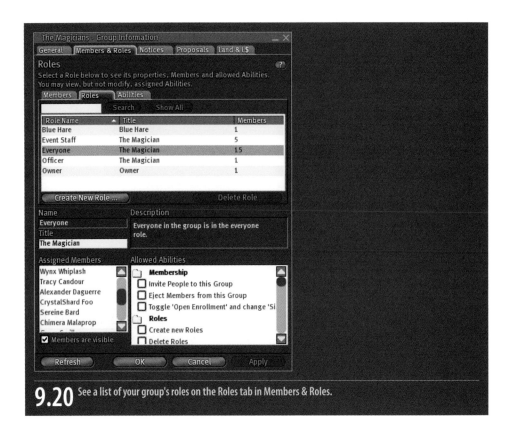

9.20 See a list of your group's roles on the Roles tab in Members & Roles.

This tab also shows the title associated with each role and the number of members in each. Highlight a role and select Delete Role if you no longer find it useful or click Create New Role to make a new one. While the role is highlighted it shows in the Name field, with the role's description next to it. You can change the role's title at any time in the Title field. When an avatar has chosen to activate a group (using the Groups tab seen in Figure 9.17) this title will appear in front of their avatar's name over their head, as well as when you mouse over them. The lower part of this window shows a list of members who are assigned to this role, and the abilities associated with the role are checked in the Allowed Abilities list. You can check or uncheck abilities at any time. Below the list of members is a check box that allows you to select whether the members will be visible—on the General tab, for example.

The Abilities tab (Figure 9.21) lists all possible group abilities. When you highlight one, its description appears in the Description box, and below it the list of roles that have that ability appears, along with a list of all group members who have the ability. The list of possible abilities is extensive, and it's hard to remember the details of what each ability allows. But as long as you remember where to find the Abilities tab, you can look them up. The abilities are broken down into 13 categories:

Membership: Add or remove group members and turn open enrollment on or off.

Roles: Add, remove, or change group roles, assign or remove members' roles, and assign abilities to roles.

Group Identity: Change public visibility, charter, and insignia.

Parcel Management: Deed, modify, and sell group land.

Parcel Identity: Change the parcel's name and its Search-related settings and configure landing point and teleport routing.

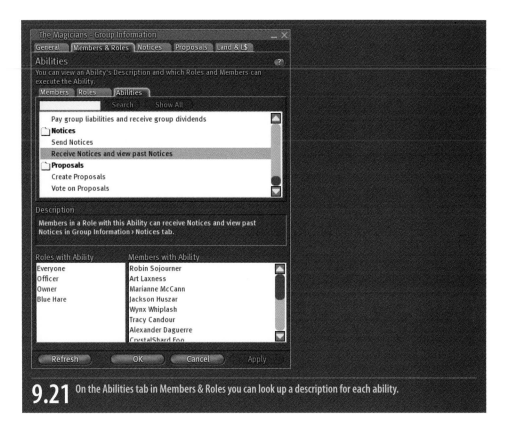

9.21 On the Abilities tab in Members & Roles you can look up a description for each ability.

Parcel Settings: Access controls for enabling Create Objects, Edit Terrain, and parcel Media settings.

Parcel Powers: Bypass parcel restrictions on things like flying and creating objects.

Parcel Access: Permit or ban parcel access.

Parcel Content: Manage objects on the parcel and place Linden Library plants.

Object Management: Deed, modify, and sell group-owned objects.

Accounting: Pay group liabilities and receive dividends.

Notices: Allow members to send, receive, and view group notices.

Proposals: Allow members to initiate and vote on proposals and see proposal history.

Setting up project roles can be complicated, but it's certainly worth the time and effort.

The Notices tab on the Group Information panel (Figure 9.22) allows you to send a message to all group members, which they will receive immediately if they are online, or upon login (and via offline IM). It also contains an archive of up to 200 messages for 14 days. To send a new message, click the Create New Notice button, enter a title in the Subject field and then enter your message. If you would like to send any inventory with it, drag the item from your Inventory and into the Attach field. If you change your mind and don't want to send the item to everyone in the group, click Remove Attachment.

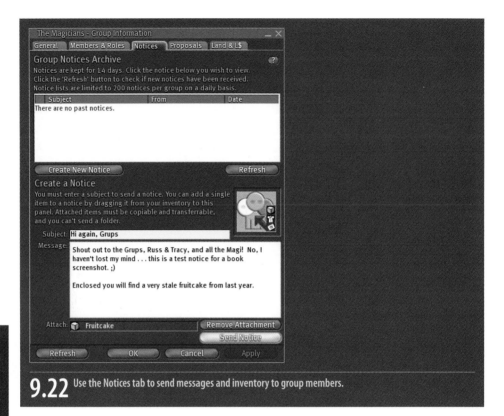

9.22 Use the Notices tab to send messages and inventory to group members.

⤳WARNING

Eventually you'll get a group invitation from someone you have never met. Usually this is for a group that's been formed to promote a specific product or venue. This sort of spam is against the *Second Life* Terms of Service. What's worse is that some fraudsters spam invitations for groups that charge a huge signup fee, hoping that you'll just accept without reading the details!

The Proposals tab (Figure 9.23) is useful for getting member feedback. You can select and view a proposal from the list of those that are currently open, and in the Group Voting History archive you can review past proposal outcomes. Click Create Proposal to open a new dialog. Here you can write a description of what you propose; choose whether it must pass by a simple majority, a 2/3 majority, or a unanimous decision; and specify how many members make a quorum and the length of the voting period.

The Land & L$ tab lists all parcels owned by the group, their locations, and their sizes in square meters. It also shows how much tier members have contributed to the group, how many square meters are currently being supported, how many more the group can support, and how much tier you have contributed. In Figure 9.24 you'll notice that some parcels appear to have no tier supporting them. This is because those parcels are on private regions where tier is not being charged.

The Group L$ section of this tab has three tabs. The Planning tab shows the projected group income and expenses for the week. The Details tab shows this data for a given date, and the Earlier and Later buttons allow you to see data for other days. The Sales tab displays data related to sales of group-owned objects.

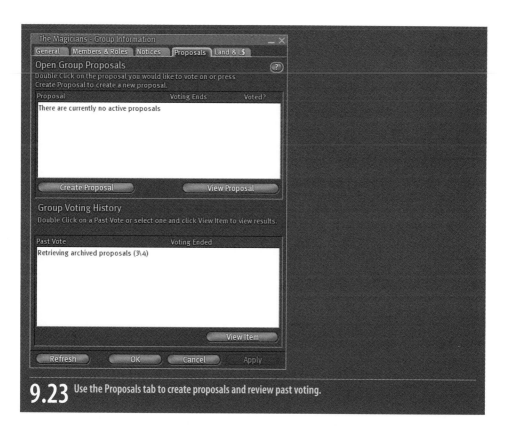

9.23 Use the Proposals tab to create proposals and review past voting.

9.24 On the Land & L$ tab, view a list of all parcels your group owns.

THE PERMISSIONS SYSTEM FOR INVENTORY: HOW TO CONTROL YOUR INTELLECTUAL PROPERTY

When a *Second Life* Resident refers to *permissions*, or *perms*, they're usually talking about the next-owner permissions for inventory items, a system designed to help control virtual intellectual property. It's sort of like the *Second Life* equivalent of a copyright notice and digital rights management rolled into one.

To see the permissions on an object in-world, right-click and select Edit. On the General tab of the Object Editor (Figure 9.25) a section called Permissions indicates if you have permission to modify the object. Below this are check boxes:

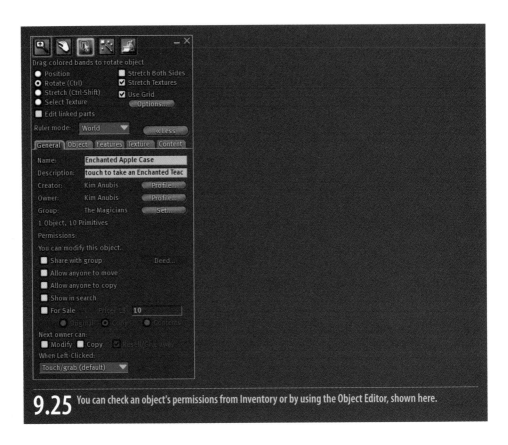

9.25 You can check an object's permissions from Inventory or by using the Object Editor, shown here.

WARNING

You can't undeed an object, so keep a backup if possible.

Share with group: This allows other group members who have the appropriate group abilities to treat this object as if they own it. Other next-owner permissions set on the object will still apply, though. If you check this box, the Deed button will be enabled. Some parcel-related scripts must be owned by the parcel owner in order to work, so if your group owns the land, you have to deed the scripted object to the group.

Allow anyone to move: Any avatar can move the object.

Allow anyone to copy: Any avatar can take a copy of the object, but next-owner permissions still apply.

Show in search: Check this if you want the object to show up in Search.

For Sale: Set the object for sale and type your price in the field. Under this are three radio buttons. Most of the time you will select Copy, to allow anyone to purchase a copy of the object. If you select Original, this instance of the object will be sold. It stays in place unless the new owner moves it. Before you set an object for sale, make sure the permissions are correct; you can't undo the sale. Also make sure the item will not be accidentally autoreturned. This is handy for transferring something like a building that the purchaser doesn't want to rerez—just set the original for sale for zero L$. The Contents button sells everything contained in the object's Content tab, rather than the object itself.

Now we are down to the nitty-gritty of permissions: Modify, Copy, and Resell/Give Away:

Modify: Check this to allow the next owner the ability to edit the object. This is also known as *mod*. An inventory asset without this checked is called *no mod*.

Copy: This allows the next owner to make as many copies of the object as they wish; otherwise the item is *no copy*.

Resell/Give away: Also known as *transfer* or *trans*, this allows the next owner to give away or sell the item, or copies if they have permission for that. Leave this unchecked if you want the object to be *no trans*.

Seems simple enough, right? There are a few more things to consider, though. You must have one of those three boxes checked. In other words, you can't set this object no mod/no copy/no trans. You have to allow either copy or transfer of the object. This means you have to make a decision when you sell or give things away.

Some items are usually sold with copy rights, such as avatar parts and clothing, which can be saved with multiple outfits. Vehicles are also sold this way because they sometimes get lost during bumpy region-border crossings. However, gifts and objects of which you might want to sell multiple copies are better off set as transferrable.

Nested permissions complicate all of this a bit. Figure 9.26 shows the Inventory Item Properties for the object in Figure 9.25. We got from the view in Figure 9.25 to the view in Figure 9.26 by right-clicking the About the Enchanted Teachers' Apple object in the Content tab of the Object Editor and selecting Properties. This shows the name of the notecard, a description, the names of the owner and creator with links to their profiles, and the date the object was acquired. It indicates what permissions you have on the item, whether it's shared with the group, if anyone is allowed to copy it, the next-owner permissions, and, if the object is for sale, the price and whether the original or a copy is for sale.

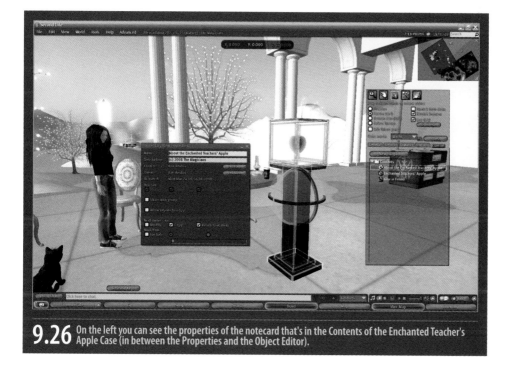

9.26 On the left you can see the properties of the notecard that's in the Contents of the Enchanted Teacher's Apple Case (in between the Properties and the Object Editor).

So this is the tricky part. You have to set permissions not only on the object, but also on the object's contents. And the Enchanted Teachers' Apple Case in this example contains the notecard, the script, and the apple. The apple has contents, as well, but you can't get at those without taking it out of the case. And if the contents have contents . . . well, let's just say that it can be a bit like nested Russian dolls. Sometimes the disassembly and reassembly of objects to set permissions can be quite complicated, with many items in various prims with different permissions on different parts.

 RIGHTS INFRINGEMENT

The permissions system is intended to help content creators control their creations. It is not, however, a replacement for real-life copyright documentation or rights transfers. It's just too easy for someone to make a mistake or for something to go wrong. Additionally, there are crooks everywhere, even in the virtual world.

Unfortunately, an inherent aspect of a platform like *Second Life*, or even the Web, is that anything you can see can be copied. Various programs and tools are used to steal *Second Life* content, usually for resale for L$ in a shop somewhere in-world. These include bots, scripts, and applications like GLIntercept. Occasionally in the past, some crooks have found exploits that allowed unauthorized duplication of *Second Life* assets. And then there's plain old plagiarism.

What if you've been ripped off? File a Digital Millennium Copyright Act notification with Linden Lab. There's information here: **http://secondlife.com/corporate/dmca.php**. In general, you can treat IP theft in *Second Life* just like any copyright or trademark infringement in the real world.

THE INVENTORY SYSTEM

Assets your avatar owns are stored in your Inventory. (To look at your Inventory, click the Inventory button at the bottom of the *Second Life* window.) You start out with some folders in your Inventory, some with things already in them. New items will automatically be sorted into a folder when you accept them or pick them up. To open a folder and see what it contains, click the triangle next to it or double-click the folder name. Do the same to close a folder when you're done.

To create a new folder, right-click the name of the folder in which you want to make another, then choose New Folder. You can create new assets in the same way. Right-click a folder and then select which type of inventory you would like to create.

If you see an object in Inventory that looks like a couple of prims piled together (Figure 9.27), it denotes a coalesced object. It means you picked up a group of objects—or a group of objects was returned to you—all at once. They'll have the name of the last object selected when you picked them up. To get at any of those things, you'll have to rez the whole clump of objects. This is very convenient if you want to pick up, say, a block of buildings together so that you can replace them with the same relationship to one another later. It's difficult on a large scale, though, and takes practice!

Right-clicking a folder or object in Inventory also offers the Delete command. If you delete something by accident, look for it in the Trash folder. Then right-click and select Restore Item. It will reappear in the folder where it was before.

To find something in your Inventory, type its name or part of its name in the box at the top of the Inventory window and then press Return. When you're done searching, click the X in the box to clear it.

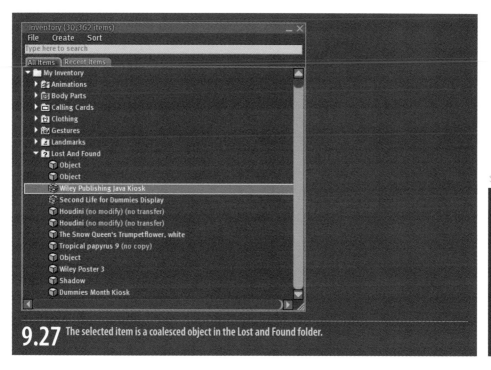

9.27 The selected item is a coalesced object in the Lost and Found folder.

◥ **TIP**

If you want to pick up a bunch of objects at once, try labeling one prim with a name like All Furniture for Kitchen Build and select that prim last. By doing this, the coalesced object will have an identifiable name.

You can also sort your Inventory to look for just the newest items in it. Instead of looking at the All Items tab, click the Recent Items tab. Or use the Sort menu and arrange your Inventory by date or alphabetically. You can use Sort to view only certain types of assets, as well.

To move things around in Inventory, just drag and drop them. You can even open a second Inventory window and move things to it. Select File ▶ New Window, and it will appear. To close the Inventory window, click the X in its upper-right corner.

You can also right-click and choose to copy or paste items. If you don't have permission to copy an item, the option will be grayed out.

If you lose an item in-world, it might come back eventually via autoreturn or because the landowner where you left it returned it manually. Be sure to check your Lost and Found folder. It's also a good idea to occasionally right-click your Inventory's Trash folder and choose Empty Trash!

MANAGING PROJECT INVENTORY

You'll find that your Inventory can get out of hand pretty quickly. If you don't watch out, soon you'll have an Objects folder full of objects with the default name Object. Then you're going to have a heck of a time finding anything!

It's vital to keep on top of sorting your assets (Figure 9.28), just as you would sort files in a real office or organize the icons that stack up on your computer desktop. Here are some tips for managing assets for your *Second Life* project:

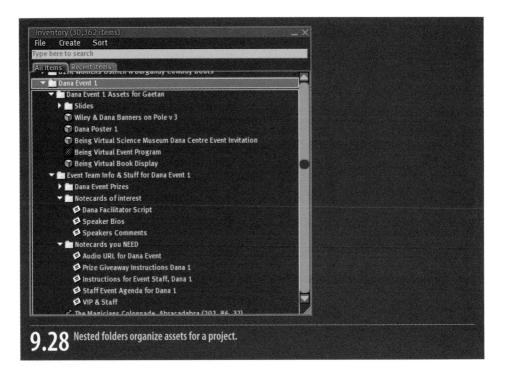

9.28 Nested folders organize assets for a project.

▸ Make a folder for each project.

▸ Create subfolders. For example, if you are building a house, you might sort the furniture into folders by room.

▸ Number different versions of the same object. It works for software, and isn't this really software, too?

▸ Use descriptive object names that will be easy to find later.

▸ If you don't have modify permission for an object, you can't rename it. In that case, name a folder and put the object in it.

MAKING BACKUPS

There's not a complete system built into *Second Life* for backing up your inventory to your local computer. Fortunately, there are some easy ways to back up most types of assets if you have the correct permissions on them.

▸ Scripts you are allowed to view can be selected (Ctrl+A), copied, and pasted into the text document of your choice outside the *Second Life* Grid.

▸ Notecards can be copied and pasted the same way as scripts.

▸ Textures and screenshots, as well as sculpted prim maps and the textures of clothing and avatar body parts, are easy to export if you have full permissions. Open the texture, then go to File ▶ Save Texture As.

▸ Terraforming may be backed up by the region owner using the Region/Estate console.

- Audio and animations cannot be backed up. However, if you or someone who works for you created them, you can keep a backup of the original file that was created in an external application anyway.

- Body parts can't be exported, but you can take a screenshot of the slider settings or write them down.

Objects can't be exported, but there are a few things you can do to protect them.

- Send copies to someone else on your team or to an alt of your own. Many developers have an alt specifically for this purpose.

- Keep a copy of the item in a box on your parcel, or just rezzed in-world.

- Drag-select the entire build and take a copy.

- Pack the build into a scripted tool such as a Rez-Foo so that the entire build can be rerezzed with the click of a prim.

What if you can't make a copy? If the item is vital, make sure you buy some backup copies. This is especially important if you buy the item from a Resident merchant. That shop could be gone the next time you visit.

What if the worst happens, and something goes missing?

- Check your Lost and Found folder.

- Make sure you haven't left the object rezzed in-world.

- Ask owners of parcels where the item might have been lost to look for items that belong to you.

- If a Solution Provider created the item for you, ask for another copy.

Sometimes inventory isn't really missing; it just hasn't loaded so that it shows in your *Second Life* viewer. If you've tried the preceding methods and your asset is still missing, try these:

- Check the *Second Life* Grid Status Report at **http://status.secondlifeGrid.net/** to see if the Grid is experiencing trouble. Particularly if the asset cluster (usually referred to as the *asset server*) is having difficulty or the whole Grid is experiencing heavy load, your inventory may not appear. During times of this sort of instability, Linden Lab will issue an advisory telling Residents not to transfer or rez irreplaceable inventory.

- If the Grid is stable and it's just a local problem, try relogging in.

- Clear your cache. Go to Edit ▶ Preferences ▶ Network ▶ Clear Cache, then relog in.

- Still no luck? It's time to file a support ticket. Go to **http://secondlife.com/support/**, and do it quickly. There's a shot that Linden Lab can recover your assets if not much time has passed.

MANAGING PROJECTS IN *SL*

This chapter included an overview of the key systems you need to understand to run a project in-world. Between About Land, Region/Estate, Inventory, Groups, and Permissions, you've learned about the administrative tools for land, assets, and people. There are plenty of added considerations for those doing real-life projects on the Grid, though.

Here are some suggestions for how to administer a project in *Second Life*:

▶ Create a group and deed your land to it unless you're doing a solo project. Otherwise, every time some-one needs to change the radio station or return some litter, they're going to call you for help. If you own a region, you can have estate managers carry part of the load.

▶ Unless you want to personally deal with every prim your avatar owns, consider giving someone else edit rights on your objects via the Friends tab in the Communicate window (Figure 9.29).

9.29 The avatar at the top of this list has edit rights on my objects, and I have edit rights on his.

▶ In general, if you're working on a collaborative project, the next-owner permissions system gets in the way. My approach is to have everyone who has to collaborate while building objects share edit rights on one another's items and work with all assets set to *full permissions*. I set more restrictive permissions only on items that will be given to avatars who are not part of my team.

▶ Don't assume *Second Life* Residents view permissions as anything other than a suggestion. Some give away full-permissions objects and then are upset when they are resold. Others will take copies of anything that's not nailed down and assume that whatever they can get away with is just fine.

▶ Be very careful as to what group role you give someone when you invite them to your group. It takes just a slip of the mouse to give someone a lot more power than you intended!

▶ You can use scripted objects that look and act like filing cabinets to organize inventory in-world and share it with group members.

▶ Systems like the boards shown in Figure 9.30 are useful for tracking assets and tasks associated with a project. This one has color-coded markers to indicate the status of tasks, as well as icons showing what staff members are working on.

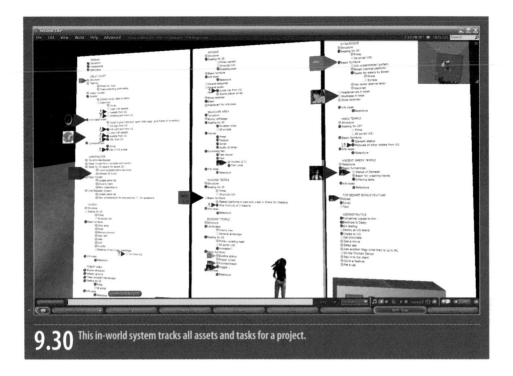

9.30 This in-world system tracks all assets and tasks for a project.

▶ Scripted objects can be made to work only for members of a group.

▶ Be cautious about sharing or deeding full-permissions objects to a group if you aren't always going to have control over who joins.

Managing a project in a virtual world is a tricky proposition if you don't have a lot of experience working with a remote team. Staying in close communication is key, and so is organization. The next five chapters cover how to conduct various sorts of projects on the *Second Life* Grid.

10

What makes *Second Life* meetings a good choice? How do meetings work in-world? For what sorts of meetings might you use *SL*? What sort of virtual space is appropriate for your project, and what should it include? What tools might be useful for your in-world meetings? Should you maintain regular office hours on the Grid? How do you use *Second Life* permissions and other tools to keep your meeting place private and secure? Those are some of the questions this chapter will answer!

SET UP A VIRTUAL OFFICE

ESTABLISH A MEETING SPACE

More and more organizations are using the *Second Life* Grid for meetings of all kinds. Some have staff meetings in-world, including employees or contractors from other locations or who telecommute. Some use the Grid for meetings with clients or to engage the public. As discussed earlier in this book, some educational institutions hold classes in-world, and the Grid enables involvement of students who live far from campus. Plus, many organizations using the Grid for their projects find it convenient to meet with project staff right in *Second Life*. Here are some reasons why the Grid is great for meetings.

Remote meetings on an equal footing. You know how it is when someone's on a conference call. If the audio is good enough, you still have one or more people who don't really feel present. They're a disembodied voice, can tend to be overlooked, and often don't get the benefit of any charts or slides others see at the meeting. In *SL*, though, everyone is represented equally.

Better than a conference call. When you're in a conference call, it can be really hard to keep track of who's saying what—especially if it's a large group. In-world, though, you have a clear indication of who's talking. And you can discuss audio, video, websites, and images that you stream in real time.

Spatial relationships and vivid avatars. Rather than being confronted by disembodied voices, names in a chat window, or a static-cracked webcam view, everyone is represented by an avatar of their own choosing. Sit next to someone, turn toward them, shake their hand, or offer them a cup of coffee. The Grid allows you to re-create many of the important nuances of real human interaction.

Reduced travel expenses. Travel is never cheap. For as little as the cost of one plane ticket, you could establish a *Second Life* location that your organization can use over and over for meetings, and for other things as well.

Reduced travel time. Travel costs a lot of time, too—time that could be spent working (or unwinding from work, which is important if you want to be efficient and do a good job). How much time does it take to pack, get to the airport, go through security, and all the rest? Compare that to the mere seconds it takes to log into the *Second Life* Grid.

3D interactive models. You can look at an artist's rendering or a tabletop model or a diagram on a whiteboard, but how much more effectively could you share your plans or explanations if you and the others at your meeting could walk through or use an interactive 3D model?

Networking. Everyone knows the value of attending conferences and conventions and how many useful connections you can make at them. What if, instead of having to travel to get to conferences or having to rent an expensive venue to set one up, you logged in from your own office and had your conference online? How many more valuable connections might you make?

Remote showroom. Sometimes you have a client or colleague who'd like to take a look at what you have to offer, but they're not interested enough—or don't have the budget—to hop on a plane. They might be willing to log in, though.

Bang for your buck. Even if your organization is small, you can probably afford an impressive presence on the Grid. A virtual office costs a lot less than one built of bricks and mortar.

Industry advantage. Remember when you realized your organization could benefit from having a website? Virtual worlds are where we're headed next, and the *Second Life* Grid is far and away the leading virtual-world platform.

The "cool" factor. Does the competition have "sexier" marketing? Do you find that trainees or students fall asleep at meetings? You can add excitement and interest by including the Grid as one of your organization's communication tools.

MEETING WITH COLLEAGUES AND CLIENTS

Meetings are a primary use of the Grid, but if you're unfamiliar with *Second Life* you might have a hard time picturing how they work. This is another reason to log in and try *Second Life*!

Let me give you an example from my own experience. My staff is spread across 10 time zones. My clients are in countries all over the globe. I work with Linden Lab staff based on a few continents. And I had only a few staff meetings and no client meetings in the real world in 2008. My entire business—of one of the most successful virtual-world development companies—is conducted online using a combination of email, voice over IP, instant messaging, and *Second Life*. The only hard-copy correspondence is contracts and payment. Think about how much this reduces my overhead, and how much larger it makes my pool of possible staff members and clients.

Meetings in *Second Life* tend to be less formal than they are in a real-world-office meeting room. As you learned in Part 2, even avatars used for education and business might not be human. Additionally, avatars don't need an office building for the traditional reasons (it's not as if it rains in the virtual world, unless you want it to). No, most meetings usually involve a few avatars standing or sitting and using text chat or voice chat, and often this takes place in a location that would not be recognizable as an office if you saw a picture of it, such as the space where I meet with clients (Figure 10.1).

10.1 Some of my staff at a meeting planning an upcoming event

However, some organizations do want an office that looks more like an office, particularly if they're working with people who aren't familiar with the conventions of Grid society!

Typically, here's how a meeting goes: Log in a bit early and make sure your avatar and your meeting space are ready for the occasion. Check if the person you're meeting is already online by looking for them on your Friends list or by checking their profile. If they haven't been added to your list or if they are blocking others from seeing if they're online, send an instant message when the meeting time comes. Then offer a teleport to your location. Expect a wait while the other meeting participants' *SL* client loads everything in view.

Depending on how resources are utilized in the area and whether these avatars have visited recently, this may happen almost instantaneously or it could take effectively forever. This is why you want to make sure your office doesn't just look good, but also doesn't hog resources. Usually people will trade small talk while waiting for things to rez. If you have a handshake attachment (which will animate you and another avatar so that you shake hands), now is the time to use it (Figure 10.2).

10.2 A scripted attachment enables avatars to shake hands.

Although some people don't care about immersion, it's usually considered polite to start off your meeting as you would offline: offer your guests a seat, and sometimes a beverage, unless they're visiting to get a tour of your build or to check out something specific. Some organizations have a special meeting area that is at some distance from the region or parcel's landing point, so you might have to walk or fly to it, leading the others, or show them where the teleporter or elevator is located.

Then you talk using the voice feature, or you type or use a combination of voice and text. Text is particularly convenient for anything that needs to be spelled correctly, numbers, or URLs (which can be clicked and loaded within the *SL* client), or if you want a log of your meeting. You might use a slide screen, video screen, or other media, or even rez objects to help get your point across.

Clients have asked me how to politely take their leave at the end of a meeting or a chance encounter. It works just like it does in real life, except that rather than walking out the door, you teleport to your own home location. It's usually poor form to log out from someone else's office, because then (unless you go to Edit ▶ Preferences ▶ General ▶ Start Location and set it to somewhere other than your last location) you'll reappear there when you log in the next time. You can imagine plenty of unpleasant consequences of having someone suddenly appear in the middle of your meeting room, especially during some other meeting! Fortunately, there are ways to avoid this problem, which I'll discuss later in this chapter.

It's also a good idea to check that you don't have your microphone button locked open while teleporting or logging off, or else those at the location you just left will still be able to hear you. Especially when you're new to *SL*, it's safer to use the push-to-talk feature.

OFFER REFRESHMENTS

Avatars don't need to eat. Why, then, do I recommend that you offer refreshments to them? First, it's a familiar politeness in the real world, and regardless of whether the coffee or bottled water is real, it's the thought that counts. But there's more to it than that.

Even in text chat in the mid 1980s, people "offered" one another ASCII cups of coffee created from typed characters. This is even more common in virtual worlds, where avatars may hold a cup and be animated to appear to drink.

There are social uses for a beverage. Want to step away from someone? Excuse yourself to go get a drink. Waiting for a casual-seeming reason to chat with someone? Catch up with them by the coffee pot. How many people who hang around chatting by the water cooler are there because they're thirsty?

It's inexpensive to offer drinks in your virtual office—they can be had for free from many in-world shops, or you could have something custom-made with your company's logo on it (like the Wiley Java Kiosk shown here, which distributes branded, scripted coffee cups that animate an avatar to drink). It's a classy touch, and one visitors will appreciate.

CONVENTIONS AND CONFERENCES

In-world conventions and conferences, as well as mixed-reality events held both online and off (with audio or video streams melding the two) are increasingly common on the Grid. Most have been educational, such as the Stepping Into series for librarians or the SLanguages conference for language educators. Rather than a single event, these are most often made up of a series of events over the course of one or more days. The events are usually held at the in-world offices of one or more organizations, perhaps with "field trips" to various builds around the Grid. For example, the Stepping Into Literature conference included presentations by various speakers, and a panel in a large event space with a slide screen, along with a few examples rezzed on the spot and visits to different locations on the Grid where educators teach literature, including a library and re-creations of scenes from novels.

Although educators are leading, as is often the case in *Second Life*, government agencies and businesses are starting to follow. In Chapter 12, "Run an Event," you'll learn more about what's involved in putting on a large event in-world.

BUILD A VIRTUAL SHOWROOM

There's been increasing interest in using the Grid as a virtual showroom. By this I don't mean selling in-world products to avatars (which you will learn more about in the next chapter). Rather, some businesses use 3D models in *Second Life* to display or demonstrate their products to clients.

Various things are designed or prototyped on the Grid or displayed to clients there (Figure 10.3). The earliest use of this sort, and perhaps the most common, is architecture. For instance, W Hotels had a model of a planned hotel built on the Grid, and they gathered feedback from Resident visitors before building the actual structure in the real world. In another case the Grid was used to design a public park and solicit input from the public. More than one organization uses the Grid to show model homes to prospective buyers. This requires accommodating the usually larger-than-life-size of avatars as well as the camera position in-world (above and behind your avatar's head), and may mean some adjustments to scaling for building models in-world. For example, your doorways or ceilings might need to be higher, and very small spaces (closets, narrow halls and stairways) may not work out without being built at much larger than scale.

10.3 I use this space to demo some of the games my company offers to clients.

 PROTOTYPING IN *SL*

Organizations use the Grid for all sorts of product testing and prototypes. When Touchstone Pictures was working on a film adaptation of *The Hitchhiker's Guide to the Galaxy*, one of the characters (Marvin the Paranoid Android) was prototyped in *Second Life* .

You might not hear much news about this particular use of the Grid, but that doesn't mean it isn't happening. I know of many more organizations that have investigated and pursued projects of this type, but I'm under NDA and can't tell you about them. And so's everyone else! That's why you don't read about them—they're considered too valuable to let competitors know they exist.

A few other examples include a Solution Provider that operates a virtual exhibition center for trade shows, an interactive pavilion to promote a Cisco product launch, and numerous virtual replicas of real-world locations to promote travel. (A cruise line has used the Grid to show off a cruise ship to prospective vacationers, for instance.) One Spanish Solution Provider created a conference hall where Spanish manufacturers are able to showcase products for Asian buyers. And, of course, there's the Tech Museum of Innovation, which you read about in Chapter 5, "Conduct Business." Hypnotherapists and surgeons have held conferences in-world, and if you were to do a web search for "trade shows" and "*Second Life*" you'd turn up even more examples.

One of the most prominent and successful ventures in *Second Life* is showcased in a recent case study by IBM and Linden Lab (**http://secondlifegrid.net.s3.amazonaws.com/docs/Second_Life_Case_IBM.pdf**). In it, IBM estimates the return on investment for their Virtual World Conference (which had over 200 participants) was "roughly $320,000." IBM also held their Annual Conference in their virtual conference space at one-fifth the cost of a real-world event.

Creating a virtual showroom is a particularly tricky area of *SL* development, and you probably don't want to try to build one yourself. You're unlikely to find prefab objects in-world that will look and function like your real-world product line! You'll want to work with a developer who not only has the skill to create very realistic objects, but who also has the experience to steer you away if your plan isn't going to function practically using the tools available in-world. You'll learn more about how to select content creators and other Solution Providers in Chapter 13, "Select a Solution Provider."

Some organizations have Residents or their customers log in with their own avatars, and others have a salesman familiar with the Grid at the keyboard, with the customer watching. If you choose the former approach, make sure your customers really meet the hardware requirements for *SL*. If you choose the latter, be sure you have a backup plan in case your net connection goes down or the Grid is having a bumpy day.

DEVELOP AN APPROPRIATE SPACE

The type and amount of space you need, and what it should contain, depends on what sort of meetings you intend to hold. How many avatars will need to be in the space at one time, and will you need to display complex 3D models? How important is privacy? There are a lot of considerations, which we'll look at in this section.

The good news is that developing your space does not have to be expensive. For little more than the cost of one premium *SL* account, you can set up a small office that contains the most important tools you need for small meetings. Small parcels are inexpensive, and so are prefab buildings and furnishings purchased from in-world merchants. The first thing you'll need is land.

CHOOSING A LOCATION

As you've already learned, the resources available for your office, particularly how many prims you can use, depend upon how much land you have. Furthermore, things like privacy, security, and the view from your window depend on your location, as does the amount of foot traffic. Here are some more considerations to keep in mind as you shop for land for your office.

▶ How important is privacy to you? Do you need to keep your space private all the time, or do you have only occasional meetings that you'd rather not share with passersby? You can learn more about privacy issues in *SL* in the "Privacy and Security" section later in this chapter. Depending on your needs, you might be able to have a small mainland parcel covered by the tier included with a premium *SL* account, or you might require an entire private region.

- How many avatars do you need to have at your office at one time? If you're going to have large meetings, you should consider an entire region—which you can rent or own—or else you run the risk of other avatars on other parcels filling the region to capacity. Remember that an Openspace or Homestead region can't support as many avatars as a normal region.

- Does the land have a covenant? Be sure to read the covenant for any land you're considering. You might find that it's limited to residential use or that large events aren't allowed!

- How does the area look? Is it presentable and will you have a good view that gives the right impression? Keep in mind that things around you can change at any time: parcels and regions are sold, builds are replaced, and regions arise in formerly empty seas!

- Will you have room for expansion, or will growth require relocation? You may not be able to rent or purchase more land adjacent to your parcel. If you plan on expanding beyond one region, be sure to purchase your land in a location where there's room to add more. If neighboring islands are too near, you may end up in a bidding war or having to pay Linden Lab to move your region.

- Are you qualified to take advantage of subsidized land or to have your location be a part of a larger continent created by organizations with interests similar to your own? You learned about these considerations in Part 1 of this book.

 MOVING MAKES LANDMARKS OBSOLETE

If you change your office location, the landmarks people are accustomed to using to visit will be obsolete. This is true whether you move to a different parcel or you have your region relocated by Linden Lab. Just like moving in the real world means you have to notify everyone of your new location and change your letterhead and business cards, you'll have to take action if you relocate on the Grid. Be sure to update objects that give out landmarks, or notecards that have landmarks embedded. And don't forget to change any SLURLs in your email signature, on your website, or on business cards.

SHOPPING FOR LAND

You can tell whether a parcel is for sale by the color of its property lines. Go to View ▶ Property lines. Land you own has green property lines. Land owned by a group you're in has aqua property lines, land owned by someone else has red lines, land with orange lines is for sale, and purple lines indicate that Linden Lab has slated the land for auction. Fly around an area that interests you and look at the colors!

Search ▶ Land Sales brings up a list of land for sale all over the Grid. You can sort the listings by parcel name, price, size, and price per square meter, and see an image and description of the land, if the seller has chosen to display them.

Of course, as you've already learned, you don't necessarily have to buy land. You can rent it or your Solution Provider may provide it as part of your agreement. There's general information about land and how to go about buying it in Chapter 9, "Manage Your Infrastructure."

HOW YOUR OFFICE SHOULD LOOK

When you select and outfit a real-world office, you consider things like what colors you'd like for the interior and whether you want a modern look or something more traditional. On the Grid you consider those options, but there are a lot of others to consider, as well.

You don't need to have a building. Many organizations don't use one, and instead simply sit on rocks, logs, toadstools, or benches in a park. However, buildings do have their uses, even when you don't need them to protect your photocopier from the weather and your petty cash from theft. They're useful for defining space, setting a tone, and projecting a sense of focus (though these effects can also be gotten—using few prims—through well-thought-out and effectively executed terraforming and landscaping). When working with people unfamiliar with the Grid, it can be very useful to conduct business in a location that looks at least somewhat like a real office, for the sake of making them feel more comfortable.

Beyond that, so long as your location isn't distracting—so no one's gawking at a rapidly approaching lava flow or a UFO swooping overhead—and isn't a resource hog, you can set up an office that has any look you like. So then the questions are whether you will be building your location in-house or buying prefab parts (both of which will probably limit your options a bit), or if you're going to have something built for you. We'll take a closer look at those considerations in Chapter 13.

Although it's probably possible to re-create your actual real-world office, it's rarely a good idea. For one thing, as you've already learned, the layout and dimensions are unlikely to be a good match for avatars. Additionally, there's probably a lot more space in your real-world office than you can use in-world. While your real location probably has lots of offices or cubicles, you're not likely to have that many people at your in-world office at once, and even if you do they probably don't need a virtual desk, let alone a virtual computer on it. And unless you're going to keep it staffed, you don't need a reception desk; an unmanned one doesn't make anyone feel welcome.

Also keep in mind that some *SL* Residents will be unimpressed (and a few might be downright critical) if your office is a simple re-creation of your real-world location. After all, avatars don't need a cafeteria or a supply closet unless you're running an in-world cafeteria-staff training simulation or using a model in *Second Life* to work out how to redesign your office-supply storage system.

Instead, think about what image you'd like to impress on visitors, what function the space is to serve for avatars, and how your virtual presence can best represent your organization's purpose. If you own a company that charters steamboat excursions, you could have a region with a river through it plied by a working steamboat, and have your meetings aboard it. A company that sells hats can have an office shaped like one, or you could re-create the exterior of your campus administration building but have the interior contain a scene from a book your class is studying. Or, as the British Council has done, you can have buildings that look similar to your real-world location as part of a much more diverse build (Figure 10.4).

Of course, your company's branding may be carried through to the virtual world. You can go beyond decorating in your brand's colors or putting up a sign with your logo on it, all the way to having a building that's shaped like your company's logo (as you saw in Chapter 5).

If your location is interesting enough or done especially well, a lot of Residents might visit to see your build, and you might find that the *SL* press takes an interest. Of course, a few press releases here and there can help with that.

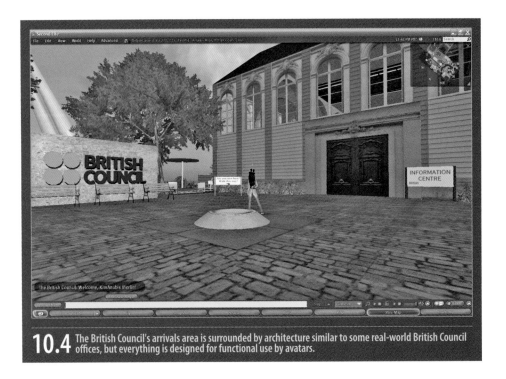

10.4 The British Council's arrivals area is surrounded by architecture similar to some real-world British Council offices, but everything is designed for functional use by avatars.

WHAT TO INCLUDE

Once you know what sort of land you need to accommodate your office and you've considered what sort of look you'd like your office space to have, it's time to plan what you want to include there. Although you can—and many do—conduct meetings using little more than a plot of land and a few chairs purchased from an in-world office-furniture shop (Figure 10.5), if you'd like to create a presence that looks more substantial and settled, as well as one that is useful for more functions, you'll probably want to create areas with different purposes.

ARRIVALS AREA

In the previous chapter you learned about the ability to set a specific landing point on your parcel. One great reason to do this is to route visitors to a dedicated arrivals area so they don't appear in the middle of your conference table with their foot in your teacup. Furthermore, if you have the space, you can set this up at a distance from the most rendering-intensive parts of your build so that visitors don't have to load everything at once.

The actual landing point is frequently indicated in some way, partly for purposes of immersion but also to keep avatars from standing where someone is likely to appear at any moment. There's a basic Telehub available in your Inventory, or you can use something a bit more novel. At my company's island, for example, visitors arrive in a fairy ring of icy mushrooms, whereas at the British Council Isles you'll find yourself arriving at a more traditional Telehub (Figure 10.4).

10.5 Many Resident-owned shops offer prefab furnishings appropriate for an office.

This arrivals area is analogous to the lobby of a real-life office, and it's likely to contain things such as the following:

Greeter. This is a scripted gadget that welcomes visitors, often by name. In Chapter 15, "Locate Resources," you'll learn more about this useful tool, along with others mentioned here.

Visitor counter. This lets you know how many visitors you've had, and may give you information about them, as well.

Notecard giver or information kiosk. A notecard giver offers a notecard to those who click on it. An information kiosk does the same, along with added functions. Some more-elaborate greeters may also do this.

Some other things you might find useful at your arrivals area include a suggestion box and an online indicator (the latter lights up or changes color or shows different text to indicate its owner's online status. Some of these are scripted so that a visitor can click it to send an instant message, essentially paging you if you're online). If your office will be staffed all or part of the time, you might want to include a reception desk.

FORMAL SEATING

If your office is small, you can place a couple of chairs near the landing point and call it good enough. However, when possible it's nice to have a meeting space that isn't right next to the landing point, so that everyone who shows up won't interrupt or "overhear" text chat. For tips on how to keep a voice chat private, see the "Privacy and Security" section at the end of the chapter.

Seating is the main thing your meeting space needs, and you can build it in-house, buy it from an in-world merchant, or have it custom-built to suit your needs and to match the look of your location. Don't "cheap out" on your chairs. Unscripted chairs can be difficult to sit on, especially for those new to *Second Life*. It's embarrassing and disruptive to have to try repeatedly to seat your avatar—not an experience you want to offer to your colleagues, clients, or students (let alone Residents who will take note and tell others about it).

Sit-scripted seats are easy to use and may contain custom poses. Unfortunately, for some reason many offices contain seats with poses inappropriate for business use. It's bad enough trying to sit on an unscripted chair; imagine sitting in one that is scripted so that everyone has a view right up your avatar's skirt! Don't purchase any chairs for your office without trying the animation first, and keep in mind that avatars of different sizes will fit differently in the chairs. Avoid animated poses that are very active. It can really ruin the tone of the meeting if avatars are stretching, yawning, and checking their fingernails. It makes people feel uncomfortable when their avatars look uncomfortable.

My solution is scripted chairs that do not contain poses, which means they will not conflict with the animation-override sit poses used by many avatars. My office chairs are scripted to offer or automatically change sit offsets to adjust for avatars of different sizes, so no one has to hover in the air over their seat or have their feet stuck in the floor.

Placing seats in a circle, while nice in real life, is less pleasant in *Second Life* because it takes more effort to look around, and you can't do it while typing. A half-circle is usually a better choice, allowing you to adjust your camera view and to see everyone at once. This is much better for newbies, in particular, who may not yet be adept at adjusting their view.

CASUAL SEATING

Sometimes it's useful to chat with someone outside of the confines of the office, both in real life and on the Grid. Although there are places like restaurants and cafes in-world, they're usually not ideal locations for a business lunch or student conference. So it can be a good idea to have some casual seating at your office (Figure 10.6).

TIP

If you expect to have a large staff or a lot of activity going on in-world, be sure to provide enough seating so that more than one group can converse without their chat overlapping in a distracting way. However, you might not need two complete meeting spaces. Some casual seating here and there might do the trick.

10.6 This casual seating area at Robin Wood's (*SL* avatar Robin Sojourner's) office is a nice place to chat.

For your casual seating area, you might add a room to your building with comfy upholstered chairs by a fire-place, or maybe you'd rather sit on a bench outside next to a working fountain, or on a log in the birdsong-filled woods, or on a rock by a shore while watching scripted crashing waves. If your casual seating area is especially nice or unique and your office is open to the public, don't be surprised if you find Residents hanging out there!

 TOYS FOR VISITORS

I like to see people hanging around the areas I create on the Grid. Not only is it nice to see someone appreciating my work, but it also ensures that your space will never feel like a wasteland. It's good for your Traffic score, too, and perhaps you'd like to market products to or offer classes to some of the Residents who drop by.

At my company's region, Abracadabra, along with casual seating, I offer things like scripted snowballs for throwing and working snowboards, and there are vendors that sell ice skates. Abracadabra is rarely empty for long. All of the visitors will see any posters, information kiosks, or event invitations I have placed in the arrivals area, too!

DISPLAY AREA

If your office is open to the public or you intend to use it for demonstrations or as a virtual showroom, you might want a dedicated space for setting up models, information kiosks, vendors, or freebie boxes, if you haven't placed them in the arrivals area.

EVENT SPACE

For most meetings, your regular meeting space will do. However, if you intend to put on large events, you need a larger space (Figure 10.7). In Chapter 12 we'll take a close look at what you should include in your event space, as well as how to run events, meetings, and classes in it.

10.7 The University of Queensland's event area looks like the ruins of an ancient stone circle.

SANDBOX

At one time or another you will probably want to try to build or script something yourself, or perhaps someone on your staff will. Even if you never want to build anything, you'll need to rez objects like clothing boxes and event invitations. It can be very nice to have a sandbox area where things can be rezzed without cluttering up your meeting area or making your arrivals area look like a junkyard!

You may limit the ability to build things in the sandbox area so that only members of your group can use it, or you can have it open to the public. In fact, a large, well-administered sandbox with a lengthy Autoreturn period can be a real draw if you would like Residents to stop by—that is, if you are willing to deal with the occasional complication. In the "Privacy and Security" section later in this chapter, I'll talk about how to manage what goes on in this space.

A sandbox may be as simple as an empty patch of ground or even a skybox, or it might include things like a building platform with a grid that's used as a guide in placing and measuring prims, posted rules for using the space, free content-creation assets (such as textures), or even content-creation tutorials.

LANDSCAPE

People new to the Grid tend to choose similar landscaping: either a tropical beach look, complete with palm trees, or an environment where nearly everything is paved, with a few manicured flat lawns and trees and flowers in planters, sort of like an office park or corporate campus. The latter look is often favored by real-life organizations in-world and is the subject of jokes. Why not try something different, like a magical winter land (Figure 10.8)?

Whatever type of landscape you choose, it's important to choose something. Even if your landing point and everything in your office happens indoors, you probably still have windows! And if there are outdoor areas, they're going to look barren and unwelcoming without a few trees and plants. As mentioned before, you can eschew a building and work with the landscape instead. This does take careful planning and skill with terraforming and other *Second Life* content-creation tools, however.

Keep in mind that, while avatars can fly, many prefer to walk, so keep your terrain walkable. Whenever possible, keep the distances short, so they can be walked in a reasonable length of time. Also, you don't want visitors getting lost between the landing point and the event area. Consider putting up signs or teleporters, or laying down paths to lead the way. Some organizations go so far as to have their Solution Provider create scripted transportation, such as the Carnaby Taxi (Figure 10.9) and Loch Ness Monster rides my company created for the British Council. Each of these rides announces important locations as it passes them.

For more information about designing functional spaces and landscapes, check out my previous book, *Creating Your World: The Official Guide to Advanced Content Creation for Second Life* (Wiley, 2007).

10.8 The landscaping around The Magicians Colonnade always draws appreciative comments from clients arriving for meetings.

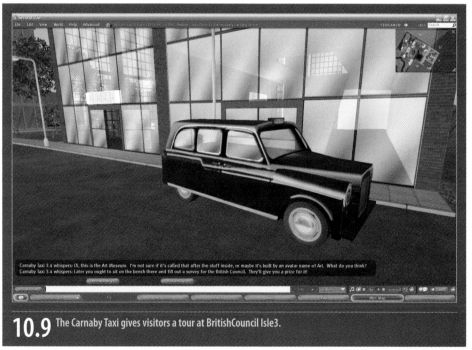

10.9 The Carnaby Taxi gives visitors a tour at BritishCouncil Isle3.

There are many other tools you might find useful for your office. Here are a few:

Handshake attachment. Wear one of these scripted gadgets to greet your visitors the same way you would offline.

Bot or artificial avatar. These scripted stand-ins, made of prims and driven by scripts, can welcome visitors or answer questions (Figure 10.10).

10.10 The British Council's Information Centre includes an artificial avatar, an answering machine, a map, and many other useful tools.

Landmark giver. This makes it easy for visitors to find your office again.

Video synching device. Use one of these to make sure everyone watching a video stream is synched up and viewing the same part of it.

Opt-in logger. Use this to log only the chat of those participating in the meeting, and to get permission to publish the log, too.

Chat queue system. If there are many people at a meeting, class, or event, it can be hard to keep track of whose turn it is to speak next, but this gadget provides a solution.

Art. Consider including some interesting or attractive artworks to make your space more inviting. You can purchase all sorts of artwork from Residents or have something created for you by a Solution Provider.

The following tools are especially useful for meeting spaces:

Announcer. This scripted gadget lets you know when someone has just arrived or is in text-chat range so you know if you're being overheard.

Slide screen. One of the slides can be the parcel media texture (the texture that is replaced with your media stream), allowing you to use the same screen for both purposes.

Whiteboard. I haven't found one that works spectacularly well yet, but with new advances in the Linden Scripting Language, whiteboards are likely to be greatly improved by press time.

Web browser. Like whiteboards, these are primitive right now, but on the horizon is a new shared web-browsing feature from Linden Lab.

Notecard giver or distro box. Rather than distributing your meeting agenda or other materials to meeting attendees, you can load them into one of these, and everyone can receive the handout with a click of their mouse upon arrival.

Refreshments. It's a nice touch to offer a scripted cup of coffee or other animated treat.

You'll learn more about these gadgets and others in Chapter 15.

SET OFFICE HOURS

More and more organizations have regular office hours on the Grid so it's easy for someone to tell when you will be available. What time will work best for you depends on who you expect to show up and what time zone they're in. Time zones, in fact, are one of the greatest challenges of those holding lots of remote meetings and conducting business on the Grid. One of my favorite—and free—online tools helps to face this challenge: **www.timeanddate.com/**. It's helpful for calculating ideal meeting times, and you can even save a list of cities that you look up often.

Here's how office hours usually work: Once you select your time, which would usually be at the same time every week (or day or month), you need to make sure others know about it. Include it in your avatar's profile, along with any real-world contact info you've put there. It's also good to include it in your office's parcel description, and sometimes it's a good idea to put up a sign or to include it in any informational notecards you might distribute. If you issue any press releases to announce your new office on the Grid, be sure to mention your office hours. And, of course, you can include your hours on the official *Second Life* events calendar.

At the appointed time, be online, in your office, and ready to receive visitors. Anyone could turn up—colleagues, competitors, Linden Lab staff, someone you met at an in-world event, or *Second Life* Residents interested in learning about what you're up to. It's usually a good idea to have at least a few seats available. Fortunately, it's inexpensive to purchase a few extra chairs that you can rez if you need them. If you built your own furniture in-house or had a developer create furniture for you, you can probably make as many copies of your chairs as you like, provided your land can support the additional prims.

Usually office hours are simply a time when you're available for walk-in discussion. Don't expect everyone to show up on time; this is an informal event. Some organizations like to keep their office staffed during business hours in their area. Others are staffed around the clock. If it's within your budget, 24/7 staffing can be a good idea. If there's often no one at your office and it's open to the public, you may catch some flak from Residents who equate a low Traffic score with a company that's not doing well, and who might feel that your place is their personal playground if no one's around.

One alternative, of course, is to restrict access to the area when no one is around to greet visitors, or to provide resources visitors can explore themselves. Some organizations use bots or scripted artificial avatars. Although these can add a lot of value, their ability to answer questions is limited, and of course they're not as engaging as a regular avatar.

Some businesses have hired Residents to do things like greet people for what's considered a reasonable in-world wage. This might work for you, but I can't advise you regarding the legal ramifications. Government authorities have already stepped in to question employment of Residents by a Solution Provider, despite the fact that they were paying the equivalent of more than the real-world minimum wage. The Residents were said to be required to work at specific scheduled times, so that they were allegedly being treated like employees rather than contractors. This is an area your legal department should investigate if you're considering it.

PRIVACY AND SECURITY

If you're using the Grid for meetings, you might want to keep your discussions private. And of course you won't want just anyone to be able to terraform your land or grab a copy of everything you own, and if the place is open to the public you might not want to have to police the place all by yourself.

CREATING A PRIVATE, SECURE SPACE

If you want to make sure that no one outside your organization hears your chat or sees what's going on in your space, there are two possible approaches:

▶ Use the upcoming offering, when it becomes available—a stand-alone minigrid solution, even behind your own firewall.

▶ Use a private region on the Grid with no adjacent regions that are open to the public. This is a good option if you don't need the security of the previous option or if your project or budget doesn't warrant it. I recommend the following measures if you elect to use a private region and keep it truly private.

   ▶ Disallow public access. Go to World ▶ Region Estate ▶ Estate ▶ Allow Public access and uncheck the box.

   ▶ List individuals or groups you'd like to allow to visit the region. No one else will be able to enter.

LINDENS ARE EVERYWHERE

Even if you disallow public access, Linden Lab staff will have access. Sometimes they need to stop in and check region performance, for example. The one exception would be if you opt for the stand-alone solution to your privacy needs.

The following are some additional settings you might consider:

▶ Disable terraforming at the Region/Estate level so that no one accidentally digs a pit or otherwise disrupts the terrain.

▶ Set permissions on objects that are given to avatars by unchecking Copy or Transfer, and consider unchecking Modify to keep people from getting at your scripts.

OPENING YOUR SPACE TO THE PUBLIC

Most organizations keep their land open to the public or put it to mixed use. There are many ways to manage permissions and settings, and they vary depending on exactly what you're up to. However, here are some guidelines.

First, if you have enough space, consider subdividing your land into more than one parcel.

▶ Create a small parcel for the arrivals area. On this parcel, you'll want to set your landing point and any Telehub.

▶ Stand on any other parcels and go to About Land ▶ Options ▶ Teleport Routing and select Blocked for each. Now everyone who teleports to your office will arrive at the arrivals area, and nowhere else. Only the land owner will be able to teleport anywhere at will. Furthermore, if someone logs off elsewhere, they will still reappear at the arrivals area—not in the middle of your meeting room.

▶ Selecting Blocked as in the previous bullet does pose the problem of teleporting people directly to you, which you might want to do from time to time. Just pop open About Land, enable teleporting on the parcel where you are, teleport your visitor, and then disable teleporting once more.

With these settings and a meeting space some distance from the landing point and any adjacent spaces open to the public, you can maintain some privacy. In fact, at my company's own island, Abracadabra, I use an announcer that lets me know when someone gets within range so that they might overhear my conversation. Here are some other options:

▶ Put your private meeting space on a parcel with restricted access using About Land.

▶ Put your "top secret" meeting space in a skybox (Figure 10.11), and use a scripted object to warn visitors away—and then keep them away. For this, I have a virtual pet dog that can fly (of course!) that barks and growls before resorting to a "deadly" bite that sends intruders straight to their home point.

10.11 This skybox office is up high enough so that no one on the ground will overhear meetings.

VOICE CARRIES

Keep in mind that text chat can be read from 20 meters away, and that voice chat can be heard from as far as 110 meters. And if people can rez objects and run scripts on your land, they can leave scripted objects that will repeat your text chat to them! Such objects are very rare, though, and won't pick up IMs or voice—and you can stop them by returning objects that belong to people you don't know.

It can take a bit of consideration to figure out what other restrictions to put on the land that hosts your office, and no one setup is the right fit for every organization and every office. However, here are a few considerations.

> If you want visitors to be able to use scripted items that you give to them (such as animated coffee cups), you have to allow their scripts to run. Even if you aren't giving away scripted items, some people don't like to visit places where their scripts don't run. For example, it can be uncomfortable if your Furry avatar's eyes are unable to open because scripts won't run!

> If you do allow visitors to run scripts, you're more likely to run into trouble with griefers. Unless you have something special going on that might be disrupted, or your organization is particularly likely to be a target, try leaving scripts on and see what happens. You can always restrict scripts to group members later.

> Turning off object creation (rezzing) not only helps to keep down griefing, but also stops most littering. However, if visitors are buying things that come in a box, you need to let them rez it!

> You can restrict object entry, as well, to control griefing attacks from the neighboring parcel or region, but it can hinder some fun, like snowball-throwing.

> You can shut off "push," but doing so can stop certain scripted objects from working. Try it out and see.

> You probably won't want your office to be damage-enabled!

> You'll probably want to restrict what visitors can do with items you give away or sell to them. I'll talk more about this in the next chapter.

WARNING

Associate parcels with a group and turn on Autoreturn to automatically clean up any litter left by visitors. But before you do it, be very sure that all items you want to stay on your land are owned by the landowner or set to the group associated with the land, or they will be returned (including your building or displays)!

Take my own region as an example. I have an arrivals area on its own parcel, as I've already described (Figure 10.12). Residents were showing up and finding out that I had object rezzing turned on, and those without land of their own would pop in to rez boxes they wanted to unpack, invitations they wanted to read, etc. and weren't always good about cleaning them up. I didn't want the first thing people saw at my region to be a pile of litter. So I have Autoreturn set here to one minute.

Why is object creation still turned on? I give away snowballs, snowboards, and other items at the arrivals area. If visitors can't rez them there, they might well not think of trying another place on my island, and just leave.

The rest of my region has a one-hour Autoreturn. It's a giant sandbox (or, in the case of my snowy island, a giant icebox). This is long enough for visitors to have a good time, but keeps down litter. It doesn't control griefing, though. Object creation, object entry, and scripting are all on (though terraforming is off!). Obviously, I don't have a lot of griefers at my region . . . at least, I haven't until now!

However, I also have help. The parcels on my region are all set to my group, The Magicians, and some group members have group roles that allow them to manage objects that are not set to the group. Also, I have a couple of estate managers who are able to deal with anything that comes up, even when I'm not around.

Sometimes I do set more restrictive permissions in my region, especially when I'm hosting a large event. You'll learn more about that in Chapter 12.

10.12 The arrivals area at Abracadabra is on its own parcel, which you can see outlined by an aqua property line. The litter of boxes will be autoreturned within one minute, leaving behind the fairy ring of mushrooms, logo sign, freebies and info kiosk, vendors, and Greeter's Sty.

SECOND LIFE ISN'T ALL THINGS TO ALL PEOPLE

Currently, *Second Life* does not offer full integration with common office software such as Microsoft Word and PowerPoint; it's not great for sharing documents—yet. However, some scripted solutions provide work-arounds, such as Immersive Work Spaces (more about that in Chapter 15).

You can manually load a slide at a time into your slide screen or show a video, or (in the near future) scroll through a website with others in-world. But the Grid isn't the right tool for every task. Despite this, some people seem to feel *SL* must do everything. They'll attempt to conduct all correspondence via offline IM instead of email, share documents on notecards, refuse to use the telephone, and insist on paying their Solution Provider in Linden dollars. Sometimes this is because they're new to the Grid and they think this is what they're supposed to do, but other times it's because they're more immersed in *SL* than is good for conducting business.

The Grid offers a lot of tools perfect for what you're trying to do, but don't hesitate to just email someone a document! Make the Grid a part of your toolbox, but don't expect it to replace everything.

MARKET AND SELL
YOUR PRODUCT

How is marketing in *Second Life* different from doing it in the real world or on the Web? What *Second Life* advertising and marketing channels are available? What's involved in bringing people in-world for your marketing experience? Can you have your own stand-alone community? How do real-world marketing tactics apply on the Grid? What can go wrong, and what works best? Can you really sell things in-world, and how? Is there any money in it? This chapter will answer these questions and more.

THE EVOLUTION OF IN-WORLD MARKETING

Early marketing projects on the *Second Life* Grid were hardly appealing to actual Residents of the virtual world. They focused on things like re-creations of real-world locations that would look good and be easy to explain in reports to upper management who might be unfamiliar with virtual worlds. Most importantly, these sorts of builds looked good in press releases, and getting real-world press was the goal of these pioneer marketing projects. After all, while it was unclear what sort of return on investment might be expected when marketing to avatars, the potential for getting lots of press was obvious. These projects attracted some Residents, who came out of curiosity or even to protest and grief these corporate incursions.

Back then, *Second Life* Residents tended to be resistant to commercial projects on the Grid. Many were offended by builds that they felt had little to do with them and everything to do with looking good in a screenshot that would appear on some corporate website with a headline about how they were the first to do whatever it was they were doing on the Grid. This habit of corporations claiming they were the first of their type or in their industry on the Grid has become a joke among Residents. Generally, some Residents' perception that they are being "used" in projects of this sort is congruent with similar attitudes about being studied like guinea pigs by educational researchers. That being said, educational uses of the Grid were often praised and even held up as examples of positive, real uses of the Grid by Residents who were getting flak about the "game" and "spending real money on imaginary chairs."

Later marketing projects—the good ones, at least—focused on *Second Life* Residents rather than external media. One criticism of this is that the in-world population is relatively small. However, that's a misconception. Philadelphia, Barcelona, and Johannesburg are each about the size of the 60-day active population in *Second Life*. Plus, *Second Life* Residents spend an increasing amount of time in-world. They tend to be heavily invested in the platform (sometimes financially) and therefore a good marketing project can make a deep impression.

Few projects involve selling merchandise directly to Residents, and these days most focus on building Resident relationships with brands. It's a good example of long-tail thinking. There are exceptions, of course, such as Wiley offering *Second Life*–specific books for sale along with those of interest to content creators (books about things like Photoshop and 3D modeling), or manufacturers of computer software or equipment building islands to showcase products Residents might use for *Second Life* content creation (Adobe and Dell have used this approach). Also of note are the ongoing and reportedly successful uses of the Grid to market employment and educational opportunities to Residents, including college fairs, job fairs, and even involvement in *Second Life* by agencies like Kelly Services and Manpower. And institutions such as Virtual Texas State University, which offers for-credit in-world courses, have to market their services, too!

HOW MARKETING IN *SL* IS DIFFERENT

Most corporate marketing managers that approach me about projects on the Grid have a very shallow idea of what it is. In fact, almost none of them had ever logged in to *Second Life* before contacting me, so they have tended to present plans that resemble either a 2D website or a real-world store. Many still think the best approach is to create an exact duplicate of their real-world shop or products.

Marketing projects that look like 2D websites are worse than pointless on the Grid. These tend to be "rows of tombstones"—kiosks with pictures that may be clicked to open external web pages or to receive a notecard of information. It's not just an unambitious approach; it's an embarrassing one because countless Residents running shops just for fun do a better job, often with no budget or experience, and a corporation that presumably has more resources is expected to do at least as well. If you want a 2D website, that's what you should have. Creating something in *Second Life* that doesn't do anything differently from your website is like buying a horse to pull your car.

The other common approach, creating a shop that looks just like your real shop, full of things that are intended to look like your real product, will perhaps look good to superiors who don't know anything about the Grid, and will yield understandable screenshots for press releases. But they won't impress Residents, no matter how good they look. Aside from problems of scale (things built to real-life scale aren't going to work well without adjustment for typical avatar sizes and camera angles), Residents will find it boring. In a world where you can go to an elven land or be a dinosaur in a jungle or visit a futuristic spaceship or another planet, most people aren't going to beat a path to your shop to see something that looks just like the local real-world mall. If they want to go to a mall, they'll go to one run by a Resident and purchase products for their avatar. In fact, your company is likely to be mocked for a lack of imagination and for not offering something that is really of interest to Residents.

An added complication of building examples of your product in-world is that it may be difficult to represent your product—particularly its functionality—with complete accuracy. This can give an incorrect impression of your product. Be certain that your product can be re-created accurately if you are considering this approach, and think through whether it would offer value to Residents in-world.

The best approach is to consider ways to translate your product or corporate image into a metaphor easily understood by Residents. Say you were selling cars. You could set up a space with lots of clickable images of the cars so that Residents will be linked to web pages with further information. Or you could have a Solution Provider create models of the car in a variety of colors and let Residents have free copies to drive. Both of these approaches have been tried, with varying degrees of success, but apparently none of them were profitable enough that they lasted long. What would work better? How about a contest where Residents create concept cars for your line? That'll get them visiting your location (especially if you use it to distribute content-creation tools such as vehicle scripts and textures). Or, instead of simply giving away copies of real-world vehicles, you could build the sky city of the future and offer free copies of the car company's latest jetpacks.

Whatever you develop in-world for marketing purposes, keep in mind that the strengths of the platform are social activity and interactivity. For instance, instead of giving away virtual dog dishes or models of boxes of your company's dog treats, you could hire someone to build a virtual pet dog that Residents would want, along with virtual dog treats that make it do special tricks—say "speak" gets you the Gettysburg Address and "up" commands the dog to fly. Maybe you could start an in-world dog owners' club? No matter what approach you take, it needs to be imaginative and involve interaction. This will get Residents talking about your brand in association with those values. Engagement times in *Second Life* tend to be measured in dozens of minutes; in contrast, web engagements are often a minute or less.

⏌NOTE

From time to time I'm approached by a prospective client who wants to re-create a real-life store, including every piece of merchandise on the shelves. Now that you've read this far you can imagine what sort of system resources that would require! Instead you might want to focus on showcasing a few carefully chosen products, and include a URL-loading kiosk of some sort to allow visitors to go to your website to see the rest of your products. Lag sure isn't a feature you want associated with your product!

ADVERTISING AND MARKETING CHANNELS

A common complaint of those interested in promoting products and events in-world is a lack of advertising channels. In fact there are plenty of them, but the problem is a lack of imagination, and unfamiliarity with the platform and its available tools. Many of the channels are just like real-world ones, including print ads and billboards. Through a combination of *Second Life* features, Resident or Solution Provider tools, and a knowledge of how information spreads in the *Second Life* world, you can get the word out very well.

SEARCH

Search is a vital feature for advertising in-world. You learned a bit about this feature in Chapter 9, "Manage Your Infrastructure." Residents will find you in Search in a variety of ways:

▶ The About Land parcel description when searching Places

▶ Classified ads you place

- ▶ Event listings

- ▶ Favorites in your profile or in others' profiles

- ▶ Group listings, if you set up a group related to your project

- ▶ Items set for sale and marked to show in Search

IN-WORLD RENTAL LOCATIONS

Most projects involve an in-world location. This might be a shop or an interesting build to explore, or it might be a place to pick up free content or a location with some sort of interface or rules for entering a contest. Most projects overlook the value of in-world rental locations.

Before I began to develop *Second Life* content for clients, I had a shop in-world on my own land where I sold products to other Residents. I also rented over 20 additional locations! Why, in a world where you can go to a shop in the blink of an eye via teleportation, did I need so many locations? Advertising!

I rented many small shop locations in malls, and even a tiny 15-prim kiosk in Linden Lab's Luna Oaks Galleria (Figure 11.1). In each of those locations I displayed a few of my more eye-catching products—and not in vendors, either. They were there, where anyone could walk around them or interact with them. And alongside them in each location I had a sign with my logo and a landmark-giving device. These drove a lot of traffic to my main shop! Surprisingly, although I have done this sort of thing for a client or two, I rarely see other enterprise projects that do anything of this sort—they usually stick to just their own islands. This is a lot like using search ads or banner ads on related websites to attract attention and bring people to your main site.

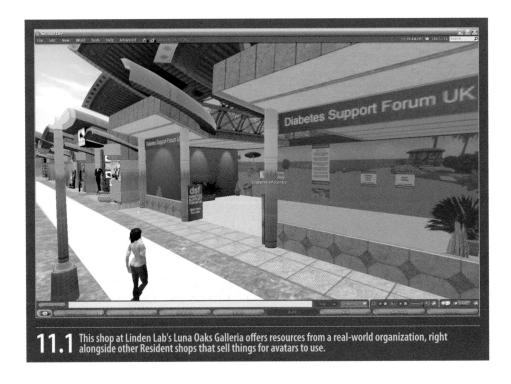

11.1 This shop at Linden Lab's Luna Oaks Galleria offers resources from a real-world organization, right alongside other Resident shops that sell things for avatars to use.

You can also rent billboards and signs in-world, or hire an ad network to display your ad for you in locations across the Grid. However, it's important to be very choosy. Most Residents are not happy to find a billboard or a stack of ad signs impinging on their view, and you don't want that dissatisfaction to reflect on you. Plus, there is the risk that you will accidentally hire a notorious "ad farmer." An effective option that won't upset Residents is to rent signs within a build (such as a mall) where it doesn't hurt the view for the neighbors.

You can find locations in-world that are appropriate for advertising. For example, many publishers and authors rent booths at the annual *Second Life* Book Fair, and all sorts of educational institutions participate in events such as in-world college fairs. Some large annual Linden Lab events provide opportunities, as well, such as Burning Life or the Winterfest, where you can develop (or have a Solution Provider develop) something fun or interesting that has your logo all over it.

EVENTS

You just read about renting booths at in-world events. Hosting your own events is also a great way to promote your offering. (In the next chapter you'll learn about what it takes to develop and run a successful event on the *Second Life* Grid.) Many more Residents than can attend will see any advertising you do to publicize the event, and the avatars who attend your event will tell their friends about it. In other words, for marketing purposes it's not just the event itself that gets the job done (though quality execution is still vital!). It's what people are reading and saying about it that matters—the buzz you create using the other tools and tactics in this chapter.

You don't need to have your own event venue; you can rent a venue or use one owned by your Solution Provider. In fact, you don't even have to host your own event; you can sponsor someone else's and have your logo large and bright behind the speakers onstage. You can watch for popular events that might appeal to your target market and then approach the person running it to offer sponsorship for one or a series of them. Or you could ask your Solution Provider for suggestions.

In addition, you might have the opportunity to speak at someone else's event. There are many in-world conferences and conventions these days, and someone needs to speak at them! There are even in-world game shows that require participants, and some of them are broadcast live or made into podcasts.

Finally, you might consider sponsoring, participating in, or purchasing advertising in the program of real-world *Second Life*–related events such as the *Second Life* Community Convention, which is held at a different real-world location each year (see **http://www.slconvention.org/**).

BUILDS

Most marketing projects on the Grid involve a build of some sort, most often an entire region. And this is where you can learn a thing or two from established *SL* Residents.

While some Residents are trying to make a profit, many simply want to support their build by earning enough L$ to cover tier. It's traditional for cool Resident builds, even many that aren't primarily commercial in nature, to be supported by their own shop, other shops (a mall), or residential rentals. Some Residents who need to raise funds to support their builds sell copies of parts of the build itself, which are simply marked for sale right where they stand. For example, they might have a great forest built to facilitate the roleplaying game they enjoy as a hobby, with some of the trees or wildlife marked for sale so that you can purchase a copy and take home a part of this build you like, and thus contribute to covering tier and other expenses that maintain the build.

This approach can work for you, too, even if you're a newcomer to the Grid and don't yet think of yourself as a Resident or are concerned that Residents might see you as an outsider. Think about developing a cool location that happens to have a display of merchandise and your logo on it, or even sponsoring or renting a shop at a Resident's popular build. After all, a build that Residents want to visit is still cool, regardless of whose products support it and whose products it supports.

The important thing here is that the build *does* have to be cool. It's got to be fun or interesting or it has to offer something else that Residents want. One good example is artist AM Radio's The Far Away, a popular art installation where you can purchase copies of parts of the build, such as the train in Figure 11.2. See the sidebar "What's Cool" here and the section "What Works Best" later in the chapter for more about what to include in your build.

11.2 AM Radio, creator of The Far Away, sells copies of parts of the build, such as this old train. Proceeds go to Heifer International.

Just as you can sponsor events, you can sponsor cool builds. To get value out of a sponsorship you need only to include your logo, maybe with some URL-loading signs or a small Infokiosk, and to send around a few press releases or arrange for some branded print ads.

A good example of this is the International Spaceflight Museum (Figure 11.3), which has a number of sponsors. The museum even auctions sponsorship of individual rocket displays—using eBay! Just as in real life, product placement works!

11.3 The International Spaceflight Museum is supported in part by sponsors, some of whom are shown in this screenshot.

One critic accused me of overusing the word *cool* in describing effective *Second Life* content. But the word captures the meaning perfectly. *Cool* sums up fun, interesting, creative, innovative, and a sense of wonder. Here are some examples of build components that would have this cool factor:

▶ Elaborate working machinery, especially if it does something functional and can be interacted with by avatars

▶ Beautiful immersive environments, especially those suited to roleplay and exploration

▶ Rides

▶ Games

▶ Quests

▶ Puzzles

▶ Artworks

▶ Surprises

▶ Interactivity

▶ Functional tools and gadgets for avatars

A cool, branded landscape with interesting things to explore or play with, which simply affords Residents a nice place to hang out or roleplay, might well get better results than a store full of information about your products.

PRINT

Print advertising is a staple of any marketing project, be it in the real world or the virtual world. However, it requires some familiarity with the *Second Life* community to discover appropriate publications and to compose advertising that will really engage Residents.

In-world publications. The quality of these varies widely and circulation figures aren't clear. These publications are usually in the form of a magazine or book that you can take from a newsstand or other kiosk. Some are made to wear as a HUD attachment, and others you would simply rez in-world. Often using various virtual "printing press" tools or services, publications may include features such as pages that turn, and embedded URL loaders. (Some newsstands simply open a web-based publication in your external browser.) Still other publications are simply text on a notecard, sometimes with embedded images. You can purchase advertising in in-world publications, or why not create one of your own?

Web-based publications. Publications outside of the *Second Life* Grid appear on many websites and in a wide range of formats, including PDF newspapers and magazines. Some of these are professional-quality, plus there are countless amateur publications. Ad rates and offerings vary quite a bit, including display ads, classifieds, and banner ads on sites. Some publications have different pricing structures for *SL*-only businesses and for real-world organizations that have an *SL* presence. Most will also accept and make good use of press releases. You can find a list of some publications in Chapter 8, "Keep Up with Current Events." Some of these may occasionally produce a hard-copy edition for a specific occasion, traditionally in conjunction with (and for distribution at) the annual *Second Life* Community Convention.

 MARKETING *SECOND LIFE* PROJECTS OUTSIDE OF *SL*

Second Life is a fantastic tool, but it's not the only one that should be a part of your marketing campaign. Be sure to integrate your *Second Life*–specific plans with real-world marketing. For example, a website that offers coupons or a promo code can be mentioned in your press releases, print ads, and notecards, or opened by an object in-world.

Additionally, tie your *Second Life* project with whatever you're doing in the real world. Mention your build, include a SLURL, and post some screenshots and even a referral link so that you can send people in-world to see what you have to offer.

Forums, blogs, and LISTSERVs. All sorts of forums, blogs, and LISTSERVs surround *Second Life*, including the official ones maintained by Linden Lab, which you learned about in Chapter 8. Those that are moderated will make use of press releases, and some also accept paid advertising. However, what works best of all for this sort of thing is participation by a member of your organization or your Solution Provider. You wouldn't want your first forum post ever to be an ad for your company . If you're going to promote your project or product by posting on forums or LISTSERVs, you or your (hopefully well-established) Solution Provider should be a part of the community first.

BROADCAST

There are lots and lots of Resident-run radio stations and television stations in-world. You can buy advertising on these, sponsor entire shows, or produce a show of your own. Many of these shows are recorded for later rebroadcast. You can learn more about them in Chapter 8 and at **http://wiki.secondlife.com/wiki/Second_Life_Radio_%26_TV**.

CONTESTS

One great way to involve *Second Life* Residents is to have a contest. In Coca-Cola's Virtual Thirst competition, for instance, Residents were asked to design and build in-world the ultimate vending machine for the product. Some companies, following the lead of Resident merchants, have prize drawings, building and scripting competitions, machinima and screenshot competitions (like the one in which Residents were able to pick up an official and free *Iron Man* avatar and use it to create screenshots).

Another approach, which has succeeded for Resident merchants but hasn't been explored much by enterprises, is to sponsor established Resident games (like Devil May Care and Pizza), giveaways (such as Sploders, objects that give small amounts of money to random Residents who are present), and trivia competitions.

Another established Resident tradition is the Show and Tell event, where Residents bring things they have created to demonstrate. Event attendees vote and prizes—usually a token amount of money—are awarded to the top three entrants. Show and Tell events are always packed. Imagine all those participants and audience members looking at a stage with your logo on it.

 CROWDSOURCING

Crowdsourcing is a popular buzzword these days. It means having a task done by people who respond to a general call. One example might be a contest a company runs looking for designs for a new product, with the winner receiving a prize and all entries being kept by the company. The term might also be stretched to apply to volunteers moderating an online community or building out a region on the Grid.

Residents are particularly savvy and particularly cynical about this sort of thing. Remember that you're going to get what you pay for, one way or another. Don't expect volunteers to build everything and run everything for you for free. Offer them a fair exchange, even if it isn't in cash, and be sure you can follow through on whatever you promise them.

WORD OF MOUTH

Word of mouth is a vital and enduring way of selling any product or making people aware of your project. Many of the approaches discussed already in this chapter will help with word of mouth, and there are other things that can help, as well.

Don't ever underestimate the power of networking in virtual worlds. This is a social network and an online community—networking is what it's all about! It's a good idea to really get around, to attend events and meet people in-world, and to join groups and get involved in community projects. The more people you know, the more people to whom you will be able to send invitations, ask for advice, or get or request referrals. Look for a Solution Provider who has a large network in the community, too!

I don't know how many times I have appeared at in-world events where, in talking about what I do, my clients received some extra buzz. And I don't know how many people I've run into in-world who checked out my profile and followed my Picks to clients' builds. But I know the number isn't small!

Residents talk a lot. Gossip makes the virtual world go around. You want buzz, so whatever sort of marketing project you plan, make sure it's something that gets attention. Rather than, "I read an article that said such-and-so company built a boring shop that looks just like RL," you want people saying, "Wow, we went to so-and-so's build the other night, the one they did for such-and-so company, and it was *so* fun—never saw anything like it before. Here's a landmark. You should check it out!"

> **NOTE**

The *Harry Potter* movie promotion discussed in Chapter 5, "Conduct Business," was a great buzz-generator, and involved just a few Residents in unique uniforms wandering the Grid and giving away freebies.

COMMUNITY

You already know that many products are marketed by development of online communities. You can create your own community in the *Second Life* world by bringing your existing community into it or by becoming involved in an existing *Second Life* subculture.

Community-building for marketing has been approached in a variety of ways. For example Pontiac's Motorati project involved offering free land rentals for other projects that supported "car culture" in *Second Life*. Other examples include various ISPs that have been at the forefront of creating their own worlds-within-a-world, with interesting continents of content and ongoing events and activities aimed at involving Residents in their communities. One great example is Telstra BigPond, which maintains a lot of interesting places to visit and things to do in-world (Figure 11.4).

11.4 Telstra BigPond's regions offer a lot of activities for Residents.

If you decide to take this approach, it's vital that you have someone with experience in online community management, and you'll probably also need moderators who are available to handle any griefing issues.

OTHER CHANNELS

There are plenty more methods to help get the word out. Some of these you would use in conjunction with the things discussed earlier, and others can also be used on their own.

Groups are one great way to keep in contact with your target audience. Resident merchants routinely start "update groups" that will receive notices of new product releases and even free, discounted, or exclusive merchandise. Unfortunately, there's no script function to enable automatically adding someone to a group by, say, clicking on an object in-world. There are workarounds, though! One is a gadget that presents a clickable link that can be used to go to a group's Search listing where Residents can join. The other is a gadget that maintains a mailing list instead of a group. Some of these gadgets work entirely in-world, while others (those with a greater capacity) store data on an external server. Some Residents have set up businesses that will host this mailing-list service for you. Using the system, you can send instant messages or inventory to Residents on the list. This sort of system is popular because it doesn't use up an in-world group (remember, Residents can only be in 25 at a time). However, joining an actual group comes with the benefit of your group title appearing over members' heads, as well as in their profiles.

Other people's groups can be useful, too. For example, you can join a group like the *Second Life* Press Club, which is specifically meant to receive announcements of newsworthy events. And, of course, you can join groups that have members who might be interested in whatever you're promoting, or just to cultivate a larger network. For example, I was involved in the International Spaceflight Museum (ISM) planning committee when I was about to do a large event for a client. As a favor to me (and any members who wanted to attend), the ISM group's leader decided to forward an invitation to my client's event to all of the ISM members—and even rescheduled an ISM meeting to make sure everyone could attend my client's event.

SLURLs are another useful tool, which you can include in chat and IMs in-world or along with clickable ads or even in print advertising or classifieds—anywhere you would normally include a URL.

Notecard givers and other automated distro gadgets serve many purposes in-world, including distribution of landmarks, informational notecards, and freebies. You can have one of these gadgets built into a greeter item that automatically senses visitors and offers them inventory, but these are so common and the things they offer usually so dull that most Residents don't pay them much attention. Your offering might be ignored, so it can be a better idea to let visitors opt in.

Sales representatives can be useful for promoting your product in your in-world shop or showroom. They're rarely available all the time in most shops and are sometimes replaced by bots or artificial avatars made from prims and driven by scripts that allow them to greet visitors and answer questions. In many cases, rather than a sales rep waiting around, you'll find one or more online status indicators or portraits of staff members who are on duty and who'll respond to your click for assistance. In Resident shops, these sometimes are also scripted to accept tips.

Invitations can be useful for more than just events. They usually take the form of a scripted gadget that may or may not look like a greeting card. When clicked, it usually gives a notecard and a landmark. It's a good idea, by the way, to make sure any notecards or landmarks can be copied and transferred so that people can pass them on.

Freebies are even more popular in *Second Life* than they are in the real world. You can give away branded items that will remind Residents of your organization, give an example of what you have to offer, or get Residents to come to your shop to pick them up. You might want to make freebies nontransferrable so you make sure someone has to come by to get their own copy. Or maybe you want to encourage passing them on, by scripting the gadget to do something special when someone gives it to a friend!

Machinima and podcasts can be created from events in-world or streamed in for Residents to enjoy in-world.

Camping chairs, lucky chairs, Mobvend, and money trees are gadgets Resident merchants use to draw additional traffic and shoppers to their location.

BRINGING IN NEW RESIDENTS

If you intend to build a community in-world or to bring in your existing community, there are a few factors to consider.

REGISTRATION API

Using the Registration API, you can create a custom experience for people you'd like to bring into the *Second Life* Grid. For example, you could have a website with information about your in-world offerings, with a custom *Second Life* account sign-up page (even including a custom last name, such as your company's brand name). Then people who sign up using it will appear at your in-world location, with no stops along the way.

Linden Lab expects to add group functionality to the Registration API, which will allow users to set group membership and roles at the time of account creation. However, use will continue to be limited to those who require it for setting access controls, creating custom names, creating accounts for an institution, and for those creating special branded registration. For other uses, consider using SLURLs instead, which incorporate registration if required; take people directly to a location; and don't require coding, testing, and monitoring of use as the Registration API does.

NOT ALL FREEBIES ARE EQUAL

A few years ago, in the early days of real-world organizations doing work in-world, I surprised a client by including with their build a virtual coffee mug with their logo on it, scripted so that an avatar could hold it and animate as if they were drinking from it. My client was so excited! Of course, Residents had been handing out mugs of cocoa or coffee for years by then to promote their own shops. Soon after this, I created a logo T-shirt for another client—something else Residents had done to promote their own businesses and groups.

Back then it was way cool. Now it's been done to death. Unless your coffee mug has a really good particle effect or is remarkably well done, or your T-shirt is especially attractive or funny, no one's going to be too excited about your free marketing asset masquerading as a "gift."

So you need to come up with something a little different, a twist on the usual, or something brand-new. Some companies have been very successful with this approach, giving away things that are both logically associated with their product and are something Residents really want. (For instance, makeup company L'Oreal arranged to give away quality avatar skins with, natch, nice makeup; Aveda Institutes offered hairstyles from a top hair designer, ETD, for a bargain price.) This approach was particularly interesting because the companies didn't set up their own shops. Instead the freebies were offered in very popular, established Resident shop locations.

Keep in mind that many Residents don't have land, and those who do might not have a lot of free prims, so you don't want to give out primmy objects. Avatar clothing and attachments are usually a good bet.

SOME CONSIDERATIONS

If you intend to bring a lot of brand-new Residents into the Grid to visit your build, attend your event, or join your community, keep the following in mind:

▶ Regions have a limited capacity, so if everyone signs up at once you may need more than one location at which they can arrive.

▶ Test your build ahead of time with plenty of new Residents to be sure your features will not be confusing or difficult for your newbies.

- Remember that you can't do any direct marketing or sales in Teen *Second Life*.

- Be sure that your target audience can meet the hardware and bandwidth requirements, and exceed them if you want them to use resource-intensive features.

- You may want to create an orientation experience for your new Residents, who will bypass the normal new-user experience by coming directly to your region.

- Be certain that your build is newbie-friendly and especially easy to navigate and use.

- Try to have someone available to offer help and assistance to your new Residents and to get them involved in your community.

WHAT WORKS AND WHAT DOESN'T

Many things can go wrong with a marketing project, online or off! Here are some more tips for what to do and avoid when marketing on the Grid:

Don't disrespect Resident attitudes toward corporate projects. It's important to understand the resistance some Residents have to corporate projects "invading" their world. Many expect that you are there only to use them, to get their money—and heck, aren't they right about that in most cases? Don't pretend otherwise; if you are going to make like you're a part of the community and that you care about it, do or offer something that demonstrates that. Otherwise your community-pandering press release will bring you nothing but derision.

Remember to check out existing content. You don't want to do something that's been done over and over, and well to boot. Trends come and go in *Second Life*, more quickly than they do in the real world. You might think Residents will be thrilled by the fishing area you set up or the parachuting . . . but only if you don't know that was all the rage recently and everyone's moved on to something else by now! Over and over I encounter people doing real-life work on the Grid who are amazed by something as simple as a quality pair of blue jeans or a logo coffee mug. These things are not going to impress Residents. You—or your trusted Solution Provider—needs to know what's in and what's passé. One of Residents' favorite things about *Second Life* is the creative, unique, and often downright strange things they'll encounter in-world. Unoriginal builds are the subject of derision, but builds that are really cool, fun, or interesting—and unique—will get a lot of attention from Residents. They'll return again and again, bring friends, and blog about it, shoot machinima videos of it, and otherwise appreciate it and spread the word for you. This is one of the most important things to keep in mind. Doing something cool is far more important than doing something slick.

Don't use spam, ad farms, or other *SL*-specific forms of blight. After reading this book, you know not to involve yourself in these things, right? Make sure your Solution Provider knows better, too. Be sure to check that messages and inventory offers targeted at visitors to your build aren't spilling over onto the neighbor's land, and do your best to ensure your build doesn't have a negative impact on the neighborhood. Imagine how you'd feel if you spent weeks or months—or even years—building something and then the view was ruined by an ugly billboard! Do your best to fit in with the neighbors.

Prepare in case of griefing. Anyone can be hit by griefers, and depending on what you're promoting and the nature of your organization, your project could be a likely target. On a related note, if you or your Solution Provider has offended Residents somehow, don't be surprised to find picketers waving signs at your shop, someone shooting visitors, or an attack of self-replicating objects. Builds can be designed to discourage griefing, and the correct parcel permissions can help to control many forms of it (see Chapter 10, "Set Up a Virtual Office," for more on that). It's important that someone is available to respond if a visitor reports a problem. Although many Residents enjoy the story of the real-world media company's interview that was interrupted by griefers because the event moderator either didn't have or didn't know how to use parcel powers, that isn't the sort of thing that reflects well on an organization.

Avoid ineffective builds. Maybe your build isn't bad and the freebies you're giving away are very well made, but they're not especially fun or interesting. This lack of imagination or accurate targeting of your audience attracts attention: the wrong kind. Make sure that whatever you do is original and innovative and cool! And make sure it's cool to Residents, not just to you! Sometimes, for unpredictable reasons, a build that should have really caught on just doesn't, or parts of it don't work out as expected. It's always a good idea to keep some extra money in the budget for revising your project based on early results and feedback. Sometimes even minor changes, such as moving a Telehub or adding a few signs or pathways, can make a difference. It's also important that anything you build in-world be designed specifically to work well in *Second Life*, including attention to conventions of layout and user interface that Residents expect. If you aren't very familiar with these things yourself, you'll need a Solution Provider with applicable experience. Otherwise people will click on your map or signpost trying to get teleported somewhere and end up sitting instead of teleporting!

Make sure your build is well executed. Many *Second Life* Residents create some content, and most have a great appreciation for a good build. They also enjoy studying a build to see what's wrong with it, and they aren't shy about pointing it out. If your build has misaligned prims, a poor design, textures that don't wrap correctly, scripts that spam everyone instead of just talking to the object owner, gadgets with confusing interfaces, expect Residents to discuss it among themselves and to tell their friends about it. And blog about it. And write articles about it. In *Second Life*, everyone's a critic, and they have seen a lot of content. If yours isn't up to snuff, it's going to be mocked mercilessly and possibly publicly. Particularly if you are running a for-profit organization, do not settle for low-quality content, or you'll find out just how much recreational value people can find in mocking it. Everything you put in-world or associate with your project needs to be of the best quality your budget will allow, because Residents are recreational build critics even when they aren't content creators themselves.

Check the reputation of your Solution Provider and others involved with the project. I've already stressed the importance of hiring a Solution Provider with a good reputation. It's also very important to be careful about the reputations of others involved with your organization. All it takes is one person saying something foolish like, "These people need to get a life," where a Resident can read it or hear it, and it's going to be in those blogs, the *SL* media, and on notecards passed from avatar to avatar, with predictably bad results for your project.

 YOUR SOLUTION PROVIDER'S REPUTATION MATTERS

Particularly if you are doing a marketing project in-world, it's very important that you be aware of the reputation of any Solution Provider or content creators you hire.

If you hire a famous content creator, many more people are going to be interested in coming to see your build. A Solution Provider with a wide network can also be very helpful in bringing in more traffic. However, a Solution Provider or content creator with a bad reputation (for spamming, scamming, griefing, shoddy work, mistreating or ripping off content creators they hire, sending out press releases that prove to be false, or just generally being a jerk) can reflect horribly on your project. You don't want your company's image associated with someone who might be reviled in the community!

You can't judge reputation by any means other than talking with community members, reading *SL*-specific press, and getting referrals. Remember that the name of the content creator or project manager from the Solution Provider company will probably appear as creator and maybe as owner of objects in your build and given to visitors. Even if it doesn't (if a special "alt" avatar is used for this, for example) word is likely to get out, and it'll look even worse because of the attempt to hide it.

Check upcoming Grid status. Unexpected Grid downtime, even your region going down for five minutes at the wrong time, can have a negative effect on your project. It can blow your grand opening or a big event, or make your content developers run late. Be sure to keep up-to-date with the planned-downtime schedule at **http://secondlife.com/status/**, allow plenty of time in case of surprises, and have a plan for what to do if the Grid has a bumpy day.

Beware of broken content. Things wear out and break in the real world, and they do in *Second Life*, too, especially when the laws of physics change! From time to time, Linden Lab will change script functions or other features of the Grid, and sometimes things just break. Keep an eye on your build to watch for problems of this sort so that they can be fixed. It won't look good for you if someone clicks on a sign to get a really cool freebie or coupon, only to see a script-error message!

Update outdated content. Newer features and the increasing facility of *Second Life* content creators mean that eventually your content is going to look about as hip as a leisure suit. If your content will be in use for more than a few months, consider refreshing it from time to time to take advantage of improvements in quality and functionality. Residents who haven't visited in a while might come by to see what's new if they hear about your updates.

Sustain interest. Some organizations start off just blazing, with lots and lots of Residents excitedly engaged with their offerings. But, naturally, that interest will fade once the novelty wears off. One of the biggest mistakes organizations make is deciding that when usage declines their project has failed. Time in *Second Life* moves quickly, sort of like "dog years." To sustain interest, you need to offer something new from time to time—a renovated build, new freebies, or events.

Beware of missed publication deadlines. Many *SL*-specific publications are hobbies or labors of love. With other things getting in the way, like jobs and family, these publications come out late from time to time. When running an ad or sending out a press release, keep this in mind and make sure you have plenty of lead time! Submit your copy well ahead of the deadline and consider running your ad before your event rather than the day it's supposed to happen.

Follow through. Some companies announce huge plans for *Second Life* projects, and then those projects never materialize, or they do but without the big cool features people expected. Remember that anything you say in your press release that doesn't actually occur is going to thrown in your virtual face over and over. Also, too many organizations create a build, send out a few press releases, and then leave their empty buildings around to collect dust and stray prims. It looks terrible. However, a location that always has something new to offer, where there's always something going on will bring Residents back again and again.

Don't blame the equipment—or the Residents. Sometimes plans just don't work out, or don't work out *at first*. A few organizations have publicly (and somewhere their chat might be logged) announced that the failings of the Grid or even its Residents were the reason their project bombed. The thing is, other organizations' and Residents' projects do just fine, and they (and their friends, and their friends' friends, and everyone who reads their blog or newspaper or listens to those Residents' podcasts or views their streaming talk shows) are going to know just who to blame for the failure of your project. If your project doesn't work out, fix it or exit with grace.

Offer value. Make sure you're offering something Residents want or need—entertainment, tools, objects, information, or the opportunity to excel. Even if your build isn't huge and elaborate, it can provide a space where people can interact in valuable ways.

Be a Resident yourself. Residents will notice if no one actually from your company is ever in-world. If someone is in-world, though, and they're likeable and engaging and helpful, attending events and doing normal Resident things, that can help immensely. It's beneficial if your Solution Provider gets out into the world, too!

Know *SL* culture. Even small things, like using the correct terminology, make a big difference with Residents. Some organizations, like the American Cancer Society, have woven themselves into the culture of the Grid so successfully that they become a part of Resident identity. When someone hassles them about spending time in "that game," they can bust out statistics about how much money was raised in *Second Life* to fight cancer!

Build community. Except for content developers and people making money in-world, the main reason people stay in *Second Life* is to interact with others, usually within a particular community or circle of friends. So if you want people to stay engaged with your product or to hang around on your land, offer them a community to get involved in, or get your project involved in an existing *Second Life* community. For example, the Library Alliance co-sponsors events with many Resident groups at their own locations.

Include interactivity. Static builds aren't interesting for long. No matter how cool your build is, if Residents can't interact with it in some way, they won't stick around for long. If there are things to poke at, to explore, or to play with, then they're going to hang around—and they'll come back again with friends! Many Residents are always looking for something fun to do, so offer it!

In general, your best examples of how to market to Residents will be at popular Resident builds; visit them to see what works. Don't forget that you can often hire a Solution Provider that employs some of those famous content creators!

SUCCESSFUL VENTURES: TWO EXAMPLES

As I've already emphasized, you should look to existing shops to see what's working. The following are examples of successful builds.

GRENDEL'S CHILDREN AND THE BIRDWORX

For example, visit Grendel's Children and The Birdworx in the Avaria regions. You will arrive in a huge, multilevel shop that sells all sorts of interesting avatars and accessories. And you'll encounter most of the other things discussed in this chapter, too. You'll be greeted automatically upon arrival and a distro will hand you a notecard of rules of conduct for the regions. There are online indicators showing which of the shop's merchants are available to help you or answer questions. There are signs indicating where you can find different types of products, and there are many vendor or sales box displays on the walls. It's a busy shop.

It's busy not just because people are there to shop, but because there's stuff to do there. If you wander around a bit you will find adventure game sets for seeking out and capturing pets (Figure 11.5) or for collecting items from the environment, which can be crafted into useful items. These are very inexpensive, easy to use, and fun. And you have to use them on the Avaria continent. That means people hang around, and the longer they're around, the more opportunities they have to purchase things—plus it drives up the Traffic score.

The shop is in the sky (essentially a giant skybox), and when you jump off one of the balconies you can fly or just let yourself fall to the ground, hundreds of feet below. Here you'll find yourself in a rich, varied landscape with what appear to be different ecosystems—desert, swamp, savannah—all marvelously detailed, beautiful, and interesting to explore. Here's where you use the adventure game sets to capture a cool pet or collect materials for crafting, plus there are always Residents hanging around (many wearing the avatars sold in the shop), exploring, and roleplaying (Figure 11.6).

Wouldn't you like to have a bunch of your customers hanging around your virtual continent and inviting their friends to come play, too? Sure! And this is what is typical of a great *Second Life* build. There's a cool place to visit and hang out, interesting activities, and great things to buy—which many Residents would purchase just to support the build, but are worth purchasing on their own.

This is the approach I take to my clients' builds, as well—an immersive environment full of interactive activities and surprises, and that's good for hanging out or having fun—and of course it displays whatever product is supporting the whole thing.

11.5 Using the inexpensive Compendium Tools, I'm able to catch a pet for my avatar while shopping.

11.6 A Resident wearing a dinosaur avatar purchased in the shop roams the virtual plains of Avaria. Vast open spaces like this are rare and valued by Residents accustomed to clutter.

WILEY

One of my clients—this book's publisher—wanted a build on their small mainland parcel to replace their existing shop, which looked like a real-life bookstore. There wasn't much to do there besides get coffee or click on something to open a website. I replaced it with an "old-growth heshroom forest" (giant hexagonal platforms on stalks, sort of like huge, flat-topped mushrooms) and a massive dome housing information-vending displays that bear more resemblance to the opening crawl from a *Star Wars* movie than to job-opportunity kiosks. I also included freebie distros (including one that worked only for Residents who joined the Wiley group) and a greeter (but not a spammer!). Trees grow up through the build, and a stream runs under it, with "steam bees" flying around and a waterfall-fed pond containing a gear-shaped island with seating. Stepping stones in the pond respond when stepped on, chiming and triggering an answering chime and the release of colorful particle "seeds" from gear-shaped "hexseven" flowers floating on the water (Figure 11.7). Avatars can hop from stepping stone to stepping stone, getting different-colored particle effects.

11.7 Wiley's unique build is located on the mainland, among homes and businesses.

When the build was ready, I sent out press releases, posted on the forums, got the event listed in Search every way possible, and did everything else you'd normally do to announce an event—because we did events along with the build (more about events in the next chapter). Residents came to see the build, and even wrote about it because it was just plain cool. No one had ever built anything like it before. Soon I'll be adding fresh freebies and hiding a few new surprises around the build (plus putting out press releases and otherwise generating renewed buzz, including offering guided tours).

When the build went live, thousands of Residents saw the print ad for the build in *The Metaverse Messenger*, read the articles based on the press releases, got copies of the freebies at the build or from friends, attended the events or received invitations, heard about the build from a friend, heard about the events from someone who won the real-life books or other prizes or pegged a Wiley staff member with a snowball, heard about the stepping stones from someone who was talking about them, and so on. And that is what my client was after . . . the buzz, more than someone clicking one of the Infovendors (which open a website in an external browser where the company's products are for sale) and buying a book right then and there. As a result the buzz isn't, "Hey, this company is trying to peddle us something." It's more like, "Wow, did you see this cool Wiley build?"

 FRANCHISE COOL

All of this "build tons of cool content" stuff is well and good for corporate clients with a big fat budget, you might think to yourself, but what if you're an educator with hardly any funding and you want to provide something fun to do at your place? Fortunately, you can purchase all sorts of fun games and gadgets from Resident shops. In fact, some Residents sell franchises! Examples include Moopf Murray's skate vending machines, which will give you a cut of the sale price, or the 7Seas Fishing system, which you can set up to allow other Residents to purchase fishing gear (from which you get a cut) and use it at your location.

SELLING THINGS IN *SECOND LIFE*

⬐ NOTE

For some sources of market research data, visit **http://wiki.secondlife.com/wiki/Market_Research_Suppliers**.

Most of what I've talked about here is focused on engaging Residents and building their relationship with your brand. However, Residents make about about US$1 million worth of L$ transactions in-world daily. (You can find more information about things like *Second Life* economic statistics at **http://secondlife.com/whatis/economy-data.php**.) Many Residents are able to defray all of their *Second Life* expenses by selling items in-world, and many others pay part or all of their real-life bills with revenue from in-world shopping. Whether selling things in *Second Life* is a good idea for you depends on what you're selling.

SELL OR GIVE AWAY?

Think carefully about your goals before you put a price on anything you set for sale in your shop. What is more important to you: making a few cents selling a virtual item to a Resident, or gaining that Resident's good will and having them use your branded item? Some Residents have a negative attitude toward some companies that set up in-world shops in which they sell virtual copies of their real products. Why? Because Residents could have gotten similar, but better-quality items for lower prices from established, familiar Resident merchants. Do you really want to try to compete with that? And are you really going to make much money, considering your overhead? Unless your company's primary goal is to make money selling virtual merchandise, you'll probably be better off giving things away for free.

Some Residents will disagree—often those with shops of their own. They feel that it will hurt their business if someone can pick up things for free from you rather than purchasing them. However, Residents give away piles and piles of free, quality merchandise themselves, and your freebie's not going to change that a bit.

SELLING REAL-LIFE ITEMS IN-WORLD

Most items sold in-world are virtual items for use in-world. What about selling real-world things in-world?

There are a couple of ways to go about this. One is to use something like the Infovendors discussed in the "Wiley" section earlier in this chapter, to direct shoppers to a web-based shopping experience. The other approach is to use the Risk API to sell items for Linden dollars right in-world. For example, Stonfield Inworld sells a variety of real-world goods through *Second Life*, including insurance and chocolates, by providing shopping assistance in-world via IM and voice chat. Avatars select the items, but they're shipped to a real world address.

If you would like to try this approach, remember that you'll have all those Linden dollars to convert using the LindeX. This means you'll be subject to market fluctuations. But Linden Lab has been keeping the exchange rate fairly stable by careful management, so these days that's not the risk it once was.

The main problem of selling real items to Residents is how many of them want to remain anonymous behind their avatars. Suppose someone can pay an in-world vendor and, say, order a real-life pizza to be delivered to their home. That means associating their avatar name and identity with their real-life identity and address. Many, probably a majority of *Second Life* Residents, would balk at this.

Does this mean this sort of business plan can't work? There have been some successes, such as Residents paying for their *Second Life* Community Convention memberships with Linden dollars, but Residents usually attend this real-world gathering wearing badges with their avatar names on them, not their real names. Amazon and Circuit City have both experimented with selling real merchandise in-world, but such virtual world/real world intermeshing is new and still experimental.

A couple of years ago I turned down projects of this sort. Today it would depend on the product being offered and the measures being taken to assure Residents that their identifying information would be safe and confidential.

What are the technological considerations when holding an event in *Second Life*? How many avatars can attend an in-world event? How can you maximize performance when there are many avatars to render at your event? What sort of venue is right for your event, and do you have to buy land and build the venue yourself? How does your intended communication interface affect venue design? What should you consider when scheduling an event? How do you publicize it and prepare for it? How can you prepare your staff? What moderation techniques and tools work for an in-world event? What should you do to prepare for any surprises? How do you document an event in-world? Read this chapter to find out!

RUN AN EVENT

TECHNOLOGICAL CONSIDERATIONS

Some people might tell you that it's impossible to put on a worthwhile event in *Second Life*, which is pretty crazy, since hundreds of people—or thousands—do it every day! I've put on successful events for myself and for my clients, and I can tell you it's actually not all that different from running online events in a text-based interface (something I did for decades before coming to *Second Life*).

The reason in-world events get a bad rap is that most are run by hobbyists. Some hobbyists live up to professional standards, however, and some subpar events are run by professionals without online-event experience or without any *Second Life* experience. Although many things you or your Solution Provider will deal with are pretty much the same issues you'd face in real life—such as making sure you have contact info for all your guest speakers—there are plenty of considerations specific to this technology. Let's take a look.

DEFAULT AGENT LIMIT

The most important technical considerations to keep in mind are the agent (avatar) limit for your event space and the limitations of the systems and bandwidth used by those attending and running your event. After all, even if you are technically still allowed another 10 agents in your region, if your keynote speaker's computer is lagging under the load of rendering all those avatars and your speaker can't type, what good does it do you?

 UPCOMING FEATURES FOR EVENTS

Using the new SLim technology, it's possible to include a greater number of participants at an event or meeting by patching them in using a voice or text instant message. And on the horizon are new features to increase the number of simultaneous participants at events. One will allow event or meeting attendees to call a phone number to participate without being at a computer. Another will be a web-based interface for sharing an avatar's view—and using camera controls—without logging into *Second Life* at all. These tools should allow hundreds of people to "attend" an event at the same time.

The default agent limit for a full-prim or "normal" region, as well as the limit for all mainland regions owned and managed by Linden Lab, is 40. Homesteads have a limit of 20 (which cannot be increased), and Openspaces are limited to 10—and they may not be used for events, anyway, according to the Terms of Service. If you want to have events at your Openspace, you'll need to upgrade your region.

This means that unless you have a very small event in mind, you need to do it in a full-prim private region. Because, as mentioned before, there's no way to know if other Residents in a mainland region are going to have an event at the same time as you're having one, filling up all 40 slots, or if you're going to fill up the whole region and upset neighbors who aren't able to log into their homes or have visitors to their shops. As always in the gossip factory that is *SL*, you can expect that this would be talked about and possibly even picked up by the press.

Rented land in a private region can also be subject to this sort of problem. Be sure that your covenant allows events, especially large ones, and think about what arrangements you might need to make with the region owner or neighbors. Events on rented land are prone to other challenges, such as less control over permissions in case of griefing at your event, which I'll discuss later in this chapter.

IF YOU DON'T HAVE A REGION

What can you do if you don't have a region of your own but need to run a large event?

▶ Rent one of Linden Lab's event regions for as low as US$50 per day (less for nonprofits). For info go to **http://secondlife.com/land/rentals.php.**

▶ Purchase a region and keep it for as long as it takes to prepare for and hold the event, then sell the region.

▶ Rent a region from a Resident.

▶ Rent or borrow an event space from another organization.

▶ Hold the event at your Solution Provider's region.

▶ Consider alternatives to holding one huge event.

FUNCTIONAL AGENT LIMIT

Although the default agent limit is 40, if you own the region or are the estate manager you have the ability to increase the limit to 100 (Figure 12.1). However, having that many avatars in one place hurts the region's general performance, slowing everything down and possibly even crashing the sim. In particular, it taxes people with slower connections or systems—they might be barely able to move or might simply crash. If you have some control over or knowledge of what sort of systems attendees will be using—such as if the attendees are your class or employees—you can test their systems or similar systems to see what the weakest system among them might bear. But if your event is open to the public, you can't really meet the lowest spec; some people can barely function in-world with 10 avatars in view!

The functional limit is also affected by things like how complex your build is to render, how many particles are flying around, what scripts are running, and how complex any neighboring regions in view are to draw. This means it's very important to hold your event in an optimized, low-lag build. Performance will also be very heavily affected by what avatars are wearing, including their clothing and skin textures and any prim attachments, such as hair.

Typically, 30 to 50 avatars at one event at the same time (unless it's spread out so that some of the other avatars aren't in view) will work for most people, with varying degrees of performance depending on their systems and broadband speeds.

12.1 Use the Region/Estate console to adjust the agent limit.

▶ TIP

You can improve your system's performance at a busy event—or anywhere performance is suboptimal due to rendering load—by adjusting your *Second Life* Preferences. Go to Edit ▶ Preferences and then to the Graphics tab. Reduce your Graphics settings to the minimum and see how much more quickly everything renders for you! Other applications running on your system use up resources, as well, and quitting them will help.

COMPENSATING FOR AGENT LIMITS

An agent limit of 30 to 50 might be enough for a meeting or a class, but it is pretty restrictive. Fortunately, a variety of solutions allow more avatars to participate in an event.

USE NEIGHBORING REGIONS

One of the oldest and best ways to include more avatars at the same event is to set up your venue so that it spans two to four regions. This is usually called a *four-corners* approach. So, for example, if you hold your event at the point where four regions meet, you can have (assuming default agent limits) 160 agents at your event. You can see an example of a four corners event space in Figure 12.2.

Remember, however, that performance in one region with 40 avatars in it will be slower if there's another region next door with another 40 avatars to render!

There are a few more considerations if you take this approach.

▶ Make certain that event attendees are aware the event will be held in more than one sim, and that they have landmarks or SLURLs for all of the regions. Otherwise they will all try to teleport to the "main" region (the one where the speakers are!) and if they can't enter because the region is full they might be unable to figure out where else to go, and give up.

▶ Be aware that an object that's placed so that it crosses a region border, while solid in the region where the root prim (the last one linked in an object) is located, is phantom (insubstantial) in other regions. You will need to have additional prims for avatars to stand upon there. Otherwise they will fall right through the floor or stage when they cross the region border.

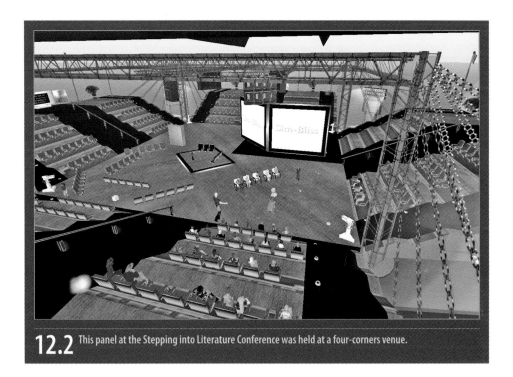

12.2 This panel at the Stepping into Literature Conference was held at a four-corners venue.

▶ Region-border crossings are prone to lag or failure under heavy load. During a busy event, expect avatars crossing the sim border to briefly appear to fall through prims and the ground before the new region picks them up. For those with poor system performance or slow broadband speed, this can lead to a crash.

▶ Having multiple regions for an event, such as the one in Figure 12.3, is, of course, more expensive than having just one region. If this would overburden your budget, you can consider renting an event space or some regions, borrowing a region, or using your Solution Provider's regions.

12.3 The balcony seating at The Magicians Colonnade is located over a region called xyz, while the main venue is on Abracadabra.

EMPLOY MULTIPLE LOCATIONS

Another approach, which can be combined with the four-corners approach, is to hold your event at multiple locations. This can be done in a variety of ways. For example, one company hosted simultaneous Christmas-tree lightings in many duplicate regions.

The main difficulty here is creating the duplicate regions! While Linden Lab used to "clone" regions and their content for customers, this service is no longer available. This means that you or your Solution Provider will have to manually copy and duplicate the regions (including the terraforming, buildings, and everything else) or build or use regions that aren't copies. You'll also want to include a way for attendees at satellite or second-ary locations to listen in (or read the text) of your presenters or speakers. For the text, there are chat repeaters. For listening in, you'll want to use streaming media (discussed next).

USE STREAMING MEDIA

NOTE

A collaborative, interactive web viewing feature is in the works and coming soon from Linden Lab.

Streaming media is a great way to reach out to a larger audience. As a bonus, it can be accessed by people outside of the Grid, too, if you provide them the URL where the stream is hosted.

You can stream audio, video, or a static snapshot of a website into a parcel on the Grid by simply pasting the URL of a QuickTime video or SHOUTcast stream into the About Land Media tab. Using a scripted object, you can also stream YouTube videos. And using the Immersive Work Spaces solution (**http://riversrunred.com/ immersive-workspaces/**) offered by Rivers Run Red, a partner of Linden Lab, you can even have the ability to show your own system's desktop or anything else on your screen.

Of course, you have to create and host a stream or have someone do it for you. However, if you don't have someone in-house able to manage this, your Solution Provider or a company that specializes in media streams for *SL* can assist you. Depending on the size of your event, you might want to hire a specialist, because a stream for a large event can require substantial bandwidth and sometimes special hardware. You might consider partnering with an in-world radio or television station that specializes in this service.

In addition, streaming media (using the audio channel) is the method usually used to present live music, which is very popular in-world. Another approach is to capture video and audio of the event in *SL* and stream it on the Web or post it for people to view after the event. This is a good solution for training or updates when some people may be unable to attend the event.

Streaming media can be tricky. Your host could run out of bandwidth, which means that once you have as many listeners or viewers as it can support, the rest won't be able to connect to the stream. There can be a long delay between speaking and hearing the stream in-world. Audio quality depends on the hardware, settings, and bandwidth of your event participants. And streaming media puts added load on the listener's or viewer's system. Don't wait until the day of your event to test your media stream! Test it well in advance, so that you will have enough time to find (and test) another solution, if necessary.

Streaming media works on a per-parcel basis. So if you have viewers or listeners in more than one parcel (or region), you will need to make sure your stream plays on all of them; you will see and hear only the stream that is playing in the parcel where your avatar is standing. The streaming feature allows you to display only one video and one audio stream at a time on the same parcel. If you want to display more than one, you will need a scripted solution.

Do keep in mind that if someone comes in late or crashes and returns, they will see the video stream from the beginning—not from the point where the other viewers are seeing it. A scripted gadget my company built provides a way around this; you'll learn more about it in Chapter 15, "Locate Resources."

TIP

It can be a good idea to make the URL of your stream available for those unable to attend your event at the in-world location. You can include the URL in press releases and invitations. Also, it's a good idea to make the URL available to those at the event in case they have difficulty with their in-world stream—if you don't provide it, someone is certain to ask your staff for it.

SPREAD ATTENDANCE OVER A LARGER AREA

Linden Lab usually holds their Concierge Party events (a sort of appreciation party for region owners and other Residents who own a comparable amount of mainland) with activities spread across many regions. This is different from a four-corners event, because, of course, many of these regions aren't next to one another! Linden Lab uses the same approach for their Winter Festival, for Burning Life, and for other big parties. The regions are not duplicates; each is unique, with different events, activities, or artworks to check out.

This spread-out technique is great for in-world festivals or any sort of event where you can have something for your audience to see or do in multiple sims. The challenge, of course, is in coming up with enough content to fill all these regions, along with staff to patrol and manage all of it.

SPREAD ATTENDANCE OVER A LONGER TIME

Rather than holding a one-hour event limited to the number of avatars that will fit into an event space simultaneously, you can have an event that runs over a longer period of time—even days or weeks. Not only does this allow more people to attend, but it's convenient for people in more time zones.

Events appropriate for this solution include Linden Lab's aforementioned annual Burning Life festival, a display of Resident-built artworks and events that takes place over the course of many days. For example, the 2008 Burning Life ran from September 27 to October 5. If you want to maximize the number of people able to attend your event, this is the ideal approach. The challenge here is to have compelling content or speakers scheduled over the duration of your event, along with staff able to respond in case of any problems or questions.

It is not unusual for those running events in-world to ask event attendees to help reduce the load on the region and on attendees' computers by reducing their avatars' resource use. The things avatars are often asked to take off, turn off, or leave in Inventory include the following:

▶ Scripted attachments, especially animation overriders and "bling" or particle-scripted objects

▶ Prim hair, or specifically resource-intensive prim hair

▶ Other prim attachments, including clothing and avatar parts

Usually these requests are included in pre-event promotional materials, such as invitations and event announcements, and an event facilitator might also make an announcement at the start of the event, and sometimes during the event, asking that animation overriders and other scripted attachments be turned off or taken off.

Although these measures can help to reduce load at an event, many Residents will resist them for a variety of reasons, and they might not come to your event if you impose restrictions instead of making requests. Some simply don't want to look less than their best. Others are unwilling to change from their usual avatar, with which they identify, are used to, or are recognized by. For this reason, some event hosts allow exceptions, such as, "Please remove all attachments before teleporting to the event, unless you are a full-time Furry."

No matter how many times you make the request, some Residents will continue to use their scripted attachments and wear their primmy things during your event unless they are simply thrown out if they don't comply. Ejecting attendees can lead to negative buzz about your event and organization.

You can always look for solutions through skillful online community management. For example, 2008's Hair Fair specified that attendees remove their prim hair—but for good reason. Low-resource bandanas were made available to attendees to wear on their bald avatar heads, cultivating solidarity between attendees and the hair-loss sufferers whom the fundraising event was intended to benefit.

👁 HOW LAGGY AM I?

You can get a ballpark estimate of the resources required to render your avatar. First enable the Advanced menu if you haven't already. Press Ctrl+Alt+Shift+D (yes, all at once). Then select Advanced ▶ Rendering ▶ Information Displays ▶ Avatar Rendering Cost (ARC) to display avatars' estimated rendering costs over their heads (as shown in the image here). These appear as color-coded numbers floating where you're used to seeing nametags. Green numbers mean a good ARC, yellow is so-so, and red indicates a very high ARC that means your avatar might be a walking lag machine, slowing down system performance for everyone in view.

It might seem tempting to restrict event attendance to avatars with an acceptable ARC. Unfortunately, the calculations give an estimate that is not always accurate. For example, ARC doesn't recognize any difference between a complex sculpted prim and one that just looks like a cube. Though ARC is useful as a general guideline, it's not always entirely correct.

VENUES

No one design is ideal for all events, in *Second Life* or in the real world! However, the sort of space you create as a venue for your event has a big impact. Many meetings and classes in-world are held without the benefit of a purpose-built venue. Avatars just stand or sit in a circle or face a slide screen, and that's that (Figure 12.4). Others take place in virtual offices and classrooms, which are often built with events in mind. And for a larger, more complicated, or more impressive event, you need a venue. Several factors dictate what sort of venue will be the best for your needs.

12.4 This event at Frontier Spaceport didn't require an elaborate venue.

EVENT SIZE AND TYPE

Both the size and nature of your event will dictate the sort of space you need. Typical venues seat 20 to 50 avatars in one region, with audience seats facing seated presenters and a slide screen on a stage. However, larger attendance or use of multiple regions require a more complicated design. For example, if you are going to host an event across multiple adjoining regions, you have to puzzle out things like where to place the stage so that everyone has a good view.

Available region resources make a big difference, as well, especially if many avatars will attend. If the region doesn't have many free prims you won't have many to use for your venue, and it's likely to lag anyway. In fact, if you find yourself in a situation like this it might well be time to consider finding another location for your event or simplifying your build. Of course, as I already mentioned, if your event will be spread across multiple regions, you're going to have to come up with enough content to fill the space!

Whatever you do, try to make sure there's enough seating for every avatar who attends. While avatars don't "need" to sit, most people feel more comfortable when their avatar looks comfortable; virtual or not, avatars convey important social cues.

COMMUNICATION INTERFACES

The communication interfaces you intend to use for your events also dictate certain aspects of your venue's design.

TEXT CHAT

Most events in-world are conducted using text chat. To accommodate the range of text chat, each of the audience seats usually should be no more than 20 meters from the avatars on stage. Otherwise your presenters will need to shout or use a scripted gadget such as a chat repeater. If you're staging an event across multiple venues, you might need a repeater system to allow remote attendees to read the text chat, too. Across large event spaces, some event facilitators find group instant messages and region/estate messages (via the Region/Estate panel) to be a useful way to keep everyone in the loop.

VOICE CHAT

TIP

It's helpful when using voice chat to have the speakers list (the bubble to the left of the Talk button) visible. Press the left box above the dots to sort by active speaker.

More and more events are conducted using voice chat. When choosing your venue, keep in mind that there is a 60-meter limit to voice range. And if you are holding an event across more than one region, voice won't carry across the region border unless the regions are part of the same estate. You'll find it's easier to hear someone at a distance if you select Preferences ▶ Voice and choose to hear spatialized audio from your camera location rather than your avatar's location, then cam in on the stage.

While voice chat allows audience seating to be placed farther from the stage, it also poses a variety of problems. Many Residents have trouble getting voice to work for them, often because their system or broadband connection is already at its limit. Particularly if you have no control over or knowledge of the sort of systems of those who'll attend your event, if you know their systems aren't the fastest, or if you expect a very large audience, voice might not be the best way to go. Remember that many Residents don't enable voice at all. At the least, be sure your event announcements indicate that voice will be used. Keep in mind that under heavier load the voice system is more prone to difficulty, particularly client-side.

The exception here is business (and some education) events. People who are in-world to do real-world work are usually much more likely to be using voice.

PAIRING GROUP IMS WITH VOICE CHAT

Voice chat can be difficult if it's not conducted in your first language, and impossible if you're hearing-impaired. For this reason, many events that might be conducted in voice are instead held as text-chat events. If you do use voice, though, you can still be inclusive. A quick, accurate typist can keep up and type a transcript (including translation, if appropriate) in real time, using a scripted translator if you can't find a human one for the occasion. A group instant message is great way to share the live transcript with specifically interested audience members. Remember to note in your pre-event announcements and invitations that this service will be available, and how to join the group!

Even before voice chat was added to *Second Life*, Residents were using streaming audio and video for live events, often mixed-reality events. Whereas streaming video can be too much for an already overburdened system, streaming audio is very reliable. It's the safest choice if you want to maximize the number of Residents able to hear your event. As a bonus, you can make the URL available to those unable to attend, or stream at multiple locations on the Grid.

It's important to make certain that your land has been parceled appropriately so everyone there is seated on the correct parcel and able to hear or view your stream.

MIX AND MATCH

Sometimes it's prudent to use more than one communication method, especially if you are hosting an event across multiple regions. For example, when my company facilitated a mixed-reality event for the Science Museum/Dana Centre in London, the event was conducted in-world via voice (Figure 12.5). A video stream of the action in-world was shown on a screen in London, where the guest speakers sat onstage in front of their computers logged into *Second Life*. To include Residents who didn't use voice, the audio portion of this stream was made available in-world on the media channel. And for those attendees sitting in the second region (part of a different estate), this same stream allowed them to listen, as well. My team also included chat repeaters, so those in the second region were able to follow side comments and backchat.

12.5 The panelists' avatars on stage at the Science Museum/Dana Centre mixed-reality event

⇘ WARNING

If you're using chat repeaters, voice, streams, or other gadgets and features to allow you to place the audience more than 20 meters away from the stage, don't forget about draw distances. Some event attendees will have theirs turned down to the minimum of 64 meters. Make sure that things are laid out so that they can still see everything!

SEATING AND LAYOUT

Along with the size of your audience, seating and layout needs will vary and must be based on your communication method and the type of event you're holding. Some venues have a flexible design that works well for many types of events, but others work well for only very specific purposes.

SEATING

If you're having a dance or a festival, you don't need a lot of seating. But you'll need it for most events, if only to give attendees a place to sit down and chat about what they just saw. In other chapters you've read about the sorts of problems you can run into with seats, such as AO conflicts or seats that are too large or small (or avatars that are, depending on your point of view). Even if you really, really like some chairs you have found in a shop, don't buy them without checking out the animations and considering your needs: Is this formal enough? Informal enough? Would an avatar in a skirt look trampy in this pose? You can always find other chairs, and most Residents are going to be uncomfortable if their avatar looks uncomfortable.

LAYOUT

If you are hosting an event for relatively new *Second Life* users, make it especially easy for them to have a clear view of the stage without using their camera controls. You want them to be able to easily get into the venue, as well—make the entrances large, obvious, and easy to navigate. The same goes for any hallways or walkways. You may consider using scripted seats or attachments (Figure 12.6) that automatically take over camera controls to give an ideal view of the stage.

⩗NOTE

Designing functional, attractive spaces in *Second Life* is a complicated subject. Want to learn more? Check out my other book, *Creating Your World: The Official Guide to Advanced Content Creation for Second Life* (Wiley, 2007).

12.6 An avatar in the audience uses a pair of scripted opera glasses to get a perfect view of the stage at The Magicians Colonnade.

CREATING A MOOD

One of the best things about events in *Second Life*, as opposed to using a regular online chat room, for example, is that you can develop a venue that evokes exactly the mood you want for your gathering. Do you want a huge, impressive location? A more intimate setting? Should attendees be in a serious mood or a playful one? You can influence this by creating the right venue. For example, my company's event venue is set up for a magical, special feeling of anticipation, to get people excited about the event as soon as they arrive (Figure 12.7).

12.7 A member of my staff flies past the entrance to The Magicians Colonnade during a fireworks display.

Should it be day or night? Should attendees be in businesswear or eveningwear—and will there be dancing or a speaker? It's all up to you. In fact, as you saw in Part 1, events can include things like a living-history re-creation of Abraham Lincoln's inauguration (including free period clothing for visitors), a real-life shareholders' meeting, or a huge music festival. Doing something that is interesting and a bit fun always draws more attendees—and more press.

SCHEDULE CONSIDERATIONS

Scheduling an in-world event can be a bit tricky. Even if you're holding an event in a region that's not open to the public, certain Grid-wide activities might affect it.

Peak concurrency. The Grid gets very busy at certain times. During peak concurrency, the Grid is more likely to experience slowdowns or slightly wonky behavior. Times of peak concurrency coincide with heavy broadband use in the US, so a lot of people are already going to be having trouble just because they are short of bandwidth. The busiest times are usually weekends, especially Sunday night, and US holidays. While there might be more people online to attend your events at those times, there's also a greater chance of technical difficulties. This can affect every region on the Grid, both public and private.

Schedule conflicts. Peak times are also more prone to schedule conflicts, because there are more events scheduled at those times. When planning your event, be sure to check the official events calendar (**http://secondlife.com/events/**) to see what else is happening at the same time as your event. You don't want a schedule conflict for the attendees you're targeting. And you certainly don't want a schedule conflict for the press that might cover your event, spreading word of it to a much larger audience than can actually attend!

Scheduled downtime. This is another important consideration. Be sure to check Linden Lab's downtime calendar (at **http://status.secondlifegrid.net/**) while planning your event. Sometimes the Grid stays up but certain features, such as voice, will be down for maintenance, or there will be rolling restarts, which might affect the region where you're holding your event.

Time zones. The trickiest part of scheduling an event has to do with time zones. *Second Life* Residents are based around the world, and that means that they're not all going to be awake or available at the same time. Give careful consideration to your target audience and when they're most likely to be awake and available to log in. Some events are held over several hours or days to include multiple time zones. Other organizations choose to hold more than one event, often duplicates, at different times of day to cater to Residents in different parts of the world. The time zone of your Solution Provider and your staff might also be a consideration. A company that is based in a different time zone from yours might not have staff available or they might charge extra to make them available at a time that is convenient for you.

Target-audience demographics. Is your audience made up of people who log on after work? Or do you plan to reach stay-at-home parents, retired people, or disabled people who are most likely to be in-world during the day in their time zone? If you'd like to attract educators and businesspeople, keep in mind that many of them log in from work and won't log in after business hours, and others cannot log in during business hours because there's a firewall at work—they have to log in from home. If you aren't familiar with the best time of day to reach your target audience, your Solution Provider may be able to offer some suggestions.

Don't forget that you can (with permission) post a transcript of the event, a podcast, or even a video. In fact, depending on the type of event you're doing (such as a lecture, class, or meeting), this will probably be expected.

PREPARATION

The primary reason events fail is a lack of preparation. I mean, think about it: if you were going to host an event in real life expecting 40 to 70 people (or more!) to arrive, wouldn't you do more to prepare than send out invitations tell your guest speaker when to show up? Sure you would! And it's no different in-world. There are a lot of things to do to prepare for an event.

NOTIFY LINDEN LAB

If your event will involve significant media coverage—viewed by over 10,000 people—or an in-world audience of hundreds, you or your Solution Provider needs to notify Linden Lab. (Those numbers look large for an event, but keep in mind that *The Metaverse Messenger*—the highest-circulation *SL*-specific newspaper—claims a readership of over 100,000 Residents.) Although the notification you are required to submit to Linden Lab doesn't mean they'll provide you with additional support, it does make Linden Lab staff aware of your event so that they can prepare for it if necessary.

To do this, email **events@lists.lindenlab.com** with the following information:

- ▶ Event name

- ▶ Event date

- ▶ Event time (PST)

- ▶ *SL* location(s)

- ▶ Expected attendance

- ▶ Any special conditions (invited only, public, etc.)

- ▶ Event sponsor (developer)

- ▶ RL name of event manager

- ▶ SL name of event manager

- ▶ Email address of event manager

- ▶ Phone number of event manager

⬂ TIP

You can find links to the Grid Planned Outages listing, Status Blog, and *Second Life* Grid Status Report, as well as information about notifying Linden Lab of your upcoming event, at **http://wiki .secondlife.com/ wiki/Event_ Notification.**

PR

Here are some ways that you can get the word out:

- ▶ Print ads

- ▶ Press releases

- ▶ Official *SL* events calendar

- ▶ In-world Classifieds

- ▶ Posters

- ▶ *SL*-specific radio and webcast television stations

- ▶ Parcel descriptions

- ▶ *SL* Press Club

- ▶ Group announcements

- ▶ Invitations (discussed in the following section)

Consult Chapter 8, "Keep Up with Current Events," for more information on where to advertise, including popular *Second Life*–specific publications and blogs.

INVITATIONS

Event invitations in *SL* are usually clickable objects that give a notecard of information and a landmark. They're usually larger than real-life invitations and often are interesting works of art in and of themselves (Figure 12.8).

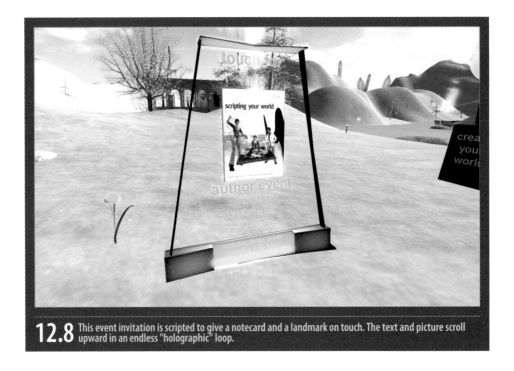

12.8 This event invitation is scripted to give a notecard and a landmark on touch. The text and picture scroll upward in an endless "holographic" loop.

Your invitation should include the following:

- ▶ Name or purpose of the event

- ▶ Date and time

- ▶ Contact person

- ▶ Who to contact for a teleport offer

- ▶ Where to submit questions for speakers (if they are collected in advance)

- ▶ Location

- ▶ Additional locations

- ▶ Whether you're using voice, chat, or streaming media (and what kind)

- ▶ The URL of your stream, if you are comfortable sharing it

- ▶ Requests or requirements for dress (such as formalwear or period costume—if the latter, it can be a good idea to provide SLURLs or landmarks for shops that provide fashions for less-well-known historical periods)

- ▶ Other requests or requirements, such as an RSVP, a group that must be joined, an admission fee, or removal of some or all attachments

Invitations are usually passed on from avatar to avatar if the event sounds interesting—and if the object permissions allow copying and transferring. People may also set up a copy of the invitation at their own parcel or region, either to admire, to remind themselves of the upcoming event, or so that visitors and friends can simply click the invitation to receive the notecard and landmark. Be sure permissions allow copy and transfer, unless you are limiting event attendance.

 TELEPORT OFFERS

It's usual to have someone at your event detailed to provide teleport offers to those who need them. I usually have at least two avatars named for this task in all pre-event press and invitations, in case one of them can't get in-world or in case of crashes or other obstacles. If you don't provide the name of a specific avatar, whoever Residents discern as being in charge of or working at the event will be IM'd to ask for a teleport. This is no good if you or your guest speaker is getting these requests in the middle of a presentation, so be sure to have someone else ready to handle them. If possible, choose someone with an easy-to-spell name for this role.

You may find it necessary to Friend someone in order to offer them a teleport; this is a small bug that comes and goes. But don't worry; you can drop their calling cards after the event—but why not maintain a bigger network?

STAFF AND SUPPORT

Although one person can run a small event in-world, if you intend to put on an event of any size you will need staff to help manage it. Event staff roles will include a variety of tasks, and one person can usually take on a few of them. I typically run events (across one or two regions) with a staff of three to five. Part of the reason for a larger team is to have backup if one or more staffer's net connection goes down.

Here are some of my event team's tasks:

▶ Greet arriving avatars and direct them to the seating area

▶ Point out freebies, displays, and event programs

▶ Help get guest speakers, presenters, or clients to where they need to be and to talk them through whatever they may need help with

▶ Offer assistance with technical issues, like enabling voice or streaming video

▶ Emcee the event

▶ Provide entertainment

▶ Take screenshots

▶ Watch for and deal with griefers

▶ Maintain a chat queue, if necessary

▶ Take audience questions, if necessary

▶ Clean up litter

▶ Offer teleports

- ▶ Direct traffic to another venue, if available, when the region fills

- ▶ Keep time and count visitors

✋ EVENT STAFF UNIFORMS

Your event staff will probably be in a specific group with a tag that identifies them, but that's still pretty easy to miss, especially in a sea of tags at a crowded event or if someone has tags disabled. That's why I find it useful to dress my event staff in something distinctive. My team wears Magicians-staff top hats, along with clothing in my brand's colors, as shown here. If you expect a large crowd—or if you just want to look slick—consider trying something like this for your next event.

MODERATING EVENTS

Unless your event is something like a casual gathering of a few friends or a small meeting or class, you will have to put some time, effort, and thought into moderating it. Otherwise things can become chaotic very quickly, especially for the newbies, with overlapping speakers and text chat flashing by too quickly. The event moderator's job is to make sure the event runs smoothly up on stage so that the audience and event participants all have a good experience. That means keeping order, facilitating communication between the audience and event participants, and keeping things interesting.

There are several techniques for moderating in-world events. Some are easier than others, some are better for a particular audience size, and some are just more fun for the audience. Let's take a look at some different approaches.

PRESUBMITTED QUESTIONS

If you are not very familiar with moderating online events or if you expect a huge audience, you might want to limit your event to presubmitted audience questions. Wherever you announce your event, as well as in event invitations, provide a channel for attendees to submit their questions. They might send them to a specific avatar via IM or put them into a suggestion box via notecard, for example. This allows you to review all of the questions, pick and choose, and ask them in a logical order, and your speaker will be able to prepare and not be caught flat-footed. Furthermore, using presubmitted questions means your speaker or event host won't be as slammed with incoming questions—or at least won't need to manage them on the fly!

Typically, you'll want to copy and paste each question into chat or read them in voice, usually with the name of the avatar who asked them. Keep in mind that some people will still IM questions or shout them out. You'll need to have someone on staff ready to ask them to stop, and be sure they have the ability to get rid of a persistent shouter if they just won't shut up.

QUESTIONS SUBMITTED DURING THE EVENT

Audiences are often asked to submit questions through a prescribed channel during the event. This can be done in a few ways, including notecards or IMs sent to the speaker, an emcee or host, or another event staff member. This allows a bit of time for screening, sorting duplicates, and putting questions in order, as well as keeping down the chaos a bit.

At a large event or one where the audience will participate a lot, you'll want to have a staff member dedicated to this task unless you have an event host with a lot of experience who is able to manage this on the fly (Figure 12.9).

⟩TIP

Always keep on hand some filler material or questions in case the audience doesn't have enough questions, the speaker crashes, etc. Be ready to carry the event for a while if you have to, and have your team ready to help.

⟩TIP

Remember that, if you're running your event in a region where you have access to the Region/Estate controls, you can make an announcement to everyone, such as, "Please submit your questions to Kim Anubis via IM." That blue pop-up message will get everyone's attention!

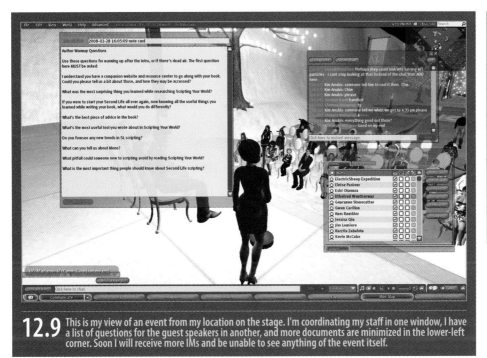

12.9 This is my view of an event from my location on the stage. I'm coordinating my staff in one window, I have a list of questions for the guest speakers in another, and more documents are minimized in the lower-left corner. Soon I will receive more IMs and be unable to see anything of the event itself.

SHOUT IT OUT

At small or informal events, or those with a very quick-witted speaker, a very experienced event host, or a very polite audience, you can get away with minimal moderation. Let the audience converse with the speakers and see where it goes. When this works well, it provides a great experience for the audience—they might get the chance to have a real conversation in-world with someone they'd probably never get to meet in real life. When it doesn't work well, though, things can get out of hand very quickly. Innocent chaos has a way of spawning griefing. Be ready to rein things in before that happens. If you don't have experience moderating in-world events, you probably shouldn't try this approach without help.

AUTOMATED SYSTEMS FOR FACILITATING EVENTS

Certain scripted tools can help you to moderate in-world events. Chapter 15 will provide more information, but here's an overview of a few things you might find helpful:

Chat-queue systems. Rather than having a staff member keep track of whose turn it is to speak next, you can have one of these systems do it for you.

Repeater system. Made up of a microphone (Figure 12.10) and "speakers" or "repeaters," this allows text chat to be read by avatars outside of normal chat range.

Microphone (shouting). This is a simple gadget that picks up the chat of a specific speaker and then shouts it to be heard by an audience farther away.

Chat logger. Rather than logging all chatters, this logs specific avatars' chat.

Slide screens and video screens. These allow you to display slides, web pages, or streaming video in-world (Figure 12.10). Some come with very advanced features.

12.10 In this shot you can see a microphone for a chat repeater system, and a slide screen.

Camera tools. Some scripted seats or attachments give audience members an improved view of the stage without requiring experience with the *SL* camera-control system.

Infokiosks and distros. These may be loaded with instructions for enabling streaming video or voice chat, event programs or agendas, information about the speakers, etc. (Figure 12.11).

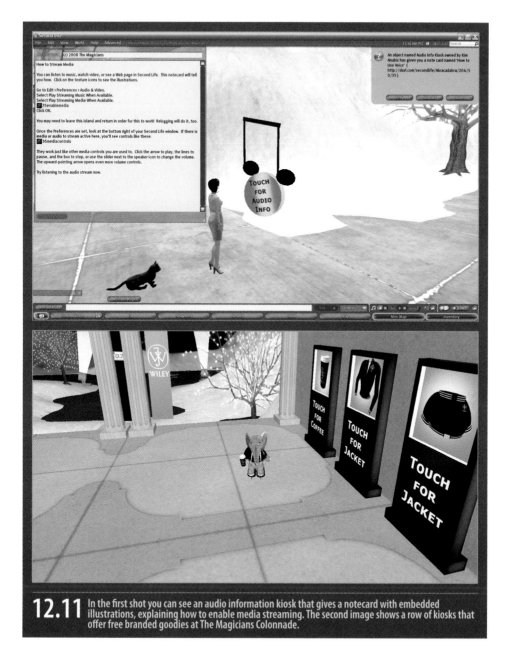

12.11 In the first shot you can see an audio information kiosk that gives a notecard with embedded illustrations, explaining how to enable media streaming. The second image shows a row of kiosks that offer free branded goodies at The Magicians Colonnade.

Immersive Work Spaces. The company Rivers Run Red will, for a nontrivial fee, set up a special island for you that offers tools for improved streaming media, including allowing others to view your computer desktop. This means you can actually make PowerPoint presentations and show other applications or documents in-world. You can read more in Chapter 15 or visit **http://www.immersivespaces.com**.

MIXED-REALITY EVENTS

Mixed-reality events are those that occur in both *Second Life* and the real world. One example would be the Science Museum/Dana Centre event described earlier in this chapter. Typically, however, such events are actually held in one or the other location, with streaming audio or video of that event displayed for those at the other location and with some provision for being able to submit questions. At an event like this in-world, there is much ongoing discussion among event attendees, often with the added participation of special guest speakers who appear in-world and comment.

The tricky bit here, of course, is setting up the streaming media. If you don't have someone in-house who's able to do this, you can find a specialist to assist you.

 RESIDENTS EXPECT TO PARTICIPATE

Second Life Residents are not like a typical real-world event audience. Because of precedents set by early Resident-run events (when everyone knew everyone else and everything was casual) and the expectation that this is an interactive environment, audiences in-world are rarely passive. They don't expect to, and rarely will, simply sit their avatars down and silently watch a presentation or speaker.

Just watching an avatar stand still, rotating through its five different standing poses, is not very exciting. The audience will look around at the build and at any slides you show them, they'll listen to the audio stream, and they'll watch your video if it works for them. But really, it's just not as vivid as watching a live person. So those slides or special effects or dancing chickens or whatever you have to liven things up really make a difference, especially if such things involve the audience.

Interactivity is key. Give the audience something to mess with while they're sitting there—a freebie to try on, a program to read, or even a building lesson or demo that they can participate in right there. (The image here shows avatars at an event learning to script a gadget during a demo. This is a busy event—note the avatars in the balconies in the neighboring region.) At least let them ask some questions or voice a few comments. Otherwise they're going to be unhappy, there might be disruption, and your audience will wander off to go to some other event or catch some TV.

A related phenomenon is called *backchat*. This is when the audience engages one another and the presenters directly, just talking to the people on the stage. Only a very rude person at a real-world event would do this, but it's common and even expected in-world. Even if you are holding a formally moderated event with all questions submitted in advance, expect backchat. *Second Life* Residents expect you to speak *with* them, not *at* them.

Usually backchat occurs in text. This means you might have a conversation on stage using voice or streaming media, and at the same time the audience will be conversing with the speakers on the stage and with one another in text chat. It can be confusing at first, and alarming to an event moderator unfamiliar with this dynamic. However, it can actually work quite well—so well that some event hosts will set up chat repeater systems or group instant messages specifically to facilitate backchat.

CHALLENGES

Things can go wrong during an event in *Second Life*, just as in the real world. Fortunately, you can be prepared for these situations, with a recovery plan and staff in place. Here are some situations to prepare for.

Event staff is missing. Suppose one of your event team members can't get online, or crashes—or you can't be there yourself. I prepare for this by providing my event staff members with a folder of plans and objects they will need in case something goes wrong. There's a notecard outlining everyone's tasks and instructions for doing them, along with a chain of command so that it's clear who takes over and how they should do it if one or more person isn't there. I make sure there's at least one backup for each task or duty. If I have two staff members using the same net connection, there's a third staff member able to take over if their connection goes down.

Region goes down. Sometimes sims crash or there's a rolling restart without warning. Don't freak out. Longtime *SL* Residents will often say that you can tell an event was a success if the sim got so full that it crashed! As great as that is, your staff needs a plan for where to regroup until the region comes back up, how to contact one another if you can't do it in-world (phone, Skype, AIM, etc.), how to contact your speakers or other event participants, and—if possible—some or all of your audience members (such as via a group message). Be ready to offer a lot of teleports or landmarks when the region comes back up!

Speaker crashes. Suppose you have the most wonderful guest speaker ever on your stage and then . . . her avatar types and types but there's no text, and then—pop—she disappears. In the middle of the stage. In the middle of your event! Well, you need a plan, don't you? Have something in mind: who's going to get up on stage and say something to the audience, and how will you keep them amused while the speaker relogs? Can you contact the speaker via phone or other method to help shepherd her back in? If she can't get back in-world, can you patch her in on the phone or transcribe what she says in text chat?

Last-minute speaker cancellation. A nightmare, right? But at least you can have a plan in place so that someone's ready to get up on stage and explain what happened and maybe even offer a rescheduled date.

Voice or other feature fails. Once in a while things go wrong, and voice chat, streaming video, or some other feature you were going to use for your event just isn't working right. So you need a backup plan, like resorting to text chat. Do you have chat repeaters in place if you might need them?

Bad Grid weather. Sometimes it rains on your real-life parade, and other times the Grid is just under too much load or otherwise not working optimally for your in-world event. Suppose log-ins or teleports aren't working correctly. Who's going to field incoming IMs about it, and how will you inform everyone else about what to do? If you're really on top of things, you might be able to announce a rescheduled date or a URL to go to for info about it.

HANDLING GRIEFERS

Some things go wrong on purpose . . . but not your purpose. Griefers are a fact of any world, not just this virtual one. So you need to be prepared for the possibility that your event might be griefed. Here's a basic plan.

Make sure you, and at least one (or preferably two) other people at the event or able to show up immediately have permissions on the land where the venue sits, at the parcel level, and preferably at the Region/Estate level, as well. Neighboring parcels where you do not have control are possible locations from which a griefer could launch an attack, so if at all possible don't hold your event with a neighboring parcel where object rezzing is enabled and scripts can be run by just anyone.

Depending on the nature of your event, you'll want to restrict object creation, object entry, and scripts. Remember, though: If you hand out scripted cups of coffee, you had better leave scripts running. And if you want to have a snowball fight with visitors, they need to be able to rez snowballs. If your staff is sufficiently vigilant and there are enough of you to cover the space, you can leave build and scripts enabled, and just be ready to immediately shut them down (Figure 12.12). You'll also probably want to turn off push and damage.

12.12 Well-prepared event staff covering two regions during a scripting demo, joking and discussing a potential griefer they're keeping an eye on.

If someone does grief your event, your staff needs to have a plan for response. Who does what, and what should they do? It's vital to have this planned ahead of time, because something like a self-replicating griefer object can crash your region and ruin your event very quickly. For each parcel and region, decide who'll watch what area for trouble, who'll clean up litter, who'll change the parcel and estate permissions (or shut off physics if things get very bad, such as cartoon bombs with lots of laggy bits), who'll kick the griefer, and who'll ban the griefer. Then have a backup plan in case one or more of your staff crashes. And make sure someone is detailed to submit an Abuse Report to Linden Lab.

DOCUMENT THE EVENT

Invariably someone will arrive late, even just after your event has ended, and ask if there's a log or if there'll be a podcast later. Plus, much of the PR bang you'll get from an event comes from the press surrounding it rather than from the avatars who were at the event. So you need to document it.

Logging an event can be a good idea, and you can do this automatically, as you learned in Chapter 7, "Understanding Social Interaction in *Second Life*." However, distributing or publishing the log is something else! It's against the rules of *Second Life* to distribute logs in-world or on the forums without getting permission from everyone logged. Of course, you can edit the log and remove chat of and references to everyone but the event staff. Still, it is considered polite to let everyone know that the event will be logged and where that log will be posted. It's similarly courteous to let folks know if you intend to make an audio or video recording of the event.

You'll also need screenshots, and lots of them, because you'll always find something wrong with a few of them (someone's arm through their body or blinking at the wrong time, for example). I usually have a staff member specifically detailed to shoot pictures at events (Figure 12.13).

12.13 The only reason I have pictures of events like this one to include here is because I detailed a staff member to take pictures during events. You never know when you'll need this sort of thing, so be sure to go to the trouble of getting pictures!

Visitor counts are also good to have. Counts can be done in a variety of ways, including counting by hand, using standard visitor counters (Figure 12.14), and employing more elaborate metrics tools. This can be a little tricky with simple tools if you are covering a large space or multiple venues, but the numbers are important, right?

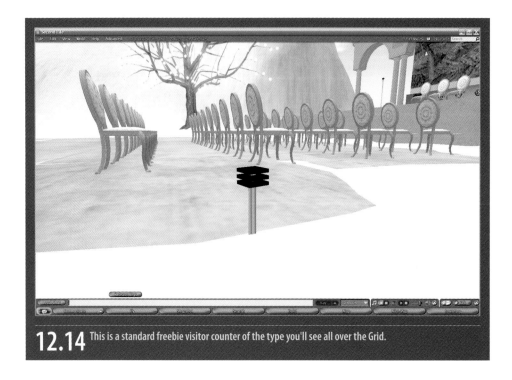

12.14 This is a standard freebie visitor counter of the type you'll see all over the Grid.

While you're at it, save all the links to press, event programs, and all the rest in a folder so you have it handy.

BE CREATIVE

Whatever you do, do it with style. *Second Life* Residents are used to all sorts of crazy, beautiful things. And anything you can do to keep people focused in a class or meeting is probably a good thing. Consider ending your event with fireworks (Figure 12.15) or a snowball fight, have a treasure hunt, contests, dancing. . . . What would make you want to be there yourself? Yes, you can have an event where avatars simply stand in a circle on empty ground, but it just won't make the same impact or hold attention as well as a carefully thought-out event.

12.15 An event closes with a dramatic fireworks display.

 MORE INFORMATION ON HOSTING EVENTS

You can learn more about how to host good events, including classes and meetings, from articles on the *Second Life* wiki:

http://wiki.secondlife.com/wiki/Presentations

http://wiki.secondlife.com/wiki/Events_in_Second_Life

13

What's a Solution Provider, and why would you need one? How much does it cost to hire one and how long does it take to develop a project? Do you pay in Linden dollars? What are the tax implications? How do you select the right Solution Provider for your project? Where can you find a Solution Provider? How can you judge if a Solution Provider's any good? What sort of agreement can you expect? How does the process work? This chapter will answer all of these questions, so keep reading!

SELECT A SOLUTION PROVIDER

DO YOU NEED A SOLUTION PROVIDER?

Throughout this book you have seen mentions of *Solution Providers*. This is the term Linden Lab uses to describe members of its Solution Provider Program who work to bring clients' in-world projects to fruition. Solution Providers are not employees of Linden Lab. They're third-party developers whose services include the following:

▶ Providing or creating custom content (such as buildings, tools, scripts, avatars, and terraforming)

▶ Planning, running, or facilitating events

▶ Training in *SL* skills

▶ Property management

▶ Community development

▶ Consultation

Some projects you can do in-house, but others require professional assistance. It all depends on the type of project you're doing, how complex it is, and what skills and resources are available to you and your own team.

For example, many small, educational projects are developed using student labor. Some pilot projects begin with prefab *SL* content purchased from Resident shops. However, it's very common for someone to start developing their project in-house and then discover they don't have the required skill or familiarity with *SL* and its content-creation and administrative tools to finish the job or do it right. Says Dr. Helen Farley of The University of Queensland, "We lacked the expertise to build [some] things ourselves. I wanted to learn how to do it and that was the original plan, that I would build them. But it quickly became obvious that I wasn't up to the job—skillswise and timewise. That's when we recruited an experienced and talented builder and her team—that was a great decision!"

In fact, one of the main purposes of this book, and the goal of this chapter, is to equip you with the information you need to gauge how much of your *Second Life* project you can really do yourself and to evaluate and select the Solution Provider you need for the rest.

Some projects are run entirely by a Solution Provider on behalf of a client. The client never has to rez an object, deal with inventory, manage groups, or even log in at all (which isn't something I recommend!). Most projects, though, require client participation or are run by the client once the Solution Provider has developed them. In the latter situation, it's especially important that you select a Solution Provider with skills and resources beyond those required to create and manage *SL* content. You'll need someone with the ability to train you in how to manage it and keep your project rolling.

WHAT DOES IT COST?

Since budget is likely one of your first concerns when planning your *Second Life* project, I'll talk about that first. Rates for *SL* content development and services vary a lot, in part because there is more than one *Second Life* economy. There's the in-world Resident economy (largely made up of hobbyists), and there's the economy of business between Solution Providers and clients. There's a lot of crossover between hobbyists and professionals: a professional Solution Provider might also have an in-world shop, and a hobbyist might do an occasional job for pay. And then there are in-world businesses that certainly aren't hobbies, that make enough Linden dollars to convert and pay the real-life bills. In general you'll find, unsurprisingly, that hobbyists charge much less than professionals. Because of this, when you seek quotes, you'll find that the range can be huge.

For example, when assessing a project so that I could provide a quote to a client, I spoke with a number of possible subcontractors to whom I might outsource construction of a simplified 3D re-creation of a historical building. I didn't approach any hobbyists, but I did approach some professional artists who only do occasional *SL* work. Estimates ranged from around US$600 to about US$3,000. The artists' work indicated a connection between skill level and the size of the quote. However, there were exceptions on both ends of the scale, and what was offered varied quite a lot. Each person had a different approach to how they intended to work with me, what source materials they thought of requesting, what rights they offered, how much artistic freedom they expected, and how clearly they explained what I would be getting for the money. Some gave a quote in an instant message, while others wrote proposals.

Generally you can expect a professional Solution Provider to charge at least US$20 per hour. This Solution Provider would most likely be working on in-world projects part-time and would simply be a single independent contractor. Rates climb steeply from there. An island full of cool content might cost US$10,000, or it might cost hundreds of thousands of dollars—or someone might catch a bargain. But remember that, broadly, you get what you pay for; it always costs added time and effort to work with hobbyists or volunteers!

> **NOTE**
>
> The highest price doesn't necessarily reflect the highest-quality work. A project's cost is sometimes a function of a larger company having more overhead.

 PRICES TOO GOOD TO BE TRUE

You can get very inexpensive development work done, and some of it might look pretty good. But if the rate you pay is so low that your Solution Provider can't pay their staff a wage competitive with what companies outside of *Second Life* pay for similar work (3D graphics, programming, facilitating online events, etc.), the working relationship won't be sustainable. A company you hire for a bargain rate might do good work but is prone to inconsistent business dealings. The staff can't last. Even if the person running the company keeps hiring replacements, they'll keep moving on, and when you need your wall repaired or your script modified, the person who built it will be gone. Maybe the feature you want can't be done because the artist who makes it left to work somewhere outside of *Second Life*. People who aren't in it for the money can be great—their passion inspires them to do amazing work. But they are also prone to taking a hike at any time.

Some Solution Providers won't quote an hourly rate for anything other than consultation. I'm one of those myself—for most projects, I quote a flat fee. The number of hours of work required is not the only—or often even the main—consideration in figuring out a quote. Here's some of what's involved:

▶ Who on my team needs to do this, and what's their rate?

▶ Do I need to bring in a subcontractor? If so, what's their rate and how much added time and effort will it take to work out the terms with them?

▶ What real-world rights and *SL* permissions will the client be getting for this project? What parts of the project will I be able to repurpose later, and how valuable are these assets to me?

▶ How many pieces of this project can I supply by repurposing something I already have?

▶ Even if I can supply parts of the project from something I've already developed, how much would it cost the client to have someone else build it from scratch?

▶ How much time will be required for meetings, paperwork, correspondence, setting permissions, managing inventory, and other administrative tasks?

▶ Will the project contract restrict me from discussing the project with the press or using it for demos or presentations and in my portfolio?

▶ How relatively difficult will the project be to complete?

- What special considerations are involved (such as the client having a very low number of free prims or other region resources available for the project)?

- How quickly does the client need the project completed?

- Will the project assets be developed at the client's location in-world or at mine?

- Does the client have enough facility with *SL*'s toolset to take the project and run with it once I hand it over, or will I need to train them how to use it?

There are many considerations like these, and you'll learn more about them throughout this chapter.

BUDGET YOUR TIME, TOO

"Time is money." An individual contractor, particularly one who's only doing this part-time and not for a substantial amount of money, is likely to produce more slowly than a company that has staff. If your project is small, if budget is important to you, or if you especially like the style of a particular part-time developer's work, you might not let that stop you. Most of the top Solution Providers, some who now work on *SL* projects full-time with an entire staff they've hired, started out as hobbyists, then worked part-time to grow their businesses. Most of them hire part-time workers themselves as their businesses grow.

I cannot stress enough that developing your *Second Life* content can take a lot more time than you might expect. Often, someone approaches me with a large, elaborate project that is certainly good and workable but that will take weeks or months to develop, but they've begun discussing it only two weeks before they need it to launch. Well-known Solution Providers, small ones, and very good ones get booked up. Even if they could complete your project in two weeks, they might be booked ahead for months.

As you've probably gathered from this book, *SL* can be relatively complicated, and it can take a fair bit of time to design something that fits your needs. Make sure to allow enough time for it! Most Solution Providers won't be able to give you a quote after chatting for a half an hour. They'll have questions, they may need to meet with specialists on their staff to discuss it, and they'll have more questions for you then. Depending on the scope and complexity of your project, and especially if you're doing something unique, this process can take days or weeks. Then the project still has to be built! Budget time accordingly.

HOW DO YOU PAY?

In most cases you don't need to go out and buy a wad of Linden dollars to pay your Solution Provider. Although some will accept them, most prefer or require payments in real-world money, often in a specific currency, such as US dollars. (Note that Solution Providers usually don't keep their real-life identities secret like most Residents do.) Beyond that, the payment method can vary. For my own projects I accept check, wire transfer, or even PayPal.

One common problem Solution Providers face is being paid late or not getting paid at all. Some institute late fees and other approaches to ensure timely payment, like any other business. Keep in mind that many Solution Providers, while very skilled at the work they do for clients, are new businesspeople who may not have much cash on hand. For a small, new company, that can be a serious problem: the developer may be counting on your payment arriving on time in order to pay to maintain their *SL* tier and their staff. If you miss a payment, don't be surprised if it leads to stoppage of work on your project.

TAXES AND RECORDKEEPING

I'm not an attorney or an accountant. That said, perhaps my experiences related to taxes and *SL* will be useful to you.

The point at which Linden dollars become taxable income varies from country to country. Most in the US find it prudent to report any Linden-dollar income that is converted to US dollars. You can access your Linden-dollar transaction history via your *Second Life* account profile and dump the data into a spreadsheet.

I repeatedly encounter clients who cannot or will not purchase Linden dollars. That's fine in that I require payment in US dollars, but it can be a hassle if a client wants to rent an in-world shop location or ad kiosk or pay Linden-dollar prizes to Residents or purchase content from Resident shops. This is another situation in which a Solution Provider can help. I have had more than one project in which I was hired to bridge the currency gap, for example, by paying the Linden-dollar fee weekly for maintaining an in-world Classified ad on my client's behalf.

Why do some organizations avoid purchasing Linden dollars, and why would a Solution Provider prefer US dollars? The main reason has to do with the conversion between virtual money and real money. Administrators or accounting departments that are not familiar with *Second Life* might have trouble with the concept that converting money on the LindeX is not like buying tokens at an arcade. It's more like exchanging foreign currency. The rate changes depending on supply and demand. So, if you spend US$100 to purchase Linden dollars to pay for something in-world, if you don't spend the Lindens right away you might find they have increased or decreased in value. If you contracted to pay L$20,000 for a project, that could translate to a lot more or less in real-world money when it comes time to pay. Because of this, you might find it useful to agree on a real-world-money rate, regardless of the currency used to pay it.

This can also mean some added bookkeeping. If you purchase Linden dollars to pay a Solution Provider, what is the invoice they provide for your tax records going to say? Maybe someday it will become practical to submit a 1099-Misc that says you paid someone L$20,000, but you can't do that today. So instead you deduct as a business expense the value of the US dollars used to purchase the Linden dollars, and you don't have a good paper trail to show that the money was actually spent to pay for development of software and 3D graphics for your project. This is another reason to pay with real-world currency—real-world dollars paid directly to a Solution Provider results in a much better paper trail.

HOW TO CHOOSE A SOLUTION PROVIDER

As you've gathered by now, there are all sorts of Solution Providers with different specialties doing business on different terms. How can you tell them apart and determine whether you need a big company or a little one? Read on to find out.

WHAT KIND OF SOLUTION PROVIDER DO YOU NEED?

Companies of all sizes, as well as individuals, provide *Second Life* services for real-world organizations. In general, they can be broken down into three categories by size: big companies with dozens of employees, midsize companies that have a staff of up to about 20 people who might or might not be part-time contractors, and small companies that might just be one developer or a team of two or three.

As I mentioned earlier, bigger companies mean more overhead, so they are in almost every case going to be your most expensive option. On the other end of the spectrum the rates could be more affordable, but your project might stall if the person doing it catches the flu and has no one to take over. And although the smaller developers may be very familiar with *Second Life* and what works there, they may also be inexperienced in doing business. The flip side is big marketing companies that have a long track record but very little *Second Life* experience; some of them tend to create beautiful content that looks great in a screenshot but that bores or even insults Residents. A midsize company that has been around for a while is often your best bet.

For a one-off project that involves building one stand-alone object, you can probably get away with hiring an individual. However, if you need someone to manage your project for you or if your project is large, you'll want to hire a bigger Solution Provider. Similarly, a big event cannot realistically be handled by one person. Maybe a one-person shop you like will hire some contractors to help? It's important to ask.

Naturally, most Solution Providers have specialties, such as scripting, events, or region design. It's important to remember this, because while these activities all take place on the Grid, they require different skill sets. You need to make sure you select a Solution Provider who has experience doing projects similar to yours. For example, someone might be the best scripter in the world, but that doesn't mean they know how to run an event!

Some Solution Providers offer particular advantages, such as these:

Enrollments in LL programs or clearances. Not all Solution Providers can offer access to or experience with all specialized tools or features, such as the Registration API or clearance to work in Teen *Second Life*.

Useful venue. A Solution Provider's land or a location—such as an event area—might be used for your project so that you don't have to rent or purchase it yourself. The venue might be modified or redecorated for your event, as The Magicians Colonnade is in Figure 13.1.

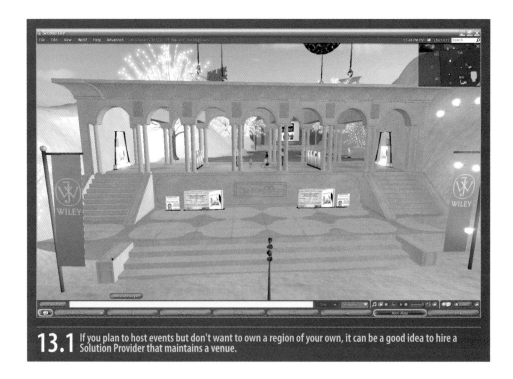

13.1 If you plan to host events but don't want to own a region of your own, it can be a good idea to hire a Solution Provider that maintains a venue.

Existing assets. An established Solution Provider probably has a large inventory of existing content and tools that might be repurposed for your project. This can make it quicker or less costly to develop what you need.

Good reputation. A good reputation will enhance the image of your project. If your developer is a company already known for doing great work, people are more likely to come check it out.

Media attention. If your Solution Provider gets press, they're likely to talk about your project while being interviewed.

Large in-world network. Networking is important on the Grid for finding resources and people and for getting the word out about a project. For example, a developer with a big network is likely to be able to draw more event attendees.

Unique skills. Some Solution Providers have staff that can do things no one else can. One example is the prim avatar "Noobs" created by William Segerman (avatar Art Laxness), a member of my staff, which (at the time of this writing) is created by a process no one has replicated. Your options are to hire the specific Solution Provider that has a unique skill or product, or invest a lot of time and money in paying a different Solution Provider to do research and development, which may or may not succeed.

Complex systems. It can take a long time to develop software, and *Second Life* scripting is not an exception. Some companies already have in place scripted tools, toys, and systems that have been developed over the course of years.

Keep in mind that you can hire more than one Solution Provider if necessary to get your job done. You could hire separate companies to make your custom avatars, build your region, and run your events, or you might find one able to do a great job of all three. Also, some companies sell copies of things like complex scripted systems (which might need to be set up by them or another Solution Provider you hire) or work under subcontract for other Solution Providers. So you could hire one Solution Provider to manage your project, with that company purchasing some specialized tools or subcontracting when necessary.

 **ANOTHER CAVEAT**

Don't select a Solution Provider just because the company's big and has been around for a long time. Some marketing companies, especially, have decided to add *Second Life* development to their offerings without having sufficient background in it. Sure, they can hire *SL* Residents to work for them, but that doesn't mean they know how to manage a project in this unfamiliar space, how to identify quality content, or how to design things that are going to be a hit with Residents. Some of the highest-profile, most expensive flops on the Grid were built by companies like these. It's great if a Solution Provider had a solid track record before coming to the Grid, but if they haven't performed as well in-world, keep looking!

WHERE DO YOU FIND ONE?

When you've figured out what sort of Solution Provider you need, it's time to take a look around and see who's available.

One of the first places to check is the Solution Provider Directory (Figure 13.2), which is maintained by Linden Lab at **http://secondlife.com/solution_providers/listings.php**. The Solution Provider Directory is searchable in multiple categories, such as Full Service, Consultant, Teen Developer, and Gold Solution Provider. Consultants are individuals or small companies that work in specialized areas. If you need someone only to create a custom skin or a desk, this might be the right category for your search. If your project is larger, consider Full Service companies, which are able to do things like develop whole regions or facilitate events or your entire in-world project.

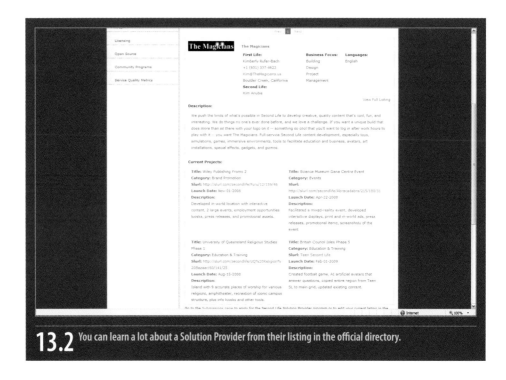

13.2 You can learn a lot about a Solution Provider from their listing in the official directory.

Solution Providers in these first two categories have met specific requirements to be listed, such as completing a required number of projects and providing real-world contact information. Gold Solution Providers take this a step further. Linden Lab's requirements for this category are higher, including references from clients, and it takes into consideration things like awards won, substantial innovation, and long and successful relationships with clients. Linden Lab intends Gold Solution Providers to include only cream-of-the-crop developers.

Solution Providers who are a part of the Gold Solution Provider program also must pay an annual fee to Linden Lab, and in exchange are rewarded with the opportunity to work even more closely with Linden Lab staff.

Linden Lab disclaims affiliation, endorsement, or oversight of any Solution Provider you might find in the directory. So, while the directory is helpful in offering you numerous options in a convenient way, it is not a substitute for doing your own research as you select your Solution Provider.

You can search the Solution Provider Directory by category, company locations, name (in case you're checking up on a company you've already heard of), languages spoken by staff, and business focus (such as landscaping, programming, or project management). The directory also offers a keyword search. Each directory listing includes contact information, business focuses, a description written by the Solution Provider, and brief examples of their recent projects, often with SLURLs to make it easy for you to check them out yourself.

There are other ways to find a Solution Provider. Some Residents maintain external directories, but the quality of these is uneven. It can be difficult to tell the roleplayers from the real businesses, especially if you are unfamiliar with *Second Life*. (We'll take another look at this in the section "Winnow Out Roleplayers.") In general, if you are not very familiar with *SL* culture, you may want to stick with the official Solution Provider Directory.

NOTE

As you peruse the Solution Provider Directory you will find that some developers' project descriptions don't include SLURLs. This is because many projects are, for one reason or another, not open to the public.

Just as in "first life," an awful lot of business is based on referrals. And referrals are usually the best way to find a Solution Provider, too. This way, you know that they have at least one client who thinks highly enough of their work to send you their way. Also, you'll probably be able to check out the referrer's build or whatever else was provided to them by the developer to see if you like it yourself. If you spend some time in-world exploring and networking, you will find many opportunities to seek referrals from other people doing projects or in a field similar to your own.

Other ways to find a Solution Provider include simply finding a build you like while exploring the Grid, then contacting its builder; responding to an ad you see in an *SL*-specific publication or blog; seeking out a Solution Provider you read about in a magazine or newspaper or saw on television, or one who has written about *Second Life* themselves.

Once you have a lead on one or more Solution Providers, you have a bit of investigative work to do!

INVESTIGATE YOUR CANDIDATES

Your next step is to check out Solution Providers you're considering. There are a few ways to go about this. If the Solution Provider company has a website, you'll want to have a look at that, and you should also check out their projects if there's something in-world you can go see yourself. You can also contact the Solution Provider and ask to meet with them in-world to see their work or get a demo. Additionally, they might have a portfolio they are able to show you. You can perform a Web search to see what press or accolades have accrued about the Solution Provider and, of course, you should get and check references.

WINNOW OUT ROLEPLAYERS

Both in-world and on *Second Life*–related websites you might encounter someone who appears to be running a real business when they really aren't. I became aware of this issue after having spent a fair bit of time in negotiations and in-world meetings with some people who represented themselves as the owners of a *Second Life* work-referral agency. They intended to connect content developers and clients, taking a percentage for themselves. Over the course of a couple of days, it finally dawned on me: these people weren't really running a business at all, and the prospective clients they were talking about were entirely imaginary. They weren't Solution Providers (and this happened before there was a directory); they were roleplaying that they were business owners—for fun, like other Residents who roleplay that they are dragons or pirates or fairies— and seemed to have assumed I was doing the same! And yes, there was paperwork involved . . . on in-world notecards. This incident directly contributed to my decision to not work with anyone who wouldn't give their real-world name and contact information immediately.

Can you really work with someone who goes by avatar name instead of their real, legal name? Some people do it all the time, and I used to do it, but I don't anymore. I insist on real names signed on real contracts, even if they come to me via electronic means such as fax or email attachment. A contract signed by an avatar might be legally binding, but imagine the messy situation of having to pursue a lawsuit under those circumstances. My advice? If the amount of money is minimal and if you are purchasing something that is not critical, not having a real-world name probably isn't such a risk. However, be prepared for the worst.

Similarly, there are people who, while competent at content creation or other skills, are so involved in roleplay that professionalism suffers. For example, I came to the conclusion that I would no longer do business with anyone who'll deal only in Linden dollars instead of real-world currency. I had arranged to have some content created by someone who appeared to be very professional in correspondence and in the detail and quality of their work, and they didn't hesitate to give me real-world contact details. However, when it came time to pay that person, they insisted that payment be made in Linden dollars because they were hiding from their spouse the fact that they were still using *Second Life* and didn't want a payment to appear on any statements! How could I work with this person again, not knowing when they might be caught or if they'd finish the project if they were?

> There are plenty of Solution Providers who aren't listed in the official directory. Some don't yet qualify because they haven't yet met requirements, such as completing a certain number of projects. Some simply missed a deadline when it was time to renew their listing. Others aren't aware of it—not a good sign at all. It's certainly possible to find a competent Solution Provider who isn't in the Solution Provider Program, though.

Along with sorting the real Solution Providers from the roleplayers, you can ask a bunch of other questions that will be helpful in selecting the right Solution Provider for your project.

▸ Are you listed in Linden Lab's Solution Provider Directory?

▸ How long have you been doing *Second Life* projects?

▸ How many clients have you had?

▸ Would you please show me some of your work?

▸ Do you think my project idea is a good one, or do you have ideas about how to improve it?

▸ What projects similar to mine have you done in the past?

▸ Would you please give me some references?

▸ What are your specialties?

▸ Will you please give me some real-life contact info?

▸ Who would I contact in case you were not available?

▸ Will you sign a hard-copy contract?

▸ What forms of payment do you accept?

▸ How do you plan to engage Residents (or employees) in this project? What will keep them coming back?

WHAT TO LOOK FOR IN BUILDS

One of the reasons I repeat that you need to log in and try *Second Life* before planning your project is that it is necessary to look at builds and gain enough experience to recognize quality content. If you never had a look around the Grid, you wouldn't have any idea whether the first build you visit is laggy or of particularly good quality.

You can ask the Solution Provider's references about the quality of their work and Resident reaction to their project, but it won't substitute for checking out the Solution Provider's work yourself. You or someone from your organization should log into *Second Life* and have a look at Solution Providers' work. You probably won't be able to recognize the finer points, but some pretty easy-to-spot things to check include the following:

Prim alignment. Look carefully at the build and see where prims meet. Do you see gaps? How about prims that overlap so that they flicker? Are they aligned correctly? (See Figure 13.3 for an example.)

Texture quality. Are the textures applied correctly, or are they distorted? Do the colors seem consistent and appropriate? Do the textures seem to fit the prims? Does the image quality seem pretty good, or is it blurry or jagged-looking? Are the textures themselves attractive? (Figure 13.4 shows an example.)

Load time. When you arrive at the build, how long does it take to load? Slow loading might not be the developer's fault, particularly if the build is on the mainland or if the client has added a lot of content, but a quick load time can probably be attributed to the builder.

Engagement. Does the build incorporate features that keep visitors coming back, such as community, contests, games, or ongoing activities?

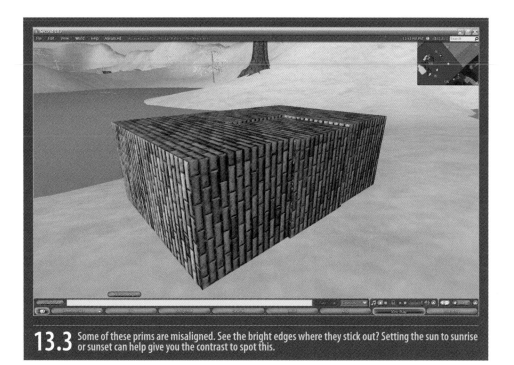

13.3 Some of these prims are misaligned. See the bright edges where they stick out? Setting the sun to sunrise or sunset can help give you the contrast to spot this.

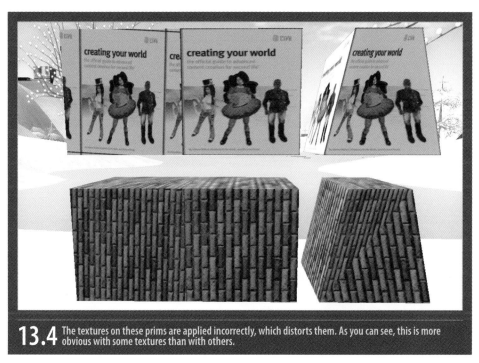

13.4 The textures on these prims are applied incorrectly, which distorts them. As you can see, this is more obvious with some textures than with others.

Lag. How much lag do you experience in the area as you move around and check the place out? Again, lag might be due to causes beyond the builder's control, but a place that's markedly lag-free probably indicates the builder took care with its design and implementation.

Functionality. Does everything work as it should? Does the design make sense (from the viewpoint of a Resident)? Are you able to find your way around? Try using interactive parts of the build. Broken assets might not be the developer's fault—but it is still important to check. You should be looking at more than one build belonging to the Solution Provider you're investigating, or at their own region, so trends will become apparent.

Attractiveness. Do you like this place? Is it somewhere you'd like to spend time?

Use of resources. Closely related to load time and lag, use of resources is very important. This is also going to be hard for you to check if you are unfamiliar with *Second Life*. Consider how well the prims are budgeted: Are there any left? Could that chair have been built and look as good with half the prims? Were resource-heavy sculpted prims used where regular prims would have done the job? How many unique textures are used? Are they loading with marked slowness? Are there similar but not identical textures where one would have been fine?

If you aren't very familiar with these things, how will you judge if a Solution Provider is really qualified? If you have someone at your organization, or even a family member or friend, who is more familiar with *Second Life*, why not ask for some advice? If you don't know anyone who can help you, you have a couple more options: purchase a book like *Creating Your World: The Official Guide to Advanced Content Creation for Second Life* (Wiley, 2007) to study what to look for, or network in-world and ask for help from someone experienced. There's some useful information in Part 1 of this book about networking opportunities available to you no matter what sort of organization you run.

PROPOSALS, AGREEMENTS, AND RIGHTS

I've mentioned a few times that you need to have a real contract with your Solution Provider. Certainly there are variations in how this might be approached. However, I can tell you a bit about the sort of paperwork I provide to my own clients.

PROPOSALS

The first piece of paperwork a client receives from me is a proposal. This document might run as long as 15 or 20 pages, depending on the scope of the project. It includes a few main sections: a detailed project specification, project risks, deadline and fee, rights and permissions, and client participation.

Typically, the proposal starts with a detailed description of everything that my company will provide or do for the client as part of the project. These descriptions are usually approached from the viewpoint of whoever would be using the assets we create or attending an event. Where necessary, there's also a description of some things from the client's viewpoint, such as the sort of user interface they'll use to administer a scripted system. It is vital to make sure that client and Solution Provider are both clear on exactly what the project includes.

Project risks are outlined, as well. Things can go wrong with any project, and I always feel I'd be remiss if I didn't make sure my client was aware of them. Some of these might include events interrupted by unexpected downtime, scripts or other assets broken by changes in *Second Life* functionality beyond my control, and the limited ability to make backups of assets created for clients.

The proposal also includes at least one deadline and fee for the project. There might be more than one deadline if, for example, a project includes more than one phase or event.

I quote the project fee, which might be divided into multiple payments, usually with partial payment due in advance and the balance due upon completion of the project, and a late fee for payments that don't arrive on time. For a longer project, however, the fee might be broken into more payments. I also specify the currency in which the payments must be made. The proposal might include a breakdown of how much each part of the project will cost, in order to allow a client on a limited budget to select only those parts that are most important. The proposed deadline is usually contingent upon a specified signing date and often also upon my company's availability, because the calendar fills up and I often have a waiting list. There might be an expiration date for the quote.

Rights and permissions offered vary depending on the nature of the project and the client's requirements, but I have a standard approach, usually offering the nonexclusive right to modify and copy assets, but restricting transfer of scripts to only members of my client's staff —no transfer or resale to anyone else. We'll take deeper look at rights and permissions in just a bit.

Every proposal includes a section outlining what sort of client participation will be required. These might be things like providing a copy of a logo to use on branded assets, supplying text included on a notecard given by an information kiosk, or arranging to make myself or members of my staff managers of the client's estate. There are usually deadlines for these things, to make certain that I have them in time to use them so that I can complete the project in time. Without them, some parts of the project might not be able to be done at all.

AGREEMENTS

Once my client has approved my proposal—of which there might be several drafts—I prepare an agreement to sign. This is a fairly standard independent-contractor agreement making reference to the proposal, which is attached to the agreement.

RIGHTS AND PERMISSIONS

As you learned in Chapter 9, "Manage Your Infrastructure," the in-world permissions system can be a bit tricky to manage, and in-world permissions are not the same as real-life intellectual-property rights. Your agreement with your Solution Provider should address both.

It's not uncommon for a client to request all rights to assets developed for a project. However, that's usually not practical for the Solution Provider. Solution Providers reuse assets all the time. For example, say one of the many things you need for your project is an information kiosk that distributes notecards and opens a browser directed to your website. Odds are that if you are working with an established Solution Provider they've built kiosks like this before; they'd normally reuse a script they've already developed, and it's possible that the code won't need any modification at all. Asking your Solution Provider to give up all rights to that script they rely on all the time is akin to asking a carpenter to give up using a hammer.

Similarly, Solution Providers reuse textures, animations, and other assets. While you might be able to talk someone into giving up all rights to their go-to content-creation tools, it's going to cost a lot.

Some assets are just too valuable to give up. Imagine your project will include a scripted system that is your Solution Provider's bread and butter—something they've been improving upon for a couple of years and of which they sell copies—a networked vendor system, for example. If they sell you all rights, how much future income would they be giving up? You'll be charged at least that amount.

Another factor that can complicate matters is assets the Solution Provider purchases from an in-world shop or a subcontractor. To give you the very best tools for your project or in order to keep the cost from being excessive, they might purchase things like trees or clothing from specialists. They're not likely to be getting all rights to these, so they certainly can't give all rights to you. For example, many trees and clothing items are traditionally sold with copy or transfer permissions, but not both, and they might not be modifiable. However, it can substantially reduce the cost of your project and the time it takes to develop it if your Solution Provider can purchase some items rather than create them. (In fact, this is so typical that it's usual to assume that your project will involve purchases.) Besides, a specialist's work can be far superior, particularly if it's a specialty that is very complicated, such as making avatar hair.

You'll learn even more about permissions in the "Inventory and Permissions Management" section of this chapter. This is a very important area to discuss with your Solution Provider. Be sure to talk about it early on.

WORKING WITH YOUR SOLUTION PROVIDER

The success or failure of your project, as well as your enjoyment or misery, depend in part on your relationship with your Solution Provider and how well you work together. In most cases, you really do have to work together; particularly because of the way the permissions, land management, and group tools work.

HOW THE PROCESS WORKS

Naturally, different Solution Providers go about things in different ways. I have found that the process I use is generally very successful and as painless and enjoyable as possible for my clients. So, I'll continue to use my methods as an example.

Prospective clients contact me in a variety of ways, usually via email or in-world instant message. If I am contacted by instant message, I usually request that we continue our correspondence via email. Instant messages, while very useful for real-time conversation and brief offline IM notes, are not ideal for extended discussion. Plus, I like to see a real email address and contact info before things go too far. (See the earlier discussion of the importance of obtaining real-world contact info from Solution Providers.)

I'll review whatever information is provided, perhaps correspond to discuss it a bit, and then we'll have an in-world meeting, or perhaps a teleconference. I have never traveled to a client's location for a meeting, nor have I ever had a client to my office for one. Some other Solution Providers jet around to meetings, but I don't find it necessary. After all, the Grid is well suited to meetings! In-world meetings are a nice way for prospective clients to learn a bit about how well this can really work, not to mention that the project will cost less than it would if I had to pass on the cost of travel as part of the project fee.

Depending on what sort of project is under discussion, I might bring one or more members of my staff with me, most often an engineer. I'll discuss the prospective client's needs, ask questions, and answer questions. I'll show examples of my work that are related to what the client needs for the project. We might even teleport around to see a few different builds. I'll want to see the prospective client's land, if they have some, to ascertain things like how many prims are available and how stable the region seems.

The questions I'm likely to ask a prospective client include these:

▶ How many buildings do you need?

▶ Please tell me a bit more about them: size, number of rooms, architectural style, and function.

▶ Do they need to be based on specific existing or historical structures? If so, how closely do these need to match the actual buildings? Will you do the research, or will I? Will you provide photos and floor plans or blueprints?

▶ Photosourced textures, or hand-drawn? If photosourced, will you provide the photos?

▶ How detailed do you want the buildings to be?

- Do you need only the structures, or do you need furnishings, as well? If so, please tell me what you need.

- What's the prim limit for the build? That is, what percentage of your land's resources do you want to use for these buildings?

- What sort of interactive/scripted objects will you need (objects that give inventory to avatars, animate them for things like bowing or sitting, open web pages, etc.)?

- Will you need any other objects or clothing?

- Do you need any landscaping or terraforming of your island, and any particular landscape features (caves, rivers, pathways, gardens, mountains, etc.)?

We'll also discuss the options of continued support, community building and management, events, and other ongoing activities that build engagement and use. Most of my clients take over long-term projects themselves after development has been completed, but some prefer to have my company continue to manage their projects. Just building a location isn't enough; there needs to be something going on there to encourage return visits. If my client does want assistance with this, such as an event (or a series of them), then I ask questions like these:

- What's the purpose of the event?

- Do you want to use voice, text chat, or both?

- Will there be streaming media, and are you hosting the stream yourself?

- What sort of attendance do you have in mind?

- Do you need a venue built for you, or do you need to rent one?

- Do you want me to provide an event host, or will you emcee it yourself?

For more about considerations involved in planning an event, check out Chapter 12, "Run an Event."

After our meeting, I will probably have to meet with members of my staff to discuss the project, and I'm likely to email the prospective client a few more questions. We might meet again to look at some demo items or to discuss more details. Then I'll write and submit a proposal. When terms are settled, I'll send the agreement for signing and get started on the project.

I'm likely to require some things from the client to get started, like photographs of items to be built and the client's logo and branding guide. In fact, I might request some of these during the process of working out a proposal, in order to get a clear understanding of what is desired.

Additionally, there are certain ways in which the client will need to participate in the project, unless they don't own and won't manage the land themselves. These usually include inviting me to or allowing me to set up a group for the client, with a role that allows me to add my team to the group and manage the land and assets on it, at least for the duration of my involvement in the project. Depending on what sort of project the client is doing, I might need additional group powers. I'll also probably need estate management permissions if the client owns a region, and some members of my staff might require them, as well. There's more information about groups and permissions in Chapter 9.

My team will probably not develop all of the project at the client's location. Content developers use a variety of tools and usually maintain their own workshops, which are set up specifically for their work style. Also, I usually set up an area at my region or the client's where I track all aspects of the project, including assets, tasks, and who on my team is doing what (this was shown in Figure 9.30, in Chapter 9).

As my team works on the project, from time to time I'll have questions or want to show the client a demo of what we're developing. The client might be asked to meet with a member of my staff to test certain items. Some completed assets might be transferred to the client immediately, before the final handoff.

When the build is complete, I arrange to meet with the client and to give a tour or demo of whatever we have created. If necessary, we can tweak a few things. And then I transfer assets to the client, something that can be fairly complicated, so I'll focus on that specifically in the next section.

If the project was something like an event, afterward I will provide the client with a summary that includes links to press received, ads and other announcements my company has placed, attendance figures, and screenshots of the event or links to screenshots.

Finally, I'll send an invoice for the final project payment.

INVENTORY AND PERMISSIONS MANAGEMENT

More than once I have worked with a client who has had to completely or nearly abandon assets created for them by their previous Solution Provider. How could this be?

Suppose you have a Solution Provider develop your entire project for you on land they hold, and they manage everything for you. Sounds great, right? No hassle, no muss, no fuss, no learning any of this stuff about managing inventory or parcel permissions!

But then, you never get a copy of the build. Then you decide to work with someone else for whatever reason . . . your old Solution Provider retired, you didn't like their work, you needed someone with a different specialty. But your build is still on your former Solution Provider's land and you don't own any of it. Unless you can track them down and get them to transfer all of it to you—and unless your contract requires them to do it—you might be out of luck!

In fact, even if you did everything right, if you wait too long and your Solution Provider hasn't been paying attention to details, you might still be out of luck. For example, one of my clients who was new to the Grid wasn't aware that this could be a problem, and it had been a long time since they'd worked with their former developer. By the time I pointed out the problem, some of the artists who'd worked on the build had left the company, and (brace yourself) though the objects were there in place, they were still owned by those long-gone folks and no one else had a backup. Fortunately for my client, the Solution Provider was able to round up their former staffers and get the objects transferred, but it could have turned out very badly, and has in other cases I have seen.

TRANSFER METHODS

Having your assets transferred to you by your Solution Provider can be a little bit tricky, and it takes organization and planning on their part from the outset. There are a few ways to go about this.

> **Sell the build with the land**. In Chapter 9 you learned how a parcel can be sold along with everything on it that has transfer permissions. However, parts of your build, such as store-bought trees or plants, might not be transferrable. Also, in order to do this your Solution Provider has to at least temporarily own the parcel. Be sure that all of the permissions on the assets on the parcel are correct before the transfer is made; the transfer can't be undone, and if it's done with incorrect permissions it could break some assets or make them unreusable. I have seen this particular feature lead to heartbreak enough times that I don't use it myself. I can't warn you enough times to be very cautious about doing this!

Sell in place for zero. This method seems straightforward. The Solution Provider sets the objects for sale for a price of zero Linden dollars and you walk around the build purchasing the items in place (Figure 13.5). Making sure permissions are correct first is vital. If the next-owner permissions are set incorrectly you might find that you now own the only copy of the item, or an item you can't modify or transfer. Selling in place for zero is a great method for transferring specific parts of a build but is far less practical for a large project, which might span one or more regions. In particular, landscape-heavy builds can be problematic, because you will probably have to individually purchase a lot of trees and rocks, some of which may be difficult to reach due to their placement.

13.5 The pop-up system message in the lower-right corner indicates that you have purchased the original prim, rather than a copy. Be sure to take a backup!

Transfer a copy from Inventory. This is something I do often. I select sections of the build and take a copy into Inventory for a backup. Then I give a copy of the backup to my client. When I do this, I normally leave my team's originals in place, which is more convenient for any repairs or additional development undertaken by my company in the future. Be sure, when you take out a copy of your build, that you are in object-editing mode so that you can hang onto all of the pieces that come out of Inventory together as a coalesced object (Figure 13.6) and move them into place.

Share with group. Another approach, though a rare one, is the Solution Provider sharing or deeding the build with a group that is administered by the client. This can be problematic because you can't undeed objects. It's important to make sure permissions are correct before you do this and to be very aware of who is in the group or who might be added to it later. You don't want just anyone to be able to mess with your build!

Put it in a rezzer. Scripted gadgets, such as the Rez-Foo, may be used to "pack" a build. In this case, your Solution Provider adds a script to every object in the build and then puts all of the pieces into a box. You can take out this box, click it, and rez your build and even move the whole thing around until you have it where you want it. This can be very convenient, but it does mean a lot of added work. Additionally, those added scripts can impact region resources. It's a good solution, though, if you expect to deploy copies of your build often.

13.6 This shows a coalesced object: a bunch of objects selected and taken into inventory at the same time.

⬎WARNING

As soon as you have received your build or a copy of it from your Solution Provider, be sure to take a backup copy into Inventory. If possible, send a copy to a member of your staff or your own alt, just in case something goes wrong.

Use a dedicated avatar. This is a really powerful approach that, unfortunately, has some big drawbacks. You or your Solution Provider can create a *Second Life* account for an avatar who will be used to place all assets for your project. When they're done, you change the account password and that's that. However, many Solution Providers use nontransferable tools to create things. Without purchasing or building copies of these tools, they probably can't use a different avatar to actually create everything. That means building with their usual avatar and lots of inventory-transferring and permission-setting, which is added work that will cost you. Additionally, content creators' names and object owners' names appear in the object properties. Traditionally, you check out who did this cool build by looking to see who owns it or built it. If your Solution Provider's content creators can't get credit in this way, it's likely to inflate your project fee. Furthermore, if you want to have more work done on the project, the Solution Provider might need to have access to that avatar again.

WHEN YOU DON'T OWN YOUR PRIMS

It's not always necessary to own all of the prims on your land, and sometimes it's not practical at all.

As mentioned earlier, content creators prefer to have their names show on their work. This has added benefits, though. If you need to have something more done to the build, your Solution Provider doesn't need to have you transfer the prims again.

Sometimes you just can't own the assets—for example, because they were purchased from a Resident shop without transfer permissions. In this case, ask your Solution Provider for a landmark to the shop so that you can buy another copy if you need a replacement. If the item is especially important to your project, it might be a good idea to purchase backup copies.

The permissions system can complicate object ownership in other ways, as well. Suppose you have hired a Solution Provider to create a scripted kiosk that gives copies of branded propeller beanies to visitors to your build. But you don't want everyone who gets a beanie to be able to give copies to just anyone, and you don't want them taking a copy of the script that spins the propeller (or the one that makes your logo light up and blink). This means the permissions all have to be set correctly on the beanie and the scripts it contains, including no-transfer permissions.

So, no problem, the Solution Provider just sets the permissions on the thing, stuffs it into the kiosk, and gives it to you, right? No, wrong! If the Solution Provider sets the permissions on the beanie so that it's no-modify, copy, and no-transfer (the usual permissions for something like this) and gives it to you, that means you can't modify it or transfer it to the visitors who click the kiosk.

The answer here is for the Solution Provider to set up a full-permissions copy of the kiosk and beanie and give them to you for backup. Then they rez a copy in-world with the permissions set correctly for use by visitors. There are other approaches, but they also require either the Solution Provider to set things up and own the prims, or you to set some permissions yourself, perhaps with your Solution Provider's assistance.

Remember: it's typical for the content creators to own all or most of the objects actually instantiated at your build. It's usually not a problem so long as you have a backup copy and a trustworthy Solution Provider.

YOUR PARTICIPATION IS REQUIRED

Although, theoretically, it's possible to simply select a Solution Provider from the Solution Provider Directory, throw your plans and money at them, and never log into *Second Life* or participate in any way in the development of your project, it's not a good idea. It's important to go in-world to familiarize yourself with what's possible and best practices and to check out the work of Solution Providers you are considering for the job. Plus, if you never log in, how are you going to get a backup of your build?

It's also possible to be what I call a *permanoob*—someone who, although they've had a *Second Life* account for a long time (even years), never learns basic skills. If you don't learn a few things, you're not going to be able to set permissions or place a backup if you need to, and your Solution Provider is going to have to charge you for the additional time and effort required if they need to walk you through everything step-by-step.

CHAPTER

14

What is Teen *Second Life* (TSL)? What sorts of projects may be undertaken there, and what are the restrictions on them and on the people working on them? How does an adult access the Teen Grid or bring in students? Is it safe? How do you go about doing a project in TSL and how can you find a Solution Provider qualified to help? What resources are available for organizations that would like to work on the Teen Grid? This chapter will tell you what you need to know.

WORK IN
TEEN *SECOND LIFE*

WHAT IS TEEN *SECOND LIFE?*

No one under 18 is allowed on the *Second Life* Main Grid, which includes both the mainland and private regions. For teens age 13 to 17, however, there's Teen *Second Life*. It offers almost all of the same features as the Main Grid, but is accessible only by teens and by adults who Linden Lab has cleared to work on certain types of educational projects (more on that later in this chapter).

Teens do most of the same things adults do on the Main Grid, including building things, running shops, buying and selling virtual land, and going to events. When a Teen Grid Resident turns 18, they receive a notice that they need to sell any TSL mainland parcels they own, and then their avatars, along with their Inventory and any private regions they own, are transferred to the Main Grid. They are no longer able to access TSL or to interact with or exchange inventory or Linden dollars with TSL Residents. A Bridge program helps to acclimate them to the Main Grid— on the Main Grid, they're invited to a special group for teens who have been transferred.

Mystery seems to shroud the Teen Grid because of these restrictions. It's a fabled land where few adults can go—and only when they have been background-checked and their educational projects have been approved by Linden Lab. Once Main Grid avatars go to the Teen Grid, they never return (so you'll need an alt for TSL use). Spurious rumors abound, full of misinformation about what is and isn't allowed in TSL, and these are traps for the unwary, who may find themselves banned from all of *Second Life* for violating rules about interactions with teens.

Fortunately, you don't have to guess or rely on rumors, because you have this book. I was the first Solution Provider to work in the live Teen Grid, way back in 2006, and I'm still working with clients there today. However, do keep in mind that Linden Lab changes rules and procedures from time to time. Particularly when working on the Teen Grid, double-check the latest information (see the resources at the end of this chapter), and don't hesitate to contact Linden Lab if you have any questions.

TEEN-GRID SAFETY

Linden Lab takes many precautions to ensure that the Teen Grid is a safe place. Teens are not allowed to reveal personally identifying information while in-world, and even interactions with adults cleared to work on the Teen Grid are curtailed. Teens must verify their identity upon signup using either SMS or PayPal (unless registering via the Registration API, which I'll discuss later in this chapter). There are limitations on how much money teens may spend in-world. Plus, no "adult" material is allowed on the Teen Grid, where all regions are rated PG. You can read the Teen *Second Life* Community Standards at **http://teen.secondlife.com/footer/cs**.

APPROPRIATE PROJECTS

There are some restrictions on what sorts of projects you can undertake in TSL. Educational institutions are allowed, and government agencies, nonprofits, and enterprises may be allowed to purchase private regions and work on the Teen Grid if their projects are made up of educational content. Selling to teens, and other commercial activity by anyone other than teen Residents, is not allowed. So while you might be able to offer a branded educational experience, you can't sell or market your products directly to teens.

Some projects you might be planning will need to be developed within the Teen Grid; namely, those that involve any participants under 18. Although you may hear a rumor that it's OK to allow teens into your private region on the Main Grid as long as it is closed to the public, that's simply not true. No teens are ever allowed on the Main Grid for any reason.

The age of 18 might seem to be an arbitrary and downright inconvenient cutoff if you're in a country where the age of majority is lower. However, 18 is the age at which one becomes an adult in the US, and Linden Lab abides by US law. You are not going to be able to, as some have hoped, convince Linden Lab to make an exception for your project, even if it means you will have added challenges if you want to use *SL* for a class in which some of the students are under 18. Later in the chapter, I'll discuss what to do about that.

If you have questions or want to double-check that your project is acceptable for TSL, submit a support ticket to Linden Lab and be very specific in your description of your project plan. Your Solution Provider may also be able to provide helpful insights.

ACCESS THE TEEN GRID

Linden Lab allows Approved Adults (Figure 14.1) to work on educational projects on the Teen Grid. What's an Approved Adult and how can you become one? Read on, and keep in mind that this is not an instantaneous process. As you plan your project, be sure to allow time for it!

14.1 Approved Adult avatars must wear this group tag at all times while in TSL.

BACKGROUND CHECKS

Every adult who enters the Teen Grid to work on a project must be background-checked. Unless you are an instructor of a bona fide educational institution that has background-checked you already (and is willing and able to verify this for Linden Lab), you will be required to use the services of third-party background-checking company, Ascertain Screening and Investigations **www.ascertainsi.com/secondlife/bgConsent.asp**. You must

NOTE

Every staff member of a Solution Provider who works for you on the Teen Grid must be background-checked, as well. If they are not already cleared when you hire them, you will be expected to be their point of contact for this process.

complete the order form, which includes some information about yourself, such as all previous residences within the last 10 years, government-issued identification number, and more. This form authorizes Ascertain to check for criminal records and particularly sex offenses. You will have to pay a fee of at least US$40, with possible additional charges, particularly for searches that must be performed outside of the US. If you would like a quote or have more questions, contact Ascertain. At press time, the *Second Life* contact at Ascertain was Dee Igo, **DIgo@Ascertainsi.com**.

Be certain to allow time for this process. It has occasionally taken as little as a week, but depending on how many times you or your staff members have moved around, and where to, it can take several weeks. It's a good idea to have a backup plan in mind in case one of your teachers or other staff members' background check takes longer than expected.

Upon completion of the check, Ascertain will send results to you and to Linden Lab. Linden Lab will not receive any details; they'll only learn if you pass or fail.

LAND REQUIREMENT

On the Teen Grid, the avatar you use there will be restricted to the estate on which you're working. Your avatar will not be able to visit the Teen *Second Life* mainland, or private regions that aren't a part of your estate. And it can't go to the Main Grid, either—there's no returning it to the Main Grid once it's gone to the Teen Grid. This means you need a place to go on the Teen Grid, as well as an alt to use there. You have three options: buy land, rent it, or arrange to share an estate.

The education and nonprofit discounted rates for regions apply on the Teen Grid, as well. You'll need to use the Special Island Order Form (**http://specialorders.secondlife.com/**) to make your purchase.

When you do this, make sure you place your order using the alt account you have created to use on the Teen Grid (which I'll discuss further in the section "Prepare for Transformation"). The estate cannot be transferred in Teen *Second Life*, so this account must be the permanent landowner. That means your Solution Provider can't purchase the land for you and transfer it to you later. Plus, a Solution Provider can't get the educational rate for land.

What if you don't want to, don't need to, or can't afford to purchase an entire region? You may be able to purchase a parcel in an estate operated by another organization, such as Virtual World Campus, which is operated by Global Kids and FireSabre. This works similarly to purchasing land in a private region on the Main Grid.

Other organizations arrange to borrow land from or collaborate with one another on the Teen Grid. A great way to connect with others to discuss this sort of collaboration is to participate in one of Linden Lab's educational mailing lists, such as SLED or Educators and Teens.

 VISITING AS A GUEST

Many people wish for a way to visit the Teen Grid to check it out before planning their projects. But to access the Teen Grid, you need to be an estate owner there or a staff member of a project on a Teen Grid estate. However, some organizations will occasionally sponsor a guest or visitor. The estate owner will be responsible for you, and you will have to provide them with an Ascertain background check. Then your sponsor will need to send Linden Lab an updated staff list that has you included.

PREPARE FOR TRANSFORMATION

If you've ever thought it would be cool to be stranded on a desert island with only your own cunning and the items you brought with you, you'll find working on the Teen Grid a dream come true.

Once you know that your project is appropriate for the Teen Grid and you've been cleared by Ascertain, and once you have arranged for a place to work in TSL, it's time to prepare your alt. You do this in the usual way, on the Main Grid. However, a Resident can have only five accounts. If you need to exceed this for business reasons, contact Linden Lab support by submitting a ticket.

Prepare your avatar carefully, because once it has been "transformed" it cannot return to the Main Grid, and you can only take with you what you have in its Inventory when the move is made—you will not have an opportunity to go back for anything you forgot. Everything must be PG in nature. Be certain to include all of the tools, textures, and objects you might need, because you won't be able to leave your estate to shop, you won't be able to have anything sent from the Main Grid, and you will not be able to use web-based shopping services. Anything you don't take with you initially will have to be brought in by another member of your staff when they come to the Teen Grid, or must be made by you, a member of your staff, a Solution Provider cleared to work on the Teen Grid, or a teen.

Once your avatar is ready, you (or your project leader) must contact Linden Lab to request transfer to the Teen Grid. The request must come from an estate owner or approved project coordinator, who will receive instructions from Linden Lab in an approval email in response to their private-region sales order. This procedure can vary (Linden Lab handles projects on the Teen Grid on a case-by-case basis), and is always improving. It may involve signing a Social Contract regarding your presence and behavior on the Teen Grid, or the estate owner might be required to update a list of approved staff members. If there are any questions, the estate owner can file a support ticket. Linden Lab prefers to have just one point of contact from an organization.

Linden Lab will notify the estate owner when your avatar has been moved to the Teen Grid. This is when the real fun begins! Unless you're joining an ongoing project, you will find yourself on an empty island—a giant blank 3D canvas just waiting for your educational content.

> **TIP**
>
> Some assets are much more portable than others. If you forget to pack up a script, you can copy and paste it. And you can reupload any textures (including sculpt maps), too. But if you forget to bring your folder of megaprims, you're out of luck!

> **NOTE**
>
> There is no official event calendar for TSL as there is for the Main Grid.

RULES FOR APPROVED ADULTS

For the safety of teen Residents, Approved Adult avatars are bound by rules and technical restrictions.

The following restrictions will apply to you while you work on the Teen Grid:

▶ You can't leave your estate.

▶ You cannot exchange Linden dollars with teens.

▶ You cannot sell, advertise, or pursue commercial activity on the Teen Grid.

▶ You can't post on the TSL blogs or forums.

▶ You cannot transfer avatars or inventory from the Teen Grid to the Main Grid.

▶ Search is limited to your own estate.

▶ The Grid map is disabled.

You have a choice about some additional restrictions: you can select either a Closed Estate or an Open Estate on the Teen Grid.

OPEN VERSUS CLOSED ESTATES

A Closed Estate is where you use the Registration API to sign up teens with TSL accounts so that their avatars appear directly at your region upon their first login. To do this, you will need to work with a Teen Grid Approved Solution Provider that has also been approved to use the Registration API.

Teen accounts' avatars created using the Registration API can never leave your estate, not even to visit the TSL mainland. You will be able to be in groups with "your" teens, IM them, and exchange inventory with them. If the teens would like to travel elsewhere on the Teen Grid or interact with others outside of your estate, they will need to create another TSL account on their own. And teens who are not a part of your project (created using the Registration API) may not visit your Closed Estate.

An Open Estate may be set open or closed to the general population of the Teen Grid. In other words, if you choose, you can allow any teens in TSL to stop in and visit or participate in activities at your region. Or you may restrict access to only "your" teens (such as your students), but let them create or use their pre-existing TSL accounts and come and go as they please.

> **NOTE**
>
> Sometimes you need to use the Registration API even if you intend to have an Open Estate, because if you are outside of the US many students will not have access to US-based SMS or PayPal, so they won't be able to confirm their identities to get their own accounts.

If you choose to have an Open Estate, you will need to follow these rules:

▷ Give Linden Lab notice that you plan to have an Open Estate, and notify Concierge (support) when you are about to open access (after development is complete).

▷ Set up a single point of entry (Telehub) for your region, with direct teleportation disabled.

▷ Set up a notecard giver (provided by Linden Lab) that announces to all avatars who visit your region that there are Approved Adults in the region (Figure 14.2).

▷ All adults must be members of the Approved Adult group (an invitation will be sent to you upon transformation to TSL) and your avatar must wear the Approved Adult group tag at all times.

▷ Your parcel description must include "Approved (non-Linden) adults may be present."

Keep in mind that if you have an Open Estate, you cannot transfer inventory to teens, IM them, or be in the same group with them. Your interaction will be limited to text or voice chat, interactive objects, and media streams.

14.2 Open Estates must use a Linden Lab–provided notecard giver to let teens know there are adults in the region.

Once you have established a Closed or Open Estate, you can't change your mind, so choose carefully. While the Closed Estate allows you a lot of control over your student experience, it also restricts their activities and you will not be able to let other teens visit or participate. An Open Estate allows visitors, and you can use the Registration API to bring in students if you choose; however, your interaction with teens will be greatly restricted, often requiring some tricky workarounds, which I'll discuss in the next section.

You can also set your own rules for your staff, of course. Some organizations might require notification every time a staff member logs into the Teen Grid, logging of discussions, or limited conversation with teens by staff members who don't need to interact with them directly.

WORKAROUNDS

Particularly if you choose to run your project in an Open Estate, you are going to need to come up with some workarounds to get certain things done. This section presents some workarounds you might find useful.

Have teens do what you can't. You can have your own students, teen volunteers, or even paid teen content developers build things, create groups, post on the TSL forums, and do most other things you can't do yourself. Do be aware, however, that in most cases teens probably can't sign a binding contract, and remember that you are not allowed to ask teens in TSL for personal information, including contact info.

Use scripts to solve your problems. The ramifications of Teen Grid restrictions are many. For example, if you cannot look up a teen in Search, you can't ban them from your region without clicking on their avatar, something they own, or their name in chat. You can't add teens to an access list for a specific parcel or to a group so that they can use parcel media controls. You can't give out L$ prizes. But with some creativity, you can use scripted tools to work around most of these challenges. I design a lot of solutions of this type for clients on the Teen Grid. For example, for one client who was not able to receive instant

> **WARNING**
>
> Be careful when transferring scripted systems to the Teen Grid when your avatar is converted. Those that are built to give inventory, including notecards or objects, are likely to break.

> **WARNING**
>
> Be aware that there may be a difference between what's possible on the Teen Grid and what is actually permissible. So if you want to try a workaround that will allow you to do something that technological restrictions would normally keep you from doing, it's a good idea to contact Linden Lab first.

messages from teens, I developed an in-world answering machine that relayed messages from open text chat (Figure 14.3). It was allowed by Linden Lab specifically because the messages were typed in open chat, where they were as visible as they would be during a normal in-world conversation. Scripts can also be useful for things like controlling media streams or access to parcels, even when you can't add teens to your group.

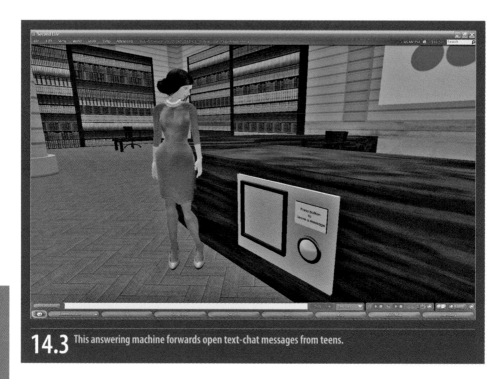

14.3 This answering machine forwards open text-chat messages from teens.

⩗**NOTE**

With Linden Lab's stand-alone offering on the horizon, working with teens will probably become much easier. You will be able to set up your own mini-grid at your own location, with or without a connection to the *Second Life* Grid. The rules surrounding this feature are not yet available, but it's probably reasonable to assume that you will be able to run your own classes, without technical restrictions, on a grid unconnected to the *Second Life* Grid.

Work outside the box. Or outside the Grid, in this case. It's usually permissible to use scripted objects on the Teen Grid to launch web pages or to give URLs in chat, depending on the nature of the site to which you're directing teens. So, for example, my Bard in a Box—a sort of information kiosk featuring a shifty-eyed bust of Shakespeare—directs teens to a website where they can download a texture to make their own British Council T-shirt, since the British Council was unable to give shirts directly to teens in-world. Another device does give shirts in-world in a roundabout way. Instead of giving the item directly to a teen, it contacts a distro box—a scripted box that hands out inventory—and the distro is owned by an avatar able to give things to teens (Figure 14.4).

Mix reality. Suppose you have a class you want to teach in-world in which some students are over 18 and some are not. There are two approaches to this. Some educators run simultaneous projects in both grids. It's even possible to connect the two groups using streaming media, such as a 2006 mixed-reality award ceremony held by Global Kids and the MacArthur Foundation. It took place in TSL and the real world, and a video stream from TSL (including the video teens were watching from real life), was viewed at the same time on the Main Grid (Figure 14.5).

Have your over-18 students background checked like other adults. This is often a necessary approach if some of your students will be turning 18 during the project.

14.4 Using Highlight Transparent will enable you to see the invisible distro box that hands out T-shirts at British Council Isle.

14.5 This is a view from the Main Grid of a mixed-reality event that took place on the Teen Grid and in the real world.

TWO SUCCESSFUL PROJECTS

Let's take a look at two examples of projects in TSL, each approached in a different way.

GLOBAL KIDS

Global Kids is a nonprofit organization that focuses on educating young people, particularly urban public-school students (many who might be at risk of dropping out), about international affairs and their role in making policy. They're encouraged to develop leadership, communication, and critical-thinking skills, and to participate in school and community affairs. Students participating in Global Kids programs often help to educate and train their peers.

In 2005 I was contacted by Barry Joseph (avatar globalkids Bixby on the Main Grid, Barry GKid in TSL), director of the Global Kids Online Leadership Program. He had spent some time in-world on the Main Grid, familiarizing himself with *Second Life* and experimenting on his organization's small mainland parcel. He wanted to put together a team to develop a private region for TSL that would be used initially to gather entries for a MacArthur Foundation–funded essay contest, and later as a virtual home base for Global Kids in *Second Life*.

After discussion with Linden Lab, it was decided that my company would develop a private region on the Main Grid and then Linden Lab would move the whole thing to the Teen Grid. This had never been done before, and my team and Linden Lab spent much time and effort on planning so it would go without a hitch, testing things and endeavoring to design our scripted systems so they would survive the trip. (It's important to note that all of these meetings occurred in *Second Life*. Imagine the savings over traveling for real-life meetings!)

We developed a quest, where on arrival an automated system gave teens a special translation ring that would allow them to understand what was being said by various objects around the island. A talking stone idol would give them the first clue in their quest. This would send them to find the Globe Quiz, which asked a trivia question about teens and media. A correct answer would grant them access to a volcano called Fire Mountain. They would encounter a talking palm tree (frightened of the approaching lava!) and bats, and finally, inside the volcano itself, they would have the opportunity to enter the essay contest by submitting their essay in-world via a Magic Envelope that forwarded their entry to Global Kids. For entering, they received prizes, including a pet iguana their avatar could carry.

After a launch party on the Main Grid, Linden Lab moved the island to TSL, where a number of scripted systems, despite everyone's best efforts, broke. To make repairs, Linden Lab arranged to bring me to the Teen Grid. That was when I became the first Solution Provider on the live Teen Grid, setting some of the precedents for the way projects work on the Teen Grid today.

The project worked out very well in the end, despite the challenges of being the first project run by adults in TSL. Teens responded as expected, puzzling out the quest like any other adventure game they'd play online, and then showing their friends around. In fact, some teens even created markers and arrows to indicate important clues. And I was sure the project was a success when a teen set the Frightened Palm Tree on fire with scripted objects and Global Kids used a screenshot of that in the parcel description—it was exactly the half-entertained, half-sarcastic attitude I expected of the teen Residents.

When the essay-contest winner was announced in the mixed-reality event mentioned earlier in the chapter, a teen who'd entered the contest in-world accepted the award from in-world.

Global Kids has since expanded their estate and has their own minicontinent. Additionally, they've brought in many notable guest speakers, such as Kofi Annan, Desmond Tutu, and Henry Jenkins (Figure 14.6), and partnered with organizations like the National Oceanic and Atmospheric Administration to bring interesting activities and exhibits to the Teen Grid, where they are enjoyed not only by Global Kids students but also by other interested teens in TSL.

14.6 Henry Jenkins (director of the MIT Comparative Media Studies Program) and other major figures have appeared in TSL.

The volcano still stands, three years later—which is ages in *Second Life* years. When Global Kids wanted to remove it (because it took up so much space and its purpose had been served), teens protested, and have even added scripting themselves to make it erupt at regular intervals. In fact, these days most Global Kids content is built by the teens themselves, along with machinima, games, and other educational tools.

Says Joseph, "You have to have a lot of grit to work as an educator in Teen *Second Life*. Imagine yourself as a resident of a Western town at the start of the gold rush—everything feels new and resources are sparse but the company is interesting and the potential to strike gold is ever-present."

We came up with some interesting workarounds over the years to make some of Global Kids's wonderful ideas functional in-world, including the GK Light Bulb System (used to maintain and manage a chat queue) and a Global Kids currency.

While you can't visit Global Kids on the Teen Grid, you can visit their small location on the Main Grid, Global Kids HQ.

THE BRITISH COUNCIL

The British Council is, according to their website, "the UK's international organisation for educational opportunities and cultural relations." Working in 110 countries and territories across the world, they were ready to expand into the virtual world.

⌐ TIP

If you work on multiple Teen Grid estates, you will need to create a different alt for each one. You will not be able to transfer inventory between them, so be prepared to pack up anew each time you send another avatar to the Teen Grid.

In 2007 I was contacted by Graham Stanley (avatar Baldric Commons on the Main Grid, Graham Bluecoat in TSL), the product manager of the Learn English Second Life for Teens project with the British Council. He wanted to do a language learning project in TSL.

Rather than building the British Council's content on the Main Grid and having it moved, my team built their assets right on the Teen Grid. This meant that, while by this time I had staff working on the Teen Grid already, additional members of my team had to undergo the background-checking and conversion process. And I made sure I packed everything I could think of into my Inventory!

We arrived at a blank island, made our *Lord of the Flies* jokes, and then got down to work, eventually creating (as of press time) three regions on the Teen Grid and a duplicate of one of them on the Main Grid (British Council Isle). They feature quests and places to explore and discuss based on UK history, legends, modern-day locations, and even a glimpse of a possible future.

Although it's an Open Estate, the British Council uses the Registration API to bring in students from all over the world. This allows them to register teens who don't have PayPal or US-based SMS, and restricts their avatars to the British Council's estate. By February of 2009, the organization had registered over 1,000 teen students from 12 different countries.

Says Stanley, "We can repurpose a lot of the British Council's output from elsewhere on the Web and link to it. Much of it is lost [overlooked] on various sites, the Poems on the Underground [Figure 14.7], etc. With *SL*, we can point people to what is there and also try to adapt it so it is relevant for our learners." The Poems on the Underground exhibit, for example, has been revived in a brand-new venue, getting added value out of this existing asset.

However, the regions are packed with original content (Figure 14.8), such as a Loch Ness Monster that gives tours, and a variety of quests. "I was attracted to quests because I think it's a great way of delivering learning content. Not only that, but although *SL* isn't a 'game,' there are some people (especially teenagers) who would like to see more of this type of activity," says Stanley.

"The idea of the quests was to give the teens things to do on the island that would be fun, to appeal to a sense of adventure and pique their curiosity. We have tried to make them fun in their own right and then to add the learning content to them in the background. With language learning, it's easy in a way. If someone decides they want to do one of our quests, then they'll have to start to decipher and decode the audio and textual clues to follow it. The trick for us is to make it not so easy for advanced speakers of the language (boring) and not so difficult for lower-level learners (frustrating). So we have lower-level quests (Merlin Quest) with short pieces of audio and the Finn McCool Quest which has no audio, then the Robin Hood Quest which is meant for higher-level learners, as the audio is more complicated. However, a learner with a lower level can always simply follow the crossword clues (this quest requires learners to fill in a crossword), and by doing so they can complete it," Stanley explains.

There's even a missing-person mystery, with roleplaying staff members interacting with teens. Content is constantly added to the regions, both by my company and by my client—most recently a full-scale football game built into a stadium.

If you'd like to learn more about the British Council's work in-world, visit their Main Grid region, British Council Isle.

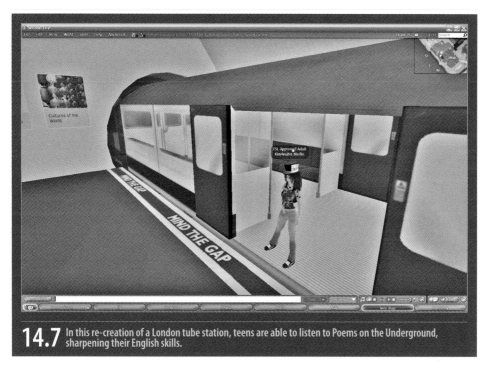

14.7 In this re-creation of a London tube station, teens are able to listen to Poems on the Underground, sharpening their English skills.

14.8 This view of the British Council estate on the Teen Grid gives a glimpse of Stonehenge, Right on Pier, a farm with a field that changes with the seasons, 1960s Carnaby Street and modern Carnaby Street, the UK of the Future, a stadium, the London Eye, Giant's Causeway, and the Learning Centre.

RESOURCES FOR TEEN GRID PROJECTS

There's more information and assistance available to you if you want to learn more about working on the Teen Grid.

Teen *Second Life* website. The most current answers to basic questions about TSL can be found at **http://teen.secondlife.com/**.

Solution Providers. If you need assistance developing your project in TSL, check the Solution Provider Directory for companies that are cleared to work on the Teen Grid. Go to **http://secondlife.com/solution_providers/listings.php** and search in the Teen Developer category.

***Second Life* Wiki.** Get even more information on TSL from Linden Lab at **http://wiki.secondlife.com/wiki/Teen_Second_Life**.

SimTeach Educators Working with Teens. Pick up some useful information compiled by educators at **http://www.simteach.com/wiki/index.php?title=Second_Life:_Educators_Working_with_Teens**.

Educators and Teens mailing list. Maintained by Linden Lab, this mailing list is a good way to keep in touch with others working on the Teen Grid: **https://lists.secondlife.com/cgi-bin/mailman/listinfo/educatorsandteens**.

SLED (*Second Life* EDucators). This list offers many useful resources and networking opportunities for educators: **https://lists.secondlife.com/cgi-bin/mailman/listinfo/educators**.

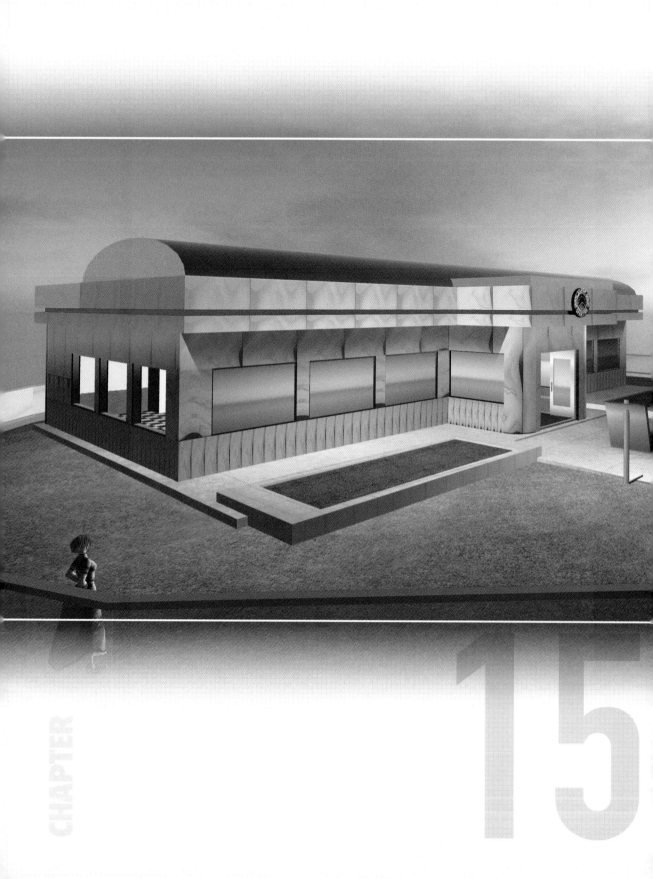

How do you find prebuilt content for your project? Is there anyone who can help? What's up with those web-based shopping sites for *Second Life* content? Is there a way to get Linden Lab to add a feature you wish you had? What tips will help you shop wisely on the Grid? How can you tell if a merchant or their products are likely to be reliable? What features should you look for, and how can you judge if you're looking at quality work? Where can you get quality freebie content? What sorts of common in-world tools can you find for free or off the rack? How can you get feedback on your in-world project and metrics to show how well it has succeeded? What new features are in the future for *Second Life* Residents? Read on to learn about all these things and more!

LOCATE
RESOURCES

FIND WHAT YOU NEED

No matter what sort of project you're doing in-world, you probably need more than an empty patch of virtual ground to make it work. You'll need tools and content and assistance of all sorts, many of them described in the preceding chapters. In this section you'll learn how to go about finding the tools you need—and about shopping wisely!

WHERE TO LOOK

Many of the things you need for your project on the Grid may already be available, sometimes inexpensively or for no charge. The tricky bit is finding them. There are a lot of ways to go about getting the things you need.

Have it made. As discussed in Chapter 13, "Select a Solution Provider," you can probably have a Solution Provider create exactly what you need. This is sometimes the only way to get what's necessary for your project, plus you can have things tailored exactly for your needs, branded, and so on. For more information about hiring a Solution Provider to build for you, check out Chapter 13.

Use Search. The first stop for most *Second Life* Residents who are looking for a particular item is Search. Mostly you would search for your keywords in the Places tab, to bring up shop locations. Remember that results are listed in order of location popularity, which might be augmented by bots (avatars controlled by a program on a computer external to *Second Life*), campers, or a dance club.

⚠ WARNING

Searching the Classifieds will skew your results; these listings are ranked by the amount paid for the ads.

Check the Classifieds. You can watch the Classifieds section of the official forums to see ads posted by in-world merchants (doing this will also keep you in the know about what's new). Additionally, there's a sub-board where you can post asking for help in locating the product you need. If the item is available somewhere in-world, it's very likely someone will post to let you know where!

Use web-based shopping sites. One great way to look for a particular item is to use web-based shopping sites such as Linden Lab's own Xstreet (**www.xstreetsl.com**). Using a site like this, you can shop on the Web while you're not logged into *SL*. Or you can simply use the site as a sort of catalog to locate likely items, then Search in-world for a shop owned by that merchant, where you may be able to see some of their work rezzed in-world or available as samples or freebies, to make a more-informed purchase.

 WEB SHOPPING

How do web-based *SL* shopping sites work? Usually merchants register, then each one puts copies of their items in an in-world server box on their own land or someplace that offers hosting for it. The shopper associates their avatar and their web-based shopping account, usually by visiting an in-world kiosk. They also deposit some Linden dollars in their account if they aren't using a credit card–based site. Then, when the shopper sees something they want on the website, they can select it for purchase and pay with the Linden dollars in their shop account. The web shop "talks to" the in-world box and tells it to send the item to the buyer.

Keep in mind that sometimes there is a brief delay while the parts of the system contact one another, so it can take a few minutes to receive your purchase, especially when the Grid is under heavy load. Occasionally there will be technical difficulties and you won't receive your item. If that happens to you, check the web shopping site for support info.

Ask a consultant. A good Solution Provider is likely to have a solid idea of what can be found for sale in-world, and where to get the best example of the tool you need or the best price. You can hire your Solution Provider to consult or even shop for (or with) you. I do this with clients from time to time, especially when a newbie client needs to outfit their avatar quickly.

Make a feature request on the PJIRA. Maybe the tool you want is something that really needs to be a built-in feature of the *Second Life* Grid. If that's the case, you can make or vote for a feature request on the public JIRA at **https://jira.secondlife.com/secure/Dashboard.jspa** and see if it will get enough votes for Linden Lab to decide to develop it.

Hire a Resident-run shopping service. Some *Second Life* Residents run professional personal-shopping services. If you'd like to consider taking advantage of such a service, check the Classifieds section of the *Second Life* official forums to find one.

Network. One of the best ways to find a tool or anything else you need is to network. Post on SLED or other professional mailing lists, or ask around the next time you're in-world at an event or a meeting. Sometimes a couple of organizations who share the need will end up coming together to have something developed. Or sometimes a Solution Provider will see the request on a mailing list, realize a lot of people would be interested in the new tool, and develop it.

Keep abreast of current events. If you are a regular reader of *Second Life*–specific news sources, such as blogs and newspapers, you will usually be aware of what the most current tools are and who's building them. If you're interested in a particular sort of product, such as fashion or architecture, you can follow related publications, even via RSS feed. You can learn about some of these in Chapter 8, "Keep Up with Current Events."

Look for freebies. Lots of useful *Second Life* content, including tools used by educators and businesses, can be had for free or at very low cost. Sometimes you'll find these as giveaways in a merchant's shop, but those that have fairly open permissions tend to be available at central locations, such as YadNi's Junkyard (Figure 15.1). Other locations are discussed in the section "Where to Get Freebies" later in this chapter.

15.1 YadNi's Junkyard is the granddaddy of all freebie locations in *Second Life*.

SHOP WISELY

You can often find things that might look OK in an ad or in the picture on a vendor, but they aren't always a good buy. Sometimes you'll buy the thing, unpack it from its box, and then find out that it doesn't look nearly as good as it did in the ad because the ad had a real-life picture of a real-world item instead of a picture of the virtual version you're actually buying. Sometimes it is a picture of the in-world item but it's been Photoshopped and the real (virtual!) thing doesn't look nearly so good.

So, how do you shop wisely in *Second Life*? Here are some tips.

See the items up close. Unless you're already familiar with a merchant's work, visit their shop before you buy (unless you're "buying" a free sample or something very inexpensive). You might be able to see a copy of the item in-world. You usually just can't tell as much from a picture of an item as from the item itself—particularly if the thing has moving parts or interactivity, or if the screenshots don't show all sides of it.

Assess the shop itself. Additionally, you should note whether the shop itself a good-looking build. This matters even more if this is the merchant's own shop, but still has some bearing even if it's a shop rented in a mall built and maintained by someone else. Someone with a good, successful product isn't likely to stay for long in a rat-hole of a mall. (There are exceptions, of course. The merchant might be good friends with the mall owner or shop builder, and that might be a higher priority for them than the appearance of their shop. Remember: many Residents aren't in this as businesspeople as much as for fun, and someone who's great at scripting or making clothes might not find building a shop fun.) Sometimes, even when the shop doesn't look spectacular and there are no demos to try, the builder has such a stellar reputation that you won't be put off.

Verify identity. While at the shop, you might find that the merchant or sales staff are present. Do not give money to anyone claiming to be the shop owner or sales staff until you've checked who owns the land to verify the shop owner's name. You may find that the owner's profile lists authorized staff, or there may be a signboard, notecard giver, greeter, or screenshots on the wall indicating who's on staff, and perhaps even on duty—there might even be an online indicator with a pager.

Contact the merchant. If there is no one to help you and you have questions or would like to see the item in-world (such as someone modeling a gown or demonstrating a scripted gadget), or if you need to purchase a no-transfer item as a gift, contact the merchant for assistance. There may be contact info posted in the shop; otherwise, check the merchant's profile to see if they prefer instant message, notecard, or some other method of contact.

Seek out demos. Many in-world merchants offer demo versions of their goods, particularly hair, skin, or shoes (Figure 15.2). When these are available, be sure to try them out. Even if you are purchasing clothing or other items that are not available as demos, it can be a good idea to try the demos that are available, just to get an idea of the quality of that artist's work. Of course, some shops do contain products built by more than one artist, so keep that in mind. If you find freebies or samples available, try them, too. If there are no demos or freebies, consider buying some small, inexpensive item to try out before buying something costly. Another option is to find someone who has your more-expensive item and will let you try it out. At the least, try other things built by the same content creator to see how their standards are.

Check permissions. It's vital to be sure the permissions are adequate before you purchase, or else you might be out of luck. First, check the vendor picture and see if the permissions are indicated there, or if there's a sign posted in the shop. If that doesn't help, you can right-click an object, select Edit, and then look at the next-owner permissions. If the item is inside a box or vendor, you do the same thing then go to the Content tab, find the item, right-click, and select Properties. There you should see the next-owner permissions (be sure you aren't looking at current-owner permissions). If the item is in a vendor and there is no indication what permissions will be, you'll have to contact the merchant or their staff.

⚠ **WARNING**

If you purchase a copiable (and probably also) no-transfer item, you probably are not going to be able to return it or exchange it. Because it's no-transfer, you can't give it back to the merchant. And if it's copiable, you could give it back and still make plenty more. When purchasing items with these permissions, take care; the sale will probably be final!

15.2 Demo attachments, like this hair, usually have the merchant's sign attached or the word *DEMO* printed over their textures.

Test the scripts. If you're buying a script, not a building or object, then the question is, do the scripts running in the shop seem to work well? If you're able to get a copy of the item or something else to test, you'll of course want to make sure it's quality work. Does the item spam a lot in open chat? Is it easy to use? There are more pointers about how to check the quality of a build in Chapter 13, "Select a Solution Provider."

Make sure the administrative tools meet your needs. Sometimes a scripted object or other item, due to permissions or design, can be used by only one person. If your staff will also be able to use it, what will be involved in that? Is there some sort of administrative interface on the object, or do you have to give edit rights on your objects to anyone who might need to add a picture to the slide screen, for example? Often vendors will distribute notecards of information that explain this sort of thing, but if there isn't a resource like this for an item you're considering, don't hesitate to contact the merchant.

Assess a scripted item's interface. Some scripted items will require you to enter data in open chat, others have a notecard-driven interface, and some have a HUD or push-button interface, or some other kind. Some are better for certain situations or are more flexible. If you aren't comfortable with the interface (for example, if you don't want to look up commands to type in chat every time you use the item, or you don't want to wear a HUD because you find it gets in your way), keep shopping.

Look for expandability. Will you be able to expand this building, scripted system, or whatever it is, as your project grows? Will you be able to match the textures, and is the item modifiable at all? This is important to know while you're planning your project, because you need to know if you're buying only a short-term solution. If you think you might want to ask the merchant to expand the system for you later on, contact them right away to find out if that can be done.

Know how to handle updates. Many merchants offer free updates for items you purchase from them. Check to see if these will be available, and by what process they happen. Sometimes you need to take the item to the shop and rez it or put it into a kiosk. Other times you contact the merchant. And sometimes an automated update system will inform you of or directly send you an updated item when you rez yours.

That last bit is important: most systems don't do a random check for updates, and only check when you rez an item in-world. If the item stays in your Inventory or if it's already in-world, the system isn't going to check for updates!

Consider your backup needs. Backups can be very important. If the item isn't copiable, maybe you need to buy some spares. And if you are purchasing a scripted item that collects data, if the information is vital to your project, you might want some sort of backup functionality. Otherwise, what happens if your system tries to email you daily results, for example, when your email is down or the region the system's in is down?

Ensure compatibility. Make sure that what you buy is compatible with what you already have or intend to have. Does the item use a channel for commands that conflicts with something else you already use? You might not even know, until you buy and test the item, if it communicates on the same channel as other items in your region, and this can cause all sorts of conflicts. A merchant who offers good support might be able to help you figure out compatibility.

Know what support is offered. Do not assume that objects you buy from in-world shops are going to come with good—or any—support. Remember that many Resident shops are run by hobbyists, and that means they might not be around when you need support, and they might even leave *Second Life* altogether or stay in-world but decide that something else going on is more fun. Check to see if support is available for the product.

Ensure server stability. Some in-world systems you purchase require that the items you have attached to you or rezzed in-world communicate with a server of some sort, either in-world or external to the Grid. Are you relying on an external server run by a hobbyist? While it might be a great tool, is there some sort of actual contract that ensures that this thing is going to be around for a while? Remember, there's a chance it could break or the person could move on to other things, leaving you with something that doesn't function right—or at all.

Think through security. Unless you know something about the reputation of the person and/or have a hard-copy contract, you are at risk of all sorts of things when running unknown software. Bots, for example, are operated on an external server. If it's not your server, you can't see any of the code. Do you really know what it's doing? What keeps the bot merchant from, say, logging all of the chat the bot picks up, then reading it for their own and their friends' amusement later? Sure, it's a violation of the *Second Life* rules. But someone who'd do this doesn't care about the rules anyway. Similarly, a scripted item like a vendor system could steal your Linden dollars. Whenever you purchase a scripted item or an item that might contain scripts, keep this in mind. Although this sort of thing is extremely rare at this time, it might be an important consideration if you, for example, are having NDA-laden business meetings. Be sure you are purchasing scripted items from a reputable merchant.

Think about modification possibilities. Sometimes you'll find something that's almost—but not quite—what you need. If the item is modifiable you can perhaps fix it yourself. And if it's transferable or if you give your Solution Provider rights on your things, a Solution Provider might be able to make the change for you. Approaching in-world merchants about customizing something that's not quite right is not a bad idea, either, if you have confidence in them. For example, I recently purchased an item in-world for a project, wrote a new piece of code for one of its functions, and sent it off to the merchant, who incorporated it into the gadget and sent me a free copy of it with my modification (which will be included in the retail version she sells). That worked out great all around and helped to keep my overhead down (plus enabled me to add a little something extra to my client's project without passing on an additional fee).

While there is almost always a better custom solution, tailored to your purpose and bearing your branding, you can purchase many valuable and useful tools and other content you need for your project, right off the virtual rack. Especially if your budget is limited, it's worth spending a little time shopping around.

PREFAB CONTENT

You've probably noticed that certain sorts of objects and gadgets are mentioned repeatedly in this book, such as vendors and notecard givers. You can have these custom-made for you with your branding and tailored to your needs, or you can get some of them for free or inexpensively in-world. Let's take a look at some of the most common ones.

Slide screens and media controllers. These are available with all sorts of features, including frame-number displays, converters that let you stream YouTube videos in-world, configurable administrator lists, and just about anything else you can think of. (One feature that you won't find in in-world video players at the time of this writing is rewind/fast-forward capability; however, my company is developing that!) To show slides in-world, typically you have to upload each image as a texture and then add it to the content of the slide screen. Occasionally you'll see a slide show that works in a different way, displaying images that were uploaded to a website instead, but this is rare. While you can play video on any prim, provided you set up a media stream (as easy as pasting a URL into About Land), this does not give you control over playback for visitors to your land. Everyone sees the video stream from its start as soon as they turn it on, so if you and colleagues were 10 minutes into a video then someone else arrived and started watching the stream, they'd be seeing scenes 10 minutes after you. My company has created a scripted gadget (Autosynch Video Controller) that addresses that problem, but most people do without it and either use a regular prim video player or a freebie video player. Some video systems available for purchase allow different avatars on the same parcel to view different streams simultaneously. Some allow changing from stream to stream via an in-world interface accessible to anyone; you can find audio and media stream controllers that work the same way.

Prefab buildings. You can find free buildings of all sorts in-world, and a quick search will quickly bring up a host of merchants who offer prefabs. The best offerings usually include features like scripted, locking doors; privacy glass, blinds, or curtains; and a rezzer that makes placement and setup easy. (Keep in mind that locks can't keep anyone out, and blinds don't stop camera controls from working!) Most buildings are sold with copy/mod/no transfer permissions—be sure to check before buying. Some merchants will assist you in deploying your purchase, sometimes for a fee.

Rezzers. Like the first commercial offering of its type, the Rez-Foo, these gadgets will make other objects appear (and sometimes disappear). Usually they're used for things like packing up a building or even an entire island of content so that copies can be rezzed easily wherever you need them. Top-quality rezzers include the ability to move the entire build by moving the rezzer itself. Sometimes a rezzer is used for changing the furniture layout of a room quickly, and some can even manage an entire region of content. Do keep in mind that whatever you add to the rezzer needs to have copy and modify permissions.

Holodecks. These are like huge, walk-in rezzers. Picture a room (or a larger space) with walls that may have any sort of panoramic image on them, so that it appears you're standing in a desert or undersea and, with the click of a button, the image changes and you're somewhere else. Sometimes holodecks rez objects, as well, so you can display all sorts of things or even change the entire purpose of the space. For example, my company built a stadium that, at the click of a button, becomes a football field, a swimming pool, or an auto-racing track, and other playing fields, including all of the goals, kiosks for a swim HUD or football HUD, etc. (Figure 15.3). If something that elaborate and customized isn't in your budget, you can buy a prefab holodeck and add your own furniture.

Furniture. You'll find every kind of furniture imaginable at shops in-world, with widely varied prices and quality. Be sure to check permissions, as well as try any animations or scripts.

Whiteboards. These are scripted tools that work like real-world whiteboards, though not nearly so well. These are mostly a novelty, and you would often be better off using an external tool in another window. However, you can find free whiteboards, so it won't cost you to try them out.

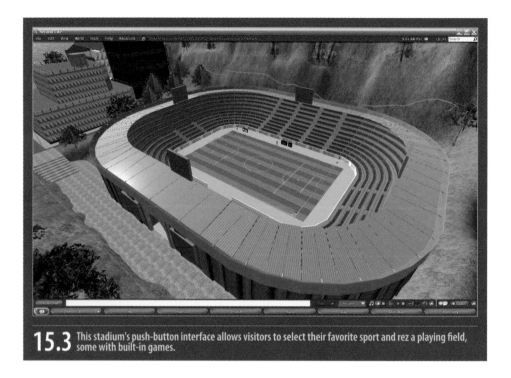

15.3 This stadium's push-button interface allows visitors to select their favorite sport and rez a playing field, some with built-in games.

Notecard givers. These do what you'd expect: give out notecards, usually when someone clicks them. You can find a freebie script to do this, particularly if you're not afraid to open up a script and add the name of your notecard instead of the one it was giving away for the last person who used it—a very straightforward bit of code. It's important for a notecard giver to be labeled or designed so that it's obvious that people can click it to get something!

Landmark givers. These are just like notecard givers, except they give landmarks—in fact, the same code will usually work for both. You'll see some landmark givers in-world that look like giant red thumb-tacks, as you would see on a map.

Vendors. There are all sorts of vendors in-world. The simplest is a single prim with a picture on the front of the content set for sale, and sometimes a hovertext note over it indicating the selling price and other details. Vendors of that simple type are also sometimes called *sales boxes*. A typical scripted vendor looks just like a box with arrows on either side (or pointing hands or something similar) that you click to advance or back through images of items for sale. More-advanced vendors offer things like an info button you can click to receive a notecard, more than one view of the item, or the ability for the merchant to split the incoming payments automatically (the vendor sends the correct percentages to various people). A gift vendor allows you to purchase an item to be automatically sent to someone else. A *holovendor* rezzes temporary copies of items instead of displaying images. Networked vendors talk to a central database system so the merchant can update their inventory or prices at multiple locations at once.

URL loaders. These are scripts or scripted gadgets that load a specific web page in an external browser when someone clicks them. By press time you will find one of these available for free at Wiley's in-world location.

Infokiosks. Usually a combination of a URL loader and inventory giver (notecards, landmarks, or other items), an Infokiosk is a valuable tool for almost any real-world project in-world. You can pick up a free Kiosk Kit at my company's island, Abracadabra (Figure 15.4).

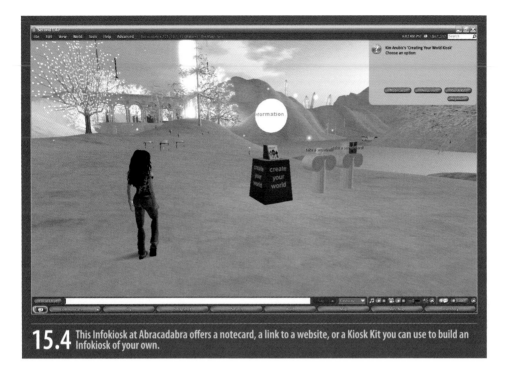

15.4 This Infokiosk at Abracadabra offers a notecard, a link to a website, or a Kiosk Kit you can use to build an Infokiosk of your own.

Greeters. These scripted tools sense avatars and welcome them, usually by name. Most greeters operate in open chat, though some will send an instant message directly to the new arrival. Some greeters also distribute inventory, such as a notecard of rules for visitors, or a gift.

Scanners. Scanners, or radar, check for nearby avatars and report them to the owner. Some of these are land-based, and occasionally they have nifty features like prim icons to show the relative location of the avatars. Others IM their owners directly. The range varies, and some have an adjustable range.

Flight assists. All avatars can fly, but maybe you'd like to fly faster, or higher, or not sink when you're working on something way up in the sky. You need a flight assist. These are available in many forms, often for free. More-advanced flight assists offer features like configurable acceleration rates and particle trails.

Finders. These scripted gadgets help you locate your friend when you get separated in a mall, or to figure out where you lost that stray prim. Some finders feature a particle trail or a pointer that moves to show you your target. By press time, you will be able to pick up a free finder at Abracadabra.

Multitools. Most *SL* Residents I know don't leave home without their multitool. This is a scripted attachment that combines the features of other tool attachments, such as a scanner, flight assist, finder, and more. There are a lot of brands, and each has its fervent adherents. If you really want to start a ruckus, ask a group of people to debate their favorite multitool! (I use a Guardian Angel from Jessica Qin's Wo & Shade Imports.)

Tip jars. Usually shaped like a jar or cup, but taking a variety of forms, tip jars are a very important part of the in-world economy. When you pay a tip jar, the money goes to its owner. You can find freebie tip jars to use.

Teleporters. Click one of these scripted objects to be instantly transported. Some teleporters have a menu-driven interface that allows you to access multiple locations. Teleporters do require a bit of setup, usually changing the coordinates of the destination in the script. Keep in mind that these have limited range, so you won't be able to teleport from one region to another across the Grid. (Some special teleporters force open the in-world map so that you only have to click the Teleport button to get where you're going. There are also *teleport maps*, which you can click to go to various pictured destinations. However, I have not seen either of these available as a prefab.)

Sculpty makers. You'll find some in-world tools you can use to make simple sculpted prims. They usually are not inexpensive, though!

Shape makers. Some merchants will sell you a tool that helps you to find or make whatever shapes you need.

Particle engines. While you can find lots of free particle scripts in-world, some of them with lots of useful instructions, you may have an easier time with a particle engine, which has controls and readouts that allow you to see your particle effect as you tweak it.

Online indicators. Shops in-world often employ these to let visitors know by a glowing light or a green indicator that their owner is online. Some of them also have a pager function.

Security systems. Want to keep someone away from your skybox even though you allow them to roam the land below? For that, you'll want a security system. These can be problematic if they aren't accurate about range, so be very sure you purchase from a reputable merchant.

WHERE TO GET FREEBIES

Some locations in-world offer a selection of free content that has been gathered from other places on the Grid (Figure 15.5). Especially when you're starting out, you might find it helpful to check some of these places for resources. Keep in mind that some places charge L$1 for "freebies," usually to make tracking transactions easier or to defray upload costs or to maintain the parcel where you pick things up.

Wiley: The publisher of this book offers a lot of free content-creation assets, like textures and scripts, and even a free gadget or two.

ICT Library: Visit the Info Islands to pick up free (or low-cost) tools for educators and trainers.

YadNi's Junkyard: The granddaddy of all freebie markets in *Second Life*, YadNi's is a cornucopia of free content-creation goodies, furniture, buildings, clothing, and all sorts of other handy stuff.

New Citizens Inc. (NCI): NCI offers all sorts of freebies for newbies starting out, as well as other assistance and information to get your *Second Life* off to a great start.

The Free Bazaar at Stillman: Linden Lab maintains this location where some donated Resident content is available for free. It's especially well organized, so it's easy to find what you need.

Abracadabra: Home of my own company, The Magicians, here you'll find a free Enchanted Teacher's Apple visitor counter/greeter, a Kiosk Kit for building your own multifunction Infokiosk, a finder, and more.

There are countless wonderful free or inexpensive tools like these available on the Grid—more than would be practical to list here. This should give you an idea, though, of what's out there. In the next section you'll learn about a few important, specialized tools that are of particular interest to people doing real-world work in *Second Life*.

15.5 You can find some useful free tools at ICT Library, the Stillman bazaar, and NCI.

METRICS AND FEEDBACK

When I think of metrics, I think of a little grade-school song about measurements, which then gets stuck in my head in an unfortunate way. But in a *Second Life* context, metrics means measuring the effectiveness of your *SL* project. If you're running a real-world-related project in-world, you probably not only want but really *need* to know how well it's working so you can write an academic paper, report it to your boss, seek a grant, or plan the next phase of your project. Fortunately, there are tools you can use to make this process easy, document-able, and even automatic. Most of them involve scripted systems in-world, a few require back ends outside of the Grid, and some of them can be quite complex. Let's take a look at some systems for gathering feedback and counting visitors.

GATHERING FEEDBACK

You can gather feedback from Residents in a variety of ways. This section discusses some methods for collecting both direct and indirect feedback about your *Second Life* project.

Surveys are an old favorite both offline and on the Web. The simplest way to conduct a survey is to set up a web-based one, then link to it with a clickable URL loader in-world. You don't have to build the external survey software, either—there are plenty of web-based services available (such as Survey Monkey). This isn't a very immersive experience, though, and it's not a lot of fun for survey takers.

Fortunately, there are in-world survey tools. These usually offer multiple-choice questions and answers. The range of features available for a system like this is very broad. I believe my company's Survey Machine (Figure 15.6) is probably the most elaborate system of its type. It includes features like notecard-driven question-and-answer sets (so you can easily swap them out), notecard validation (the system lets you know when you have made an error), a daily emailed anonymized summary of results, a backup system, a prize distro for those who complete the survey, a built-in URL loader for those who want more information (such as a link to your privacy policy), and more. Because it's customized for clients, the Survey Machine has taken on forms such as a giant mainframe computer and a teleporter that sends survey takers to an in-world science-fiction museum. A system with so many features is going to cost more than a simpler one, but it offers more flexibility; your decision of what survey tools to use depends on what you need.

If your budget is small or if you just want general feedback, a suggestions or comments box can work very well. This is a scripted box that allows a visitor to drop a notecard into its inventory. Depending on the way the system is designed, either the system's owner comes along and removes the notecards manually, or the system automatically forwards them (or the data on them) to the owner. The name of the person who created the notecard will show as its creator, which means user-created notecards do not provide anonymous feedback. However, if you set up a distro that hands out notecards that have you as the creator, and specify that those should be used, then you can get anonymous results. However, you can't create a form with fields in a notecard, so you may not get the sort of information you requested.

Comment boxes can have all sorts of features, such as rejecting items that are not notecards or are not labeled correctly. This can help keep down the amount of trash people throw in there. As for appearance, you can have just about anything. I once created a comment-forwarding system that looks like a magic envelope with my client's real-world mail address on the front. Created on the Teen Grid, it allowed the teens to take an envelope, put their essay into it, and then click it, and it disappeared in a puff of magical particles, with a twinkly sound, ostensibly on its way to my client. Then it called to a distro that gave a prize for participating! As you can see, these systems can be as simple or as complicated and customized as you want. It depends on your needs and your budget.

15.6 This version of the Survey Machine flashes a message to invite passersby to take a survey.

Answering machines perform a similar task. Someone can walk up to one of these, click it, and then enter a brief message in chat. The message is recorded (there's a time limit per message), and either saved for playback by its owner or, less commonly, forwarded immediately, usually via IM. Variations abound. For example, for a client on the Teen Grid I created an answering machine that forwards, via email, messages spoken in open chat. This is vital, because as you learned in Chapter 14, "Work in Teen *Second Life*," teens cannot send an instant message to an adult's avatar. (As noted in Chapter 14, if you're thinking about a solution of this sort for the Teen Grid, you need to check in with Linden Lab about it before you set it up or have it built!)

Getting direct feedback from Residents isn't the only approach. Suppose you have a URL loader or two in-world. How do you know if people are using it? That's easy! Whoever administers the website to which users are being directed can check the hits. This is especially easy if you direct the traffic to a web page that is used only for this purpose. Gathering metrics about URL loaders is an especially nice solution because even those in your organization who are not familiar with *Second Life* will understand the value of those web hits, plus you don't have to count on unfamiliar in-world tools or on reports from your Solution Provider to see how things are going.

There's another way you can check metrics related to your URL loader (or just about any other interactive gadget in-world): a *click counter*. This is a script that counts how many times an object has been clicked, and it typically reports results when the object owner comes along and clicks it or says a specific command. These sorts of things can be very effective, and in some cases can be built to autoreset so you don't have to rush to reset them before they exceed their script memory and crash, and to email results so you don't have to run in and check the counters.

VISITOR COUNTERS

Visitor counters are ubiquitous in *Second Life*. Anywhere you go, the odds are high that somewhere in the shop or region there is a visitor-counting gadget that has added you to the tally and probably made a note of your avatar's name. The visitor counter you'll encounter most often is a freebie that has been available in-world for years (you saw it in Figure 12.14 in Chapter 12, "Run an Event"). Not all counters look like this, of course, but many do.

The standard visitor counter scans for avatars within a certain range, usually around 10 or 20 meters, and silently adds their names to a list that the counter's owner retrieves by giving a chat command. Then the gadget dumps the data into open chat. There's also a reset command for clearing the list. Such visitor counters are the most common metrics tools on the Grid.

Some visitor counters perform a similar task using different methods of sensing avatars. Scanning scripts are considered laggy, though, especially if they scan frequently. You can instead find a system, usually including a greeter function, that works when avatars pass through a phantom prim. This is less laggy but covers a smaller space.

There are all sorts of variations on this sort of system. As I mentioned, some also greet visitors by name. For example, my Enchanted Teacher's Apple scans, greets, and keeps a visitor count, with a cool apple shape that has cute sound effects and gold-star particles, as well as communicating on a channel other than open chat so it doesn't spam the world or let everyone see its data when it dumps it. (And you can get one for free at my island, Abracadabra!) Another system I have alerts me in real time, via IM, when someone arrives at a particular location or leaves it, but only when I'm in-world, so I don't wake up in the morning and find a mailbox full of reports on who's arrived or left.

Script memory is a factor for these sorts of gadgets. There are various ways of working around the problem, though. A few years ago my company developed a Welcome Machine that greets visitors, gives them items only on their first visit since the system's been reset, and remembers upward of 1,000 visitors before it's at risk of overloading—all without an external server for storing data. But of course this forgets everyone after it's reset, and it scans only a 96-meter range, which is the maximum for the script function that handles scanning. That means it can't cover an entire region. One solution is to have a dedicated parcel for arriving teleports and to disallow teleportation to other parts of the region. But such a system can miss anyone who flies in from over the sim border.

Getting an accurate visitor count across an entire region is usually accomplished by setting up a bunch of scanner-type visitor counters all across the sim. You can manually dump the counts and hand-collate them, or the system might be networked with a database on an external server. Sensor grids of this type are usually used for a "heat map" sort of visitor-tracking system. One, offered by Maya Realities, gives the user a web-based interface with a nice visual representation of where the most avatars were sensed.

This sort of approach has holes in it, though. For example, how many scanners do you intend to put in the sky? And what happens if you want to or need to frequently rearrange your build or to reterraform? Getting those scanners spaced out correctly without overlap can be a real challenge.

My company developed a system that uses a proprietary method for tracking every avatar in the region. It maintains anonymized data on an external database, tracking the number of unique visits and repeat visits, where avatars go, and how long they stay, and it is all owner-configurable. Furthermore, it requires only three or four prims, total, which can be placed almost anywhere, or moved, and can also work across additional regions with only two or three more prims on each of them. It can even track a specific event or space within a region, and remember those settings if you want to use them again, and it allows for relocating a region or adding another to an established setup. The problem with this system? Its complexity; someone brand-new to the Grid would have trouble setting up this system, and even someone familiar with the Grid must follow the instructions carefully. Systems like these may be set up by your staff or by the company from which you purchased it (usually for an additional fee), plus there is an ongoing charge for hosting your data (unless you host it yourself). For most projects this sort of system is overkill, but sometimes it's exactly what you need!

If you intend to use a visitor counter that maintains a database of some sort or tracks any detailed information, you need to be aware of and conform to Linden Lab's requirement that this system provide a privacy policy. This might be a kiosk that gives a notecard or opens a URL, or it might be something more elaborate. For example, my company's system greets every avatar upon their first visit and gives them a folder of inventory, including the privacy policy.

Of course, there are other, more traditional ways to check how you're doing. You can monitor how well your products are moving, and conduct an exit survey at your real-world location or website to see where people learned about your product or service. You can see if your students are doing better and if they seem more engaged. Almost all the methods you'd use to track progress on a real-world project work in-world.

TIP

In a pinch, you can check your parcel's Traffic score to see if a lot of avatars have been there during the preceding day. However, this isn't always an accurate measurement, and it can be gamed by someone using bots or camping chairs!

ADVANCED TOOLS

Systems such as the avatar-tracking setup described in the previous section are advanced tools that you probably won't want to (and possibly won't be able to) purchase and set up without the assistance of a Solution Provider. Some things are just too complicated to set up and maintain without expertise. Similarly, Linden Lab offers some tools and programs you can't access without signing up or working with a Solution Provider who has. View it as the *Second Life* equivalent of needing an IT department to keep your organization's network running.

 WHY SOME TOOLS AREN'T SOLD OFF THE RACK

Some tools and systems, and even unscripted objects, are quite complex, require customization, or are full of proprietary code or created by proprietary methods, so you can't just buy them from a vendor in-world; the Solution Provider will require a hard-copy contract for purchase. Additionally, any advanced object or system that is sold with modify rights requires personal contact, discussion, and paperwork. Keep in mind that Solution Providers often need to sell copies (albeit customized or with slightly different features) of systems that are expensive to develop or that undergo continued development, so protecting that intellectual property is important.

Let's take a look at some of these advanced tools and programs.

APIS

Linden Lab has available a number of APIs to facilitate third-party development. These include the Exchange Risk API, DirectSLURL, and the Registration API.

The *Exchange Risk API* is used to facilitate the exchange of Linden dollars for any real currency. You can learn more about it at **http://secondlifegrid.net/technology-programs/virtual-world-api/risk**.

A *DirectSLURL* (usually just called a SLURL) allows you to provide a web link that a user can follow to your indicated location within *Second Life* upon login. If the user doesn't have an account, they'll be directed to the registration page, download the client, and when they log in they'll arrive at the location set in your SLURL. Build your own SLURL at **http://slurl.com/build.php**. You can also get a SLURL from the *SL* world map; the "Copy SLURL to clipboard" button creates a SLURL for any location you search for or visit using the world map.

The *Registration API* can allow you to register *SL* users from your own website, sending them on login to a location you select in-world. You can even customize and brand the registration process, provide access to selected avatar names, and bind accounts to your estate. Learn more about this program at **http://secondlifegrid .net/technology-programs/virtual-world-api/reg**.

CUSTOM ORIENTATION EXPERIENCES

If you decide to use the Registration API or if you have many people new to *Second Life* involved in your project or visiting your estate, you might find it helpful to provide an orientation experience for them. You can find some very basic orientation tools in the Library section of your Inventory and there is a public orientation area on the mainland (Figure 15.7), but you may want something branded, specialized, or in a particular language. The best approach in this case, if the offerings in the Library won't do the trick, is to work with a Solution Provider on a custom orientation experience.

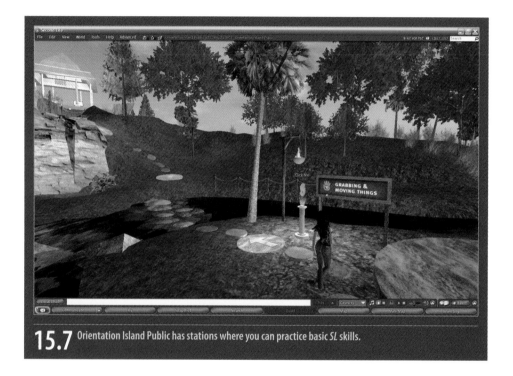

15.7 Orientation Island Public has stations where you can practice basic *SL* skills.

COMMUNITY GATEWAY PROGRAM

The Community Gateway program can allow you to publicize your community to people registering for *Second Life* on Linden Lab's site. This allows you to reach out to people to engage them in your community. Upon their first login they will arrive at your location, where they will experience your orientation. This is great if you have a strong themed, language-based, or focused community. You can learn more about it at **http://wiki.secondlife.com/wiki/Community_Gateway**.

CUSTOM LAST NAMES

You can't change your account name, but you can get a new account with the last name you choose. Linden Lab, upon reviewing your request, may create a custom surname for a US$500 setup fee, plus an annual $500 fee. This must be an organizational or corporate name, not a personal surname. To create additional accounts with this last name, you will need to use the Registration API.

Custom vanity names are available at Linden Lab's discretion, usually for events that involve major press or television coverage with substantial publicity value. The name owner will be billed a US$50 setup fee plus an annual US$50 fee. The name you choose must reflect a real-life name.

There's a discounted rate for nonprofits and educational projects that would like to take advantage of these programs. For more information, go to **http://wiki.secondlife.com/wiki/Custom_Name_Program**.

BOTS AND ALTERNATIVES

Bots are used for a variety of purposes in-world, often simply to make a venue seem more popular (a controversial practice). Others are designed to do things like automatically greet visitors, copy objects (such bots are *copybots*), or travel the Grid collecting data. Some Solution Providers may offer this service, and there are Resident-operated businesses that offer them as well.

There are alternatives to bots for many purposes. For example, my company and others have developed objects that look like avatars with varying degrees of "artificial intelligence" and animation (Figure 15.8). These are usually less resource-intensive than bots, as well as less controversial, for purposes like answering visitor questions.

15.8 This "noob" developed by The Magicans looks just like an avatar and has rudimentary AI. It greets visitors and offers to answer their questions.

CUSTOM VIEWERS

Linden Lab has open-sourced the *Second Life* viewer. It's relatively straightforward to skin the viewer (information at **http://wiki.secondlife.com/wiki/Skinning_How_To/Add_custom_artwork_to_the_viewer**). For more information about complex customization of the viewer, visit the Open Source Portal, **http://wiki.secondlife .com/wiki/Open_Source_Portal**. (The *Second Life* viewer is available under multiple licenses; for more information, see **http://secondlifegrid.net/technology-programs/license-virtual-world/viewerlicensing**.)

IMMERSIVE WORK SPACES

In partnership with Rivers Run Red, Linden Lab offers Immersive Work Spaces. These are prefabricated regions that include meeting rooms, screen sharing (including the ability to broadcast your desktop in real time), media sharing (including PowerPoint), news feeds, and more. Users administer the system via a 2D interface external to the Grid. However, it does have limitations, including a nontrivial price and the inability to make any modifications or additions to the region. If you even rez a prim, you may make the system malfunction, so if you want any other content (besides various streams, like those described earlier in the chapter) you will need to do it somewhere else. For more information see **http://immersivespaces.com**.

MORE RESOURCES FROM LINDEN LAB

The best place to check for all sorts of resources, information, programs, tips, and contact info is the *Second Life* Grid site at **http://secondlifegrid.net/**.

NEW FEATURES ON THE HORIZON

Second Life is constantly evolving, with more and improved features coming from Linden Lab all the time. Here's a glimpse at what Linden Lab is planning for its Residents.

CONTENT-CREATION TOOLS

Support for mesh imports. While sculpted prims are very useful, support for actual meshes has been at the top of many people's wish lists for a long time. Linden Lab will be granting their wish; this feature is in the works. You'll be able to import content you already have, though at least for the time being your ability to edit it will be limited, similar to sculpted prims.

Linden-dollar API. Want to sell your real-life products for Linden dollars? Soon you'll be able to using the upcoming Linden-dollar API, which will allow use of L$ microcurrency on the Web.

Dynamic shadows. When Linden Lab introduced the Windlight rendering system, with its customizable skies and reflective water, there was talk of eventual dynamic shadows. Some in the press and blogosphere have noticed that code for this exists but isn't yet enabled (and at least one Resident developed an open-source viewer that uses it), but many feared the feature would be put to rest or delayed. But it's on the way, probably in 2009.

HTTP-in script function. This major new feature will facilitate the creation of robust, persistent servers in *SL*. It will obviate the need for XML-RPC services, providing greater reliability and scalability, and should be particularly useful for things like networked vendors.

COMMUNICATION TOOLS

Collaborative media sharing. One of Residents' most requested features will become a reality: true native collaborative web browsing on a prim. How soon? That's hard to say, but probably by the middle of 2009.

SLim. Currently in beta, this chat client allows *SL* Residents to text chat or voice chat with their *SL* Friends without having the regular viewer open. It has a small footprint and you may be able to run it when it's just not practical to go in-world. You can try the features available so far by installing SLim (find it at **http://secondlife.com/SLim/**. (You must be logged in to a valid *Second Life* account to access to this page.)

You will be able to associate SLim with an email address to have your voicemail sent to you. Although you will be able to use SLim to monitor only one account at a time, you will be able to have multiple accounts. So, for example, you could be logged in with one account in-world and another in SLim, and voicemail for other accounts would be emailed to you. Eventually it will be possible to communicate with other online communities via SLim. In fact, eventually multiple people should be capable of sharing your in-world camera view via SLim, and even of manipulating the camera controls. This will be a great way to give someone a taste of your in-world project, and will probably be available sometime in 2009.

This feature will make it possible to greatly increase the number of participants in an in-world meeting, class, or event. In fact, there are plans in the works to associate SLim accounts for individual users or even a group with phone numbers that can be called from any phone, with the option of using a local-access number or a direct-dial number (for a fee). There also are plans to add an SMS feature, but not a way to dial out for voice calls. In early testing, this feature has supported over 400 voice chatters simultaneously.

Web-based communication tools. Also under development are web-based communication tools that will allow someone to contact *SL* Residents without even the SLim client. This is likely to be available during 2009.

STAND-ALONE GRIDS

Government agencies, enterprises, and educational institutions have longed for a stand-alone solution that would allow them to run their own grid, even behind a firewall, and I've mentioned this upcoming feature several times throughout this book. Seeking to fulfill the need, some Residents have turned to reverse-engineered platforms that work with the *Second Life* viewer, but these aren't very stable and just don't have the user base, Resident-created content, and momentum of *Second Life*.

At press time, stand-alone grids were in alpha tests. Alpha-test customers report that deployment, from opening the box to having an operational grid up and running, has taken as little as 30 minutes. Users will be able to bring up 4 to 8 full regions (on preconfigured, rack-mounted servers shipped to them by Linden Lab) and will have a simplified, easy-to-use suite of administrative tools and preloaded content. (For example, IBM recently hosted a sensitive meeting of high-level senior engineers—300 of them. They didn't need to fly around the globe to share best practices and white papers, but instead met in 16 regions behind their own firewall.) As a bonus, because you'll only have a few regions, compared to the entire Grid, you can expect an increased level of stability and high performance if your regions remain unconnected to the rest of the *Second Life* world. It will be up to you whether to remain behind your own firewall. If testing goes as hoped, you'll be able to order a grid of your own by the end of 2009.

THE FUTURE

We can already see glimpses of the *Second Life* Grid's future. MIT's Media Lab is working on a cross-reality system using *Second Life*. They've created models of their real-world conference rooms. Some staff meets in the real-world rooms and others as avatars in *SL*. In meeting rooms, intersections of hallways—key points—there are video screens where everyone can watch and hear their counterparts in the "other" world in order to collaborate naturally, as if they were all in the same real-world location.

You can learn more about these new features as news becomes available by visiting **http://secondlifegrid.net**—or just stick around in-world and see how the future unfolds.

APPENDICES

What does backchat mean? What's concur-rency? What are the official *Second Life* community standards? Find answers to these questions and more in the following appendices.

APPENDIX A: GLOSSARY

/me: Typed in chat before a line of description. For example */me waves at you* would appear in open chat as *Kim Anubis waves at you*.

512/512M2: Often considered the basic parcel size, 512 square meters, referred to as "a 512."

abandon land: Allow Linden Lab to reclaim a parcel without any compensation.

About Land: Panel used to control land at the parcel level.

Abuse Report (AR): A report sent to Linden Lab to report griefing, harassment, etc. Also used as a verb for the act of sending in an AR.

account: Associated with a specific avatar name.

ad farm: A parcel full of advertising signage.

agent limit: The number of avatars that may be in a region simultaneously.

allow list: The list of Residents specifically allowed to enter a parcel or estate.

alpha: *1.* Textures with invisible layers. *2.* To make something invisible using a script (to make it "go alpha").

alt: Short for "alternate account;" a secondary *Second Life* account, often kept secret.

animated texture: A texture on an object that appears to move or animate through use of a script.

animation override (AO): A scripted object used, along with animations, to replace default animations for walking, sitting, standing, etc.

animation: *1.* A file uploaded from an external program (such as Poser) used to make an avatar move or pose in a specific way. *2.* Describes textures or objects scripted to appear to move.

announcer: A scripted object that heralds the arrival of an avatar in range.

AO conflict: The problem of freaky animations or poses caused by a conflict between an animation override worn by an avatar and an animation contained by another object, such as a chair.

Appearance mode: A feature of *SL* that allows Residents to edit their avatars' appearance or to create clothing.

army: A Resident group that roleplays as an army.

artificial avatar: Prim sculptures that look like avatars and are scripted to do things like greet visitors or answer questions. See also *noob*.

asset cluster: See *asset server*.

asset server: The Linden Lab servers that host inventories, as well as information related to things like logins.

attachment: An object made from prims that is worn on an avatar.

attachment point: A point on an avatar on which prim attachments may be worn.

augmentationist: A philosophy that combines immersionist and platformist views.

Autoreturn: A feature that can be set to return objects on a parcel to their owners after a configurable length of time.

autoupdate: A script that automatically sends updated versions of objects when they become available.

avatar: The representation of a person in a virtual world.

avatar imposter: A 2D sprite that stands in for an avatar when many avatars are present, in order to reduce load and thus lag.

avatar mesh: The shape of an avatar, controlled using the Appearance sliders.

Avatar Rendering Cost (ARC): A number that gives a rough estimate of the resources required to render an avatar.

Away: A setting that may be selected or to which an avatar defaults after being idle for a while; the avatar slumps over as if asleep.

away from keyboard (AFK): Typed in chat to indicate one is stepping away from the computer or otherwise distracted.

backchat: Comments and discussion by the audience at an in-world event.

bake: Replace a cached/default version.

banhammer: The mythical object used to ban someone.

ban lines: Lines that indicate you are not allowed to enter a parcel.

ban list: The list of Residents banned from a parcel or estate.

Basic Account: A free *Second Life* account type with certain limitations, such as the inability to own land or receive a weekly stipend.

blind teleport offer: A teleport offer sent with no prior warning, such as an IM. Usually frowned upon, especially when sent by a stranger.

bling: A particle effect used to imply sparkle.

boot: To eject someone from a parcel, region, or estate.

bot: An automated avatar run by a program on an external server.

build: *1.* To create things in *Second Life*. *2.* A developed area or even object in *Second Life*.

builder: Someone who develops *Second Life* content, usually objects (as opposed to scripts).

Burning Life: Annual Linden Lab event featuring regions full of Resident art.

busy: A setting used to indicate one is not to be disturbed; a "busy" avatar sends out an automatic busy message and refuses all inventory offers.

cager/cage gun: A scripted weapon used to trap someone in a cage.

calling card: Inventory asset used for organizing in-world contacts/Friends.

camera controls: Used for controlling your view while in-world.

camming: Using the camera controls.

camping chair: A scripted object an avatar sits on to be paid a small number of Linden dollars at intervals.

camping: Sitting on a scripted object, such as a camping chair, in order to be paid a few Linden dollars per hour; intended to increase the Traffic total for the parcel.

cash out: Common Resident term for selling Linden dollars for real-world currency.

channel: Text chat usually happens in open chat (Channel 0), but particularly for scripted objects it is sometimes useful to have them communicate on another channel.

channel 0: Default chat channel.

chat: Usually assumed to mean conversing via text/typing.

chat log: Log of all chat or just IMs in *Second Life*; can be turned on or off.

chimera: An attachment that is scripted to make avatars dance.

Classifieds: Set up via a Resident's profile, these in-world Classified ads will appear in a Resident's profile and in Search listings.

click counter: A script that records the number of times avatars have interacted with an object.

client: The *Second Life* application.

clothing layer: A layer of an avatar on which clothing may be worn, such as undershirt layer, shirt layer, or jacket layer.

clothing mesh: The shape of clothing that is controlled using the Appearance sliders.

coalesced object: Objects taken into or returned to Inventory together, which cannot be taken out separately.

collision: Physical objects coming into contact.

collision map: The invisible outlines of an object that define its physical borders (which often do not match the visual borders).

color sims: Very old regions on the mainland named after colors.

Concierge: Higher-level support services provided to Residents who own one or more private regions or an equivalent amount of mainland.

Concierge Party: A periodic Linden Lab event that is a themed multiregion party for Concierge-level Residents.

concurrency: The number of Residents logged into *Second Life* at the same time.

content: *1.* Objects, clothing, animations, scripts, or other assets inside the *Second Life* world. *2.* Assets contained within an object.

copy: A permissions setting that allows the object owner to make copies of the asset.

covenant: Agreement between an estate owner and purchasers of parcels within the estate.

damage: An avatar that is damaged by weapons, falling, etc. will "die" and return to its home point.

dance ball: A scripted object that makes avatars dance.

dance machine: See *dance ball*.

default prim: A 0.5×0.5-meter box textured like unfinished wood.

derez: To delete something.

Devil May Care: A popular casual game played in-world.

direct teleport: Ability to teleport to a location directly rather than only to Telehubs.

distro/distro box: A scripted object that gives inventory assets; often called to by a script in another object.

donation kiosk: An object that Residents can pay to make a donation. See *tip jar*.

DOS attack: An attempt to stop someone from using or accessing a site or the Grid by keeping the system too busy. See *self-replicating object*.

drama: Complicated virtual personal life or gossip about the same.

drama-free zone: Usually used in jest; refers to an area or serves as a request that drama be avoided.

draw distance: How far one is able to see; up to what distance objects are rendered.

draw: See *render*.

Dwell: The original name for Traffic.

edit rights: Permission to edit objects that belong to another avatar.

emote: A keyboard shortcut that causes an avatar to animate in order to express emotion. See *gesture*.

emoter: A scripted object used to more easily or automatically trigger emotes.

estate: A set of regions belonging to the same owner.

estate manager: Someone given estate administration powers by the estate owner.

events: In-world activities.

facelight: An invisible light-emitting object an avatar wears to light their face to best advantage.

Feral: A Resident roleplaying a wild animal.

feted inner core (FIC): A supposed clique of favored *Second Life* Residents who get special treatment from Linden Lab.

finder: A scripted object used to locate another object or avatar.

First Land: Defunct Linden Lab program that made low-cost land available to newbies.

first life: See *real life*.

flight assist: A scripted object worn to make an avatar fly faster or higher than the usual limit.

floating text: See *hovertext*.

force(d) teleport: A teleport initiated by a Linden with no teleport offer or warning.

frames per second (FPS): A measure of performance; how many times per second your view of *SL* is redrawn.

free group: One of the 25 group slots a Resident has that isn't already filled with a group.

freebie box: A box of free items, usually intended for newbies or as a promotional item from a merchant.

Friend: *1.* Someone with whom you've exchanged and accepted Friendship offers; someone on your contact list. *2.* The act of adding someone to your Friends list.

Friends list: A contact list.

full bright: An object setting that makes the object immune to the effects of local lighting and the sun and moon.

full permissions: Object permissions set so that an object may be modified, copied, and transferred by the next owner.

full-prim sim/region: A normal region.

full-service Solution Provider: A Solution Provider that offers a wide range of services to clients.

Furry: Part human, part animal avatar; distinguishing feature is a prim animal head attached to a humanoid body.

gesture: Made up of one or more animations, sound clips, and text strings used to make an avatar perform basic or custom activities, such as bowing or expressing excitement, by typing a keyword.

global time: The default day/night cycle in-world.

god mode: An increased feature set available to Lindens in-world.

god teleport: See *force teleport*.

Gold Solution Provider: Linden Lab program intended to offer additional resources and support to the cream of the Solution Provider Program.

Gor: *1.* A fantasy world created by author John Norman. *2.* A *Second Life* subculture based on John Norman's Gor novels.

Gorean: A Resident involved in Gor roleplay.

Governor Linden: The traditional figurehead of the *Second Life* world.

greeter: A scripted object that welcomes visitors; may or may not offer inventory.

grey goo: See *self-replicating object*.

grid: A system of connected regions.

griefer: Someone who tries to upset other people for amusement's sake.

griefer object: A scripted object used to grief someone.

griefing: The act of trying to cause trouble for or upset other people for one's own amusement.

ground textures: See *terrain textures*.

group adder: A scripted object intended to make it easier to join a group.

group build: An area where only members of a specific group can rez objects.

group IM: An instant message sent to all members of a group, in which they can share a discussion.

group limit: The maximum number of groups a Resident can be in simultaneously; currently this is 25.

group notice: A notice sent to members of a group.

group-only: Parcel or other settings which restrict certain abilities to members of a specific group.

group proposal: A proposal sent to members of a group who may then vote on it.

group role: One's role in a group, which comes with a title and abilities.

Groups: A feature used for organizing people and managing land and other assets.

handshake attachment: A scripted object used to animate avatars to shake hands.

Havok: A physics engine used to simulate realistic physics in *Second Life*, as well as in some video games.

HB: Abbreviation for *hurry back*.

heads-up display (HUD): Special attachment points (or objects worn on them) that are viewable only by the wearer.

holodeck: A space in which scripted wall textures and perhaps objects may be made to automatically appear and disappear, in order to change the space's look or function.

holovendor: A scripted vendor that displays temporary copies of the items for sale.

Help Island: A Linden Lab-owned location where Resident volunteers help new Residents learn *Second Life* skills.

home: An avatar's default start location, to which they return if damaged or if the region to which they were attempting to teleport is unavailable.

Homestead: A low-prim region that supports a limited number of avatars but more avatars than an Openspace.

hovertext: Text that floats above a prim through use of a script.

hub: Short for *Telehub*.

hug attachment: Scripted object used to animate avatars to hug.

immersion: The feeling that one is "in" a virtual world.

immersionist: The philosophy that virtual worlds are just that: worlds in which one lives (part of one's life, or a literal *Second Life*).

Infohub: A Linden Lab–owned location where Residents may go to get Linden information, hang out, or set their home location.

Infokiosk: An object that may be clicked to get information.

instant message (IM): *1.* Instant-messaging system. *2.* A message sent by an instant-messaging system. *3.* The act of sending an instant message.

instant-message cap: The limit to how many offline instant messages will be displayed when you log in.

inventory: *1. (capitalized)* Where a Resident accesses stored in-world assets. *2.* An asset, like an object or script.

invitation: *1.* An offer to add you to a group. *2.* A scripted object that typically, when touched, gives you information about and a landmark to an event.

in-world: Within the virtual world.

island: Usually refers to a private region.

JIRA/PJIRA: Linden Lab database where Residents are encouraged to post bug reports and to read about workarounds.

Kk: A common abbreviation for *okay*, quicker to type than *ok*.

Knowledge Base/KB: Linden Lab database where you can look up information; takes the place of a manual.

lag: Catch-all slang for slow response.

lagmire: An especially laggy area.

land baron: A Resident who buys and sells (or rents) virtual land for profit.

Land for the Landless: See *First Land*.

land griefing: Purposely building ugly or laggy things on a parcel to harass the neighbors.

landing point: A preset location where avatars appear when teleporting into a parcel.

landmark: The *Second Life* equivalent of a bookmark.

landmark giver: A scripted object that gives landmarks on touch.

level of detail (LOD): The degree of detail rendered based on how far the viewer is from the object.

Library: A folder in Inventory where free Linden Lab–provided content is available to all Residents.

Linden: *1.* Used as an adjective to describe something owned or developed by Linden Lab. *2.* A member of Linden Lab staff. *3. Second Life* microcurrency (short for *Linden dollar*).

Linden dollar: *Second Life* microcurrency used as the medium of exchange in-world.

Linden Lab: The creators of *Second Life*.

Linden Scripting Language (LSL): Proprietary programming language used in-world.

Linden Village: An area where many Lindens maintain offices open to the public.

LindeX: The currency exchange operated by Linden Lab where Linden dollars are bought and sold for real-world currency.

linkset: A group of prims that are linked together.

Locked: A setting that will make instantiated objects immobile.

Lost and Found: The Inventory folder where objects that have been autoreturned, that have "gone off the world," been returned (manually), or that have been lost some other way will usually reappear.

lucky chair: A scripted object that displays randomly chosen letters and gives a prize to a Resident who sits in it if they have a name starting with that letter.

Luna Oaks Galleria: An in-world shopping mall operated by Linden Lab. Linden Lab periodically raffles shop locations here.

M2: Common shorthand for square meters.

machinima: A video shot using avatars in a virtual world or game instead of real-world actors or cartoon characters.

mafia: A Resident group that roleplays an organized-crime family.

Main Grid (MG): The *Second Life* world, except for the Teen Grid.

mainland: The continents within the *Second Life* world that are owned and administered by Linden Lab.

map: *1.* The complete world map of *Second Life*. *2.* To find or track a Resident's location in-world (using the map).

media texture: A texture that is replaced with a streaming video image when video streaming is enabled.

megaprim: A prim created through use of a script that exceeds the limit on prims larger than 10 meters square.

Mer: A Resident subculture for mermaid/merman roleplay.

mesh: Short for polygon mesh.

Message of the Day (MOTD): A message from Linden Lab that appears upon login, usually with tips or info about upcoming events, downtime, or new features.

metaversal development company (MDC): A company that develops content for virtual worlds.

metaverse: One overarching virtual world, a term coined by Neal Stephenson in the novel *Snow Crash*.

minimap: A small map that indicates your location, those of other avatars, and objects around you; used for navigation.

mixed-reality event: An event conducted simultaneously in *Second Life* and the real world, with media streams bridging the gap.

mobvend: A special vendor that lowers its price based on how many avatars are in proximity.

modify (mod): A permissions setting that allows the object owner to edit/change the asset.

money tree: A scripted object that accepts donations and makes small payments of free money to newbies who visit it.

Mono: An improved compiler for scripts written in LSL.

mouselook: An alternate, first-person camera view.

multitool: A scripted object that combines a number of features, such as a scanner, flight assist, pushgun, etc.

Mute: A feature used so that you no longer have to see the chat of a specific avatar.

neko: Part human, part cat avatar; distinguished from Furries by the lack of a prim head.

nested permissions: Permissions on assets contained within objects.

networked vendor: A vendor system with a central control that makes it easier for a merchant to change their offerings, prices, etc.

newbie (newb, noob): A new *Second Life* Resident.

no-build: Describes an area where the ability to rez objects is disabled.

no-copy: A permissions setting that prevents the object owner from making copies of the asset.

no-damage: Describes an area where the damage feature is disabled.

no entry: See *ban lines*.

no-fly: A restriction on the parcel level that disallows flying.

no-modify (no-mod): A permissions setting that disallows the object owner from editing/changing the asset.

noob: *1*. See *newbie*. *2*. An object made from sculpted prims by artist William Segerman (*SL* avatar Art Laxness) that looks just like a *Second Life* avatar.

no-push: Describes an area where the push feature is disabled.

no-script: Describes an area where the ability to run scripts is disabled.

notecard: A very simple document type used in-world.

notecard giver: A scripted object that gives notecards on touch.

no-transfer (no-trans): A permissions setting that prevents the object owner from giving or selling the asset to someone else.

object: A virtual thing made from prims.

object entry: A permission on the parcel level that controls whether objects may enter from a neighboring parcel.

object spam: Spam delivered, on purpose or not, by an object. See *spamming*.

official events calendar: *Second Life*–specific event calendar maintained by Linden lab.

official forums: *Second Life*–specific forums maintained by Linden Lab.

offline IM: An instant message received while offline. May receive these via email, or only upon login.

online indicator: A scripted object that shows whether a specific avatar is currently online.

open: Using the pie menu to "open" an object (such as a box packed by a merchant) and transfer its contents to Inventory.

open chat: The default chat channel.

open permissions: See *full permissions*.

Openspace: A low-prim region that supports a very limited number of avatars and scripts and is to be used only for things like scenery and boat races.

Orientation Island: Now defunct; used to be the starting point for new Residents, where they learn basic *Second Life* skills.

owner say: Refers to messages sent using a script function, llOwnerSay, which enables a scripted object to communicate directly with its owner rather than where everyone has to read it.

P2P teleport: See *direct teleport*.

parcel: A piece of virtual land; smaller than or up to the size of an entire region.

parcel description: A description of a parcel written in About Land that appears in Search.

particle: A 2D sprite generated by a script, usually used for special effects like fireworks or smoke.

particle engine: A scripted object that provides a convenient interface for editing particle scripts.

partners: *Second Life* Residents who have registered a partnership with Linden Lab so that their names appear in one another's profile, in the Partner field.

peak concurrency: The highest number of Residents logged in at the same time.

permanoob: A Resident who has had an account for a long time yet still has not learned basic *Second Life* skills.

permissions: Settings used to limit how others may use or interact with your objects or on your virtual land.

Phantom: A setting for an object that removes its collision map so that avatars and objects can pass through it.

phishing: A form of fraud whereby someone is tricked into giving up their login info or other personal information by something like a fake login page.

Photo Album: The Inventory folder that is the default location to store snapshots.

photosourced: Describes textures created from photographs.

Physical: A setting for an object that makes it subject to simulated physics. Avatars are also physical.

Picks: These are listed in the Picks section of a Resident's profile. Intended to showcase a Resident's favorite in-world locations, Picks are often used to present other information, such as pictures of friends or in-world shop policies.

Pizza: A popular casual game played in-world.

PJIRA: See *JIRA*.

platformist: The philosophy that virtual worlds are platforms, like a word processor or a drawing program.

poofer: A scripted attachment that fires a particle effect when someone teleports or otherwise triggers it.

pose: A static animation.

poseball: A scripted object that contains an animation to pose an avatar.

pose stand: A scripted object used to make an avatar hold still while adjusting attachments.

prefab: Any Resident-created content that can be bought in a shop in-world. (Usually refers to buildings.)

preferences: *Second Life* settings administered via Edit ▶ Preferences.

Premium Account: A fee-based *Second Life* account type, which has added features over the Basic Account, such as a stipend and the ability to own land.

prim/primitive object: The basic building block from which objects are created.

prim baby: An artificial baby made from prims. May talk in open chat.

prim clothing: Clothing made up completely or partly by prim attachments.

prim count: The number of prims used to build an object or used in a specific area.

prim drift: Describes the problem of the prims in a build gradually becoming misaligned due to rounding errors.

prim hair: Hair made from prims and attached to an avatar instead of through use of sliders.

prim-heavy: See *primmy*.

prim limit: The number of prims available to use in a specific area.

primmy: Something that contains or is made up of a lot of prims, usually more prims than would be necessary if the item(s) were built with more care.

prim shoes: Shoes made from prims rather than through use of the sliders; usually worn over slider shoes.

prim torture: The practice of editing a prim radically to shape it.

prim tummy: An artificial pregnant stomach made from prims. May talk in open chat.

private island: A region owned by an individual other than Linden Lab that is detached from the mainland.

profile: Includes information about a person or group. Avatar profiles include buttons for things like contacting someone via instant message, giving them inventory, or sending a Friendship invitation.

property line: Indicates the borders of a parcel.

push: *1.* Force applied to an avatar or other physical object to move it. *2.* The script function llPush.

pushgun: See *push weapon*.

push weapon: A weapon that pushes avatars using the Push script function.

quad: An avatar with prim parts and an animation override that appears to be a four-legged animal.

radar: See *scanner*.

radio: Parcel audio stream.

real life (RL): Usually describes anything outside of the virtual world, although some people will always point out that virtual worlds are part of real life.

real world: See *real life*.

region: A 256-square-meter area of virtual land managed via the Region/Estate panel, often called a sim or an island.

region restart: Rebooting a region.

region/estate notice: A pop-up that may be made to appear for everyone in a region or estate.

Registration API: Used to create custom *Second Life* registration web pages and new-user experiences.

render: Make visible, draw, appear.

Resident: Someone who has a *Second Life* account.

rez: To make something appear in-world.

Rez-Foo: A scripted system by CrystalShard Foo that allows boxing up a large (up to full-sim) build so that it can be derezzed, rerezzed, or moved around easily.

rezzer: A scripted object that rezzes other objects.

rights: See *permissions*.

Risk API: An API that enables use of the Grid for real-world purchases.

rolling restart: A process by which Linden Lab updates regions on the Grid by shutting down individual regions briefly, in series, rather than shutting down the entire Grid at one time.

root prim: The main prim in a linkset, it is the last linked and its characteristics and name are taken on by the completed object.

Ruth: All avatars started out looking like the basic Ruth avatar, and defaulted to the Ruth shape when their own had not yet loaded. Ruth has now been replaced by a shifting particle cloud.

sales box: The simplest form of vendor.

sandbox: An area where all Residents or only members of a specific group may build objects, and in some cases run scripts.

say: A form of text chat that may be seen within a 20-meter range; the default text chat.

scanner: A scripted object that scans for Residents, usually reporting to its owner how far away they are and their names.

script: *1.* A program written in Linden Scripting Language. *2.* A *Second Life* asset used for this purpose.

sculpted prim: A prim shaped using a sculpt map imported from an external 3D-modeling program, such as Maya.

sculpt map: A texture created by a 3D-modeling program, such as Hexagon, or a converter and imported into *Second Life* to create sculpted prims.

sculptie, sculpty: See *sculpted prim*.

sculptie importer: A program used to convert 3D models created outside of *SL* into sculpt maps.

Search: A feature used to locate people, places, things, events, and land for sale in *Second Life*.

Second Life Community Convention (SLCC): An annual real-world gathering of *Second Life* Residents, Lindens, and others.

Second Life Grid: The virtual-world platform built and operated by Linden Lab.

Second Life Time (SLT): Pacific Time, or the time zone shown on the in-world clock and by which Linden Lab and most Residents tell time when discussing things such as events.

Second Life Uniform Resource Locator (SLURL): A special sort of URL used to link and offer a teleport to an in-world location.

Second Life world: The virtual world maintained on the *Second Life* Grid by Linden Lab.

self-replicating object: A scripted object that rezzes copies of itself, which then rez more copies, and so on.

sell for zero: A way of transferring an object in place by selling it to someone for zero Linden dollars.

send a taxi/taxi has arrived: Slang for requesting/receiving a teleport offer.

set to group: Associate a piece of land or an object with a specific group.

shape: Short for avatar shape, or mesh.

shout: A form of text chat that may be seen within a 100-meter range.

Show and Tell: An event at which people display things they have created. Everyone votes for a winner or winners, who usually receive a prize.

sim/simulator: See *region*.

sim border: The borders of a region.

sim crossing: Traveling across the border from one region to another; sometimes there are lag and lag-related problems at this point.

sim limit: See *agent limit*.

sim rating: Region rating: Mature (M) or PG.

sit offset: How far from the center point of an object a seated avatar will be placed when sitting on an object.

sit: A sit is a pose, as in, "That sofa has a nice sit in it."

sit-hack teleport: A special scripted way of teleporting that works within a limited range.

skin: The texture that is used on the surface of an avatar shape.

skybox: A box, house, or platform in the sky that is used for privacy.

SL: A common abbreviation for *Second Life*.

SL5B: The fifth annual *Second Life* birthday event sponsored by Linden Lab, featuring Resident groups' builds and events.

SL child, SL kid: A Resident who roleplays as a child.

SLED: An in-world group for educators who use *Second Life*, with an associated blog and mailing list maintained by Linden Lab.

slider: *1.* An interface used to control input, usually for avatar-appearance editing. *2.* Describes avatar parts created using the slider interface.

SLim: An external *Second Life* application that allows voice or instant-message chat with Residents by someone who's not in-world.

smile attachment: A scripted attachment that makes an avatar smile all the time or at random intervals.

smiler: See *smile attachment*.

snapshot: Screenshot.

Solution Provider: *1.* Linden Lab's name for individuals or companies that do work in *Second Life* for real-world clients. *2.* A participant in Linden Lab's Solution Provider Program.

Solution Provider Program: The Linden Lab program that offers resources and support to Solution Providers.

sounds: WAV files that may be imported and played in-world.

spamming: *1.* When a scripted object blurts information, particularly advertising, to people who aren't interested in it. *2.* When a scripted object offers inventory assets to people who aren't interested in them. *3.* When someone puts their ads all over the place. *4.* When someone chats the same thing over and over, disruptively.

sploder: A scripted object that periodically pays a small amount of Linden dollars to a random nearby avatar.

stalking: *1.* Mapping someone and then going to their location; following them. *2.* Happening to run into someone (said in jest).

stipend: Weekly allowance paid by Linden Lab to Premium Account holders.

stream: Live feed of audio or video.

tag: The floating words that appear over an avatar's head, including their group title and name. Distinguished from a title created by a Resident-built titler by being a Linden feature.

Teen Grid (TG): See *Teen Second Life*.

Teen *Second Life* (TSL): The *Second Life* product for teens ages 13 to 17.

Telehub: *1.* A preset location where avatars appear when teleporting to a region. *2.* The build surrounding the actual Telehub, especially such a build developed by Linden Lab.

teleport (TP): A way of moving almost instantly from one location to another in *Second Life*.

teleporter: A scripted object used for sit-hack teleports (touch-enabled).

teleport map: A scripted map which may be clicked in order to nearly instantly travel to the pictured locations.

teleport request: A pop-up message that appears when someone offers to teleport you to their location.

teleport routing: Setting up a Telehub on a parcel or region.

Temporary (Temp): A setting for a prim that will make it disappear after being rezzed, in typically about a minute and a half.

terraform: Modify the appearance of virtual land and water.

terrain textures: The textures that are used on the surface of the terrain map, such as dirt or grass.

texture: *1.* A 2D graphic used on the surface of a 3D model. *2.* A *Second Life* asset used for this purpose. *3.* The act of creating and applying textures.

texture tutorial: An in-world resource for teaching oneself how to work with textures, created and maintained by Robin Wood (SL avatar Robin Sojourner).

tier, tier fee: The monthly maintenance charge for parcels.

Tiny/Tinies: Very small avatars created by use of animations that fold up an avatar, which is then encased in prim attachments to give the appearance of (usually) a cute animal.

tiny prim: A prim made smaller than the 0.010 limit through techniques like cutting and dimpling.

tip jar: An object that may be paid in order to show appreciation for someone's service or build.

title: *1.* The title associated with a particular group role. *2.* The floating words over an avatar's head that shows this title. *3.* Floating words made to appear over an avatar's head through use of a titler.

titler: A scripted object that makes words appear over an avatar's head.

tombstoning: Lining up rows of kiosks or vendors so that it looks like a graveyard.

Town Hall Meeting: Large event at which Lindens speak directly with Residents about major changes or issues facing them. Usually simulcast via chat repeaters or streaming audio.

Traffic: A measure of a parcel's popularity.

transfer (trans): A permissions setting that allows the object owner to give or sell the asset to someone else.

translator: A device used to translate text chat in real time.

Tringo: A popular casual game created in *SL* by *Second Life* Resident Nathan Keir (avatar Kermitt Quirk) that has been licensed for use on other platforms.

typing replacer: A scripted object that overrides default typing animations and sounds so that an avatar may instead stand still, appear to be conducting a band, waving hands in the air, taking notes, etc.

typist: The real person operating an avatar.

unpack box: See *open*.

update group: A group created for the purpose of updating members about a shop or other organization's new offerings and upcoming events.

URL loader: A scripted object that opens web pages.

vehicle sims: Regions on the mainland maintained by Linden Lab for vehicle use.

vendor: A scripted interactive tool used to display or, usually, to sell assets.

virtual world: A computer-generated space, such as *Second Life*, where people can interact using avatars.

visitor counter: A scripted object that counts how many visitors have been in range of it; may also maintain a list of visitor names.

voice: The feature that allows Residents to use a headset/mic to chat in-world or in in-world instant messages.

void: See *Openspace*.

WB: Abbreviation for *welcome back*.

Welcome Area: A Linden Lab–owned location where some new Residents enter the *Second Life* world.

whisper: A form of text chat that can be seen only within a 10-meter range; available only through use of scripts.

wings: A very common avatar attachment, tried at least once by most new Residents.

Winterfest: An annual Linden Lab event featuring winter-themed and holiday builds by Residents, and a Lindens-vs.-Residents snowball fight.

XStreet: Linden Lab's web-based shopping site that allows purchase of Resident-created assets without being in-world.

APPENDIX B: *SECOND LIFE* COMMUNITY STANDARDS

(From **http://secondlife.com/corporate/cs.php**)

We hope you'll have a richly rewarding experience, filled with creativity, self expression and fun.

The goals of the Community Standards are simple: treat each other with respect and without harassment, adhere to local standards as indicated by simulator ratings, and refrain from any hate activity which slurs a real-world individual or real-world community.

BEHAVIORAL GUIDELINES—THE "BIG SIX"

Within *Second Life*, we want to support Residents in shaping their specific experiences and making their own choices.

The Community Standards sets out six behaviors, the "Big Six," that will result in suspension or, with repeated violations, expulsion from the *Second Life* Community.

All *Second Life* Community Standards apply to all areas of *Second Life*, the *Second Life* Forums, and the *Second Life* Website.

1. Intolerance

Combating intolerance is a cornerstone of *Second Life*'s Community Standards. Actions that marginalize, belittle, or defame individuals or groups inhibit the satisfying exchange of ideas and diminish the *Second Life* community as whole. The use of derogatory or demeaning language or images in reference to another Resident's race, ethnicity, gender, religion, or sexual orientation is never allowed in *Second Life*.

2. Harassment

Given the myriad capabilities of *Second Life*, harassment can take many forms. Communicating or behaving in a manner which is offensively coarse, intimidating or threatening, constitutes unwelcome sexual advances or requests for sexual favors, or is otherwise likely to cause annoyance or alarm is Harassment.

3. Assault

Most areas in *Second Life* are identified as Safe. Assault in *Second Life* means: shooting, pushing, or shoving another Resident in a Safe Area (see Global Standards below); creating or using scripted objects which singularly or persistently target another Resident in a manner which prevents their enjoyment of *Second Life*.

4. Disclosure

Residents are entitled to a reasonable level of privacy with regard to their *Second Life* experience. Sharing personal information about a fellow Resident—including gender, religion, age, marital status, race, sexual preference, and real-world location beyond what is provided by the Resident in the First Life page of their Resident profile is a violation of that Resident's privacy. Remotely monitoring conversations, posting conversation logs, or sharing conversation logs without consent are all prohibited in *Second Life* and on the *Second Life* Forums.

5. Indecency

Second Life is an adult community, but Mature material is not necessarily appropriate in all areas (see Global Standards below). Content, communication, or behavior which involves intense language or expletives, nudity or sexual content, the depiction of sex or violence, or anything else broadly offensive must be contained within private land in areas rated Mature (M). Names of Residents, objects, places and groups are broadly viewable in *Second Life* directories and on the *Second Life* website, and must adhere to PG guidelines.

6. Disturbing the Peace

Every Resident has a right to live their *Second Life*. Disrupting scheduled events, repeated transmission of undesired advertising content, the use of repetitive sounds, following or self-spawning items, or other objects that intentionally slow server performance or inhibit another Resident's ability to enjoy *Second Life* are examples of Disturbing the Peace.

POLICIES AND POLICING

Global Standards, Local Ratings

All areas of *Second Life*, including the **www.secondlife.com** website and the *Second Life* Forums, adhere to the same Community Standards. Locations within *Second Life* are noted as Safe or Unsafe and rated Mature (M) or non-Mature (PG), and behavior must conform to the local ratings. Any unrated area of *Second Life* or the *Second Life* website should be considered non-Mature (PG).

Warning, Suspension, Banishment

Second Life is a complex society, and it can take some time for new Residents to gain a full understanding of local customs and mores. Generally, violations of the Community Standards will first result in a Warning, followed by Suspension and eventual Banishment from *Second Life*. In-World Representatives, called Liaisons, may occasionally address disciplinary problems with a temporary removal from *Second Life*.

Global Attacks

Objects, scripts, or actions which broadly interfere with or disrupt the *Second Life* community, the *Second Life* servers or other systems related to *Second Life* will not be tolerated in any form. We will hold you responsible for any actions you take, or that are taken by objects or scripts that belong to you. Sandboxes are available for testing objects and scripts that have components that may be unmanageable or whose behavior you may not be able to predict. If you chose to use a script that substantially disrupts the operation of *Second Life*, disciplinary actions will result in a minimum two-week suspension, the possible loss of in-world inventory, and a review of your account for probable expulsion from *Second Life*.

Alternate Accounts

While Residents may choose to play *Second Life* with more than one account, specifically or consistently using an alternate account to harass other Residents or violate the Community Standards is not acceptable. Alternate accounts are generally treated as separate from a Resident's principal account, but misuse of alternate accounts can and will result in disciplinary action on the principal account.

Buyer Beware

Linden Lab does not exercise editorial control over the content of *Second Life*, and will make no specific efforts to review the textures, objects, sounds or other content created within *Second Life*. Additionally, Linden Lab does not certify or endorse the operation of in-world games, vending machines, or retail locations; refunds must be requested from the owners of these objects.

Reporting Abuse

Residents should report violations of the Community Standards using the Abuse Reporter tool located under the Help menu in the in-world tool bar. Every Abuse Report is individually investigated, and the identity of the reporter is kept strictly confidential.

INDEX

2.5D sites: 12

3D: 12; construction *36*; data visualization: 10

3D online virtual space: 6; *see also* stand-alone grid

7Seas: *228*

M

Mars, RC: 62

Marvin the Paranoid Android: *192*

Massachusetts Institute of Technology: 26

Massively: 144

mathematical notation: *36*

mathematics: *36*

Mature rating: 100-102, 139, 157, 164, 166, 172

May Day: 80

Maya: 13

Maya Realities: 308

McBrayer, Robert: 72

McCann, Marianne: *111*

McMullen, Barbara: 35

media: 10, 245, 265, 297, 301, 311, 312; publication deadlines 224; *see also specific medium*

media backlash: 18

media controls: 164-165

media in-world: 142-145

media on a prim: 124

media sharing: 10, 312

Media tab: 164-165

medical training: 27-28

meditation, teaching of: 28

meeting etiquette: 128-130

meetings/conferences: 6, 8, 10, 15, 19, 29, 30, 32, 34-35 44, 46, 49, 51, 60, 64-65, 67, 71, 72, 76-80, 88, 95-97, 105, 107, 118-119, 122, *123*, 125, 128, 133, *136*, 139, 147, 148, 187-198, 204-205, 213, 219, *232*, 234, 235, *238*, 239, 243, 244, 248, 256, 257, 261, 267, 272, 288, 297, 300, 312, 313

Members & Roles tab: 172

mental health: 64

Mer: 110

mesh imports: 312

Message of the Day: 147

message: to estate 170

Metanomics: 32, 144

Metaverse Messenger, The: 134, 144, 146, 228, 244

metrics: 142, 255, 306-309

Metropolitan State College of Denver: 67

Mexico: 83

microphone: 126, 129, 190, 250

Microsoft: 50

Microsoft Word: 207

military: 109

Mir space station: 72

Missouri: State of Missouri Job Fair 56; IT employment center *57*

MIT Comparative Media Studies Program: *289*

MIT Media Lab: 313

mixed-reality events: 191, 241, 252; in Teen *Second Life* 286, *287*

model homes: 192

moderating events: 248-252

modify content: 11

modify objects permissions: 179-180; *see also* permissions

money: *see* currency; L$; exchange rate

money saving: 188, 193, 194

Monroe College: 35

mood creation: 243

MOTD *see* Message of the Day

Motorati: 218

movies: 83

multicultural considerations: 10, 15

multilingual: 15

multinational: 15

multitasking: 118, 121

multitool: 105, 303

Murray, Moopf: *228*

Museum of Women Composers: *34*

museums: 20-21, 34, 45, *48*, 61-62, 81, 139, 193, 214-*215*, 219, 241, 252, 306

Music Academy Online: 34, *37*, 41

music/musicians: 34, 67-68, 83, 129, 130, 144, 146, 147, 165, 237, 243; *see also* media; streaming media

mute: 126, 137

name: considerations in choosing *97, 247*; custom names 85, 106, 220, 310-311; griefing 135; real life 267

naming conventions: for land 154, 157, 160

NASA: 18-20, 34, 45-47, 56, 62, 77

NASA CoLab: 20, 46, 62

NASA events: 46

National Aeronautics and Space Administration: *see* NASA

National Oceanic and Atmospheric Administration (NOAA): 44-45, 52, 56, 67, 70, 289
National Physical Laboratory (NPL): 47, 62
National Security Space Office: 72
National Space Society: 46
Naval Postgraduate School: 50
NCI: *see* New Citizens Incorporated
NDA: 53, *192*
neko: 111, 112, 114
nested folders: 182
nested permissions: 179-180
networking: 19, 32, 34, 60, 70, 72, 137, 188, 217, 219, *223*, 265, 267, 270, 297
neuropathy: 64
Neva, Prokofy: 132, 144
New Citizens Incorporated: 304, *305*
new features: 312-313
New Media Consortium (NMC): 32, 47, 62, 66-67, *154*
New Orleans: 60
new Residents: 220-222
New Unionism Network: 80
New User Tutorial: 38
New World Notes: 144, 146
New York Law School: 77
newbie: 38, 97, 98, 106, 107, 221-222, 242, 248
newspapers: 142-*143; see also media*
NMC Campus: 32, *33*, 62, 66, 72; *see also* New Media Consortium
NOAA: *see* National Oceanic and Atmospheric Administration
nonhuman avatars: 95-96
nonprofits: 60-73; land discounts for 31
Nonprofits Commons group: 72
non-uniform rational B-spline (NURBS): 13
noob: 310
Norman, John: 110
Not Possible in Real Life: 144
notecards/notecards giver: 16, 51, 86, 102, *108*, 123-124, 126, 158, 179-180, 182, 194, 197, 203, 207, 210, 216, 219, 220, 223, 225, 246, 247, 249, 251, 253, 267, 271, 284-285, 298-299, 302-303, 306, 309
notices: 124
Notices tab: 175-176
no-transfer assets: 106
NPL: *see* National Physical Laboratory

Nuclear Power Station: 47-48
nudity: 56, 100, *102*, 107, 138
NURBS (non-uniform rational B-spline): 13

O

object bonus: 166
Object Editor: 101-102, Object Editor: 178-179
object griefing 135
object permissions: 179-180, 204; *see also* permissions
object-oriented scripting language: 14
Objects tab: *162*
objects: 163; administering 162; copying for backups 183
office appearance: 194
office hours: 147, 187, 203
Official *Second Life* Community Convention: 34
online indicator: 197, 225, 298, 304
Online Programming for All Libraries (OPAL): 32, 67
Only Yesterday: 68, *69*
OPAL: *see* Online Programming for All Libraries
Open Estate: 283-285, 290
Openspace: 155, 157, 194, 232
opt-in logger: 202
Options tab: 163
Orange: 83-84
orbiters: 104
Oregon L5 Society: 46
organization of inventory: 181-183
orientation: 6, 38-39, 66, 71, 94, 148, 222, 310
Otawara, Eshi: 62
outdated content: 224

P

Pacific Time: 128; *see also Second Life* Time
panic disorders: 64
parametric surfaces: *37*
parcels: *see* land
particle engines: 304
partners: 131

Q

Qin, Jessica: 303
quads: 109-110
qualifications: for Solution Providers 263-270
quality: in builds 268
questions: at events 249-250
quests: 29, *215*, 288, 290
QuickTime: 236

R

racism: 113
radar: 104, 303
Radio, AM: 214
ratings: 56, 100-102, 114, 139, 164, 166; for land 157; for Teen *Second Life* 280
Raymaker, Potter: 72
real estate: *see* land
real life: 111-112, 131; etiquette regarding 126
real life contact information: 267, 268, 272
Real Life Education in *Second Life*: 33
Real Life Government mailing list: 52
real world media: 81-82; *see also* media
reclaiming land: 161
recordkeeping: 263
recruiting: 76
red tape: 53
reference works: 67
references: 267, 268
referrals: 267
refreshments: 190-*191*, 203
region name: 157
region resources: 239
Region/Estate controls: 165-171, *234, 249*
regional message: 166
Registration API: 7, 38, 85, 220, 264, 280, 284-285, 290, 309
Relay for Life (RFL): 9, 19, 62-64, 73; *see also* American Cancer Society
religion: bigotry regarding 113, 332-333
religious studies: 28-29, 35, 38
relocating a virtual office: 194
relocating land: 157
remote listening device: 55

rendering distance: 14
rendering load: *see* lag; system resources
rental locations: 212
renting land: 154
repeater: 250
reputation: of Solution Provider 88, 219, 223, 265, 298, 300
research/researchers: 10, 18, 39-40
research policies: 40
resell/give away object permissions: 179-180
Resident created content: 6
Resident culture: 18-20
Resident volunteers: 21
resources for educators: 30-34; for nonprofits 60; for Teen *Second Life*: 292
restart region: 167
restrictions on advertising: 86
Return Objects button: 162
Return to the Moon: 46
Reuters: 144-*145*
Revnik, Nadja: *37,* 41
rez permission: 125
RezEd: 32, 70, 144
Rez-Foo: 183, 276, 301
rezzers: 206, 301
RFL: *see* Relay for Life
rides: *215*
Right on Pier: *291*
rights: 270-272
Risk API: 229, 309
risks: 270, 274
ritual: 29
Rivers Run Red: 236, 251, 311
RL Work in *SL* group: 85
Robbins, Sarah: 31, *40*
robot avatars: 94, 95, 98, 101, 109
rockets: 46, 61-62, 71-72; *see also* ISM; NASA
roleplay/roleplayers/roleplaying: 17, 110, 131, 133, *215,* 267
Roles tab: 172-175
romance: 131-132
Rosedale, Philip: 66
RSU IBM Vimercate: 80
rudeness: 124, 134
ruins: 51
rumors: 280, 288